THE AFRO-AMERICA

NO BIB

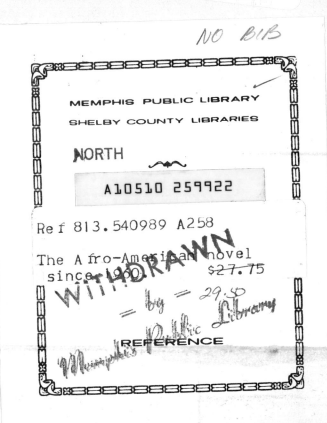

THE AMERICAN NOVEL SINCE 1960

THE AFRO-AMERICAN NOVEL SINCE 1960

edited by

PETER BRUCK - WOLFGANG KARRER

B. R. GRÜNER PUBLISHING CO.
AMSTERDAM 1982

© 1982, B.R. Grüner Publisihing Co.
ISBN 90 6032 219 3
Printed in The Netherlands

CONTENTS

PREFACE

The recent clash between J. Saunders Redding and Imamu Baraka on the issue of integrated versus Afro-American Studies Programs (*American Studies International*, Summer 1979) demonstrates again that, although the vogue of interest in Afro-American Literature seems to be ebbing, the critics and intellectuals engaged in the fiery cultural and political debates of the sixties and seventies, did leave behind a number of unresolved questions. We thought it would be useful to reconstruct the social history underlying the contemporary Afro-American novel as well as the history of criticism in order to redirect our attention to the ideological forces that have dominated, and often hampered, the reception of black fiction since 1945.

In conceiving this volume of essays with our contributors, we have tried to break with the established canon of novelists and place particular emphasis on the current generation of writers as well as on those authors who have so far been victims of tokenist neglect. Hence the reader will find no articles on either James Baldwin, Ralph Ellison or Richard Wright.

As always in such endeavors, the reader will miss one or the other of his favorite recent novelists. (We regret, for instance, that a planned for contribution on Chester Himes had to be omitted.) Still, we hope that the selection of writers will prove to be stimulating and help fostering further discussions of the rich body of the contemporary Afro-American novel. The checklist at the end of our book contains more than 700 such novels published between 1945 and 1980.

Finally we would like to thank our colleagues from both sides of the Atlantic whose contributions made it possible for this volume to appear without using previously published articles. Kurt Westermann helped us to compile the *Checklist*. Thanks are also due to Mr. B. Roland Grüner of the Grüner Publishing Company, Amsterdam, who is once again willing to embark on yet another publishing adventure in Afro-American Literature.

Peter Bruck
University of Münster

Wolfgang Karrer
University of Osnabrück

PETER BRUCK

INTRODUCTION

A: PROTEST, UNIVERSALITY, BLACKNESS:
PATTERNS OF ARGUMENTATION IN THE CRITICISM OF THE CONTEMPORARY AFRO-AMERICAN NOVEL

> A Janus-Faced question — 'who and what is Negro' — sits like a perennial sphinx at the door of every critic who considers the literature or the art of the Negro.
> Alain Locke, "Who and What is Negro?", *Opportunity*, 20 (February, 1942)

> Despite fifty years of criticism of Afro-American literature, criteria for that criticism have not been established.
> Darwin T. Turner, "Afro-American Literary Critics" (1971)

> No white critic can judge my work. I'd be a fool if I depended on that judgment.
> Statement by James Baldwin
> James Baldwin / Nikki Giovanni, *A Dialogue* (1973)

Reviewing Paul Laurence Dunbar's *Majors and Minors* in Harper's Weekly in 1896 William Dean Howells had this to say about the value and role of black literature:

I have sometimes fancied that perhaps the negroes thought black, and *felt* black; that they were racially so utterly alien and distinct from ourselves that there never could be common intellectual and emotional ground between us ... But this little book has given me pause in my speculation. Here, in the artistic effect at least, is white thinking and white feeling in a black man, and perhaps the human unity, and not the race unity, is the precious thing, after all. God hath made of one blood all nations of men: perhaps the proof of this saying is to appear in the arts, and our hostilities and prejudices are to vanish in them.[1]

1. Willian Dean Howells, "Review of *Majors and Minors*," in Edwin H.

1

Howells' attitude anticipates several lines of thought of literary criticism in the decades to follow, indeed, his utterance almost presents the history of criticism of Afro-American literature in a nutshell. Thus the first part of his comment refers to blackness both as a physical as well as spiritual category. As irony would have it, sixty years later the advocates of a black aesthetic seized precisely this point, turning blackness now into a distinctly racial entity and endowing it with such an authority that it became the sole focus of critical attention. Equally telling is Howells' emphasis on the integration function of black literature and, more importantly, his assumption that the black writer has to adapt his art to white standards. By identifying "white thinking and white feeling" with "human unity" Howells set in motion a train of ideas which associated mankind with being white, thus implicitly viewing ethnicity as a limiting factor.

Both blackness and human unity were to become major evaluative criteria and formed a dominant pattern in critical statements by black and white writers and critics alike. The symposium "The Negro in Art: How Shall He Be Portrayed?", organized by *The Crisis* during the March-December issues of 1926, is here the case in point. Among the writers and critics who participated were, for instance, Sherwood Anderson, Sinclair Lewis, Benjamin Brawley, Charles W. Chesnutt and Countee Cullen. Significantly, the majority of participants rejected both the notion of art as propaganda and the artist's primary obligation to his race. Thus Sherwood Anderson bluntly states: "Why not quit thinking of Negro art?"[2], and Charles W. Chesnutt, commenting on the fact that black writers often felt burdened with the responsibility of defending the race, pointed out that "such a frame of mind, however praiseworthy from a moral standpoint, is bad for art."[3]

Not all writers and critics shared this position, of course. Notably W.E.B. DuBois, Alain Locke, and Langston Hughes held a contrasting view, arguing that protest writing was not only legitimate but also necessary. They thought black writers should write about black people and help foster race-pride. Moreover, these literary

Cady, ed., *W.D. Howells as Critic*. London: Routledge & Kegan Paul, 1973, p. 251.
  2. Sherwood Anderson in *The Crisis*, 31 (March 1926), 36.
  3. Charles W. Chesnutt in *The Crisis*, 33 (December 1926), 29.

theorists perceived close linkages between political and literary thought. DuBois for example, called for a development of a black aesthetic ("we must come to the place where the work of art when it appears is reviewed and acclaimed by our own free and unfettered judgment"[4]), believing that art has some primary political function: "All art is propaganda and ever must be, despite the wailing of the purists. I stand in utter shamelessness and say that whatever art I have for writing has been used always for propaganda for gaining the right of black folk to love and enjoy."[5] DuBois' literary concept shows a strong undercurrent of nationalism. This term, which has become the badge of contemporary black criticism, has mostly been so poorly understood that the concept warrants clarification. Following E.U. Essien-Udom's definition of the term —

> The concept of nationalism ... may be thought of as the belief of a group that it possesses, or ought to possess, a country; that it shares, or ought to share, a common heritage of language, culture and religion; and that its heritage, way of life, and ethnic identity are distinct from those of other groups. Nationalists believe that they ought to rule themselves and shape their own destinies, and that they should therefore be in control of their social, economic, and political institutions[6] —

and in keeping with John Bracey's typology of black nationalism we see that DuBois' concept is rooted in the belief "that black people share a culture, style of life, aesthetic standard and world view distinct and different from that of white Americans and Europeans."[7]

Significantly, the nationalist commitments of DuBois, Locke and other literary thinkers of the Harlem Renaissance did *not* set in motion a revision of the accepted norms in art from a black nationalist point of view, much less a striving toward ethnic-oriented modes of evaluation. Even though these intellectuals did not follow Howells' premises they proved to be unable to move beyond

4. W.E.B. DuBois, "Criteria of Negro Art," *The Crisis*, 32 (October 1926), reprinted in Daniel Walden, ed., *W.E.B. DuBois: The Crisis Writings*. Greenwich, Conn.: Fawcett Premier, 1972, p. 289.

5. *Ibid.*, p. 288.

6. E.U. Essien-Udom, *Black Nationalism: A Search for an Identity in America*. New York: Dell, 1964, p. 20.

7. John H. Bracey Jr., "Black Nationalism Since Garvey," in Nathan I. Huggins / Martin Kilson / Daniel M. Fox, eds., *Key Issues in the Afro-American Experience: Vol. II. Since 1865*. New York: Harcourt, 1971, p. 261.

his artistic conclusions. Thus DuBois endorsed traditional forms as can be seen from the type of arguments he used in his review of Claude McKay's *Home to Harlem*. Commenting unfavorably on McKay's use of drunkenness, fighting and sexual promiscuity in the novel, he notes: "If this had been done in the course of a well-conceived plot or with any artistic unity, it might have been understood if not excused."[8] And Alain Locke, despite his deep interest in the Africanness of the black and in spite of his nationalistic stance, adhered to such 'universal' literary values as beauty, goodness and truth.[9]

Notwithstanding the fact that critics and writers remain committed to conventional aesthetic values, the literary concepts formulated by black nationalist thinkers in the 1920s provided important cultural innovations. Just like the nationalist critics of the late 1960s and 1970s, they were primarily concerned with developing a rational framework for black writers rather than with interpretations of black novels for white readers, and the black novelist saw his work as a means to extend his culture rather than to expose the racial injustice and brutality of whites. Unfortunately, however, the controversy over the aesthetic value of Richard Wright's *Native Son* dispelled the critical heritage of the 1920s. Notably, a large number of black writer-critics of the postwar era fell back to Howells' position, for as novelist William Gardner Smith remarked in 1950, "too often ... in Negro novels do we witness the dull procession of crime after crime against the Negro. ... These chronicles of offenses ... do not constitute art."[10] Hence the rebirth of the art versus propaganda debate in the 1950s and 1960s, hence the attempt of writers such as Baldwin, Baraka, Cecil Brown, Albert Murray and others to define themselves in opposition to Wright, hence also the tendency of contemporary black critics toward an ethnic absolutism.

8. W.E.B. DuBois, "Two Novels," *The Crisis*, 34 (June 1928), reprinted in Robert Hemenway, ed., *The Black Novelist*. Columbus, Ohio: Charles E. Merrill, 1970, p. 148.

9. Cf. his "The Legacy of the Ancestral Arts," in Alain Locke, ed., *The New Negro*. New York: Atheneum, 1974, p. 264 where he states: "All vital art discovers beauty and opens our eyes to that which previously we could not see."

10. William Gardner Smith, "The Negro Writer: Pitfalls and Compensations," in C.W.E. Bigsby, ed., *The Black American Writer. Vol. I*. Baltimore: Penguin, 1971, p. 73.

I

Ever since its publication, *Native Son* has been both a model and, as James Baldwin once put it, "a roadblock" for black thinkers. For those who considered it a model it suggested a new direction in which black consciousness should develop. In the words of Eldridge Cleaver: "of all black American novelists, and indeed of all American novelists of any hue, Richard Wright reigns supreme for his profound political, economic, and social reference."[11] Among those who most fervently attacked Wright, James Baldwin stands out in particular. In his famous critique he charged the novel with presenting a "sub-human" black: "The failure of the protest novel lies in its rejection of life, the human being, the denial of his beauty, dread, power, in its insistence that it is this categorization alone which is real and which cannot be transcended."[12] Similarly, novelist Albert Murray criticized Wright for his "overemphasis on protest" and then went on to say: "Oversimplification in these terms does lead almost inevitably to false positions based on false assumptions about human nature itself. Every story, whatever its immediate purpose, is a story about being man on earth. This is the basis of its universality ..."[13] The key issue surfacing here concerns the opposition between protest and universality which are considered to be mutually exclusive. This reading is clearly reminiscent of Howells' position. Moreover, it operates from the unstated assumption that there are no universal values in black culture. If we bear in mind that Murray voiced his criticism of Wright seventeen years after Baldwin, we see indeed the perseverance of Howells' racially determined views even among contemporary black novelists.

Of the two critical reactions, Baldwin's attack has had the greater impact over the years as it instigated a fiery debate about the subject matter, tone and style to be used by the black writer. This debate dominated poetic discussions up to the late 1960s to such

11. Eldridge Cleaver, "Notes on a Native Son,"*Soul on Ice*. New York: Dell, 1968, p. 105.

12. James Baldwin, "Everybody's Protest Novel," *Notes of a Native Son*. London: Corgi, 1965, p. 17.

13. Albert Murray, "Something Different, Something More," in Herbert Hill, ed., *Anger, And Beyond: The Negro Writer in the United States*. New York; Perennial Library, 1968, p. 132.

an extent that the so-called protest controversy became a ritualized encounter, the various exchanges resembling arguments running
in circles. What is more, the so-called Wright-Baldwin feud[14] triggered off among black writer-critics a series of 'parricides' which,
as I shall try to argue later, constitutes the paradigm in the evolution of black artistic philosophies.

Perhaps the most significant aspect concerns the various literary
and political concepts underlying the protest debate in the postwar years. Unlike Wright, who in his *Blueprint for Negro Writing* a-
dopted the position of proletarian realism and called for "a nationalist spirit in Negro writing ... carrying the highest possible
pitch of social consciousness",[15] Baldwin's view on the nature of
art and, ultimately, of its political implications, seems to derive
from his depressing experience that to be black meant to be "a
kind of bastard of the West."[16] In his early days as a writer this
experience prompted him to "prevent myself from becoming
merely a Negro; or even, merely a Negro Writer,"[17] for, as he once
remarked, "I can't make my alignments on the basis of color."[18]
The dilemma Baldwin faced is perhaps best expressed by his following statement: "One is always in the position of having to decide between amputation and gangrene."[19] Both metaphors refer
to different attitudes to life. Whilst "amputation" would seem to

---

14. The Wright-Baldwin controversy has intrigued critics for some twenty
years now. For a convenient summary of participants and their views see the
bibliographic essay "James Baldwin" by Daryl Dance in M. Thomas Inge,
Maurice Duke, Jackson R. Bryer, eds., *Black American Writers: Bibliographic
Essays. Vol. II.* London: Macmillan, 1978, pp. 112-113.

15. Richard Wright,"Blueprint for Negro Writing," *New Challenge* (1937),
reprinted in Addison Gayle, ed., *The Black Aesthetic.* Garden City: Anchor,
1972, p. 320.

16. James Baldwin, "Autobiographical Notes," *Notes of a Native Son*,
p. 4.

17. James Baldwin, "The Discovery of What it Means to be an American,"
Nobody Knows My Name: More Notes of a Native Son. New York: Dell,
1963, p. 17.

18. Fern Marja Eckman, *The Furious Passage of James Baldwin.* New
York: Popular Library, n.d., p. 155.

19. James Baldwin, "Notes of a Native Son," *Notes of a Native Son*, p.94;
for an analysis of these metaphors within Baldwin's thinking cf. my *Von der
'Store Front Church' zum 'American Dream': James Baldwin und der amerikanische Rassenkonflikt.* Amsterdam: Grüner, 1975, p. 8f.

convey the fate of Bigger Thomas, "gangrene" refers to the psychological disintegration of those who try to repress their rage. Trying to overcome his predicament, "Baldwin committed himself to the task of exhortation",[20] assigning the Afro-American a redemptive role in American society. Hence Baldwin's essentially moralist stance which dominated his writing up to and including *The Fire Next Time*.

Ironically, this anti-militant, integration-oriented attitude was severely attacked by the white left-wing critic Irving Howe in 1963. Arguing from the premise that the black's position in American society predisposes him to protest, and holding up Wright as a model, Howe not only reproached Baldwin but also reprimanded Ellison for creating a black world "seemingly apart from plight and protest" and for violating "the reality of social life, the interplay between external conditions and personal will."[21] In his reply, Ellison asserted his right to an individual outlook on life, rejecting anyone's prescription who "wants to tell us what a Negro is."[22] More important than this, however, is Ellison's dismissal of Howe's view of protest. In the interview "The Art of Fiction", published in *The Paris Review* in 1955, Ellison outlined his position as follows:

> I recognize no dichotomy between art and protest. ... If the Negro, or any other writer, is going to do what is expected of him he's lost the battle before he takes the field ... For us the question should be, What are the specific *forms* of [the Negro's] humanity, and what in our background is worth preserving or abandoning. The clue to this can be found in folklore ..."[23]

These lines summarize the canon of black literary thought for the postwar decade and lay down an aesthetic which seeks to preserve a specific unity within the larger cultural diversity. The most innate cultural expression is generally felt to be "music" which, as Albert Murray points out, "does contain the most comprehensive rendering of the complexities of the American Negro experi-

20. Louis H. Pratt, *James Baldwin*. Boston: G.K. Hall, 1978, p. 25 [TUSAS 290].

21. Irving Howe, "Black Boys and Native Sons," *A World More Attractive: A View of Modern Literature and Politics*. Freeport, N.Y.: Books for Libraries Press, 1970, pp. 114-115.

22. Ralph Ellison, "The World and the Jug," *Shadow & Act*. London: Secker & Warburg, 1967, p. 115.

23. Ralph Ellison, "The Art of Fiction: An Interview," *Shadow & Act*, pp. 169-171.

ence."[24] Both Murray and Ellison argue against the background of the concept of universality as advocated by Howells, who could conceive of universality only in assimilationist terms. Murray and Ellison, by contrast, stress the specific ethnic aspect of this idea, opting for cultural integration rather than assimilation.

The black writer's preoccupation with integration did not meet with the respective literary concepts advanced by black and white critics in the early part of the postwar decade. In the first monograph to appear after the Second World War Hugh M. Gloster again took up the assimilationist stance of Howells. He remarked:

> Negro writers of the future will extricate themselves from the limitations of color and stand independently as artists, interpreting racial difficulties in universal terms and providing a comprehensive representation of life.[25]

Note the value assumptions implicit in this statement. The relation between color and aesthetics, between ethnicity and universality thus remained the epitome of literary criticism and led to a number of ideological corollaries which dominated critical discussions for at least two decades.

The first corollary refers to the premise of universality which became the watchword in literary evaluations. Thus Carl Milton Hughes, in his study *The Negro Novelist 1940 - 1950* (1953),[26] espoused the doctrine that the topic of "inequality of races ... impoverishes the thematic content of [the Negro novelist's] body of literature," for, as he insisted, such topics "are hardly conducive to producing a great literature." (251) The second corollary refers to the well-known concept of mainstream literature. In the words of Hughes: "various ethnic groups like tributaries flowing into a large river contribute to the main stream of American belle lettres." (17) This stream imagery reveals that the underlying literary--political belief is the philosophy of assimilation. Together with the idea of universality and the concept of mainstream literature, the ideal of assimilation constitutes the semantic field used by critics up to the mid-1960s to discuss and evaluate both the Afro-American novel and the role of the writer. The following credo by

24. Albert Murray, "Something Different, Something More," p. 116.
25. Hugh M. Gloster, *Negro Voices in American Fiction*. Chapel Hill: University of,North Carolina Press, 1948, p. 257.
26. Carl Milton Hughes, *The Negro Novelist 1940 - 1950*. New York: The Citadell Press, 1970. [Page numbers in brackets refer to this reprint edition].

Hughes clearly demonstates the ideological interplay of these semantic forces:

> This wider perspective [humanity] eliminates the Negro novelist from literary specialization with its corresponding emphasis upon injustices and discrimination against a single minority in a polyglot population. At the same time this trend of Negro novelists indicates a favorable literary horizon. It is only in a positive affirmation of American democratic heritage that any American author can point the way of truth. .... Among Negro authors the question of assimilation in the written word is a fait accompli. (266)

An even more striking example of this assimilationist-oriented stance by which the white critic seeks to establish his hegemony over the black writer was furnished by Allen Tate in the same year. In his preface to Melvin B. Tolson's *Libretto for the Republic of Liberia* (1953) Tate had this to say:

> For the first time, it seems to me, a Negro poet has assimilated completely the full poetic language of his time and, by implication, the language of the Anglo-American tradition. I do not wish to be understood as saying that Negro poets have hitherto been incapable of this assimilation; there has been perhaps rather a resistance to it on the part of those Negroes who supposed that their peculiar genius lay in 'folk' idiom or in the romantic creation of a 'new' language within the English language.[27]

The evaluative standards set forth by Tate not only repeat almost verbatim the tenet formulated by Howells in 1896 but also surpass Howells in terms of racial bigotry. What is more, by choosing to disregard the historical body of black writing and by imposing his own scale of values upon Afro-American literature, Tate helped to support that kind of selective criticism which decisively hampered the reception and critical recognition of that literature. Tokenism was thus to become the very epitome of white critical activity. By singling out one black writer and holding him up as a model, the white critic assumed the role of expert, holding an effective monopoly over the critical appreciation of the black writer.

Only five years later, this monopolistic tradition was again administered in what has probably been the most influential monograph on the black novel, Robert Bone's *The Negro Novel in Ame-*

---

27. Allen Tate, "Introduction," in Melvin Tolson, *Libretto for the Republic of Liberia*. New York: Collier Books, 1970.

rica (1958)[28] . Significantly enough, however, Bone departs from an assimilationist reading of the idea of universality. Instead, he expands upon it by introducing the following frame of reference: "Assimilationism and Negro nationalism, concepts indispensable to understanding the cultural history of the American Negro ... provide ... a fixed point of reference from which to view the changing racial attitudes of the Negro novelist — attitudes which are often fundamental to the content of his art"(7). Consider the dualistic point of departure in Bone's argument which reflects the political and social division among black intellectuals at that time[29] . Obviously, this frame of reference follows that contextualistic tradition of American Studies which conceives of American culture in dualistic terms. Such an approach is, as Wilfried Fluck has pointed out, indeed tailored to the needs of a literary critic who, without giving up his aesthetic premises, wants to bring social relevance into his studies[30] . This becomes particularly clear when we review the logical status of the terms "assimilationism" and "nationalism" in Bone's literary value system. Since he decidedly rejects the "assimilationist novel" as "a blind alley" (248) for the black writer and since, at least in 1957, Bone could only visualize a black nationalistic novel as protest art à la Wright's *Native Son,* he takes recourse to a third category which serves as his prime evaluating tool: "to succeed aesthetically, a novel must develop a theme of universal significance from an otherwise isolated segment of human life." (249) Bone's conceptual triad clearly moves beyond the previously discussed notions of universality, since it does not exclude ethnicity *per se* but implies, rather, the idea of cultural integration. However much his concept signals a significant advance on earlier critical approaches, its application does not escape the miasma of tokenism as can be seen from Bone's selective reading list[31] . It so happened that his rigid pledge of allegiance

28. Robert Bone, *The Negro Novel in America.* New Haven: Yale University Press, rev. ed., 1965. [Page numbers in brackets refer to this edition.]
29. For the political and intellectual history of this argument see Harold Cruse, *The Crisis of the Negro Intellectual.* New York: William Morrow, 1968
30. Winfried Fluck, "Das ästhethische Vorverständnis der *American Studies,*" *Amerikastudien,* 18 (1973), 122.
31. Cf. *The Negro Novel in America*, op. cit., p. 254 where, for instance, *Native Son, Invisible Man* and *Go Tell It on the Mountain* are classified as "Major."

to universality was to have far-reaching consequences in the history of the literary criticism of the black novel. For, as Donald Gibson has recently remarked: "Bone is largely responsible for the existence of the line of thought associated with the black aesthetic"[32]. Although this may be overstating the case, Bone was indeed to become the object of much critical shadowboxing by the new generation of black critics.

Only one year after the revised edition of *The Negro Novel in America* had appeared, David Littlejohn published his *Black on White* (1966)[33]. Writing quite obviously under the impression of the beginning racial turbulences of the sixties, Littlejohn sets out to discuss the various responses a white reader is likely to feel upon reading Afro-American fiction. The rather outspoken and lucid enumeration of these responses, which comprise such diverse attitudes as "pain" and, as a form of escape mechanism, literary judgment by which the "reader slips on the rubber gloves of criticism to avoid the sting" (13), is unfortunately not followed by an equally lucid analysis on the critic's part. Instead of pursuing the interesting idea of 'white' literary judgments as "illicit self-defense against pain or as moral evasions" (13) from the racial and cultural context of many black novels, Littlejohn falls short of his own initial perceptions. Note the following statement which serves as a kind of guideline throughout his book: "The protest novels, the pain-causing works can tell only part of the story. The greater art is to contain, to hold together more, the suffering *and* the joy, the hate and the love"(17). Such a position does, of course, echo the previously mentioned dichotomy of protest versus universal art and hence does not provide a new point of orientation.

At first glance, a more promising approach than Littlejohn's confessional criticism seems to have been advanced by Edward

32. Donald B. Gibson, "Afro-American Fiction: Contemporary Research and Criticism, 1965 - 1978," *American Quarterly*, 30 (1978), 397; the critical reception of Bone's study deserves an analysis of its own. For an initial orientation on the shifting reception see the following two articles: August Meier, "Some Reflections on the Negro Novel," *CLA-Journal*, 2 (1958), 168-177 and Darwin T. Turner, *"The Negro Novel in America*: In Rebuttal," *CLA-Journal*, 10 (1966), 122-134.

33. David Littlejohn, *Black on White: A Critical Survey of Writing By American Negroes*. New York: Viking, 1969. [Page numbers in brackets refer to this edition.]

Margolies' *Native Sons* (1968)[34]. Starting from the assumption that the black American has had a distinct cultural and political experience Margolies seeks to discuss Afro-American writers "in the light of the shifting social and historical backgrounds against which they wrote"(18). These backgrounds comprise, for instance, such diverse historical and socio-cultural experiences as migration, miscegenation, the black church, the expatriate point of view as well as the newly emerging black nationalism. Despite the fact that Margolies does not state any reasons why these experiences are distinctly different from similar experiences of other Americans we must admit that his synchronic procedure does have some hermeneutic merits, particularly since it allows for an historical approach. Yet, to give a proper assessment of Margolies' study, it is necessary to relate his frame of reference to the problem of identity which constitutes his major theorem. As he chooses not to define his central term, however, one is never quite sure whether identity refers to a personal, racial or cultural plane. Moreover, the tacit assumptions that the black "has always been the most estranged and alienated of Americans" (16) and that, as a consequence, "the Negro author ... stands as an intensified image of the total American search for self" (15) are not, methodologically speaking, linked to the general frame of reference. In point of fact, the concept of identity turns out to be a dangling term behind which the notion of universality seems to be emerging once again. Consider the following appraisal of William Demby:

> Demby is one of those rare Negro Americans immersed in the culture of the West, who has discovered himself at home in a civilization that has deeply wounded him. His acceptance of the West has not negated his Negro identity but has enhanced it. (189)

In contrast to the critics discussed above, Margolies does not derive his critical judgments from such abstractions as protest or race, rather he deduces his standards of criticism from allegedly objective modes of existence. However, these modes of existence are not conceived of in terms of a historical process but are obviously viewed as facts with an ontological status of their own. Within his

---

34. Edward Margolies, *Native Sons: A Critical Study of Twentieth-Century Negro American Authors*. Philadelphia: Lippincott, 1969. [Page numbers in brackets refer to this edition.]

list of modes, the expatriate espousing western culture seems to be the most praiseworthy as he is genuinely integrationist.

Five years after the publication of Margolies' study another critical effort towards a literary typology of black fiction was launched. In his *From Apology to Protest* (1973)[35] Noel Schraufnagel sets out to delineate the evolution of the black novel since Wright's *Native Son.* Unlike the dualistic frame of reference advanced by Bone, Schraufnagel introduces a more extensive critical machinery, the point of orientation being the central terms "protest novel," "assimilationist and accomodationist novel," "apologetic" as well as "militant protest" fiction. This multiple approach allows Schraufnagel to distinguish different historical phases in terms of the degree to which they reveal the racial preoccupation of the respective writer. If we accept his major premise — "the urge to protest has been basic to the Negro novel since its inception" (99) — and, moreover, if we bear in mind the political nature of Schraufnagel's conceptual system, we come to realize that his concept does indeed embrace almost the whole spectrum of the black novel since 1940. In order to arrive at an adequate appreciation of this typology, it seems to me to be imperative to discuss some of his classifications for, after all, the utility of any typology can only be demonstrated when it is brought to bear on specific literary instances.

Schraufnagel's grouping of the novels of the fifties and early sixties well displays his ability to avoid one-sided categorizations as he carefully reconstructs the various politico-literary paradigms. This well-balanced approach, however, gives way to a rather rigid classification of all those novels which fall under the heading "militant protest." For example, to label Baldwin's *Tell Me How Long The Train's Been Gone* "an overtly propagandistic novel" (187) evidences persuasive arguing which is not corroborated by a close reading of the text. Similarly, to state that "Leo Proudhammer embraces militancy" (187) is to overlook the fact that the novel's hero is an artist who has left behind the misery of the ghetto and achieved fame as an actor. These kinds of statements are indicative of Schraufnagel's procedure which centers almost exclusively on

35. Noel Schraufnagel, *From Apology to Protest: The Black American Novel.* Deland: Everett / Edwards, 1973.[Page numbers in brackets refer to this edition.]

content analysis and hence does not cast light on intra-textual aspects. A further reservation applies to the epistemological status of his system of classification. Since his central terms are used descriptively rather than analytically, they do not provide new evaluative tools as can be seen from his concluding statement: "No novel by an Afro-American has eclipsed *Invisible Man*." (201) Here we are left wondering what evaluative category (other than universality) has persuaded Schraufnagel to commit himself to tokenism.

Although operating from a completely different set of references Roger Rosenblatt in his *Black Fiction* (1974)[36] also finds himself finally trapped in the idea of universality. In contrast to the previously mentioned monographs, *Black Fiction* starts from the assumption that the black novel "has continued to function within patterns peculiarly its own" (2), these patterns being "a cyclical conception of black American history." (12) The term "cyclical history" refers to the fact that the black has alway been the object of the "definition of someone else's manufacture" (18) which, according to Rosenblatt, entails his various attempts to break this confinement through such outlets as religion, education, love and humor. Significantly, the greatest value is attached to the use of humor because, as Rosenblatt insists, "for the characters who use it, it is a way of surviving within, not beating the cyclical system, which is why the few wholly humorous characters who have existed in black fiction have achieved a brand of universality at once unique and credible." (101/102) Despite his elaborated conceptual machinery, despite his frequent emphasis on the historical uniqueness of black literature, Rosenblatt, just like Schraufnagel, is unable to move beyond the rhetoric of tokenism. Consider his following credo: "In terms of the cyclical conception of the literature generally, Ellison's hero represents the ultimate stage." (185)

II

Speaking at the Conference of the American Society for African Culture in 1959 the novelist-critic Julian Mayfield questioned the

36. Roger Rosenblatt, *Black Fiction*. Cambridge, Mass.: Harvard University Press, 1974. [Page numbers in brackets refer to this edition.]

concept of the American literary mainstream popular at that time. He observed: "The Negro writer is being gently nudged toward a rather vague thing called 'the mainstream of American literature'. ... But before plunging into it he owes it to the future of his art to analyse the contents of the American mainstream to determine the full significance of his commitment to it."[37] Three years later, in an essay entitled "The Myth of a 'Negro Literature'" Baraka called on the black artist to "provide his version of America from that no-man's-land outside the mainstream"[38], and in 1965 Ralph Ellison, addressing the American Academy of Arts and Sciences Conference on the Negro American, remarked: "One concept that I wish we would get rid of is the concept of a mainstream of American culture — which is an exact mirroring of segregation and second-class citizenship. I do not think that America works that way at all."[39] The statements of these, politically speaking, rather diverse thinkers are a first pointer towards the growing discomfort among black intellectuals with the mainstream ideology. One important consequence of this new awareness was the rejection of protest fiction as a viable literary mode. In the words of Baraka: "The Negro protest novelist postures, and invents a protest quite amenable with the tradition of bourgeois American life. He never reaches the central core of the America which *can* cause such protest."[40] According to Baraka, the mode of protest writing suffered from the fact that it excluded a position where its writer "could propose his own symbols, erect his own personal myths."[41] If we set these views against the value systems espoused by Hughes, Bone, Littlejohn and Margolies we come to realize that universality has ceased to be the prime evaluative tool. Instead, the black critic has set out to devise an ethnic-oriented value system of his own.

37. Julian Mayfield, "Into the Mainstream and Oblivion," in Addison Gayle, ed., *Black Expression: Essays By and About Black Americans in the Creative Arts.* New York: Weybright & Talley, 1969, p. 273.

38. LeRoi Jones [Amiri Baraka], "The Myth of a Negro Literature," *Home: Social Essays.* New York: Apollo Books, 1966, p. 114.

39. Ralph Ellison, "Remarks at The American Academy of Arts and Sciences Conference on the Negro American, 1965," in Abraham Chapman, ed., *New Black Voices: An Anthology of Contemporary Afro-American Literature.* New York: Mentor, 1972, p. 403.

40. LeRoi Jones, "The Myth of a 'Negro Literature'," p.112.

41. *Ibid.*

Baraka's criticism of the protest genre constitutes an early testimony of the increasing nationalist turn that black consciousness took after 1963. The political goals of the emerging movement have been concisely stated by the late Malcolm X:

> Our political philosophy will be black nationalism. Our economic and social philosophy will be black nationalism. Our cultural emphasis will be black nationalism. ... The political philosophy of black nationalism means: We must control the politics and politicians of our community.[42]

Translated into the context of literary criticism and poetological thinking, Malcolm's teaching affected a number of important issues: (1) the assertion of an independent cultural identity and the tendency to reject everything 'western' and 'white'; (2) an increasing ethnic radicalization and, as a consequence, the denouncement of white critics as racists and of James Baldwin and, to a lesser extent, of Ralph Ellison as assimilationists; (3) an extremely functional and utilitarian view of literature; (4) the striving toward a redefinition of literary criticism from an ethnic point of view in order to destroy the hegemony of the white critical establishment, and (5) the call for independent black publishing houses.[43]

Organically related to the concept of an independent cultural identity is the tenet of a separate black experience and, as a corollary, the stress on the uniqueness of that experience. By implication, then, 'western' aesthetics is regarded as meaningless because, as Larry Neal polemically notes, it "is fundamentally a dry assembly of dead ideas based on a dead people."[44] A further corollary of this concept consists in the theorem of the colonial status of black literature. Thus Gayle laments the "cultural strangulation of Black literature by white critics,"[45] and Hoyt Fuller, editor of the now defunct *Black Scholar*, speaks of "literary colonialism"

42. George Breitman, ed., *Malcolm X Speaks: Selected Speeches and Statements*. New York: Grove Press, 1966, p. 21; for a detailed analysis of the evolution of Malcolm's ideas as well as of his rhetoric see Archie Epps, "The Paradoxes of Malcolm X," in *The Speeches of Malcolm X at Harvard*. New York: William Morrow, 1969, pp.15-112.

43. See the introductory article by Wolfgang Karrer in this volume.

44. Larry Neal, "Any Day Now: Black Art and Black Liberation," in Woodie King and Earl Anthony, eds., *Black Poets and Prophets*. New York, Mentor, 1972, p. 150.

45. Addison Gayle, "Cultural Strangulation: Black Literature and the White Aesthetic," *The Black Aesthetic*, p. 44.

which, as he maintains, has "always handicapped" black artistic achievements.[46] A third corollary refers to the cultural hermeticism by which the white critic is declared as incompetent, since he "can only summarize the work" of black writers[47] or, at the very best, has "only a miniscule place in Black literature."[48]

Significantly, the target of attack was not confined to the white critical establishment alone. As the cultural nationalists no longer ascribe to the black writer the role of spokesman *for* the race to whites, but, instead, urge him to act as spokesman *to* the race, James Baldwin caught the line of critical fire. Particularly the arguments advanced by Baraka, Cruse and Cleaver warrant scrutiny because they anticipated the current notion of a black aesthetic.

In his article "Mass Culture and the Creative Artist" (1960) Baldwin had argued for a division of responsibility between the writer and the politician:

> There is a division of labor in the world — as I see it — and the people have quite enough reality to bear, simply getting through their lives. ... This is what the writer is always describing. There is nothing else to describe. This effort at description is itself extraordinary arduous, and those who are driven to make this effort are by virtue of this fact somewhat removed from the people.[49]

Even though Baldwin was to reverse this position during his commitment to the Civil Rights movement, his concept of "division of labor" proved to be "his Achilles heel",[50] which was quickly exploited by Baraka who chides Baldwin's individualistic attitude and then goes on to say: "Men like Baldwin and Abrahams want to live free from such 'ugly' things as the 'racial struggle'. ... Their color is the only obstruction I can see to this state they seek, and I

46. Hoyt W. Fuller, "The New Black Literature: Protest or Affirmation," *The Black Aesthetic*, p. 330.

47. Ernest Kaiser, "Negro Images in American Writing," *Freedomways*, 7 (1967), 160.

48. Sherley Anne Williams, *Give Birth to Brightness: A Thematic Study in Neo-Black Literature*. New York: Dial, 1972, p. 234; some white critics did indeed fall victim to the black nationalist polemics and retired as critics of black literature. See, for instance, Richard Gilman, "White Standards and Negro Writing," in C.W.E. Bigsby, ed., *The Black American Writer*, pp. 35-50.

49. James Baldwin, "Mass Culture and the Creative Artist: Some Personal Notes," *Daedalus*, 89 (1960), 375-376.

50. Louis H. Pratt, *James Baldwin*, p. 126.

see no reason they should be denied it for so paltry a thing as heavy pigmentation."[51] Similarly, Harold Cruse labels Baldwin's work "the modern literary school of conscience-pleading civil writism,"[52] and Eldridge Cleaver castigates Baldwin for embracing white American cultural values which, according to him, reveal that "there is in James Baldwin's work the most grueling, agonizing, total hatred of the blacks."[53] An almost identical opinion, though less harshly stated, is held by the non-nationalist Albert Murray who criticizes Baldwin for "never having written in terms of the sustaining actualities of [the Negro] tradition in any of his own stories."[54] As for Cleaver and Baraka, their objections seem to be primarily self-serving in that they obviously feel the need to assert themselves by repudiating Baldwin. Moreover, their assessments illustrate the rather selective criticism of black writer-critics who have come to adopt a rhetoric of introjected tokenism. Just as Baldwin blatantly misread Native Son,[55] Baraka, Cruse and Cleaver in their hasty attacks chose to overlook the fact that Baldwin's endorsement of white culture was historically conditioned.[56] And even conservative Albert Murray tends to forget that Baldwin did make use of the blues tradition in Another Country as well as in the short story "Sonny's Blues." The enforced system of only tokenist white attention thus leads to an infighting among black writer-critics whose search for individual self-affirmation implies the "parricide' of one's literary elders. Consider the fictionalized account of the Baldwin-Wright quarrel in John A. Williams The Man Who Cried I Am where the young novelist Marion Dawes (J.B.) says to Harry Ames (R.W.): "It is the duty of a son to destroy his father ... you're the father of all contemporary Negro writers.

51. LeRoi Jones, "Brief Reflections on Two Hot-Shots," Home, p. 120.

52. Harold Cruse, The Crisis of the Negro Intellectual, p. 181.

53. Eldridge Cleaver, "Notes on a Native Son," p. 97.

54. Albert Murray, "Something Different, Something More," p. 118.

55. Like many other black intellectuals Baldwin read the novel rather selectively. In this instance he overlooked the fact that Wright had not presented with Bigger Thomas a model; rather Bigger represents historically conditioned modes of behaviour. Similarly, Baldwin disregarded the accuracy of Wright's social analysis and the nationalist implications that followed from it.

56. Cf. Louis H. Pratt, James Baldwin, p. 128, who points out that in "the 1930s when Baldwin was growing up in Harlem ... African culture was virtually inaccessible to all blacks."

We can't go beyond you until you're destroyed."[57]

On another level, the criticism of Baraka, Cruse and Cleaver pinpoints both the increasing ethnic partisanship of the black writer-critics as well as a change of artistic philosophy. In terms of literary concepts, the nationalist critics of the 1960s and 1970s resumed DuBois' position of the 1920s. DuBois' assertion that "all art is propaganda" is now taken literally and applies to both the poetics and the criticism of black art. Following Maulana Ron Karenga's dictum "that all Black art, irregardless of any technical requirements ... must be functional, collective and committing [and] must expose the enemy, praise the people and support the revolution"[58] black critics started to advocate a politicized art which is viewed purely in functional terms. Discarding the mimetic and textual aspects of literature these critics urged the artist "to change the images his people identify with by asserting Black feeling, Black mind, Black judgment."[59] The role of the artist as an image-maker for the black community involves two decisive issues. In the first place, the black arts movement aims at destroying the double consciousness as described by DuBois in 1903 in order to merge the "unreconciled strivings" into "One Committed Soul integrated with itself."[60] The problem of the double audience which had intrigued the Afro-American artist since 1903 is now, at least theoretically, resolved by the idea of ethnicity, with blackness becoming the sole poetological referent. Secondly, the function of black artistic expressions is not only "the destruction of white ways of looking at the world"[61] but, more importantly, the creation of the nation. The idea of a cultural nation-building has been

57. John A. Williams, *The Man Who Cried I Am*. New York: Signet, 1969, pp.181-182.

58. Ron Karenga, "Black Cultural Nationalism," in *The Black Aesthetic*, p. 32. Karenga borrowed his concept from Frantz Fanon, *The Wretched of the Earth*. New York: Grove Press, 1968, pp. 226-232.

59. Amiri Baraka, "The Legacy of Malcolm X, and the Coming of the Black Nation," in Abraham Chapman, ed., *New Black Voices*, p. 465.

60. Larry Neal, "Any Day Now," p. 151.

61. For the socio-literary background of this problem see my article "Black American Short Fiction in the 20th Century: Problems of Audience, and the Evolution of Artistic Stances and Themes," in Peter Bruck, ed., *The Black American Short Story in the 20th Century: A Collection of Critical Essays*. Amsterdam: Grüner, 1977, pp. 1-20.

most notably espoused by Baraka in his "7 Principles of US Maulana Karenga & The Need for a Black Value System" where he describes its purpose as follows: "To make as our collective vocation the building and developing of our community in order to restore our people to their traditional greatness."[63]

The notion of cultural exclusivism and artistic functionalism has been put into practice by a number of black critics recently. What is noteworthy in their activity is a radicalization of that prescriptive attitude to literature which was first formulated in the 1920s; indeed, the critic as textual explicator seems to have resigned and given way to the critic as ethnic partisan. One of the most versatile of these critics is undoubtedly Addison Gayle whose various writings illustrate perhaps best the direction in which ethnic criticism has moved. In *The Black Situation* (1970) Gayle proclaimed that "Afro-American literature awaits its Whitman and the chances of this Whitman appearing are better today than at any time before."[64] Translated into the cultural context of the black aesthetic, the reference to Whitman suggests that the black literary nationalists initially saw themselves as the true successors to the 18th and 19th century striving for a genuinely national American literature. Bearing in mind that Walt Whitman in *Democratic Vistas* called on the American writer to create "national, original archetypes,"[65] and following Benjamin Spencer who has pointed out that the early nationalist critic rejected "imported novels" on the ground that they "instilled alien modes,"[66] we come to realize that close parallells do indeed exist between the two movements. In the

62. Larry Neal, "Any Day Now," p. 154.

63. Amiri Baraka, "7 Principles for US Maulana Karenga & The Need for a Black Value System," *Raise Race Raze: Essays*. New York: Vintage. Baraka was later to shift his position once more. For a detailed analysis of the evolution of his political thinking see Werner Sollors, *Amiri Baraka / LeRoi Jones: The Quest for a 'Populist Modernism'*. New York: Columbia University Press, 1978, pp. 64-82, 221-232.

64. Addison Gayle, *The Black Situation*. New York: Horizon Press, 1970, p. 20.

65. Walt Whitman, *Democratic Vistas*, in Floyd Stovall, ed., *Walt Whitman: Prose Works 1892*. New York: New York University Press, 1964, II, p. 405.

66. Benjamin Spencer, *The Quest for Nationality*. Syracuse: Syracuse University Press, 1957, p. 30.

words of Gayle, who attacks the critical monopoly of Allen Tate and Robert Penn Warren:

> In propounding the thesis of a Black Aesthetic, they [black intellectuals] offer an instrument as potent as that of the early American writers who sought to break the domination of their culture by Frenchmen, Englishmen, and Germans. In freeing American letters from southern tyranny, in advocating critical rules opposed to the anti-humanistic one of the disciplines of the New Critics, in postulating a literature which functions in the interest of all mankind, they may bring about a revolution in American letters designed to usher in a new freedom for all writers — white and black alike.[67]

Note the non-ethnic stance of this statement which does not yet aspire to a black absolutism. However, Gayle was soon to change his position, thus abandoning a promising approach which might not only have yielded important historical tools for the evaluation of Afro-American literature but which might also have initiated a genuinely comparative perspective.

The most comprehensive attempt to establish and apply the "critical rules" mentioned above is to be found in *The Way of the New World* (1975).[68] Here Gayle sets out to discuss the history of the black novel in terms of the struggle for the supremacy of the ideas of assimilationism or nationalism. Significantly enough, this binary frame of reference is, epistemologically speaking, a replica of that advanced by Bone in 1958. Strangely enough, Bone, who is otherwise the continual object of Gayle's critical shadowboxing, has indeed provided Gayle with the point of orientation needed for his nationalistic evaluations; for what Gayle does is nothing but invert the values Bone attached to his conceptual triad. Hence the focus of evaluation has shifted from universality to that of "racial pride" (21) or blackness, the center of attention now being the extent to which a novelist is successful in "undertaking the war against the American imagists." (8) It so happened, however, that the application of this critical credo shows Gayle to be following the familar Howellian concept, which as the following passage indicates, has simply been tinged with blackness: "When the black novelist seizes upon images [of exploitation and oppression]

67. Gayle, *The Black Situation*, p. 185.
68. Addison Gayle, *The Way of the New World: The Black Novel in America*. Garden City: Anchor, 1976. [page numbers in brackets refer to this ed.]

to people his works, the black novel moves into the universal arena, and the black character becomes the representative of struggling humanity everywhere." (245) Within the line of Gayle's reasoning, protest against cultural colonisation gains a universal dimension, i.e. protest, by the very definition of the politico-cultural situation of the blacks, as well as the concomitant striving for new ethnic images reflects the universal concern of every ethnic minority. Yet, the attentive reader of *The Way of the New World* is soon confused by the fact that Gayle, perhaps unintentionally, also echoes that notion of universality which has been formulated by Howells, Tate, and Bone. Consider this statement: "The archetypal hero of the twentieth century is the black man evidencing, in his daily struggles, the most universal of characteristics — hope, love, determination, and courage." (340)

Apart from its obvious inconsistencies, Gayle's general approach to the Afro-American novel lends itself to a number of objections. First of all, it is narrow, operating from the assumption that content takes *sui generis* precedence over the various manifestations of literary discourse. Thus, methodologically speaking, the individual value judgments turn out to be circular as they invariably reflect the prescriptive canon of the critic. Secondly, the method is, as Henry-Louis Gates has pointed out, "reductionist," since it describes the literary discourse "mechanically by classifications that find their ultimate significance somewhere else."[69] Other strictures apply to various contradictory judgements. In his introduction, for example, Gayle argues that "traditional plots in the black novel, situations and character became anachronistic." (xxii) Yet, it is this textual category which prompts him to praise *The Autobiography of Miss Jane Pittman* for having reached "near perfection because of the unity of form and content, because the themes are interwoven into the fabric of the novel in such a way as to complement the form." (365) Here we are left wondering why Gayle employs the rhetoric of the New Critics whom he has earlier castigated for their "anti-humanistic rules." A further contradiction emerges with regard to the evaluation of *Native Son*, which is

69. Henry-Louis Gates, "Preface to Blackness: Text and Pretext," in Dexter Fisher / Robert B. Stepto, eds., *Afro-American Literature: The Reconstruction of Instruction*. New York: The Modern Language Association of America, 1969, p. 67.

praised as "the model for the novelist of the nineteen seventies" (209) as well as referred to in this way: "Neither should *Native Son* be considered the model for future black writers." (218)

Another major weakness refers to the epistemological status of his "major criterion for the evaluation of art," which Gayle has stated as follows: "How much better has the work of art made the life of a single human being upon this planet, and how functional has been the work of art in moving us toward that moment when an ars poetica is possible for all." (379) Gayle's disrespect for a critical methodology[70] seems to have prevented him from developing concise, well-defined tools. For according to what standards are we to decide if, when and how a novel has made better the life of a single human being? And, to return to Gayle's reference to Whitman, is his "major criterion" an exclusive ethnic category or does it refer to the art of any oppressed people irrespective of their ethnicity? As Gayle never clarifies these problems, his practical application of the theorems of the black aesthetic is at best thought-provoking and, at worst, a blind alley in the critical effort of coming to terms with the various textual manifestations and the thematic richness of the contemporary Afro-American novel.

III

The prescriptive canon of the black aestheticians has evoked a number of negative reactions by black writers and critics alike. Thus Julian Mayfield categorically states, "I cannot-will not-define my Black Aesthetic, nor will I allow it to be defined for me,"[71] the critic George Kent rejects the functionalist concept advanced by Karenga on the ground that "it is rather difficult not to envision a cultural commissar arriving to enforce upon the artist his ver-

70. See Gayle's statement in his introduction to *The Black Aesthetic*, p. xxii: "A critical methodology has no relevance to the black community unless it aids men in becoming better than they are." For an illuminating critique of this position within the context of literary politics in the late 1960s see Richard Kostelanetz, *The End of Intelligent Writing: Literary Politics in America*. New York: Sheed and Ward, 1973, pp. 237-245.

71. Julian Mayfield, "You Touch My Black Aesthetic and I'll Touch Yours," in *The Black Aesthetic*, p. 27.

sion of what fits the people's needs"[72] and novelist Albert Murray even suspects that the Black Arts Movement is "commercially o-riented toward white American audiences above all others."[73] One of the most piercing criticisms has been put forth by James Cunningham who in the January issue of *Negro Digest* in 1968 wrote an article directed against Karenga's manifesto "Black Cultural Nationalism." Cunningham finds fault, for instance, with Karenga's invocation of the black community as the focal point for the black artist. Moreover, he reprimands Karenga for his dismissal of individuality, pointing out that the latter's idea of collective art makes the blacks "ruthlessly streamlined and standardized for convenient over-simplification."[74] Poetologically, the Cunningham-Karenga controversy added no new ideas to the art versus propaganda debate of the fifties and sixties. What it did show, however, is the continuous tendency of black intellectuals to formulate blueprints according to which the writer is expected to create his work, and the continual rebellion of the writer against such blueprints. Hence it will come as no surprise that many novelists of the younger generation insist on their freedom of artistic expression, for, as Ernest J. Gaines has declared, "the artist is the only free man left. He owes nobody nothing. ... He should write what he wants, when he wants, and to whomever he wants."[75]

Other indicators of the anti black aesthetic attitude shared by many novelists may be observed in the emergence of such feminist writers as Alice Walker and the increasing concern with black womanhood, which underlies the novels of Toni Morrison as well as Al Young's *Who Is Angelina?* . Additionally, novelists have also started to parody the militancy of the black aestheticians in literary discourse. Consider the aesthetic confrontation between the cowboy Loop Garoo Kid and the neo-social realist Bo Shmo in Ishmael Reed's *Yellow Back Radio Broke Down* which reads like

72. George Kent, *Blackness and the Adventure of Western Culture*. Chicago: Third World Press, 1972, p. 200.

73. Albert Murray, "Something Different, Something More," p. 123.

74. James Cunningham, "Ron Karenga and Black Cultural Nationalism," *Negro Digest,* 17 (January 1968), 79.

75. Statement by Ernest J. Gaines in "A Survey: Black Writers Views on Literary Lions and Values," *Negro Digest*, op. cit., 27; significantly, of the 38 writers participating in this survey, the majority rejected the notion of a black aesthetic.

a fictionalized account of the Cunningham-Karenga debate:

> What's you beef with me Bo Shmo, what if I write circuses? No one says a novel has to be one thing. It can be anything it wants to be, a vaudeville show, the six o'clock news, the mumbling of wild men saddled by demons.

To which Bo Shmo replies:

> All art must be the end of liberating the masses. A landscape is only good when it shows the oppressor hanging from a tree.[76]

Reed's satirical attacks against the prescriptions of the black aestheticians, their hampering influence on the further evolution of Afro-American literature[77] as well as his promotion of an ethnic multiculturalism[78] illustrate perhaps best the new awareness of black novelists. The cultural concern of this direction is metaphorically encompassed in *Mumbo-Jumbo* where the multi-ethnic organisation "Mu'tafikah," an obvious ironic pun, seeks to restore the stolen objects of black art. Translated into terms of scholarship, these new concerns call for new critical ventures which must do away with the rigid, scriptural canon argued for by the black aestheticians.. In the first place, more comparative studies such as Klotman's *Another Man Gone,*[79] which analyzes the various manifestations of the black runner within the context of American and western culture, are needed in order to arrive at a proper assessment of Afro-American literary expressions. Secondly, we need to release Wright's Bigger Thomas from the enshrinement many critics put him into[80] and redirect, instead, our attention to the "in-

76. Ishmael Reed, *Yellow Back Radio Broke Down*. New York: Avon Books, 1977, p. 44.

77. Cf. Reed's criticism of the editorial policy of Hoyt Fuller's *Black World* in his article "You Can't Be a Literary Magazine and Hate Writers" which is reprinted in his *Shrovetide In Old New Orleans*. New York: Avon Books, 1979, pp. 283-286.

78. Cf. Reed's articles "The 'Liberal' in Us All' and "The Multi-Cultural Artist: A New Phase in American Writing", *Shrovetide in New Orleans*, pp. 43-50 and 291-294.

79. Cf. Phillis Rauch Klotman, *Another Man Gone: The Black Runner in Contemporary Afro-American Fiction*. Port Washington, N.Y.: Kennikat Press, 1977.

80. For the influence of *Native Son* on contemporary critics see Robert B. Stepto, "I Thought I Knew These People: Richard Wright & The Afro-American Literary Tradition," *The Massachusetts Review*, 17 (1977), 525-541.

tertextuality"[81] of black novels, analyzing Afro-American literature as an evolutionary system, thus breaking with the established canon of the critical community which is still preoccupied with the writings of Wright, Ellison, and Baldwin.[82] *Native Son, Invisible Man* or *Go Tell It on the Mountain*, for all their thematic richness, are not the yardstick by which to measure other Afro-American novels nor can they stand — as this collection of essays tries to show — as tokens for them. Thirdly, the aesthetic and political victimization of the black artist by black and white critics alike must come to an end. The tendency of critics "to denigrate older black writers while lauding the newest"[83] and the concomitant series of 'parricides' have always led to an unfortunate ghettoization of those writers who, for whatever reasons, refused to 'slay their elders.' In the words of Chester Himes:

> On the American literary scene, the powers that be have never admitted but one black at a time into the arena of fame, and to gain this coveted admission, the younger writer must unseat the reigning deity. It's a pity but a reality as well.[84]

81. Henry-Louis Gates, "Preface to Blackness," p. 68.

82. I checked the *International Dissertation Abstracts* from Vol. 25 (1964) up to Vol. 40 (1980). Of the 50 dissertations dealing with contemporary black novelists, 10 are written on Baldwin, 9 on Ellison, 16 on Wright, 3 on Himes, 3 on Baraka and 1 each on Killens and Williams. Similarly, most course outlines make use of the triad Wright-Ellison-Baldwin. See, for instance, the course outlines of the National American Studies Faculty, Stetson University, Deland, Florida.

For a re-orientation of course designs which do away with the established canon see the three articles on "Afro-American Literature Course Designs" in Fischer / Stepto, eds., *Afro-American Literature*, pp. 233-255.

The most recent attempt at canonizing black novelists is to be found in Jeffrey Helterman / Richard Layman, eds., *American Novelists Since World War II*. Detroit: Gale Research Company, 1978, who only include Baldwin, Ellison, Gaines, Himes, Reed, and John A. Williams.

83. Darwin T. Turner, "Afro-American Literary Critics: An Introduction", in *The Black Aesthetic*, p. 72.

84. Chester Himes, *The Quality of Hurt: The Autobiography of Chester Himes*. London: Michael Joseph, 1973, p. 201;

Ralph Ellison, by contrast, refuses to acknowledge this aspect, calling the father-son metaphor "a source of needless confusion." See Robert B. Stepto, "Study & Experience: An Interview with Ralph Ellison," *The Massachusetts Review*, 17 (1977), 419. It must be pointed out, however, that both Stepto

It would seem to me that serious literary criticism must cut through this vicious circle, bury the ghosts of William Dean Howells and Bigger Thomas, which still haunt the critics, and finally accept the credo spoken by one of the characters in Reed's *Mumbo-Jumbo*: "Is it necessary for us to write the same way? I am not Wallace Thurman, Thurman is not Fauset, and Fauset is not Claude McKay, McKay isn't Horne. We all have our unique styles."[85]

and Ellison discuss this problem in psychological rather than sociological terms and hence do not deal with tokenism.

85. Ishmael Reed, *Mumbo-Jumbo*. New York: Bantam, 1973, pp. 116-117.

WOLFGANG KARRER

B: INTEGRATION OR SEPARATISM:
THE SOCIAL HISTORY OF THE AFRO-AMERICAN DILEMMA
AFTER WORLD WAR II

> I maintain that since in the United States we are a most special minority, amid a majority of whites, the real issue for us is Adjustment and not Segregation. For when we come down to brass tacks, the Negro minority must depend finally on the good-will of white America.
>
> Claude McKay, "On Becoming a Roman Catholic," *The Epistle*, 11 (Spring 1945).

> The society we seek to build among black people, then, is not a capitalistic one. It is a society in which the spirit of community and humanistic love prevail. We can build a community of love only where we have the ability and power to do so: among blacks.
>
> Stokely Carmichael and Charles Hamilton, *Black Power. The Politics of Liberation in America.* (1968)

> This old hammer
> Killed John Henry,
> Can't kill me, Lord,
> Can't kill me.
>
> Traditional.

The justification for a separate treatment of the Afro-American novel remains the specific Afro-American experience out of which it arises:

In 1970 a national sample found that only 29 percent of blacks reported contact with a white neighbour. Almost as many (24 percent) had contact with white policemen, while the most interaction took place with employers or supervisors (68 percent). Thus blacks' principal social dealings are with blacks, while their contacts with whites are more often with supervisors or authority figures.[1]

1. Sar A. Levitan, William B. Johnston, and Robert Taggert, *Still A Dream:*

The underlying and continuing causes for this experience — and here Gunnar Myrdal (1944), the Kerner Report (1968) and the latest figures agree — have to be located in the open or hidden, individual and institutional racism of American society. Black social history, black integrationist or separatist ideologies, and the contemporary Afro-American novel have to be studied starting from these causes.

Gunnar Myrdal's classic study *An American Dilemma* documents fully the pervasive racism in American society: the discrimination against blacks in economics, politics, justice, and social equality.[2] It also assesses the strength of black leadership, organizations, and community institutions as well as their chances in overcoming racism.[3] Finally, it describes the political dilemma of integration vs. separatism among blacks in its social and economic setting, a dilemma that has characterized black politics for so long and continues to do so.[4] Myrdal defines the black position within a dual system of social class with black and white subsystems of lower, middle and upper classes divided by a caste line:

Percentage of Whites and Negroes at each level of
Social Status

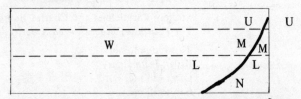

While the Negroe class structure has developed contrary to the caste principle and actually implies a considerable modification of caste relations, fundamentally this class structure is a function of the caste order. We have repeatedly had to refer to this important fact that while caste order has held the Negro worker down, it has at the same time created petty monopolies for a tiny Negro middle and upper class.[5]

The Changing Status of Blacks since 1960. Cambridge: Harvard University Press, 1975, p.156.

2. Gunnar Myrdal with the assistance of Richard Sterner and Arnold Rose, *An American Dilemma: The Negro Problem and Modern Democracy*. repr. New York: Harper, 1969, pp. 205-705.

3. *Ibid.*, p. 709-994.

4. Thomas L. Blair, *Retreat to the Ghetto: The End of a Dream*. New

This basic social situation and its changes — later restated not in terms of caste but of colonialism (Carmichael) or ethnic minorities (Glazer / Moynihan)[6] — account for much of the unity and disunity among Afro-Americans since World War II.

If Myrdal saw World War II as a possible decisive turning point for blacks in analogy to the Civil War and World War I he overrated political changes as much as ideological forces: he believed that the vicious cycle of prejudice and discrimination could be broken by confronting racism with the American Creed. Social and economic changes, not the ideological conflicts accounted for many of the developments after 1945.

THE COLD WAR 1945 - 1954

If blacks gained a selective admission to Northern industrial jobs during World War II,[7] many of them were exposed to a double economic squeeze which brought about important social changes after 1945. The traditional Southern class structure of black landowners, tenants, and farmhands all but collapsed under the impact of technological changes.[8] The majority of blacks in the South

York: Hill and Wang, 1977, p. VIII: "Integration and separatism, two opposing philosophies by which blacks have dealt with a hostile white society and in the process shaped images of themselves." Myrdal, p. 720 ff. uses the older terminology of "accomodation" and "protest."

5. Gunnar Myrdal, *An American Dilemma*, p. 692 f. The model is misleading insofar it suggests that more whites belong to the upper than the middle class. For a table that reflects the actual size of different minority groups along class lines see Dorothy K. Neuman, "The Black American Worker," in Mabel M. Smythe, ed., *The Black American Reference Book*. Englewood Cliffs NJ: Prentice-Hall, 1976, p. 262.

6. The inadequacies of the caste model were criticized by Oliver Cox, *Caste, Class and Race*. New York: Harper 1948, pp. 489-538. In the theory of internal colonialism the black middle class became part of the exploitive structure. In the ethnic-minority approach the black middle class was taken as indication that blacks would eventually follow other immigrant minorities in their upward mobility. See below, p.

7. Gunnar Myrdal, *An American Dilemma*, pp. 1004-1008 describes the struggle against discrimination in the defense industries.

8. *Ibid.*, pp. 235-250. For the decline in ownership, decline in acreage and sharecropping since 1910 compare George W. Groh, *The Black Migration: The Journey to Urban America*. New York: Weybright and Talley, 1972, pp. 32-38.

had worked as sharecroppers and farmhands in the production of cotton and tobacco. Their indispensable work on which the Southern social and economic structure had rested so long[9] was taken over by machines: tractors took over the plowing and planting, chemical weed control the weeding, and cotton picking machines did 80 percent of the harvesting by 1970. The mechanization of tobacco production followed soon.[10] A whole mode of production on which black livelihood and folkways had depended so long was rapidly disappearing. Urban blacks and newly migrated blacks, on the other hand, had to face a new wave of automation and further mechanization of industrial production which left fewer and fewer jobs for unskilled laborers. By 1961 companies were hiring 50 percent more professional people than laborers, and the role of the laborer had been reduced to one job in eighteen.[11] Industries deserting the cities aggravated the problem even more. This created new tensions in the urban ghettoes of the North and West: a pressure against the job ceiling between unskilled and skilled jobs, an increase of black unemployment, and the slow beginnings of a growth in the black middle classes.[12] The increased industrial demand for a more skilled labor force and the growing black vote in Northern cities created the necessary political pressure for the reform of the segregated school system which finally led to the *Brown vs. Board of Education of Topeka* decision in 1954.

Even so, economic and educational possibilities still seemed better in the North. Thus the migration of blacks from the South to the Northeast and West which had lagged during the Depression augmented dramatically during the forties and continued unabated during the fifties and sixties. During the decade 1910-1920 454 000 blacks left the South, 749 000 in 1920-1930, 348 000 in 1930-1940, 1 597 000 in 1940-1950, 1 457 000 in 1950-1960, and one million in 1960-1970.[13] Mechanization and decline of

9. George W. Groh, *The Black Migration*, pp. 13-22.
10. *Ibid.*, pp. 64 f.
11. *Ibid.*, p. 117.
12. For an illustration see the Chicago study by St. Clair Drake and Horace C. Cayton, *Black Metropolis. A Study of Negro Life in a Northern City.* 2nd. ed., New York: Harper 1962, pp. 287-311, 658-715.
13. *Report of the National Advisory Commission on Civil Disorders.* New York: Bantam Books, 1968, p. 240; Sar A. Levitan, *Still A Dream*, p. 4.

Southern agriculture with the resulting unemployment, discrepancies between North and South in social services like welfare and food programs, farm subsidies and school lunch programs remain the principal causes for this migration.[14] The new defense industries in California and World War II added a third to the major migration routes: north along the Atlantic Seaboard toward Boston, another north from Mississippi toward Chicago, and the third west from Texas and Louisiana toward California.[15] The mechanization of Southern agriculture did not only hurt blacks:

> Demographically speaking, it resulted in the greatest displacement of one segment of the population – farmers – in the history of the nation. Twenty million Americans, a figure comparable in scope to the 30 million immigrants who entered the United States between 1880 and 1930, were dislocated in the thirty years between 1940 and 1970. About 16 million of these people were white; 4 million were black.[16]

This rural-urban and geographic population shift is one of the basic collective and individual experiences for Afro-Americans during the whole period; it is reflected in the biographies of some of the authors and almost all the novels represented in this collection.

The continuing migration made Afro-Americans rapidly one of the most urbanized groups of the nation faced with very specific urban problems like life in the ghettoes, segregation in housing and education, family disruption, and building new community institutions. Besides the NAACP and the National Urban League the black churches helped the newly arrived to adjust to city life.[17] Urban church life had its base in the local community and showed very clear class alignments. Baptist and Holiness churches served all but found their particular strength in the black lower classes, Methodist churches had a higher percentage in the middle and upper classes. These churches were not only expected to bridge rural and urban life for those recently arrived but also, as one of the strongest community organizations, to work and speak out for

14. George W. Groh, *The Black Migration*, pp. 63-87.
15. *Report*, p. 240.
16. Leonard Dinnerstein, Roger L. Nichols and David M. Reimers, *Natives and Strangers: Ethnic Groups and the Building of America*. New York: Oxford University Press, 1979, p. 252.
17. Thomas L. Blair, *Retreat to the Ghetto*, p. 19.

the rights of Afro-Americans.[18] This last expectation, however, was almost exclusively held by the middle class congregations while lower class churches remained closer to the rural Southern traditions, often very otherworldly and less concerned with secular affairs. The increasing social, cultural and economic differentiation of black churches combined with their declining importance for urban blacks which may have forced its leaders to take a more active and militant role in the civil rights struggles of the fifties.[19]

The Cold War situation of the United States made protest and direct action against racism virtually impossible. The break of black intellectuals with the Communist Party[20] and its separatist programs,[21] the European exile of important black writers like Richard Wright, James Baldwin, Chester Himes and William Demby, the hostile critical reception of the so called "protest novel" – Gloster's book *Negro Voices in American Fiction* is a good case in point – all reflect the stifling climate of loyalty or "Unamerican activities" which made CORE's early attempts at sit-ins and Freedom rides ineffective. Political powerlessness in the North, disenfranchisement in the South, and the political and media conservatism of the Cold War restricted black activities to the legal tactics of the NAACP as the only generally accepted way of fighting prejudice and discrimination. On the other hand, the decolonization of Africa, the war against fascism and racism in Europe, and the ideological role as the champion of freedom assumed by the United States brought a certain pressure on the Federal Government to propose civil rights legislation which in face of the majorities in Congress had little chance of being passed.[22] Congress had passed its last civil rights law in 1875, and the Cold War remained in spite of some tokenism for black leaders[23] the last phase of a long hist-

18. St. Clair Drake and Horace C. Cayton, *Black Metropolis*, pp. 412-429; 611-657.

19. Norval Glenn, "Negro Religion and Negro Status in the United States,' in David G. Bromley and Charles F. Longino, Jr., ed.,*White Racism and Black Americans*. Cambridge, Mass.: Schenkman 1972, pp.452-476, esp. 464-473.

20. Harold Cruse, *The Crisis of the Negro Intellectual: From its Origin to the Present*. New York: Morrow, 1967, pp.147-170.

21. Thomas L. Blair, *Retreat to the Ghetto*, pp. 15 f.

22. John Hope Franklin, "A Brief History," in Mabel M. Smythe, ed., *The Black American Reference Book*, pp. 69 f.

23. William Z. Foster, *The Negro People in American History*. repr. New York: International Publishers, 1976, pp. 518-540.

oric period that established and carried out Jim Crow laws and racial segregation in almost all areas of life.[24] During the same period some of the economic foundations of racism in the United States began to crumble away: if there was less and less need for black sharecroppers, the expensive effort to maintain a "separate but equal" second school system for blacks in the South became more and more questionable. For its 1953 convention the NAACP adopted the slogan "We want to be free by Sixty-three."

THE CIVIL RIGHTS MOVEMENT 1954 - 1964

The continuing decline of farm tenancy and of opportunities for unskilled black and white workers hit blacks harder than whites, especially in the South. Here blacks were systematically excluded from the political and educational possibilities to make use of their rights. The control of local politics, the election of sheriffs, tax assessors, judges, school and city board members[25] became crucial in all places where it was general practice

> that the cotton gins paid a white price and a black price, that the merchants and money lenders had white and black terms, that even the county agents offered separate and unequal white and black services.[26]

Together with rising black unemployment and the permanent low status of blacks in the North these potentially explosive factors led to the Supreme Court decision of 1954 which ended *de jure* segregation of American schools and reverted its 1896 decision which had made "separate but equal" services perfectly constitutional.[27] The Court recognized two important facts which led to its decision: education determined more than it did in the past the employment chances and status of Americans, and a segregated school system discriminated against blacks, if only through the fact that segregation generated a feeling of inferiority as to their status

24. Alton Hornsby Jr., *The Black Almanac*. 4th rev. ed., New York: Barron's Educational Series, 1977, pp. 94-324 lists the occasions certain prizes or positions were given for the first time to individual blacks.
25. Gunnar Myrdal, *An American Dilemma*, pp. 432 f.
26. George W. Groh, *The Black Migration*, p. 12.
27. Albert P. Blaustein and Robert L. Zagrando, ed., *Civil Rights and the Black American*. rev. ed., New York: Washington Square Press 1970, pp. 294-311 and pp. 406-447 reprint the essential documents of both cases.

in the community and affected their chances of getting an equal education.[28] Too many studies had shown how deeply a segregated school system and hegemony of white values in curricula and textbooks impaired the sense of identity and school advancement of black children.[29] Some school districts in the South complied with the Supreme Court decision to desegregate, but others resisted with all possible means: non-compliance, lower-court obstruction, a turn to a private school system and closing public schools, internal (classroom) segregation, boycotts, picketing and physical violence. Federal troops had to return to the South. The success of the legal strategies of the NAACP had its obvious limitations.

The change to a strategy of nonviolent direct action to achieve equal rights came from the churches. The Montgomery bus boycott aimed not only at desegregating public facilities — one of the weakest links in the Jim Crow system, because it brought profit to nobody — but also at opening employment opportunities for black workers. Its success helped to build the Southern Christian Leadership Conference (SCLC), to bring the churches and the NAACP closer together, and to build strong student organizations like the Student Nonviolent Coordinating Committee (SNCC), which together with CORE and the other organizations adopted Ghandi principles to work them into effective tactics of sit-ins, freedom rides, and peaceful demonstrations. If the aim to force negotiation on the unwilling local administrations through creative disorder remained fairly stable for the SCLC, the emphasis of the students quickly shifted from desegregating lunch counters and interstate buses to voter registration in predominantly black counties and striking down black disenfranchisement in the South. The violent white reactions to the Civil Rights Movement in the South, the high personal losses in property and lives involved, and the grow-

28. *Ibid.*, p. 436.

29. A summary of the relevant literature can be found in Steven R. Asher and Vernon L. Allen, "Racial Preference and Social Comparison Processes," in David G. Bromley and Charles F. Longino, Jr., ed., *White Racism*, pp. 133-143 repr. from *The Journal of Social Issues*, 25 (1969), 157-165; G.P. Armstrong and A. James Gregor, "Integrated Schools and Negro Character Development," in David G. Bromley and Charles F. Longino , Jr., ed., *White Racism*, pp. 158-165, repr. from *Psychiatry*, 27 (1964), 69-72; compare also Kenneth B. Clark, *Dark Ghetto: Dilemmas of Social Power*. New York: Harper, 1965, pp.111-153.

ing disenchantment with the Democratic Party brought about a split between the more gradualist approach of the NAACP and the SCLC and the "Freedom Now!" demand of SNCC and CORE.[30] This split reflected tensions between the groups supporting the Civil Rights Movement: between the black middle-class leadership dependent on white support and the more radical student organizations with a newly mobilized mass support. This heterogeneous composition of the movement was also reflected in its aims: equal rights was something very definite and generally agreed on, whereas integration meant such different things as "adaptation" of the white majority culture, "adjustment" or "accomodation" to it, "assimilation" by it or "amalgation" through intermarriage with it (all these terms were used, often indiscriminately, during the Civil Rights struggle). Most of these concepts seemed to imply a tacit acceptance of a hegemony of the white majority over the black minority. White supporters continued to give to NAACP and SCLC, the money for SNCC and CORE dried up as they turned to more radical ideologies.

The split over gradualism and legal tactics had other causes as well. The resistance in Congress to pass, after the two token Civil Rights Acts of 1957 and 1960,[31] one that would work, the failure of the Democratic Party to seat the independent and nonracist Mississippi Freedom Democratic Party in 1964, and, maybe most important of all, the experience of violent retaliation accompanying and following principled nonviolent demonstrations had to be countered, according to some, by a more cautious, according to others, by a more direct violent approach of armed self defense. The mass media which helped to bring about the Civil Rights Act of 1964 also brought home to many blacks in the North the fact that nonviolence was at best a very limited instrument to abolish racism in the United States. Unpunished lynchings and police brutality in the South often made a farce of Southern justice.

30. The whole movement is succintly summarized by Thomas L. Blair, *Retreat to the Ghetto*, pp. 61-85; for a fuller treatment see Benjamin Muse, *The American Negro Revolution: From Nonviolence to Black Power*. Bloomington: Indiana University Press, 1968. A bibliography on the subject can be found in James M. McPherson a.o., *Blacks in America: Bibliographical Essays*. Garden City: Anchor, 1971, pp.314-331.

31. For the texts see Albert P. Blaustein and Robert L. Zagrando, ed., *Civil Rights and the Black American*, pp. 471-482.

The Civil Rights Movement also left its impact on the Afro-
-American novels represented here, whether through direct participation like Alice Walker or through thematic incorporation into
the novels as in the case of William Melvin Kelley or Ernest Gaines.
Mass media opened, publishers, anthologists, and critics supplied a
growing market with an increased output of Afro-American fiction, drama, poetry and essays. A second Renaissance, this time
not exclusively based in Harlem, seemed to have come for Afro-
American literature.[32]

THE BLACK POWER MOVEMENT 1964 - 1973.

The Civil Rights Act of 1964 dealt in detail with discrimination in
voting rights, places of public accommodation and public facilities,
education, federally assisted programs, and employment opportunities. The weak section on voting had to be amended by the Vo-
ing Rights Act of 1965. The conspicuously absent regulation of
the housing market was dealt with in the Fair Housing Act of
1968. Much of this took effect. Blacks, especially urban blacks,
made definite economic progress during the period. They narrow-
ed the black and white income gap, black occupational distribution
became more like that of whites, they increased educational attainments and enrollment, and they made some progress in housing.[33] As a result the black middle classes grew and were economically strengthened,[34] a fact which is reflected in the growing

32. Nathan Irvin Huggins, *Harlem Renaissance*, repr. Oxford: Oxford University Press, 1971, pp. 307 f. and Addison Gayle, *The Way of the New
World: The Black Novel in America*. Garden City: Anchor, 1976, p. xxii.
33. A full and balanced documentation of the relevant figures can be
found in Sar A. Levitan a.o., *Still A Dream*; compare also Thomas L. Blair,
Retreat to the Ghetto, pp. 163-191 and George W. Groh, *The Black Migration*
pp. 119-134.
34. Interested authors claimed that the 1970 National Census showed that
a majority of blacks belonged to the middle class which meant taking a tendency too far. For a debate on this point and a more adequate view of black
class structure during the sixties see William F. Brazziel, *Quality Education
for All American*. Washington, DC: Howard University Press, 1974, p. 20.;
Thomas L. Blair, *Retreat to the Ghetto*, pp. 185 f.; Sar A. Levitan a.o., *Still
A Dream*, pp. 44-78.

middle-class orientation of authors, readers and themes of Afro-
-American novels. If black novelists of the fifties were often alien-
ated from black middle-class values (Richard Wright, Chester
Himes, LeRoi Jones), black writers as different as Paule Marshall,
John Williams,[35] Albert Murray or Toni Morrison, tended to be-
come spokesmen for the ambitions of their class.

The net economic gains made by blacks during this period have
to be contrasted, however, with the following facts: The per capita
income of blacks had not reached three-fifths of that of whites
and the income gap was widening again after 1969. The war on
poverty had never been won, and in 1966 11.9 percent of the
nation's whites and 40.6 percent of its nonwhites were poor under
the Social Security definition ($3335 per year for an urban family
of four). The labor market problems of many blacks were not alle-
viated by the decade's progress: blacks continued to have their
earnings and employment interrupted by forced idleness, illness
and other factors. Hunger was widespread.[36] Black participation in
employment declined. Black children were still more likely to be
enrolled at grade levels below their age groups, and this differential
increased in higher grades. Black achievement in school as measured by sometimes highly controversial tests continued to lag. Blacks
were still four times as likely to live in substandard houses as
whites.[37] In spite of the evidence to the contrary presented by Levitan much seemed to point at a growing gap between the black
middle class and the black lower class which participated less in
the decade's progress.[38]

35. Compare John A. Williams' interesting essays on the new black middle
class in *Flashbacks: A Twenty-Year Diary of Article Writing*. Garden City:
Anchor 1974, ppp.112-166.
36. *Hunger and Malnutrition in America:* Chronology and Selected Background Materials Prepared by the Subcommittee on Employment Manpower
and Poverty of the Committee on Labor and Public Welfare, United States
Senate, July 1967. Washington, DC: U.S. Government Printing Office, October 1968, partially repr. in David G. Bromley and Charles F. Longino, Jr.. ed.,
White Racism, pp. 487-520.
37. Sar A. Levitan a.o., *Still A Dream*, pp. 13-43, 44-78, 79-104, 143-161
on income, employment, education and housing.
38. *Ibid.*pp. 185-204; compare Stokely Carmichael, "Power and Racism"
in Stokely Carmichael, *Stokely Speaks: Black Power Back to Pan-Africanism*.
New York: Vintage 1971, p. 23: "Integration today means the man who
'makes it,' leaving his black brothers behind in the ghetto. It has no relevance
to the Harlem wino or to the cottonpicker making three dollars a day."

The Civil Rights Movement helped Southern blacks mainly by getting them the vote: 100 blacks elected officials in 1965 compare to 1 185 in 1969 and 3 503 in 1973. "The major gains were in the seventeen states of the South which account for 55 percent of all elected black officials."[39] For the first time since Reconstruction black mayors, sheriffs and council members were elected in many places in the South.[40] Economically the decline of Southern agriculture and the increasing industrialization of the South which had started after World War II dislocated more tenant farmers, and, in spite of some agricultural cooperatives growing out of the Civil Rights Movement,[41] migration to the North and West continued throughout the sixties. Southern blacks

> acquired a political voice at almost precisely the period when they lost such tenuous economic status as they ever had. Thus it was that poverty grew worse and migration swelled throughout all the years when civil rights demonstrators were winning important victories. Over the past two decades [1950-1970] more than two thirds of all black farm families have been forced off the land, contributing some two and a half million people to the migration stream. The relentless attrition still dispossesses tens of thousands a year.[42]

In 1964 when the Civil Rights Act was passed the ghettoes in the cities of the North and West, having little hope in the change through legislation, opened a new phase of black politics: the ghetto revolts or the politics of violence.[43] Between 1964 and 1971 there were at least 1000 black revolts or riots, out of which at least 350 can be considered major outbursts of violence.[44] *The Report of the National Advisory Commission on Civil Disorders* or Kerner Report of 1968 tried to answer the crucial questions: What happened?, Why did it happen?, What can be done? A fairly regular pattern of revolt emerged in the analysis: a "trigger" event,

39. Thomas L. Blair, *Retreat to the Ghetto*, p. 194.
40. See Alton Hornsby, Jr., *The Black Almanac*, pp. 133, 248 f., and 251 for details.
41. George W. Groh, *The Black Migration*, pp. 89-111.
42. *Ibid.*, p. 63.
43. Joe R. Feagin and Harlan Hahn, *Ghetto Revolts: The Politics of Violence in American Cities*. New York: Macmillan, 1973, pp. 1-55 discard purely economic or psychological explanations of the so called "riots," and argue convincingly for a political explanation of the events.
44. For data and definition problems see *Ibid.*, pp. 101-140.

often a police action against blacks, set off a chain of violent acts against symbols of white society, authority, and property in black neighbourhoods. The revolt ended with (usually violent) riot-control actions taken by the police, National Guard or even federal troops. The causes of these revolts which cost more black than white lives were not difficult to find: "White racism is essentially responsible for the explosive mixture which had been accumulating in our cities since the end of World War II."[45] White racism led to pervasive discrimination and segregation in employment, education, and housing. Black in-migration and white exodus perpetuated the stagnating poverty in the ghettoes; frustrated hopes and the frustrations of political powerlessness generated a new mood of racial pride. Black leaders approved or encouraged violence against things or the police as a tangible symbol of that white racism.[46] The Commission ended by recommending expensive high impact programs and experiments with building community institutions.

The situation in the ghettoes had long been the concern of sociologists, psychologists, and economists. But what had seemed to them mainly a pathological deviation from American norms, a culture of poverty or a Negro lower-class culture[47] in more recent studies emerged as social organizations with their specific strengths, the main values and aims of which were sometimes in direct opposition to white middle-class norms.[48] Where Clark and others di-

45. *Report*, p.10.
46. *Ibid.*, pp. 10 f., 219-282. The *Report* tends to couch its explanations in terms of the frustration-agression hypothesis.
47. For a detailed analysis and criticism of the concept "culture of poverty" see Charles A. Valentine, *Culture and Poverty*. Chicago: University of Chicago Press, 1968. Lee Rainwater, *Behind Ghetto Walls: Black Families in a Federal Slum*. Chicago: Aldine, 1970, pp. 361-397 resumes the "Negro lower class" discussion.
48. A general criticism of all deficit theories in sociology which justified and called for programs which were often just another form of institutional racism can be found in Joan and Stephen Baratz, "Black culture on black terms: a rejection of the social pathology model" in Thomas Kochman, ed., *Rappin' and stylin' out: Communication in urban black America*. Urbana: University of Illinois Press, 1972, pp.3-16. Compare also Albert Murray's attack on the "fakelore of pathology" in *The Omni-Americans: New Perspectives on Black Experience and American Culture*. New York: Outerbridge and Dienstfrey, 1970, p.38.

agnosed the pathology of the ghetto other researchers found "Soulside" and viable street cultures with a strong network of solidarity between kinsmen, peers, and neighbours.[49] Where Moynihan found a deficient status of the black family — its basic pathology resided in the absence of the father and a resulting "matriarchal" structure leading to lower educational attainments, higher delinquency and crime rates, drug addiction and lower labor force participation — others found a particular lower-class family structure with rules and strengths of its own. Some of these strengths were extended family relationships with strong kinship bonds, informal adoptions, more equalitarian family patterns, and strong work orientation.[50] Instead of assigning the high incidence of functional illiteracy and low educational achievement of black children to cultural deprivations at home, researchers began to look more closely at the schools and text that produced and sometimes increased such results and found them wanting in their specific white middle-class bias.[51] The black family also emerges as a major theme of the Afro-American novel, here represented by the novels of Paule Marshall, Alice Walker, Albert Murray and Toni Morrison as well as the feminist theme of the new role of black women in American society.[52] A similar paradigma-change took place in the

49. Kenneth B. Clark, *Dark Ghetto*; Ulf Hannerz, *Soulside: Inquiries into the Ghetto Culture and Community*. New York: Columbia University Press 1969; for a balanced case study in which the ghetto inhabitants are given voice, too, see Lee Rainwater, *Behind Ghetto Walls*.

50. *The Negro Family: The Case for National Action*. Office of Policy Planning and Research, United States Department of Labor, Washington, DC: U.S. Government Printing Office, March 1965, partially repr. in David G. Bromley and Charles F. Longino, Jr., ed., *White Racism*, pp. 197-218. Answers by Lee Rainwater, "Crucible of Identity: The Negro Lower-Class Family" and Robert B. Hill, The Strengths of Black Families" are also repr. in *White Racism*, pp. 228-261 and 262-290. For some background on this controversy see Ulf Hannerz, *Soulside*, pp. 70-78. See also Lenwood G. Davis, *The Black Family in the United States: A Selected Bibliography of Annotated Books, Articles, and Dissertations on Black Families in America*. Westport, Conn.: Greenwood Press 1978.

51. James S. Coleman a.o., *Equality of Educational Opportunity*. Washington, DC: U.S. Government Printing Office, 1966, partially reprinted in David G. Bromley and Charles F. Longino, ed., *White Racism*, pp. 291-302; Sar A. Levitan, a.o., *Still A Dream*, pp. 86-98 summarize this discussion.

52. For a discussion of the changing sex roles among blacks see the readers compiled by Toni Cade, ed., *The Black Woman: An Anthology*. New

discussion of black language and culture.[53] Afro-American English was not longer seen as a deficient state of Standard American English but as a system with rules and patterns of its own and such expressives devices as rapping, shucking and jiving, gripping, signifying, and sounding.[54] Anthropologists discovered a rich and varied repertoire of communicative styles and urban folklore in the ghettoes.[55]

Together with these strengths of black ghettoes their poverty, segregated schools, substandard and overcrowded houses, bad health and sanitation conditions, high crime rates, exploitation by merchants and landlords, and their exclusion from city politics[56] were a sufficient cause for the impatience with the legal tactics of the NAACP or the nonviolent actions of the Civil Rights Movement and for supporting the politics of violence in form of ghetto revolts.[57] The Kerner Report was quick in pointing out a moral:

> What white Americans have never fully understood — but the Negro can never forget — is that white society is deeply implicated in the ghetto. White institutions created it, white institutions maintain it, and white society condones it.[58]

York: New American Library, 1970, and Doris Y. Wilkinson and Ronald L. Taylor, *The Black Male in America: Perspectives on his Status in Contemporary Society*. Chicago: Nelson Hall, 1977.

53. Robert Blauner, "Black Culture: Myth or Reality?" in David G. Bromley and Charles F. Longino, Jr. ed., *White Racism*, pp. 577-604 and William Labov, *Language in the Inner City: Studies in the Black English Vernacular*. Philadelphia: University of Pennsylvania Press, 1972.

54. Thomas Kochman, "Toward an Ethnography of Black American Speech Behavior" in David G. Bromley and Charles F. Longino, ed., *White Racism*, pp. 637-662; Claudia Mitchell-Kernan, "Signifying" in Alàn Dundes, ed., *Mother Wit from the Laughing Barrel: Readings in the Interpretation of Afro-American Folklore*, Englewood Cliffs, NJ: Prentic-Hall, 1973, pp. 310-328.

55. Thomas Kochman, ed., *Rappin' and stylin' out*; Roger D. Abrahams, *Deep down in the Jungle*. Hatboro, Pa.: Folklore Associates, 1964; Charles Keil, *Urban Blues*. Chicago: University of Chicago Press, 1966.

56. Compare the Chicago study by Harold M. Baron with Harriet Stulman, Richard Rothstein, and Rennard Davis, "Black Powerlessness in Chicago" in David G. Bromley and Charles F. Longino, ed., *White Racism*, pp. 442-451, repr. from *Trans-action*, November 1968.

57. Joe R. Feagin and Harlan Hahn, *Ghetto Revolts*, pp. 28,34.

58. *Report*, p. 2.

"What can be done?" was a question also raised by black leaders. Their answer seemed to lie in "Black Power," i.e. the new mood of racial pride had to be transformed and channeled into viable political and economic organizations.[59] A first solution — still derived from traditional church politics and ideologies — and a symbolic spokesman were offered by the Nation of Islam and Malcolm X. Black nationalism, combined with shopkeeper capitalism[60] (or a new Pan-Africanism and an ultimate overthrow of capitalism[61]), gained a stronger hold on ghetto inhabitants than the Civil Rights Movement could. A second solution grew out of the attempts to bring about community control of institutions and officials in the South. The experiences in Lowndes County, Alabama, led Stokely Carmichael to a political and completely secular analysis and program of Black Power:

> Black people in the United States have a colonial relationship to the white society, a relationship characterized by institutional racism. That colonial status operates in three areas — political, economic, social ...
> Black Power recognizes — it must recognize — the ethnic basis of American politics as well as the power-oriented nature of American politics.
> Thus we reject the goal of assimilation into middle-class America because the values of that class are themselves anti-humanist and because that class as a social force perpetuates racism.[62]

In this model of internal colonialism the police represented the occupying forces. The program rejected coalition-politics with whites until blacks had gained power and self-determination, it defended revolts and guerilla warfare for this purpose. Integration was not completely rejected, but postponed. It had to be negotiated from a position of strength not received as a favor on white conditions. The framework of majority-minority, assimilation-integration had given way to a concept of multi-ethnic politics where blacks competed with other ethnic groups for political power and self-deter-

59. For a bibliography on Black Power see James M. McPherson a.o., *Blacks in America*, pp. 372-389.
60. E.U. Essien-Udom, *Black Nationalism: A Search for an Identity in America*. Chicago: University Press of Chicago, 1963, pp. 143-182; Thomas L. Blair, *Retreat to the Ghetto*, pp. 163f.
61. George Breitman, *The Last Year of Malcolm X: The Evolution of a Revolutionary*. New York: Merit Publishers, 1967.
62. Stokely Carmichael and Charles Hamilton, *Black Power: The Politics of Liberation in America*. London: Cape, 1968, pp. 6, 47, 41.

mination. Mainstream and melting pot were replaced by separation and cultural pluralism, negroes became blacks or Afro-Americans in distinction to Italo-Americans, Irish-Americans and other immigrant groups.[63] A third variant, cultural nationalism, advocated and singled out consciousness-raising in the ghettoes as the primary task, something that Carmichael and Hamilton had thought of only as a first step.[64] Spokesmen like Baraka and Karenga tried to instill African value systems of collectivity and cooperation through lectures, pamphlets, theaters, or African Free Schools.[65] Black publishing seemed a realistic chance to free Afro-American literature from the cultural colonialism of the major publishing houses. Compared to the heavy concentration within the publishing industry[66] the new black publishers[67] remained very small business, indeed, but they helped to print and spread texts major publishing houses would not touch.[68] New black journals like *Black America, Black Dialogue, Black World* (formerly *Negro Digest*), *Black Scholar* helped to establish the new nationalist writers.[69] Black Studies Programs in colleges and universities stressed

63. Nathan Glazer and Daniel Patrick Moynihan, *Beyond the Melting Pot, The Negroes, Puerto Ricans, Jews, Italians, and Irish of New York.* end ed., Cambridge, Mass.: MIT Press 1970, pp. 24-85 tend to see blacks as one example of urban ethnic immigrant groups, one that arrives relatively late and — compared to other immigrant groups — has to overcome specific problems of its own. The authors underline the special situation of West Indians within this group.

64. Stokely Carmichael and Charles Hamilton, *Black Power*, pp. 34-56 outline a three-step strategy: 1) new consciousness, 2) political modernization, and 3) black power.

65. Alphonso Pinckney, *Red, Black, and Green: Black Nationalism in the United States.* London: Cambridge University Press, 1976, pp. 127-150.

66. J. Kendrick Noble, Jr., "Books" in Benjamin M. Compaine, ed., *Who owns the Media? Concentration of Ownership in the Mass Communications Industry.* New York: Harmony Books, 1979, pp.251-291.

67. Sheila Smith-Hobson, "Black Book Publishing: Protest, Pride and little Profit," *Black Enterprise*, May 1978, pp.39-47; compare the exchange between John A. Williams, "Black Publisher, Black Writer: An Impasse" and Dudley Randall, "Black Publisher, Black Writer: An Answer," *Black World*, 26 March 1975, pp. 28-37. See also the annotated directory of black publishers, *ibid.*, 73-79.

68. About discrimination in the publishing field see John A. Williams' interview with Chester Himes in "Chester Himes, My Man Himes" in *Flashbacks*, pp. 292-352.

69. Compare Abby Arthur Johnson, *Propaganda and Aesthetics: The liter-*

black contributions to American history, revised this history as a multi-ethnic one or as a distortion which stood in the way of true black identity, or they studied the African heritage as a model for black consciousness and action for the future.[70] The question of self determination also played an important part in who was to criticize Afro-American literature and in the creation of the Black Aesthetics program.[71] Textbooks and Afro-American novels increasingly reflected these new historical trends and the tendency tɔ redefine black identity and history on their own terms. Adaptations of Roots and The Autobiography of Jane Pittman, however diluted by television, reached a mass audience.

The ambiguity of the concept of Black Power reflected a widening split between black radicals and the black middle classes.[72] If there was unity on racial pride and self determination the controversy broke out on tactics of separate organizations and the use of violence. Dual organizations like black parties, black unions and, to a lesser degree, violence against things and guerilla action were supported by the urban lower classes.[73] Shopkeeper capitalism and black capitalism (supported by the Nixon administration through the Small Business Administration) found response in the black upper working-class and lower middle-class strata,[74] and the

ary Politics of Afro-American Magazines in the Twentieth Century. Amherst: University of Massachusetts, Press, 1979.

70. Jörg Becker, Alltäglicher Rassismus: Die afro-amerikanischen Rassenkonflikte im Kinder- und Jugendbuch der Bundesrepublik, Frankfurt: Campus, 1977, pp. 1-118 has a useful survey of different Black Studies concepts in the United States. Compare also Theodore Draper's chapter on Black studies programs in The Rediscovery of Black Nationalism. New York: Viking Press, 1970.

71. Compare Peter Bruck in this volume, pp. 46 f.

72. Compare Stokely Carmichael, "Toward Black Liberation" in Stokely speaks, p. 37: "the thing to do was to syphon off the 'acceptable' Negroes into the surrounding middle-class white community." Compare also Vivian Henderson quoted in the Report of the National Advisory Commission on Civil Disorders, p. 231: "No one can deny that all Negroes have benefited from civil rights laws and desegregation in public life in one way or another. The fact is, however, that the masses of Negroes have not experienced tangible benefits in a significant way."

73. Thomas L. Blair, Retreat to the Ghetto, pp. 195-243 documents some of the controversies. For lower-class support see Joe R. Feagin and Harlan Hahn, Ghetto Revolts, pp. 129 f.

74. Thomas L. Blair, Retreat to the Ghetto, pp. 164-191.

fact that black radicals failed to mobilize greaters portions of the ghetto poor shows the strength of the new black middle classes. So does the growing disenchantement of Baraka and Karenga with this middle class and their subsequent turn to Maoism and Marxism.[75] The idea of a separate state in the South or in Africa, as in the past, was only backed by a small but growing minority of blacks.[76]

The conflict between the Black Power Movement and the Civil Rights Movement, both divided internally on tactics and to a lesser degree on aims, reenacted a very old dilemma:

> From the colonial period to this day there are two identifiable modes of action which blacks have used to assault the barriers that violate their right as Americans and as human beings. One is to submerge their African heritage and despised traits of character, and by political and legal mechanisms and cultural imitation become integrated into the society as a whole. The other is to restructure black groups to resist white-imposed social deformations and to adopt to new circumstances with a revived sense of pride in their black heritage.[77]

The difference with earlier enactments of these alternatives lay in the broad mass support of the corresponding organizations during the fifties and sixties. If the lasting contribution of the Civil Rights Movement lay in ending more than 80 years of legal segregation and discrimination, the Black Power Movement formulated a however contradictory ideology of self determination which helped to bring about political and economic participation for many blacks especially on the local level. The success of black community control, however, had to depend in the last analysis on the economic development of the United States at the end of the Vietnam war.

---

75. Alphonso Pinckney, *Red, Black and Green*, pp. 149 f; Thomas L.Blair, *Retreat to the Ghetto*, pp. 152-160.

76. R.I.Hall, ed., *Black Separatism and Social Reality: Rhetoric and Reality*. New York: Pergamon Press, 1977 assembles contributions to the political debate on separatism.

77. Thomas L. Blair, *Retreat to the Ghetto*, p. 5. For a different statement of this old dilemma see Oliver Cox, *Caste, Class and Race*, pp. 545 f.

The deepening recession of the seventies ended and sometimes reverted the economic gains made by blacks during the sixties: the income gap widened again to 42 percent.[78] Employment opportunities declined inspite of a federally backed voluntary quota system. Unemployment for blacks remained twice as high as that of whites, for black teenagers it was almost 40 percent.[79] More than 30 per cent of nonwhites continued to live in poverty. The decrease in farm employment remained a driving force behind the migration to the cities. Blacks had become more urbanized than any other group in American society. About half of them lived in the South. It is too early to say whether the seventies have brought a change in the traditional black migration patterns but between 1975 and 1977 the Northeast and the North Central had a net outmigration while the South and West had net immigration.[80] The old South so many Afro-American novels return to was rapidly ceding to a new industrialized and urbanized South.

The ghettoes remained and spread.[81] Where blacks gained community control by electing mayors, council board members and other officials they found the cities in a grave crisis. Newark, for instance, where an alliance of Afro-Americans and Puerto Ricans elected a black mayor in 1970, was faced with lack of funds when

78. The table in Mabel M. Smythe, "The Black Role in the Economy" in Mabel M. Smythe, ed., *The Black American Reference Book*, p. 213, shows the opening income gap. For further figures see *The World Almanac and Book of Facts 1981*. New York: Newspaper Enterprise Association, 1980, p. 269.

79. According to *Newsweek*, June 2, 1980, 25: "The six per cent overall unemployment rate translates to roughly 12 per cent for blacks in normal times - and perhaps 18 or 20 per cent in the recession just now setting in." On teenage unemployment see *Newsweek*, August 8, 1977, 23.

80. *The World Almanac*, p. 87f. California, Illinois and New York were leading Texas and Georgia in numbers of black population, according to *The World Almanac*, p. 96. For a more detailed picture see Karl E. Taeuber and Alma F. Taeuber, "The Black Population in the United States" in Mabel M. Smythe, ed., *The Black American Reference Book*, pp. 176-205.

81. Compare *The World Almanac 1979*, p. 205: "While the white population in central cities of metropolitan areas declined by 8 percent during the 7 years since 1970, the black population has increased at a rate of 4.2 percent a year since 1970 while the white population by 1.3 percent last year."

it tried to change its desperate situation.[82] The vicious cycle of white and industrial exodus to the suburbs, downtown decay and unemployment, the cities' rising costs for social services, and high property taxes to pay for those services could not be broken up, even with considerable state support.[83] This problem was and is a general one. The cities are bearing the main cost of the farmers' dislocation and they are hardly prepared to do so:

> The average city gets back in direct federal benefits about four or five cents for every federal tax dollar that city people pay. If the indirect benefits are calculated the figure might go as high as ten or twelve cents on the dollar, it is not enough.[84]

Racial segregation and city bankruptcies are intimately intertwined. Anti-poverty campaigns, urban renewal and Model Cities programs have brought little change. The continuing growth of the ghettoes will without doubt lead to black majorities and black political control of other major American cities in the future.[85] As long as they will not succeed in gaining economic power as well, they will have to face the acute problems arising from residential segregation, concentration of poverty and unemployment, and an unbalanced tax structure. As Newark Mayor Kenneth Gibson told the 1974 NAACP Convention:

82. The literature on Newark, location of one of the gravest revolts of the sixties and of much agitation for black nationalism by Amiri Baraka, is fairly large. Essential readings are Tom Hayden, *Rebellion in Newark: Official Violence and Ghetto Response*. New York: Vintage, 1967; Nathan Wright, Jr., *Ready to Riot*. New York: Holt, Rinehart and Winston, 1968; State of New Jersey Governor's Select Commission on Civil Disorders; *Report for Action: An Investigation into the Causes and Events of the 1967 Newark Race Riots*. New York: Lemma Publishing, 1972; for Baraka's political writings see the bibliography in Werner Sollors, *Amiri Baraka / LeRoi Jones: The Quest for a "Populist Modernism."* New York: Columbia University Press, 1978, pp. 301-313. A short summary of the Newark situation can be found in George W. Groh, *The Black Migration*, pp. 157-248.
83. Nathan Wright, Jr., *Ready to Riot*, pp. 72-78 has a detailed analysis of what he calls "unplanned exploitation of the cities on the part of the suburbs and the nation."
84. George W. Groh, *The Black Migration*, p. 139.
85. In 1970 Washington, Newark and Atlanta had black majorities. By 1976 they may have been joined by Baltimore, Detroit and St. Louis; compare Karl E. Taeuber and Alma F. Taeuber, "The Black Population in the United States," 1967.

After my election many folks came to the office and asserted that now Blacks were in control of the city. They were wrong. I just hang in there by the skin of my teeth and try to shave off as many benefits as I can from the real powers and pass them along as far as I can ...

No elected official has any power. He is simply permitted to exert some influence on those who do. And if influence is to be had, then we might as well get some of it.

But we should tell our kids to continue fighting until they reach the positions that really count: – the presidency of General Motors, Reynolds Aluminum, Shell Oil Company. Kennecott Copper Company, or ITT.[86]

The Black Power call for community control had obviously underrated the dependency of local communities on their surroundings.

So the social consequences of ghetto life as outlined in the Kerner Report in 1968 continue. In 1977 38 percent (as compared to 14 percent in 1961) of black children lived on welfare. Only 47 percent of black children under 18 lived with both their parents (71 percent in 1965). 50 percent of black births in 1976 were illegitimate and the proportion of female-headed black households has risen from 24 percent at the time of the Moynihan Report to 36 percent in 1977.[87] In spite of progress made in desegregating schools, a majority of black children continued to go to segregated schools. White opposition to busing grew as court and street battles in Boston, Detroit, and Atlanta showed.[88] A changed Supreme Court and a Federal Government facing a grave economic recession were less likely to support the black struggle against the economic and social problems. It is in this situation that

The protest style of the sixties has given way to the new politics of today, a reformist strategy of political mobilization which helped to catapult a white Southerner, Governor Jimmy Carter into the presidency. The overwhelming majority of black voting opinion is apparently integrationist in outlook, aiming not at the destruction of American values but at their fulfillment.[89]

86. Quoted in Larry E. Moss, *Black Political Ascendancy in Urban Centers and Black Control of the Local Police Function: An Exploratory Analysis.* San Francisco: RE 1977, p. 86.

87. *Newsweek*, May 15, 1978, pp. 55-56.

88. Alton Horsnby, Jr., *The Black Almanac*, pp. 250, 270-272, 322 f.

89. Thomas L. Blair, *Retreat to the Ghetto*, pp. viii f.

The more radical organizations like the Black Panthers, Revolutionary Action Movement, Republic of New Africa or urban guerilla organizations like the Symbionese Liberation Army[90] had been broken up or destroyed by the FBI. Dual organization strategies have given way to work as pressure groups within the two-party system, the unions, and the traditional framework of ethnic politics. But neither the causes for the revolts nor the revolts themselves have disappeared as the 1980 example of Miami shows. In spite of reforms in justice and politics the basic patterns of social and economic discrimination as described by Myrdal in 1944 and the Kerner Report in 1968 remain a part of American Society. The 1980 elections and disturbing signs of a reemerging white racism[91] seem to point at an end of a historical phase of New Deal reforms and social legislation. The Black experience of the past 25 years and the mass support it has mobilized mark a new beginning for Afro-American history and, last but not least, for the Afro-American novel, and form a great potential for further changes to come. Whatever their individual differences may be, Afro-American novels of the last 35 years have reflected the social history of Afro-Americans faithfully, as a list of themes compiled in 1976 by Helen Armstead Johnson[92] will demonstrate:

Some of the major themes of Afro-American writing are these: 1. the folk experience (Murray); 2. double consciousness (Wright); 3. alienation from self, from race, from country, from society in general, from family, and from God and other Gods (Walker); 4. the substance of Negro life, including middle class life (Marshall); 5. a mystical sense of race, which is a kind of Afro-American negritude (Morrison); 6. miscegenation and the mulatto experience; 7. religion and the church (Murray); 8. personal, inner group and cultural identity (Young, Reed); 9. black-white relationships of multiple kinds and nuances (here integration and the love-hate ambivalence should be singled out because of a tendency in the 1970s to ignore

90. *Ibid.* pp. 86-126.
91. The shooting of Vernon Jordan of the Urban League, the reemergence of the KKK, race murders in American cities, the Senate vote to stop busing are few examples.
92. Helen Armstead Johnson, "Black Influences in the American Theatre. Part II, 1960 and after" in Mabel M. Smythe, ed., *The Black American Reference Book*, pp. 707 f. I take the liberty of interpolating the novelists represented in our collection.

51

them) (Kelley, Demby); 10. the jazz experience (Williams); 11. migration and the urban experience (Walker, Morrison); 12. patriotism; 13, nationalism (Reed); 14. the black American dream (Marshall); 15. love (Williams); 16. the ghetto as experience (Wright, Himes); 17. freedom (Gaines, Kelley) and 18. revolution.

If some of these themes reflect social problems rather directly (4, 6,7,9,10,11,13,16), others — whether through focussing on individual reactions to these problems or through a translation of these problems into fantasy or aesthetic experimentation — have a more oblique relation to the black experience during the last few decades. In all their diversity — far from being exhausted by such a thematic catalogue — contemporary Afro-American novels escape easy political or social categorizations and not seldom challenge or redefine the dominant conception of the American experience as well as the literary conventions and language to express it in.

DEBORAH SCHNEIDER

A SEARCH FOR SELFHOOD:
PAULE MARSHALL'S *BROWN GIRL, BROWNSTONES*

Brown Girl, Brownstones, Paule Marshall's first novel, was published
in 1959 and concerns the life of a girl growing up in Brooklyn,
the daughter of black immigrants from the Caribbean island of
Barbados. The "brownstones" of the title refer to the milieu in
which the central character lives, the neighborhood of Victorian
row houses around Fulton Park which, as the action of the novel
begins in the year 1939, the last white residents are leaving, rent-
ing or selling their houses to black West Indians, and Barbadians in
particular. Acquiring the ownership of these brownstone houses,
acquiring property and an identity as middle-class home owners in
their new country is the main goal — an obsession in some cases —
of many of the Barbadian immigrants; they love their houses with
a "fierce idolatry."[1] The plot of the main portion of the novel
turns on one family's disagreeement over whether or not to buy
the brownstone in which they are living, and almost every character in the book is defined by his or her attitude towards this central question. The houses play such a role in the lives of the characters that their identities become intertwined; to the main character, Selina Boyce, "her house was alive"(4), and the images linking
architecture and the human personality are numerous.[2] The
brownstones are the heart and soul of the Barbadian-immigrant
community and when, at the end of the novel, they have been
blasted into a "vast waste" "to make way for a city project"(309),
this signifies not only Selina's departure and the break up of her
family through travel, marriage, and death, but also the breakup of
the tightly-knit community which had existed in her childhood.

1. Paule Marshall, *Brown Girl, Brownstones* (New York: Random House,
1959), p. 4. Following quotations from the novel will be identified by a page
reference to this edition in brackets in the text.
2. See Kimberly W. Benston, "Architectural Imagery and Unity in Paule
Marshall's *Brown Girl, Brownstones*," *Negro American Literature Forum*, 9,
No. 3 (Fall 1975), pp. 67-70.

As the book ends in the early 1950's, the older Barbadians who can afford it are moving out into better neighborhoods, and the younger generation is scattering.

Because of its wealth of specific detail about the social and economic circumstances of its characters' lives, the novel has been cited by social scientists in a study of New York City minority groups as "remarkably revealing."[3] *Brown Girl, Brownstones* is, in spite of this, however, first and foremost a novel of family life, a novel about highly individual characters who are not portrayed as solely the products of environmental influences. It is, as critics have observed, a *Bildungsroman*,[4] "unified by the dominating presence of a bared and evolving consciousness (as in Joyce's *Portrait of the Artist as a Young Man*)."[5] A young girl's search for a stable self holds the rich and diverse material of the novel together, the author's concentration on the psychological configurations of the family rather than the relatively unobtrusive use of particular imagery.[6]

The novel is divided into four "Books." Book 1, "A Long Day and a Long Night," introduces Selina and her family, consisting of an older sister and her parents. Selina is a lively and imaginative ten-year old who has the feeling of not being quite at home either in her family or her house, although she has an especially close relationship with her father, Deighton Boyce. Characteristically Selina is first shown on a Saturday, when she is at home but restless and longing to get outside. She has not merely been born into the role of outsider, however; she pursues it with a will, always wanting something which others do not seem to want or need. The territory which she attempts to penetrate changes with each book of the novel, but her urge for freedom does not.

The second book, called "Pastorale," is as short and lyrical as the title suggests. Selina, on the verge of adolescence, goes on a

3. Nathan Glazer and Daniel Patrick Moynihan, *Beyond the Melting Pot: The Negroes, Puerto Ricans, Jews, Italians, and Irish of New York City* (1963; rpt. Cambridge, MA: M.I.T. Press Paperbacks, 1964), p. 35.

4. Leela Kapai, "Dominant Themes and Techniques in Paule Marshall's Fiction," *College Language Association Journal*, 16, No. 1 (September 1972), p. 50.

5. Benston, p. 68.

6. I disagree with Benston's emphasis on the central role of architectural imagery, although his analysis of it is full of insights.

trolley outing on a Sunday with her best friend:

> To Selina, the colors, the people seemed to run together ... Those colors, those changing forms were the shape of her freedom, Selina knew. She had finally passed the narrow boundary of herself and her world. She could no longer be measured by Chauncey Street or the park or the nearby school. "Lord," she whispered behind her hand, "I'm free." (56)

Selina's friend Beryl Challoner is still a part of her freedom at this time, a special companion. Later on the novel will have much to say about Beryl's development into a middle-class materialistic conformity which pulls them apart. The fact that this friendship will not be able to survive gives the idyllic scene in Prospect Park a particular poignancy; it is a last taste of innocent childhood pleasures before Selina's family is torn to pieces.

The title of Book 3 is "The War"; the time-span it covers corre-. sponds precisely to World War II. None of the novel's characters is involved in the fighting, however – "Thank God," says Selina's mother of her two daughters, "I ain got neither one to send to die in another white man war" (65) – so that the principal war referred to is the one which begins in earnest between Selina's parents. No matter how his wife Silla insists, Deighton Boyce refuses to sell a piece of inherited property in Barbados in order to buy the house in Brooklyn. By means of forgery and a carefully-hatched plan Silla manages to sell the land without her husband's knowledge, but when the money is sent to New York he spends it all on clothes and gifts instead of a down payment. Shortly afterwards he has an accident at his factory in which his arm is badly injured. In a despondent state of mind in the hospital, seeing his role as breadwinner and head of the family lost, he is converted to the sect of "Father Peace," a religious movement which encourages believers to sever all family ties. Deighton leaves his family and finds work managing a sect-owned business; his wife is so outraged by his desertion that she reports him to the police as an illegal immigrant and has him deported. Shortly before his ship docks in Barbados Deighton goes overboard, and is drowned.

Book 4, "Selina," concludes the novel with an account of Selina's attempts to come to terms with her father's death and her mother's life in continued quest of house ownership. Selina experiences a deep conflict between her membership in the Barbadian-immigrant community and her urge to seek a less materialistic and

55

confining life for herself outside it. She attends college in Manhattan, has a disappointing love affair, and joins the college dance group. Her discovery of modern dance as an art form in which she can express her inner self and communicate with others represents a great step forward. As the novel concludes Selina is planning a trip to Barbados, in the hope that the journey will help her to understand herself as well as the people among whom she has spent her life and the influences which have shaped her.

The author's insistence on her characters' individuality as the core of the novel is conveyed by the imagery of the opening passage. Marshall begins, as if with a film camera and a pan shot down the street, with a row of houses so similar that they appear "as one house reflected through a train of mirrors." But the reader is then asked to take a close look, to see that "under the thick ivy each house had something distinctively its own" (3), and the novel continues with introducing the all-important constellation of individuals and relationships in the Boyce family. The firstborn of Deighton and Silla Boyce's children, their daughter Ina, is a quiet and obedient girl and her mother's ally. The next child, a son, died of heart trouble as a small boy, a tragic event which Silla has irrationally blamed on Deighton. A photograph in the dining room shows the family when the boy was a baby; the impression is given that the family was in some way destroyed by his death, that it was never worth while taking another picture afterwards (7-8). Although things have never been the same, Selina feels she was born as a replacement for the lost son, and by becoming her father's ally she has re-established a balance of power within the family.

Selina's relationship to her father is greatly influenced by her female sex, however, in the form of an extremely strong Oedipal attachment which she will have difficulty overcoming as she approaches maturity. It is of fundamental importance that the phase of the parents' greatest antagonism towards each other occurs when Selina is an adolescent, when the first stirring of adult sexual feeling are directed entirely towards her father and her mother is seen as an inconvenient, even sinister and malevolent rival. Throughout the novel Selina tends to see "her" father as a heroic figure, while "the" mother is denied a possessive adjective. The language of describing her is used to reject her, a stylistic gesture which also points up the narrator's consistent partisanship for Selina's point of view. There can thus not be the slightest question about whose side Selina takes during the battle over the house and money, and the narrator's reinforcement of her attitude seeks to pull the reader in as a partisan as well. Selina's recognition, at the end of the novel, that she closely resembles her mother in feelings and personality will be the result of a long and slow growth of insight.

In 1939, when the novel begins, the Boyces are living near Fulton Park in a rented brownstone. Deighton arrived in the United States in 1920 (38) and Silla at about the same time, having left, with many others, a small overcrowded island on which for the black population poverty was great and opportunities for employment small. After nearly twenty years of hard work — typically as factory workers and domestic servants — the Barbadians have taken the first strides towards a more comfortable, middle-class way of life. They have moved out of cockroach-infested housing in South Brooklyn (38) into the neighborhood of Fulton Park, and many of them are buying houses. They are beginning to turn their attention to opening their own businesses, to educating their children and, within a few years, to forming a community association which will provide scholarships and a voice in local political and economic affairs.

Such aims receive Silla Boyce's full assent. Raised in extreme poverty, given no schooling, sent out to work in the cane fields as a small child, she tells her daughter Selina that she gave her own mother no peace until she borrowed the money for Silla to come to New York (45-46). Buying the brownstone house in Brooklyn is Silla's greatest goal; she needs to feel that she is keeping pace with the other Barbadian immigrants, and providing a better life for her children.

Deighton Boyce does not want to buy a brownstone. To begin with, on his and his wife's income as a factory worker and maid, this would mean an austerity program in his daily life, none of the luxuries such as silk shirts and fancy shoes which he allows himself. Deighton could not give these things up, for he has never known or been permitted to know deprivation for the sake of a future goal. As the youngest child and only son of a mother who spoiled him, he was always given better than she could afford; he received the education to become a schoolteacher, but not the self-discipline or ability to use it and be content with it. Deighton has always been unrealistically ambitious; he ran away, first to Cuba and then to New York, in search of a dream, and after twenty years is still hoping that some scheme or twist of luck will bring it within his grasp without too much hard work or sacrifice (32-33).

When he receives a letter informing him that he has inherited a piece of land, Silla sees only one possible course of action; if the property were sold they could make a down-payment on their house even without scrimping or taking out a loan. Deighton, however, immediately conjures up a new dream: when his big break comes, when, for example, he finds a better-paid job as a result of the correspondence course in accounting he is half-heartedly studying, he will build the family a mansion on his land back home. He daydreams about returning in style and "living like a lord" (87). Silla is infuriated at what she considers his unreasonable intransigence; finally, goaded beyond endurance by friends' accounts of all the other Barbadian families in Brooklyn who are buying houses, she hits upon a scheme to sell the land without Deighton's knowledge. She forges his signature in a letter asking his sister to sell the property because he has lost his job. When a check for nine hundred dollars arrives at a New York bank, Silla's goal is at last within reach, but nine hundred dollars in his pocket mean that Deighton's life-long dream of flashing money around and commanding respect like a rich man is also within reach. The possibility of making such a dream come true, if only for a few short hours, proves irresistible. He spends the entire sum of money on Fifth Avenue, enjoying not only the chance to buy armfuls of expensive gooods, but even more the pleasure of being adressed as "Sir" and treated with deference and respect by the white sales staff:

> Ha. When I went in these store the first thing I did was to lift muh head and not act like I come asking for a job sweeping the floor or cleaning out their toilet ... I come in looking like I was somebody big ... They look at me funny at first ... But all I did was to start counting muh money ... and I tell yuh they almost break their neck running to wait 'pon muh ... (125).

No brownstone house in Brooklyn could ever equal the satisfaction of this experience to Deighton. The dream of the mansion on Barbados is gone with the money, but he has made his gesture and had his moment of triumph. When his action becomes known, however, the other Barbadians ostracize him, and a further blow falls when he is injured working at an unfamiliar machine at the factory. The lie his wife had told about his being unemployed has come true, tragically and ironically only after all the money is gone. Silla, grimmer and more single-minded than ever, takes out a loan and takes in roomers, and finally becomes a home-owner. The final hostile act which Deighton performs, in her eyes, is moving out; in her by now implacable hatred of him she reports him to the police and has him deported. The Boyce family war ends when Deighton either falls or jumps overboard. The authorities think it may have been an accident; Suggie Skeete, the Boyce's lodger, is convinced that it was suicide. She is sure that Deighton could not face returning for the same reason that she herself would never go back to Barbados: "Do you know how bad those malicious brutes would lick their mouth on me if I went back the same way I left?" (208). To Selina it was murder, and her mother is responsible. Silla and all the other Barbadians who saw buying their brownstones as their major goal in life and shunned her father when he refused to do the same are more than merely wrongheaded; they are almost criminals living by a shameful and vicious code.

Since buying, or resisting buying, a brownstone is at the center of Selina's parents' lives and battles, this act and the house itself acquire an immense, symbolical significance to her. To own, or not to own, such a house are antithetical ways of life, carrying the broadest implications. Selina's interpretation of this act, or the intention to perform it, is complex and far-reaching; as she matures it affects every area of her intellectual and emotional life.

Selina's mother wants to buy a brownstone; therefore, in Selina's eyes, to want to buy a brownstone is to be like the mother. And the mother is, from her very first appearance in the novel, a character of forbidding aspect:

Silla Boyce brought the theme of winter into the park with her dark dress amid the summer green and the bright-figured house-dresses of the women lounging on the benches there. Not only that, every line of her strong-made body seemed to reprimand the women for their idleness and the park for its senseless summer display. Her lips, set in a permanent protest against life, implied that there was no time for gaiety. And the park, the women, the sun even gave way to her dark force; the flushed summer colors ran together and faded as she passed. (16)

It is impossible to imagine Silla lounging; she represents work, self-denial, the rejection of pleasure in any form. The house she wants is a bleak row house in a dark, wintry city. Later in the novel she is shown at the defense plant where she has found a better job during the war, and is brought into association with the grim, inhuman productivity of vast machines:

> belts slapping on giant pulleys, long shafts rearing and plunging, whirling parts plying the air, the metal whine of steel being cut, steam hissing from a twisting network of pipes on the ceilings and walls ... (98).

In the midst of this inferno Silla appears competent and deft; she "worked at an old-fashioned lathe which resembled an oversize cookstove, and her face held the same transient calm which often touched it when she stood at the stove at home" (99).

Just as she is connected with machines, Silla represents the antithesis of nature and of sexuality. The tropics signify to her merely the back-breaking labor she is glad to have escaped from, and she impresses on her daughters the need for sexual abstinence until they are suitably married: "I ain having no concubines round here and I ain supportin no wild-dog puppies. Out you'll go!" (191). Finally, in wanting to buy her brownstone Silla resembles so many other Barbadians who — or so it seems to Selina — are content with an all but faceless group identity and purely material values.[7] Buying a house like Silla's means confirming one's membership in a rigid, narrow, and intolerant immigrant ethnic group; it means admittance to the middle classes of America, that class, as Erik Erikson has defined it, "pre-occupied with matters of real estate and consumption, of status and of posture."[8]

To Selina her father Deighton is a far more appealing alternative, all that Silla is not: free and easy, pleasure-loving and generous, able to play as well as work. The house he wants is not a drab real house in Brooklyn but a dream mansion, "with tall white columns at the front like some temple or other," "every bathroom with a stained-glass window like a church" (86). Deighton loves plants; he wants a flamboyant tree, and a garden planted with ladies-of-the-night (85). This fantasy ranks far above any existing house to Selina's mind; it has grace, poetry, and grandeur, as

7. As Benston puts it, "The house Silla ... is driven to possess becomes an ominous emblem of the materialistic ambitions which the fast-moving, competitive, at best amoral 'New World' proliferates and spurs," p. 68.

8. "The Concept of Identity in Race Relations: Notes and Queries," in *The Negro American*, ed. Talcott Parsons and Kenneth B. Clark (Boston: Beacon Press, 1967), p. 249.

Brooklyn does not. Her father is a being above the common herd to be able to dream such a dream of a lush tropical island in contrast to a cold, dirty city. And the best part of this non-material, non-middle-class fantasy is that it has a special place in it for her. Deighton positively feeds Selina's own, Oedipal fantasies by saying that they will go off together if the others don't choose to come, and he will make her mistress of the house (87). Later, after Deighton's death, when Selina has discovered her preference for a life of the mind and her interest in arts such as dance and painting, she traces this development to his influence. At a party attended by other Barbadian girls she becomes impatient with their crass materialism and their lists of what their fathers have given or will give them. When her old friend Beryl is provoked into responding, "What's your father gonna give you?", Selina is unable to answer aloud, but she reflects on what her inheritance has been:

.. she would have liked to turn and tell Beryl very quietly .. what he had given her . How one cold March afternoon long ago she had found him stretched on the cot in the sun parlor in his shirt sleeves, his head cradled in his arms and humming. "Is it spring?" she had asked, her breath coming in cold wisps. He had drawn her down beside him, loosened her arms and said, "Yes." And suddenly she had sensed spring in the air, seen it forming beyond the glass walls and had not been cold anymore.

How could Beryl understand that this was what he had given her? And its worth? (197-98)

Deighton had not wanted to own a brownstone, and not to own a brownstone is to be like Deighton, warm, loving, and full of poetry.

Selina chooses to remember her father this way, although she has had to deal with the dreadful sight of him as a changed man after his accident, which robbed him of his self-confidence, of his ability to support his family or even to go out "dress back and making like a big sports" (157). His way of coping psychologically with this disaster is religion, specifically the cult of "Father Peace,' a fictional figure bearing a close resemblance to the actual Father Divine who achieved a national following from his base in Harlem in the 1930's and 40's.[9] Father Divine's cult established itself in

9. The phrases Deighton repeats, "Peace, Father. It's wonderful!" and "Thank you, Father!" (160), are identical to those used by followers of Father Divine; see Sara Harris, *Father Divine: Holy Husband* (Garden City, NY: Doubleday, 1953), p. 68.

Harlem during the Depression; his appeal rested not only on the provision of spiritual comfort but on economics as well. Since his followers were encouraged — and devout ones even required — to throw off all familiy ties and to live as simply as possible within the group, the money they earned and no longer needed to support families was available to the sect. Father Divine founded an organization based on principles of co-operative ownership of different types of business, primarily rooming-houses and restaurants. The cooks, restaurant managers, and building superintendents worked enthusiastically for pay which amounted to their room and board, and the privilege of belonging to the inner circle of the saved. Father Divine was thus able to provide lavish meals for visitors and casual followers, such as Selina observes on her visit to Father Peace (164), and decent housing for the committed faithful. This was no mean achievement, and one with which the established churches could not compete; as long as they were unwilling to make the same demand on their followers to leave their families — the cornerstone of the sect's economic system — these "competitors" had to endure Father Divine's claims to be God and the government's failure to turn up any evidence of rampant immorality or tax fraud.[10]

In the novel Deighton takes Selina with him to one of Father Peace's Sunday meetings, and she realizes with dismay that the congregation there is Deighton's new community; for the first time he has sought and found comfort and acceptance, and the cult of Father Peace offers the added advantage of excluding his wife, as wife, as relentlessly as the Barbadian community had rejected Deighton:

> God is your father [says Father Peace], your mother, your sister, your brother, your wife, your child, and you will never have another! The mother of creation is the mother of defilement. The word *mother* is a filthy word. When a person reaches God he cannot permit an earthly wife or so-called children to lead him away. God is all! (168-69)

And God is, of course, none other than Father Peace himself. Selina, watching the enthusiastic worshippers, is embarrassed and disappointed. Father Peace could not conceivably be the road to salvation for her, and she is unable to grasp how he can be for her father. She fails to understand fully why her father now needs a

10. Harris, pp. 49-61.

62

community, since he had been so strong and independent before, and to understand what Father Peace has to offer a man like Deighton. But Deighton has come back from a disaster to become the manager of a business, a "peace restaurant" (178), and a member of a community in which black and white live and work together on an equal footing, as he had always envisioned. He has regained a sense of pride and worth; he bears a strong likeness to the followers of Father Divine as they are described by his biographer:

> The men who join Father's movement have stopped worrying about being men and earning money to care for their wives and children. Father's fantasy world, where the kind of a job a man does or the amount of money he makes just don't matter, understandably becomes an ideal world to them. Certainly, they can give up their wives and sweethearts who reminded them every hour of every day that their dark skins were badges of inferiority, preventing them from being good providers and whole men ... Father gave them a chance to grow whole again.[11]

Silla Boyce will not accept being given up, however, and Deighton dies. Selina finishes high school and enters college with the war between her parents continuing in her own mind. She lives in two worlds and travels back and forth between them in Book 4, in a literal sense. The first is the old and familiar one of her Barbadian neighborhood, now organized into "The Association of Barbadian Homeowners and Businessmen." The second world is the sphere of her new experiences and friendships, her college dance group where she encounters an important new friend in Rachel Fine, who is white and Jewish, and the apartment of her boyfriend, Clive Springer, which seems to Selina more like Greenwich Village than Brooklyn, with its "books instead of dishes in the closets" (241), and paints and brushes in the sink.

Selina has always felt contempt or pity for the younger Barbadians who fail to rebel, or to rebel successfully, against the narrowness and materialism of the older generation. In Book 3 a large wedding takes place at which Selina feels a characteristic "sharp sense of alienation" (141). An imperious and formidable woman, 'Gatha Steed, is marrying off her daughter, who significantly is never given a name of her own. The girl had wanted to marry an American boy, from the South, and "they almost had to tie

11. Harris, pp. 102-03.

'Gatha down with wet sheets when she found out" (73). This show of independence, amounting to a rejection of ethnic group membership, is quickly squelched by the mother, who finds her daughter a suitable "Bajan" husband. The wedding takes place as a resounding demonstration of the mother's will power and group solidarity. The bride herself is "numb" and "broken" (138-39). Later, Selina cannot help feeling that her sister Ina's wedding will present a similar spectacle. Ina's fiancé is so "neat, cautious, Barbadian, light-skinned" and her future life so depressingly stereotyped that Selina can foresee only a "slow blurring of the self," a "steady attrition of the soul" (300).

At the first Association meeting which Selina attends she meets a group of docile contemporaries who provoke in her a silent outburst of rage:

> Prim, pious, pretentious pack! She noted the girls' tightly closed legs, the skirts dropping well over their knees, the hands folded decorously in their laps. No boy's hand had ever gained access to those breasts or succeeded in prying apart those clenched knees. Her cold glance swept the young men: Queers! (226)

In her highly emotional state Selina concentrates on the supposedly repressed or perverted sex lives of the other young Barbadians. Whether these accusations are true or not is immaterial; what Selina senses is their lack of inner vitality which should, at their age, be impelling them to embrace life, to assert themselves. They have allowed this vitality to be suppressed by their parents, however, and they sit at their parents' meeting like obedient, sexless children.

When Selina rushes out of the meeting she meets Clive Springer, whom she allows to make love to her before she even knows his name, in a gesture of defiance against all the others. Clive, an older man, a non-conformist Barbadian artist and intellectual, has the great appeal of unacceptability to Selina's mother and the rest of the community. Unfortunately, however, Clive is a failed rebel like 'Gatha Steed's daughter and has returned from Greenwich Village to live at his hypochondriac mother's beck and call. Ultimately Selina breaks off her affair with Clive because he has given up the struggle and will not be her loyal ally in rebellion. He has not lived his life to please his parents, but he has not been able to stand up to their tragic disappointment either. He ends up in a psychological no-man's land, paralyzed with guilt. "Look the poor mother!" says Silla to Selina when she learns of their romance:

> Every morning Clytie carried that boy for somebody to keep so she could do day's work. Clytie wore one coat for years so the Great Master Clive could take piano lesson ... And what she get for it? I know every hair 'pon she head is white-white and she does walk the streets talking to sheself ... (259)

Clive did not ask to be the Great Master, the recipient of his mother's ambitions and sacrifices, but it is a role he can never escape from.

Selina hates "the Association" as the organized and visible form of her mother's values and the pressures which are being exerted on her to conform to them. Although she makes an effort, she is unable fully to appreciate the needs of the older generation, which seem merely to frustrate her own. From their point of view, as an immigrant minority within the black minority of the American population, the maintenance of strong group ties was imperative. As blacks they have been forced by the white society to live in restricted ghetto neighborhoods; as Barbadians with a middle-class tradition, such as Deighton came from, which they are eager to defend, they wall themselves off from contrasts with American blacks, contacts which would mean to them a drop in status as well as a blurring of their special ethnic identity. "The Association" is a voluntary banding together in a hostile, foreign environment, a source of mutual aid and support. Its members feel proud of what they will be able to pass on to the rising generation:

> But tell me why we start this Association now when most of us gon soon be giving business to the undertaker? I gon tell you. It's because of the young people. Most of us did come to this man country with only the strength in we hand and a little learning in we head and had to make our way, but the young people have the opportunity to be professional and get out there and give these people big word for big word. Thus, they are our hope. They make all the sacrifice, all the struggle worth while. (221)

The message to the younger generation is problematical: their elders are telling them that they have not only the opportunity, but also the obligation to make the sacrifice worth while. The parents need the children to reach the goals they could not quite attain themselves, and are incapable of realizing that although they have provided amenities of life and education in quantities they had to grow up without, they are misusing the young at the same time, demanding the right to shape and control their children's lives to satisfy their own needs. The gift to the children is indeed great, but the psychological burden is great as well.

In her attempts to find positive expression for her father's values, as opposed to resisting her mother's, Selina's greatest success comes from her modern dance group at college. Dancing is a satisfactory activity for Selina in almost all respects. She is good at it and wins recognition; it stands in contrast to the professional training of her money- and career-minded Barbadian friends. It also involves her for the first time in a community of people brought together by a common interest rather than a common ethnic background. She belongs because of what she is by virtue of talent and inclination rather than by accident of birth.

The recital at which Selina dances just before her graduation is a true culmination of her college education. For once she is not a marginal figure but at the center of the stage, and as she dances she feels that more than communication with the audience is taking place; she has a sense of communion, of being truly part of a community at last:

> ... she danced well, expressing with deft movements the life cycle, capturing its beauty and exceeding sadness. The music bore her up at each leap ... until at the climax, she was dancing, she imagined, in the audience, through the rows of seats, and giving each one there something of herself, just as the priest in Ina's church, she remembered, passed along the row of communicants, giving them the wafer and the transmuted blood ... (281)

The content of this dance is particularly significant for Selina's development; it is a symbolic cycle of life that she enacts, in which she is not primarily a child of immigrants, or Barbadian, or black, or female, but a human being. Through the medium of her art she has overcome, for a brief moment, the barriers which restricted her growth, taken the wispy, intangible fragments of her father's inheritance and shared them with a random group of other human beings. She has turned her liabilities into assets, ironically profiting from her father's failure as her friends suffer from their own parents' achievements, since Selina has the opportunity of following in her father's footsteps, but of calling her success her own.

The dance recital is the climax of the novel in that it is a celebration of Selina's selfhood. She has finally become a person in her

or destroy it.

In the final chapter, which takes place a week later, Selina is awarded a scholarship by the Association, anti-climatically, since she had planned to use the money to run away to Barbados with Clive. Now she has realized that he will never be able to leave his mother. The award is nonetheless an important opportunity for Selina to reaffirm her position. Her experience of racism has not brought her back into the fold as a defeated spirit, but only tempered the exuberance in her determination to go her own way. She refuses the scholarship in quieter tones than she has ever used to the Association before, and refuses the guilt with which her mother wants to burden her, explaining that her insistence on independence is not ingratitude or rejection, but rather a tie between them, an imitation of the mother's strength. Selina leaves the hall determined to leave the country, and her past is already dead, reflected in a Brooklyn which is now a "vast waste" (309). It is far from clear what Selina will do or be on her journey, except her "own woman" (307).

In psychological terms, Selina has reached a state of inner equilibrium at the outset of her adult life, in which she can recognize the good qualities in both her parents and find them mirrored in herself, she is ready for the further experience represented by the journey she plans to make to Barbados. In sociological terms, she has placed herself in a more precarious position. She has rejected the claims of exclusive loyalty made by her own ethnic group and sought membership in a voluntary community of artists and intellectuals, which one sociologist has identified as the only substantial exception in American life to the rule of association based on race, religion, or national origin.[12] Since this community of college girls was temporary and tenuous, Selina could not feel fully welcome there, either, and she lands in the sociological category labeled "marginality":

> The individual who engages in frequent and sustained primary contacts across ethnic group lines, particularly racial and religious, runs the risk of becoming what, in standard sociological parlance, has been called "the marginal man." The marginal man is the person who stands on the borders

12. Milton M. Gordon, *Assimilation in American Life: The Role of Race, Religion, and National Origins* (New York: Oxford University Press, 1964), p. 111.

or margins of two cultural worlds but is fully a member of neither.[13]

Difficult as it is, this situation nonetheless contains much creative potential, and it is perhaps no exaggeration to say that exploring the implications of such a marginal position is the task Marshall set herself in her second novel, *The Chosen Place, the Timeless People* (1969).

The heroine of this novel, Merle Kinbona, is a separate fictional creation, but in her determination and independence she resembles Selina Boyce. Ideologically, however, Merle lives in different territory, more in the decade of the 1960's. For all her rebellion against middle-class consumerism, Selina appears as a figure quite recognizably of the late '50's, a beatnik in black tights. The ideals of social commitment and political activism, including black nationalism, lie in the decade to come; Selina's are self-expression and personal fulfillment in art. Merle Kinbona, on the other hand, is far more concerned with social problems and efforts to put an end to poverty and exploitation among blacks in Barbados, and the journey on which she embarks at the end of the second novel will take her the further step from Barbados eastwards to Africa.

The idea of seeking "salvation" in art and individualism rather than in community political action (for the first steps towards which "the Association" takes such a beating from Selina in *Brown Girl, Brownstones*) is not the only quality of the novel which links it to the 1950's. There is also the fact, striking to this contemporary reader at least, that Selina seems to show no awareness that the conflict between her mother and father is in any way related to their sex. Since Selina's perspective is that of a child, there are few hints, for example, of the pain and sexual jealousy that Silla Boyce must be feeling when her husband leaves the house every Saturday night to visit his mistress. Perhaps this omission has something to do with the fact that sexual jealousy is a major theme of *The Chosen Place, the Timeless People*, leading to the break-up of Merle's marriage and the death of another major character. In *Brown Girl, Brownstones* Selina interprets the differences between her parents as differences of values, personality, and temperament, although the novel offers evidence in abundance that other interpretations are possible.

The antithetical value structures and connotations with which

13. Gordon, p. 56.

Selina surrounds her parents are in fact her projections rather than the reflection of any objective reality. Could one not imagine a portrayal of Silla and Deighton Boyce which would reverse the degrees of sympathy the reader feels for them? Is Silla really the evil, materialistic consumer and Deighton the free spirit and artist-in-life as which their daughter sees them? Silla is, after all, a responsible and hard-working woman, who does not appear to be obsessed with status symbols in the least. She does indeed want to own her own house, but this is hardly a nefariously anti-social or exploitative desire; on the contrary, she merely wants to lessen the family's exposure to exploitation by others, to be rid — in view of all the other problems they face — at least of the problem of the gouging landlord. The grim single-mindedness with which she pursues this goal is unappealing; to be sure as is the way she crowds in roomers once she reaches it, but is she not forced into this role by her husband? She would not have to be so grim and intent if, with their two jobs and salaries, they were co-operating, if Deighton were not spending his money on silk shirts, fancy shoes and girls friends in order to look like a big man.

Silla's situation is made difficult by her husband's ideas about all the things *due to him* as a *man*. Deighton has been raised to think big and aim high by his mother, and his values and sense of reality have been corrupted in the process. He was robbed of his sense of manhood before leaving Barbados (182), and while there is no denying the pain and injustice of this experience, of what does this sense of manhood consist mainly but a feeling that only the best is good enough for him, that it is his natural right as a male? As a black male who meets with prejudice and discrimination, the best of everything is consistently withheld from him; he responds by retreating into fantasies. As a black woman his wife has to "know her place" in two senses, and since she has learned to make compromises and to aspire to only moderate aims as a female, she is less shattered by the limitations which white racism imposes on her as a black.

Selina and some critics are mistaken in thinking of Deighton as an anti-materialistic man. He is, on the contrary, obsessed with dreams of great wealth and prestige. "I ain looking for nothing small," he tells his family on the day he goes out job-hunting. "It got to be something big for me 'cause I got big plans or nothing a-tall. That's the way a man does do things" (82-83). The conflict between Deighton and Silla is not over whether to own a house at all, but over *what sort* of house to own. It is characteristic that the house she wants is of "uniform red-brown stone"; it is part of a row which shares "the same brown monotony" (3); in short, it is the sort of house that ordinary brown-skinned people in Brooklyn own. By contrast, Deighton's house will be "just like the white people own. A house to end all house" (12). It will be painted white and have white columns: "Everything gonna be white!" (86) And if Deighton cannot have this house, then he will have none at all; he would rather make do with the silk underwear and expensive shoes that rich white men wear. One critic, following Selina's emotional associations with her parents' desires, writes that "Deighton's land becomes a symbol for the long lost and ir-recoverable 'home' of Barbados — its simplicity in poverty, slow-paced living, natural beauty, and essential pre-Lapsarian purity and innocence."[14] Applied to Deighton Boyce, this is sheer wishful thinking. He does not want "simplicity in poverty," he wants stained-glass windows in every bathroom, "the best of clothes ... the swellest cars," since, in his refrain, "that's the way a man does do things" (85). He does not intend to kill himself working for them, however, "'cause a man got a right to take his ease in this life and not always be scuffling" (85). Deighton is a dreamer, in-deed, but to do this dreaming he assumes the pose characteristic for him in the novel: lying down. The scene in which he goes out to spend nine hundred dollars in one day is one of the infrequent ones which show the man on his feet. It is conceivable that he might try the patience of a more long-suffering woman that Silla.

While one can feel with Deighton over his rejection by prospec-tive employers and the process of emasculation, set in motion by his being first black and later injured, which finally overwhelms him, it is more difficult to sympathize with the dreams which frustrate his wife's efforts to live in the real world. As a fictional character Silla Boyce bears little resemblance to Nora in Ibsen's feminist classic, *A Doll's House*, but it is interesting to note that her crime is also the forging of a man's signature for money to do what she considers to be in her husband's best interests. Even at the end of *Brown Girl, Brownstones* Selina has not lost her sym-pathy with her father's dreams, however; she places the most

14. Benston, p. 68.

favorable possible interpretation of his behavior, identifying his male fantasies with the spirit of human endeavor in general, with striving for achievement and full selfhood against all unnatural boundaries and unjust limitations. Since that helps her to set out as a strong and independent woman, who is to say she is wrong?

BIOGRAPHY

Paule Marshall was born Paule Burke in Brooklyn, New York, in 1929; her parents had immigrated from Barbados shortly after World War I. She visited Barbados as a child, but grew up in Brooklyn and studied English literature at Brooklyn College, from which she graduated Phi Beta Kappa in 1952. She worked as a librarian and later as a writer for a black magazine, traveling to the West Indies and Brazil on assignments. Since then she has lived in the Caribbean and New York City, with her son. She has been a Guggenheim Fellow and received grants from the American Academy of Arts and Letters and the Ford Foundation.

BIBLIOGRAPHY

I. WORKS BY PAULE MARSHALL

Brown Girl, Brownstones (New York: Random House, 1959; rpt. Avon Books, 1970).

Soul Clap Hands and Sing (New York: Atheneum, 1961).
This collection contains four stories: "Brooklyn," "Barbados," "Brazil," "British Guiana."
"Barbados" and "Brooklyn" rpt. in *Black Insights,* ed. Nick Aaron Ford (Waltham, MA: Xerox College Publishing, Ginn & Co., 1971), pp. 104-19.
"Barbados," rpt. in *Black Writers of America: A Comprehensive Anthology*, ed. Richard Barksdale and Keneth Kinnamon (New York: Macmillan, 1972), pp. 774-81.
"Brazil," rpt. in *Cannon Shot and Glass Beads*, ed. George Lamming (London: Pan Books, 1974), pp. 253-77.

The Chosen Place, the Timeless People (New York: Harcourt, Brace & World, 1969).

"Reena," in *American Negro Short Stories*, ed. John H. Clarke (New York: Hill & Wang, 1966), rpt. in *The Black Woman: An Anthology*, ed. Toni Cade (New York: New American Library, Mentor Books, 1970), pp. 20-37, rpt. in *Black-eyed Susans: Classic Stories by and about Black Women*, ed. Mary Helen Washington (Garden City, NY: Anchor Books, 1975), pp. 114-37.

"Return of the Native," in *Sturdy Black Bridges: Visions of Black Women in Literature*, ed. Roseann P. Bell, Bettye J. Parker, and Beverly Guy-Sheftall (Garden City, NY: Anchor Books, 1979), pp. 314-321.

"Some Get Wasted," in *Harlem U.S.A.*, ed. John H. Clarke (Berlin: Seven Seas, 1974).

"To Da-duh, In Memoriam," in *Black Voices: An Anthology of Afro-American Literature*, ed. Abraham Chapman (New York: New American Library, Mentor Books, 1968), pp. 205-14.

II. WORKS ON PAULE MARSHALL

Benston, Kimberly, "Architectural Imagery and Unity in Paule Marshall's *Brown Girl, Brownstones*." *Negro American Literature Forum*, 9, No. 3 (Fall 1975), 67-70.

Bond, Jean Cory, "Allegorical Novel by Talented Storyteller." *Freedomways*, First Quarter, 1970, 76-78.

Braithwaite, Edward, "Rehabilitation." *Critical Quarterly*, 13 (Summer 1971), 175-83.

––, "West Indian History and Society in the Art of Paule Marshall's Novel." *Journal of Black Studies*, 1 (December 1970), 225-38.

Brown, Lloyd W., "The Rhythms of Power in Paule Marshall's Fiction." *Novel*, 7 (Winter 1974), 159-67.

Butcher, Philip, "The Younger Novelists and the Urban Negro." *College Language Association Journal*, 4 (March 1961), 196-203.

Kapai, Leela, "Dominant Themes and Techniques in Paule Marshall's Fiction." *CLA Journal*, 16 (September 1972), 45-59.

Keizs, Marcia, "Themes and Style in the Works of Paule Marshall," *Negro American Literature Forum*, 9 (Fall 1975), 67 and 71-76.

Nazareth, Peter, "Paule Marshall's Timeless People." *New Letters*, 40 (Autumn 1973), 116-31.

Stoelting, Winifred, "Time Past and Time Present: The Search for Viable Links in *The Chosen Place, the Timeless People*." *CLA Journal*, 16 (September 1972), 60-71.

Washington, Mary Helen, "Black Women Image Makers." *Black World*, 23 (August 1974), 10-18.

Whitlow, Roger, *Black American Literature: A Critical History*. Chicago: Nelson-Hall, 1973.

WOLFGANG KARRER

MULTIPERSPECTIVE AND THE HAZARDS OF INTEGRATION: JOHN WILLIAMS' *NIGHT SONG* (1961)

There seems to be a widespread consensus that John A. Williams has produced one great novel — *The Man Who Cried I Am* — several well-made novels and also some potboilers. This is hardly surprising for a writer who has produced books since 1960 at the rate of almost one book per year.[1] The status of *Night Song* (1961), his second novel,[2] is dubious, at best. It almost won Williams the Prix de Rome from the American Academy of Arts and Letters,[3] received generally favorable reviews, but later critics dismissed it as an "apprentice work," "derivative, literary, and ineptly political."[4] After three editions in the United States and two in Great Britain *Night Song* quietly went out of print until it was republished along with Williams' first novel *One for New York* in 1975 by The Chatham Bookseller.[5]

Night Song deals with the jazz experience, a crucial aspect of black culture, but it also reflects certain esthetic problems of technique black novelists had to face around 1960, a year that signified a critical juncture between social criticism, bohemianism and the Civil Rights Movement.[6] The so-called "protest novel" — a majority term for minority fiction and itself an example of

1. See the bibliography at the end of this article.
2. For early unpublished attempts see Earl A. Cash, *John A. Williams: The Evolution of a Black Writer.* New York: The Third Press, 1975, pp. 45 f.
3. *Ibid.*, pp. 61-70.
4. Ronald Walcutt, "The Early Fiction of John A. Williams," *CLA Journal* 16 (1972), 202; Jerry H. Bryant, "John A. Williams: The Political Use of the Novel," *Critique: Studies in Modern Fiction* 16 (1975), 87.
5. *One for New York* was first published under the publisher's title *The Angry Ones.* John A. Williams, *Night Song.* Chatham, N.J.: The Chatham Bookseller, 1975 will be the edition quoted parenthetically in the text.
6. Compare my introduction in this book, pp. 35-38.

cultural hegemony[7] — seemed to have reached its end, not so much because the causes of its emergence had disappeared but because the Cold War climate of the fifties had made black social criticism and leftist attitudes in the vein of Richard Wright or the early Chester Himes something "un-American" and had brought more acceptable writers like Ralph Ellison and James Baldwin who were willing to disclaim the "protest"-tradition, to the foreground. Williams states the underlying conditions very clearly:

> They Baldwin and Wright, were a generation apart, but they remained victims. They were artists, writers, yet they knew that only one of them at a time, were it James Baldwin, Langston Hughes, Chester Himes, Ralph Ellison, or Richard Wright, could be, would be allowed to be, the black writer of the moment. America was not geared nor did it wish to be geared for the spectacle of more than one black writer at a time. Thus driven into the arena of further oppression, like gladiators, they were forced to battle among themselves for a place of honor in the white establishment. So they hurt each other, and often they knew exactly why they were doing it.[8]

This process had displaced the naturalistic conventions and had channeled black grievances into more acceptable literary conventions. On the other hand, there was the new Beat Movement and the new East Village bohemia centering around St. Mark's Place in places like the Five Spot Café, the Cedar Tavern, the Eight Street Book Shop or Mickey Ruskin's 10th Street Coffeehouse. Here such diverse writers as Norman Mailer, Jack Kerouac, Allen Ginsberg, LeRoi Jones, Calvin Hernton and David Henderson lived, worked and met each other. Black writers founded the Society of Umbra and published little magazines like *Yugen* or *The Floating Bear*. To Hettie, LeRoi Jones' white wife, it seemed the beginning of black bohemia.[9] Williams makes this new bohemia around St. Mark's place — at the time of its flowering — the theme and setting of *Night Song* and takes one of the cultural heroes of the Beat Movement as the novel's secret hero: Charles Christopher

7. The fact that minority writers have accepted this term does not make it less discriminatory. Nobody would call works by Dreiser, Sinclair, Steinbeck or Dos Passos "protest novels."

8. John A. Williams, *The Most Native of Sons*. New York: Doubleday, 1970, p. 113.

9. Susan Edmiston and Linda D. Cirino, *Literary New York: A History and Guide*. Boston: Houghton Mifflin, 1976, pp. 124 – 142.

Parker, Jr., generally known as Charlie Parker, Yardbird or Bird (August 29, 1920 – March 12, 1955).

John A. Williams shared the Beatnik's admiration for the music of Charlie Parker. In 1959 Williams began to collect material on Parker for a biography, projected together with Robert Reisner who had promoted Parker during the last months of his life and who now wrote a jazz column for the *Village Voice*. The project was turned down and Williams found it increasingly difficult to work with Reisner, who published his material separately in 1962 as *Bird: The Legend of Charlie Parker*. Williams used his material for an article on Charlie Parker in *Swank* magazine in 1960. His first published novel had not made any money for him. But it brought him a commission for a paperback novel from Arlene Donovan, then editor at Dell. The new novel, written more or less simultaneously with *Sissie*, was *Night Song*, a fictional recasting of some of the materials Williams had on Charlie Parker. Farrar, Straus, Cudahy took *Sissie* and also bought *Night Song* from Dell, who kept the reprint rights. *Night Song* was thus clearly aimed at the general paperback market.[10] It was later made into a film version *Sweet Love, Bitter* (1967) by Herbert Danska, casting Dick Gregory as Charlie Parker.[11]

Night Song is neither a beat or jazz novel, nor a "protest" novel, nor – in anticipation of British sales – the novel of an "angry young man," though it shows traits of all these conventions.[12] Unlike Dorothy Baker's *Young Man with a Horn* (1938) which set some of the conventions for the jazz novel, *Night Song* does not make a thinly disguised jazz musician the central character of the book. In fact, critics have seen different characters as the hero of the novel. For Ronald Walcott *Night Song* is basically a novel of Keel Robinson's identity quest between black and white, of his regeneration after having been emasculated by a white racist socie-

10. Paperback covers implying interracial sex seem to have helped the sales in the United States and Great Britain. For Williams' opinions on this marketing strategy see his interview with Cash in Earle A. Cash, *John A. Williams*, p. 149.

11. Ibid., p. 152; John A. Williams, *Flashbacks. A Twenty-Year Diary of Article Writing*. Garden City, N.Y.: Anchor Books, 1974, pp. 218-221, 396 f.

12. Compare *The Angry Ones*, *The Angry Black*, *Beyond the Angry Black* and the frequent use of "anger" and "rage" in *Night Song*.

ty.[13] Earl A. Cash sees *Night Song* primarily as a mythic initiation of a prejudiced white, David Hillary, into a new knowledge of self.[14] For Jerry J. Bryant the novel has two main characters, both black and both suffering heroically, the jazz musician Richie Stokes and Keel Robinson. David Hillary serves as a white foil.[15]

The contradictions between these interpretations disappear after a closer look at the conventions used in Williams' novel. *Night Song* uses the Jamesian convention of telling the story of a group of closely interrelated people in multiperspective or different point of views. Another title for *Night Song* might well have been 'The Wings of the Eagle.' The techniques Henry James introduced to American fiction and codified in *The Art of the Novel* or his prefaces were transmitted and generalized by Percy Lubbock, Joseph W. Beach and Richard P. Blackmur. They were taught in numerous college courses all over the United States and had become something like a prescriptive poetics of the novel for writers, critics and publishers alike during the fifties. Until Wayne Booth opened his attack in *The Rhetoric of Fiction* (1961) the absence of an overt narrator, the skilful handling of point of view and scenic narration had been the criteria for a well-made novel. The impact of this tradition on the black writers who came of age in the fifties — Baldwin readily comes to mind — seems to have been great. The Henry James cult which so significantly coincides with the Cold War period served as an antidote to the naturalistic conventions of Dreiser and Wright. The international theme became a model for the interracial theme.[16]

During the cold winter of 1954/1955 former college professor David Hillary, whom guilt feelings about the death of his wife drive to alcoholism and skid row, meets the jazz musician Richie Stokes, generally known as the Eagle. Stokes saves his life and takes him to a friend, Keel Robinson, who offers him work in his

13. Ronald Walcutt, "The Early Fiction of John A. Williams," 204 f.
14. Earl A. Cash, *John A. Williams*, pp. 51-55.
15. Jerry H. Bryant, "John A. Williams," 86 f. Noel Schraufnagel, *From Apology To Protest: The Black American Novel*. Deland, Fla.: Everett/Edwards, 1973, pp. 148-150 reads *Night Song* as "an examination of prejudice from a sexual viewpoint" which, again, seems to make Hillary the main character.
16. Examples like *The Primitive* or *Another Country* come readily to mind.

coffee-shop in St. Mark's Place. Here Hillary meets and immediately desires Della Madison, Robinson's white lover. Robinson, who lost his virility with Madison during a racist attack on them in a bar, and Hillary save Stokes from an overdose of heroin. With help from Madison and his new black friends Hillary recuperates and applies for a position at his old college in Onondaga Falls, N.Y. Several weeks pass and spring approaches. Madison, who is desperate because of Robinson's impotence or unwillingness to make love with her, has ended a brief affair with Hillary. She criticizes him for being ashamed to work for Robinson, a black man. Hillary gets his former position back but misses an appointment with Stokes, who is beaten up by a brutal white policeman from Onondaga Falls. Hillary returns to New York to confess to Stokes, Robinson and Madison that he has witnessed the beating without interfering. Eagle dies from another overdose of heroin under rather mysterious circumstances. After a memorial concert for Eagle, Hillary returns to his college, Madison and Robinson, who have found a loving and permanent relationship, return to his apartment. This spare outline of the main plot has to be filled out with the details of the background: the night world of the bohemia with its artists, their fans and exploiters, interracial couples and barroom brawls, its survival economy and behavioral codes.

Night Song adapts the quadrangle construction of the late novels of Henry James with Richie Stokes as Milly Theale, and David Hillary as Kate Croy. Della Madison, the woman between two men, shares certain functions with Merton Densher and Keel Robinson is among other things a confidant for Richie Stokes and David Hillary. At least this is the way Williams sees it:

> In *The Angry Ones* and in *Night Song*, you've got this tandem pair of black guys Keel and Eagle and Obie and Steve. You've got the same thing in *The Man Who Cried I Am*. Now early I was very aware that this was the only way to deal with black dialogue; that is, to have another confidant. Or as in the case of *The Man Who Cried I Am*, Harry is not always a confidant. He is an antagonist. But at least they can dialogue. And to a larger extent having two characters function like this, you're really dealing with one character, but using two parts.[17]

17. John A. Williams, "Interview" in Earle A. Cash, *John A. Williams*, p. 132. In other interviews Williams claims he learned his technique from Malcolm Lowry's *Under the Volcano*, a novel closely modelled on *The Wings of*

This specific quadrangle convention, which has to be distinguished from the old comedy tradition of contrasting symmetrical couples (from antiquity through Shakespeare and Jane Austen to *Who's Afraid of Virginia Woolf* and *The Blood Oranges*), consists of either three men and one woman or vice versa. It often combines a love triangle with a victim or outsider figure and creates multiple relations between characters which go far beyond sexual attraction and symmetrical foils. As in *The Wings of the Dove, Pylon, Under the Volcano, All the King's Men* or *Up above my Head* this pattern tends to blur sexual boundaries and to sacrifice definite couplings to an unstable balance of conflicting forces which is generally disrupted by the more or less ritual death of one of the characters. If, in addition, as in *The Wings of the Dove* and *Night Song* all four main characters become "centres of consciousness" or "reflectors," then scenic narration alternating with reflections and flashbacks, architectural construction in blocks, mutual constrast of point of views and the theme of deception or betrayal seem to follow logically from the initial choice.[18] The plot tends to take on certain archetypal and ritual overtones of sacrifice and redemption.[19]

The arche- or stereotypes in *Night Song* stand out very clearly. For Hillary the *katabasis* or descent into the night world of black and white bohemia seems to have regenerative functions, as it does for Robinson, son of a bishop and a real estate speculator himself. But for Hillary the old adventure of the hero with a thousand faces[20] is different. Descent and ascent are inverted: the higher

the Dove. John A. Williams, "John A. Williams at 49: An Interview," *Minnesota Review* 7 (1976), 55 and "Interview with John A. Williams," *Black World* 25, 3 (January 1976), 64.

18. Henry James, "Preface to 'The Wings of the Dove' " in Henry James, *The Art of the Novel.* New York: Charles Scribner's Sons, 1937, pp. 288-306 describes this process as one that leads from idea through central figure, establishing one's successive centers of consciousness and construction of blocks to detail of treatment. James underlines the difficulties in keeping balance between the figures, a difficulty which reflects the historical process of displacing the hero from the center of the novel.

19. Northrop Frye, *Anatomy of Criticism: Four Essays.* Princeton, N.J.: Princeton University Press, 1957, pp. 216-219 establishes four constant characters in tragedy plots.

20. Joseph Campbell, *The Hero with a Thousand Faces.* New York: Bollingen, 1949.

world he returns to may be lower than the underworld he leaves, his social ascent a moral descent, his recuperation a final sickness unto death:

> "How could we be unworthy of your love [says Robinson to Hillary] and yet worthy of your confession? It's not only that you don't know where you are, you don't know where we are. Are you at the top looking down or at the bottom looking up? Has somebody been playing with mirrors? Who? Or what? Most important, why?"

Williams' play with mirrors and existentialism[21] includes Robinson who unlike Hillary is finally able to dissociate his ideas on race from his personal relation with Della Madison. Madison, another patient Griselda, has waited patiently and lovingly for him to find his way back to her. Richie Stokes enacts the tragic *pharmakos* role: his sacrificial death seems to free (by coincidence) Robinson from his sickness and may even free the man who turned out to be his Judas rather than his St. John (196), Hillary, once he finds out who is really responsible for Eagle's death. Like Kate Croy he will never be again as he was. There is the tragic flaw of heroin addiction, the unlucky concatenation of circumstances playing nemesis[22], and the final enigmatic consent with his death that distinguishes the tragic hero. On the other hand, Eagle's heroin addiction is as much a result of racism as the circumstances that concatenate, and the sacrifice of the hero leaves society just as racist as before. Eagle's deaths and rebirths, though closely matched with seasonal change, will not bring summer and maturity to anybody else but Robinson and Madison.[23]

The problem *Night Song* poses is: what happens when two whites and two blacks meet in a situation, the night world of the bohemia, where the "normal" relation of racist domination are

21. Compare John Clellon Holmes, "The Philosophy of The Beat Generation" in Seymour Krim, ed., *The Beats*.Greenwich: Fawcett, 1960, p. 15. "To be beat is to be at the bottom of your personality, looking up; to be existential in the Kierkegaard, rather than the Jean-Paul Sartre, sense." Compare also *Night Song*, p. 193.

22. If Stokes had not talked about racism, Hillary would not have written to his college; if Robinson had not rejected Madison, she would not have started an affair with Hillary; if Stokes had not slipped away to get drugs, he would have met Hillary before the appointment etc.

23. For further mythic parallels see Earle A. Cash, *John A. Williams*, pp. 51-61 and Jerry H. Bryant, "John A. Williams," 86-88.

momentarily inverted, a black man loves and marries a white woman and a white man works as a waiter for a black proprietor? Both, sexual domination and domestic service, have long characterized relations between whites and blacks in the United States.[24] The solution *Night Song* offers is neither original nor very convincing: love, whether as interracial sex or help and solidarity between black and white, can be stronger than racism as in the case of Madison and Robinson, but it can hardly be considered a solution to the institutional racism Richie Stokes has to face. Even if the disc jockey Rod Tolen, the jazz critic Stanley Crane or the recording agent Moe Alvin could be made to act in solidarity with Eagle instead of exploiting him the institutional framework of racism in education, employment and justice would remain. The vestiges of the "protest" tradition in *Night Song* are not amenable to he Jamesian technique. The literary conventions of the quadrangle and multiperspective tend towards certain "literary" or "mythical" answers like betrayal, sacrificial death and (possible) regeneration. It seems probable, however, that Williams chose this technique not so much for its inherent solutions as for its power as a tool to analyze racism on a face-to-face level. After selecting an idea (racism) and a central character (a jazz musician) the technique of "the *indirect* representation of his main image"[25] leads Williams to a series of scenes or confrontations which reveal the interaction of thought, feeling, speech and action within the successive centers of consciousness. It is with the strengths and limitations of his narrative convention for analyzing individual racism[26] that the following more technical discussion will be concerned.

Henry James had observed that in establishing one's successive centers of consciousness the author has sometimes to consent to a practical fusion of the consciousness between two characters[27] or, more precisely, to supplement the dominant point of view with an

24. Sherley Anne Williams, *Give Birth to Brightness: A Thematic Study in Neo-Black Literature*. New York: Dial Press, 1972, pp. 160 f. Gunnar Myrdal, *An American Dilemma: The Negro Problem and Modern Democracy*. repr. New York: Harper, 1969,pp. 652, 654.

25. Henry James, *The Art of the Novel*, p. 306. For the image of the jazz musician as a cultural hero see Sherley Anne Williams, *Give Birth to Brightness*, pp. 135-167.

26. Gordon W. Allport, *The Nature of Prejudice*. Garden City, N.Y.: Doubleday, 1958.

27. Henry James, *The Art of the Novel*, p. 299.

occasional opposing view. His terminology suggests that this "fusion" is not a matter of the author's plan or "idea" but is somehow forced on him by his characters during the execution or "working out." This is, of course, only a mystifying way of saying that certain of the author's thematic interests assert themselves against his plan. Something similar seems to have happened in *Night Song* where several such fusions occur:

> "You see," Keel said, "you don't belong here. What's there to focus? You live, you don't try to figure out why."
> Hillary thought: Why is he trying to frighten me? Keel thought himself: I'm trying to scare this cat. Why? (122)

The dominant point of view in chapter ten is Robinson's —signalled in the quote by the tag "himself" — but for reasons of his own Williams here interpolates Hillary's view. The following charts shows the succession of the dominant point of view among Hillary (H), Robinson (R), Stokes (S), and Madison (M) in the two blocks of the novel:

Chapter	Point of View				Chapter	Point of View			
1	H				8	H			M
2	H				9	H			
3	H				10		R		M
4	H	R	S		11		R		
5		R		M	12	H		S	
6	H				13	H	R		M
7	H	R			14			S	
					15	H	R		M
					16	H	R	S	
					17	H	R		

The most remarkable fact emerging from this chart is the preference for Hillary's point of view which dominates in thirteen of seventeen chapters. The adaptation of a "white" technique[28] is matched by a prevalent white point of view. The chart also shows very clearly how the succession in point of view multiplies in the second block of the novel. The chart cannot reveal to what extent succession and fusion become a major structuring device in *Night*

28. Robert Felgar, "Black Content, White Form," *Studies in Black Literature* 5 (1974), 28-30.

Song. If a chapter boundary traditionally signals some discontinuity in time or place[29] it sometimes, as in the case of chapters nine and ten, thirteen and fourteen, fourteen and fifteen also signals a change in point of view. Generally, however, changes of point of view are reserved to subsections of a chapter marked by extra wide spacing between two paragraphs. There are four main types of change: the gradual transition through blackout or drunkenness as in chapter four, the slow emergence of one point of view from a basically fused situation as in chapter ten, the cinematic cross-cutting between two unfused point of views in chapter twelve, and the equally cinematic rapid succession of three point of views, roughly simultaneous but in different places, in seven and thirteen. Juxtaposition is more frequent than transition. Another significant fact the chart does not reveal is the higher incidence of fusion in the second part of *Night Song* when spring brings out more clearly the (mis)understandings between the main characters.

Point of view focuses thought, feeling and perception in one character. Thought, feeling and perception sometimes appear detached from dialogue as in the memory flash-backs of Hillary, Stokes, Robinson and Madison (8, 9, 24; 45-48; 54-57; 61-67) or in the long reflective rambles by Hillary and Robinson through the streets of Manhattan. More often, however, thought is externalized through speech — something the Jamesian structure easily lends itself to — by making the member of the quadrangle confidants for each other. Here again Hillary dominates the others by making all of them confidants of his doubts and guilt feelings. Of all possible combinations only the black characters never meet alone nor do Stokes and Madison. In scenic narration thought, feeling and perception tend to supplement talk, less frequently action. Here are the richest strata of analysis in *Night Song*. By refusing to make Hillary an openly racist character Williams is able to demonstrate the contradictory workings of everyday racism in a liberal and even negrophile middle-class WASP.

Cash has assembled some of the more blatant examples of prejudice which make Hillary's racism sound rather simple and straightforward.[30] Actually, Hillary likes blacks, their lifestyles

29. Philip Stevick, *The Chapter in Fiction: Theories of Narrative Division*. Syracuse , N.Y.: Syracuse University Press, 1970, pp. 37-96.
30. Earle A. Cash, *John A. Williams*, pp. 48-51.

own right; on the stage she was "exposed," "utterly dependent ... upon her body" (281), but this body proved to be "eloquent." Paradoxically, it is this hard-won assurance of her own self which makes possible the feeling of communion with others, the feeling of "giving each one there something of herself" and "bearing something of them all away with her" (281-82).

Were the novel a fairy-tale, it would end here. Art is not life, however, and Selina's identity must prove itself in the face of rejection as well as acclaim. At the party following the recital, in the home of a wealthy white family on the Upper East Side of Manhattan, the unconscious, patronizing racism of the hostess brings Selina brutally back to earth, reminding her that she has entered a world in which her presence will not always be un-questioningly accepted, that she is, after all, not a priest but a black West Indian immigrant girl. The girls in the dance club form a group bound together by ties in which race plays no part, but each of them is also part of a family, in the setting of which the racial and ethnic barriers of the larger society quickly reassert themselves. If Selina's sense of self were firmly established at this point, she would be able to give her fellow dancer's mother a crisp and devastating reply; she would refuse to accept the mother's illusion of her and insist that she allow "her real face to emerge" (291). Only after she has run out of the party does the complexity of the whole truth begin to dawn on Selina: the problem is not that this white woman has failed to see her as she really is; on the contrary, it is as if she had instinctively penetrated beyond the façade of Selina's attractive, acceptable face or self and seen the true "bad" Selina, her "dark depth":

> Her sins rose like a miasma from its fetid bottom: the furtive pleasures with Clive on the sofa, her planned betrayal of the Association, the mosaic of deceit and lies she had built to delude the mother. They took form in the shadows around her – small hideous shapes jeering her and touching her with cold and viscid hands. (291)

Selina limps back to Brooklyn, "like an animal broken by a long hunt" (290), yet with a sense, if not a clear idea, of the difficult task ahead of her; she must consolidate her achievement, build on the identity she has already established, accept the "good" and "bad" elements of it without permitting either the pressure of her own ethnic group or the prejudice of the white majority to distort

and jazz (10, 31, 105, 93). He has sought out their company, and the childhood frienship with Borden, a black boy, is like a lost chance and dream often present in his mind (25, 78, 88, 104). But it is not simply another case of the attitude of a liberal "Some of my best friends are ..." Here are a few examples of Hillary's point of view:

"All right, for crissakes," the man said, and Hillary felt a stab of fear. Why didn't this man like him? (12)

Keel nodded to the beat of the music for a couple of bars, then said, "I don't understand why a white man can't make it in his society. You know, it bugs me sometimes."
"That's a pretty narrow view," Hillary said angrily.
"Maybe."
"What the hell are you?" Hillary asked wearily. He thought back through the conversation, checking. This had all begun when Eagle went out; Keel had become upset then, though it hadn't shown on his face. (17f.)

"Did you know," Eagle asked when he had finished the soup, "that Keel was a minister?"
The disclosure did not impress Hillary. He had known of Negro preachers; they were the butt of jokes among Negroes themselves. "Oh, yeah?"
"I don't mean an ordinary preacher. He had all that bullshit behind his name, B.D. and D.D. Went to some seminary at Harvard. A real heavy cat.'
This made it intersting to Hillary, but then, Keel being what he was, he probably took some money and had been defrocked for it — or whatever Protestant churches did with their ministers.
"He just quit," Eagle said, and there was both wonder and pride in his voice. Hillary knew that Keel, then, often puzzled Eagle. (51 f.)

The three quotes illustrate three recurring mechanisms in David Hillary's mind: his desire to be accepted and liked by blacks, in other words, his fear of rejection; his anger at being made aware of the real and pervasive discrimination of blacks which makes fraternization with whites so difficult for Stokes and Robinson; finally, the habitual stereotyping of blacks as a defensive mechanism.[31] All three are intimately connected. Perception enables Hillary to revise a feeling as in example two, but not a prejudice as in the third example, because in one his self esteem is involved in the

31. Further examples: 15, 18, 31, 38, 45, 50, 70, 75, 78, 82, 86, 88, 101 etc.

other it is not. Almost all of the stereotyped and racist thoughts in Hillary's mind go back to his insecurity about his own value. Other examples, like Hillary's uncomfortableness at the use of "nigger" in black dialogue (50) or his bewilderment when Kilroy and Background signify about black and white relations, (136) demonstrate that he knows little of black styles of communicating.[32]

Though *Night Song* is mainly geared to catch Hillary's involuntary reactions to dialogue with and between blacks, we are also given Robinson's reactions to speech acts by Hillary, Madison and other whites:

> ... Crane asked, "What's this I hear about Eagle?"
> Keel looked at him. Vulture, he thought. (57)

> Hillary didn't answer that either and Keel was overwhelmed with the urge to smash him. (119)

> Then a slow fright worked loose inside him and he had the answer. He sensed something between Hillary and Della which had somehow gotten out of his control, something which passed — Damnit! Why was he thinking like that? — only between whites. (122)

Both, Hillary and Robinson, react angrily at rejection, both want love and acceptance, both are highly introspective and self-analytical, but while Hillary defends his prejudices against better evidence Robinson questions his even before the evidence comes in.

If these examples so far show how racism interferes with understanding and communicating between blacks and whites, *Night Song* also offers moments of perfect understanding and overcoming of obstacles in Robinson and Madison:

> "Promise to take care of me." Even though she understood once the words were out that they had a double meaning, Della continued to smile at him, wishing they had not been spoken.
> But there was nothing demanding in her eyes, Keel saw, only a smile as soft, as clean, and as deep in its depths as one can see down in clear water. "I promise," he said in her ear, "to take care of you, but only if you promise to love and obey me. Obey, baby."
> Della hid her laughter behind her hand. It had been a long time since they had engaged in repartee. "What about honor?"

32. Thomas Kochman, ed., *Rappin' and stylin' out: Communication in Urban Black America.* Chicago: University of Illinois Press, 1972.

"That's for *mothers* and fathers. Save it for them."
     She took his hand and playfully dug the nail of her thumb into his palm. "Mothers" had had a double meaning. (213)

Love is shared meanings, black and white, "mothers" and marriage ceremony.[33]

Speech is more heavily censored than thought or feeling, especially between blacks and whites in the tough nightworld of the artist and the hustler.[34] But racism, prejudice or simply preference come out in dialogue as well. As the exchange between Madison and Robinson shows, speech acts can be potentially hostile or misunderstood if they are not based on common and shared assumptions.[35] For this very reason race talk alienates and angers Hillary, and Hillary's "human" generalizations offend Stokes and Robinson because they know the underlying assumption of equal rights to be false. And as most dialogues in *Night Song* center around race relations in work and sex, examples are not hard to find. But social and racial estrangement also comes out in naming.[36] David Hillary, who introduces himself as "Dave Hillary" is called "Prof" by Keel Robinson, "Jimsey" or "Prof" by Richie Stokes. Even Della Madison avoids calling him "Dave" and uses hip talk and a sarcastic "man" to put him down. Only once, Hillary has just helped to save Stokes, there is acceptance (45). Della Madison never calls Keel Robinson "man," he is "Keel" or "baby" to her. To Richie Stokes David Hillary remains "Jimsey," something he calls everybody until the betrayal after which he uses a sarcastic "baby" for him. If naming is a subtle way of offering or withholding sympathy and love then the narrator shares the likes and dislikes of his characters. Regardless of whose turn it is as a center of consciousness, he cannot bring himself to call David Hillary anything but Hillary, Keel Robinson Keel, and Della Madison Della. Richie Stokes remains Richie Stokes, but more often becomes Eagle. The author directs the reader to take his/her stand in "this quiet war-

33. Stokes' mental reactions to speech and all mental reactions to action are rarely given in *Night Song*.
     34. Compare the passages on pp. 120, 176, 181 f.
     35. Erving Goffman, *Frame Analysis: An Essay on the Organization of Experience*. New York: Harper, 1974, pp. 496 -559.
     36. Boris A. Uspensky, *The Poetics of Composition: Structure of the Artistic Text and the Typology of Compositional Form*. Berkeley: University of California Press, 1974, is useful on this point.

fare that raged in the clubs and bedrooms, in smiles and language." (218 f.)[37]

The meaning of love and its frustrated counterpart, anger, which underlie the talk, feeling and thought of the main characters, becomes much clearer by looking at the actions taken by them. The plot of *Night Song* could be broken down into a series of acts of help: Stokes helps Hillary, Robinson helps Hillary, Hillary and Robinson help Stokes, Robinson refuses help from Madison etc. If "counselling" in dialogue is also included as a verbal equivalent of help the plot reduces itself to various interrelated acts of help, accepted or denied, which connect the main characters in a mutually supportive net.[38] It is important in terms of the novel that this net of love and solidarity extends only as far as the bohemian nightworld. The racist dayworld surrounding the East Village is a constant danger to it. Hillary stands up for Stokes in the club Bohemia and fights, but he does not have the nerve, much less the impulse to do so in broad daylight in his home town. The chance and risks of integrated action[39] between blacks and whites is the generating idea behind the actions, words and mental processes of the experimental quadrangle of *Night Song*.

The indirect presentation of the main image through reflectors traditionally calls for a covert narrator,[40] hiding behind his reflectors. The loss of authorial omniscience is more than made up for by the multiperspective and its flexibility in time (flashbacks, dreams, plans) and place (change in point of view). Explicit bridging becomes superfluous. But the narrator hides, he does not exit. In *The Wings of the Dove* he emerges with an occasional "we." In *Night Song* the teachings about the "objectivity" of the novel, i.e. the absence of narratorial comment, are fairly closely observed. This leads to some awkward sermonizing on the part of Robinson

37. Even Henry James who skilfully varies between Susan Stringham, Susie, Susan Shepherd, Mrs. Stringham, the poor lady etc. according to the point of view will never call Lord Mark or Sir Luke Street Mark or Luke. Naming permits to identify social and sexual prejudices in a novel.

38. *Night Song* could easily be formalized in one of the structuralist models of narration.

39. There are very few instances in *Night Song* where thought leads to action; a notable exception occurs on p. 78.

40. Seymour Chatman: *Story and Discourse: Narrative Structure in Fiction and Film*. Ithaca: Cornell University Press, 1978, pp. 197-262.

who, in the second part, increasingly becomes the author's mouth-piece — only to give way to open comment in the last sentences of *Night Song*:

> Someday Hillary would understand. Maybe. The bus edged through the toll booths, down the bricked road into the gaping mouth of the tunnel. (219)

After the work is done, the narrator appears behind his reflectors.

But there are earlier hints of the narrator's intrusion, and these "flaws" in technique are particularly revealing of what Williams thinks needs special motivation.[41] Thus the narrator steps in with a few helpful remarks like "for the first time" (26, 44), "until the moment" (29), "here at the very end" (71) etc. in order to point out both the various stations of Hillary's journey through the underworld as well as to underline the important coincidences marking his way. The narrator is more reticent with Robinson. He sometimes deliberately withholds insight into his mind (116), sometimes he emphasizes his intrusion by an agnostic "perhaps:"

> Perhaps it was the way the question was asked or maybe something within Hillary which at the precise moment the question was asked screamed for help. It could even have been one of those rare times occurring within the lives of humans, when understanding strikes with the cleanness and power of a thunderbolt. (119)

The integrationist and even universalist assumptions underlying *Night Song* emerge quite clearly. If the rather obtrusive symbolism of water, the Statue of Liberty / the ship *Liberté*, night and day is usually tied to one of the reflectors,[42] the various descriptions of the East Village which could have been easily integrated into one of the centers of consciousness belong to the narrator. And here the paradisiacal vision of a multi-ethnic non-melting America emerges briefly but repeatedly:[43]

> On Saturday nights, above the sound of traffic and the noise of many people too close together came music from all over the world played on bongos and congas, on horns of various sizes and shapes made out of metal, wood, or plastic. Against the frenetic background of the cha-cha-cha there came the spirituals of the fearful but devout huddled in a storefront

41. *Ibid.*, pp. 51-53.
42. Hillary and water (94 f.), Stokes and Liberty (94, 180, 204), Robinson and night vs. day (39, 54, 127).
43. Compare pp. 53, 75, 111.

church, isolated from the main chorus by 122 blocks. And above this the Cantor's tremolo lingered on, sighing over the clatter of the polka.

In this part of town, it was said that people were more like people. (21)

The description, like the name-calling in the novel, points at William's reservations on whether WASPs like Hillary would be able to join this night song of multi-ethnic America ... Other more covert intrusions underline this sceptic attitude. Occasionally in the novel the narrator briefly steps beyond the four centers of consciousness to include further points of view. Almost all of these passages demonstrate the pervasiveness of racist assumptions (8, 40, 81 f., 147). An exception is the slow emergence of Candy, Stokes' white lover, as an ambiguous reflector, in many ways similar to Hillary, somebody willing to learn, but unwilling to make sacrifices outside the nightworld (204 f.).

The study of technique helps to pin down and specify some of the novel's underlying assumptions about racism and love, domination and integration, nationalism and universalism. It also helps to determine some of the limitations of this technique and some of the reasons why most black writers stopped applying Jamesian conventions to interracial problems. As powerful as this technique is for analyzing racism on a personal level of everyday life, it tends to reduce social and economic problems to psychological ones, institutional to individual racism, political problems to personal dilemmas of loyalty or betrayal. I do not agree with Bryant's "doctrine of fortunate oppression," i.e. his interpretation that Stokes owes his sentimentalized heroic status only to discrimination.[44] In terms of the novel Stokes is one of the four centers of consciousness. Stokes is a rebel to Robinson (126), a victim to Hillary (71), a hustler to Della (215 f.), an animal to Candy (202) etc., and any interpretation which fixates one of the point of views destroys the indirect and multiple presentation of the main image. But it is precisely this indirect presentation which limits the choice of main characters to such who talk, think or feel more than they act and thus to such who belong to a certain group or class. Minister Keel Robinson, son of a bishop, college professor David Hillary, social worker Della Madison and artist Richie Stokes reflect this social bias quite as clearly as the characters in Henry James. There is an even more serious limitation in Jamesian technique. If displace-

44. Jerry H. Bryant, "John A. Williams," 88.

ment of the hero and analysis of racism through opposing point of views seemed helpful in escaping the protest tradition and in presenting a more balanced view of race relations in the United States — even incorporating and thus anticipating the white readers' point of view — the ritual implications of the Jamesian quadrangle undermine any attempt to connect racism with stereotype and prejudice. Obviously, the way from stereotype to archetype and back is as easy as it is treacherous. The myth of sacrificial death and its accompanying archetypes of seasonal change, the Statue of Liberty, the Eagle, the nightworld and its tragic coincidences come uncomfortably close to the stereotypes Hillary holds on blacks. The ritual sacrifice of a bird — whether dove or eagle — absolves society from guilt,[45] and the reader from a fresh insight. Though Williams remains loyal to his depictions of black artists and middle-class intellectuals, after *Sissie* (1963)[46] he abandons or at least modifies the Jamesian technique and returns to a more heroic format. Even the inversions of above and below, of hero and dragon in the mythic structure of *Night Song* leave the structure and its inherent limitations intact.

John A. Williams once complained that white critics tend to compare black writers only with other black writers, thus cementing segregation and double standards in criticism as in life.[47] *Night Song* provides an excellent opportunity not only in technique or discourse but also in subject matter or story for a comparison with other fictional accounts of Charlie Parker who remains the most important influence in modern jazz and one of the greatest musicians the United States have produced.[48] One of the first stories about Charlie Parker, "Sparrow's Last Jump" by Elliott Grennard

45, The guilt feelings of the new black middle class as a theme in Williams's novels are analyzed by Earle A. Cash, *John A. Williams*, pp. 55, 84.

46. *Sissie*, again, is cast in a multiperspective quadrangle though the publsihed version omits the fourth point of view, that of Big Ralph. Cash, p. 89 f. describes the missing chapters. *Sons of Darkness* again makes use of multiple point of view.

47. John O'Brien, ed., *Interview with Black Writers*. New York: Liveright, 1973, pp. 227 f.

48. Robert Reisner, ed., *Bird: The Legend of Charlie Parker*. repr. New York: Da Capo Press, 1977. Max Harrison, *Kings of Jazz: Charlie Parker*, New York: Barnes, 1961. Ross Russell, *Bird Lives!* London: Quartet Books, 1973. Ira Gitler, *Jazz Masters of the Forties*. New York: Collier Books, 1974.

appeared in *Harper's Magazine*, May 1947.[49] In it Harry McNeil, a California record producer, recalls how he coaxed a recording from jazz musician Sparrow Jones before his final breakdown from drugs: "Yeah, Sparrow's last recording would sure make a collector's item. One buck, plus tax, is cheap enough for a record of a guy going nuts." The cynical hip jargon of the narrator vacillating between enthusiasm for good jazz and the profit motive reflects its own theme. Grennard exploits one of the most legendary moments of Charlie Parker's life: his breakdown after recording four titles in the Dial Studios, Los Angeles, July 29, 1946.[50] The producer Ross Russell released the recordings of that date against Parker's wish and the missed bar on the opening of "Loverman" has indeed acquired a sad fame among jazz fans and collectors.[51] The story establishes most of the conventions still used in *Night Song*: the biographical flashback which to the connoisseur reads like a *roman a clef*, the verbal rendering of an exciting jazz performance, the introduction of living jazz musicians as major characters,[52] the theme of exploitive relations between artist and producer, critic or fan, the hip talk, the drug motif.

Though Jack Kerouac never wrote a complete story on Charlie Parker, his work is full of references to Bird, and he is mainly responsible for the cult of Charlie Parker among the members of the Beat Generation. *On the Road* (1957) was supposedly written in a new spontaneous bop prosody, but its prose owed more to the talk and letters of Neal Cassady than to Charlie Parker.[53] But then Parker in Kerouac's view had something of the saintly madness he found in Dean Moriarty, alias Neal Cassady:

> Then had come Charlie Parker, a kid in his mother's woodshed in Kansas City, blowing his taped-up alto among the logs, practicing on rainy days, coming out to watch the old swinging Basie and Benny Moten band that

49. The story was reprinted several times.

50. Ross Russell, *Bird Lives!* pp. 218-227 calls the respective chapter of his biography "Sparrow's Last Jump."

51. On p.423 of his short story Grennard selfironically includes short story writers among the exploiters of jazz musicians. Russell released the records only after Grennard's success with the short story. Robert Reisner, ed., *Bird*, pp. 27, 198.

52. Hughie is a thinly disguised portrait of trumpeter Howard McGhee.

53. Ann Charters, *Kerouac: A Biography*, New York: Warner, 1974, pp. 123-125.

had Hot Lips Page and the rest — Charlie Parker leaving home and coming to Harlem, and meeting mad Thelonius Monk and madder Gillespie — Charlie Parker in his early days when he was flipped and walked around in a circle while playing.[54]

Parker becomes something like a model who in *The Subterraneans* (1958) presides over the narrator's love affair with the black girl Mardou:

Bird, whom I saw distincly digging Mardou several times also myself directly into my eye looking to search if really I was that great writer I thought myself to be as if he knew my faults and ambitions or remembered me from other night clubs and other coasts — not a challenging look but the king and founder of the bop generation at least the sound of it in digging his audience digging the eyes, the secret eyes him — watching, as he just pursed his lips and let great lungs and immortal fingers work, his eyes separate and interested and humane, the kindest jazz musician there could be while being and therefore naturally the greatest ...[55]

One year later Parker had merged completely with Buddha:

Charley Parker Looked like Buddha
Charley Parker, who recently died
Laughing at a juggler on the TV
after weeks of strain and sickness,
was called the Perfect Musician.
And his expression on his face
Was as calm, beautiful, and profound
As the image of the Buddha
Represented in the East, the lidded eyes,
The expression that says "All is Well"
— This was what Charley Parker
Said when he played, All is Well.[56]

Others, like Norman Mailer, John Clellon Holmes or Herbert Gold were quick to codify this hero worship as the hipster ideal of the "White Negro" or as a beat trinity of Charlie Parker, Dylan Thomas and James Dean.[57] Indeed Kerouac's admiration for blacks had

54. Jack Kerouac, *On the Road*. New York: Signet, 1958, p. 197.

55. Jack Kerouac, *The Subterraneans*. London: Panther, 1962, p. 19.

56. Jack Kerouac, *Mexico City Blues*. New York: Grove Press, 1959, p. 241.

57. John Clellon Holmes, "The Philosophy of the Beat Generation," p. 6; Herbert Gold, "The Beat Mystique" in Seymour Krim, ed., *The Beats*, p. 161; also Robert Reisner, ed., *Bird*, p. 26.

something in common with David Hillary's:

> At lilac evening I walked with every muscle aching among the lights of 27th and Welton in the Denver colored section, wishing I were a Negro, feeling that the best the white world had offered was not enough ecstasy for me, not enough life, joy, kicks, darkness, music, not enough night.[58]

Compare Mailer's Reichian version of this primitivism:

> Knowing in the cells of his existence that life was war, nothin but war, the Negro (all exceptions admitted) could rarely afford the sophisticated inhibitions of civilization, and so he kept for his survival the art of the primitive , he lived in the enormous present, he subsisted for his Saturday night kicks, relinquishing the pleasures of the mind for the more obligatory pleasures of the body, and in his music he gave voice to the character and quality of his existence, to his rage and the infinite variations of joy, lust, languor, growl, cramp, pinch, scream and despair of his orgasm.[59]

A less primitivistic attitude can be found in John Clellon Homes' *The Horn* (1958), a composite fictional portrait of Lester Young and Charlie Parker in eight choruses or chapters. The tragedy of Edgar Pool follows the old ritual of the slaying of the king: the ageing musician is beaten and finally replaced by a younger one. The technique is multiperspective and makes ample use of flashbacks and freely blends (disguised) facts and fiction.

The following year Julio Cortázar published "El perseguidor," another fictional portrait of Charlie Parker. The first-person narrator and jazz critic Bruno believes that altoist Johnny Carter is trying to transcend time in his music, is pursuing something rather than being pursued:

> Ahora se que no es asi, que Johnny persigue en vez de ser perseguido, que todo lo que le esta occuriendo en la vida son azares del cazador y no del animal acosado.[60]

But Bruno's white middle-class ideas are in many ways opposed to that of Johnny Carter who represents disorder, emotion, and bohemia. Bruno's failure to amend certain interpretations in his book

---

58. Jack Kerouac, *On the Road*, p. 148.

59. Norman Mailer, "The White Negro: Superficial Reflections on the Hipster," in *Advertisements for Myself*. New York: Berkley, 1959, p. 314.

60. Julio Cortázar, *Las Armas Secretas*. Madrid: Ediciones Cátedra, 1978. p. 179.

on Carter which Carter objects to symbolically coincides with the death of the musician. Bruno play Judas to his J.C., very much like Hillary does in *Night Song*. Bruno's account of Johnny Carter is full of racist stereotypes.[61] Again, the "Loverman" episode is used and material from the Parker legend appears only thinly disguised.

The year *Night Song* appeared, yet another jazz novel based on Charlie Parker's life reached the public. The same Ross Russell who had released the "Loverman" session on records now reworked his knowledge of Charlie Parker into *The Sound* (1961) in which Red Travers took the role of the tragic musician.[62] So when *Night Song* was written a formidable body of writing and a widely spread legend based on Charlie Parker's life existed. There was obviously a market for such writing. Certain conventions in technique and thematic approach were firmly established. *Night Song* is the only black contribution to the Charlie Parker fiction.

Few critics have realized so far, that *Night Song*, as its predecessors, is a *roman à clef*. The jazz fan will hardly need a key to the novel. Not only is Richie Stokes, the Eagle, a portrait of Charlie Parker, Bird, using many episodes of his life and legend, but other characters in the book are also based on well known figures of the jazz scene. Yards Brown is nobody else but Miles Davis, Rod Tolen is an acid portrait of Sid Torin, also called "Symphony Sid," Candy combines traits of Parker's wife Chan Richardson and Nica de Koenigswarter in whose apartment Parker died under much publicized circumstances. Aunt Jessie is Addie Parker, Tippy Dunbar is Tommy Douglas, Lee Jones is Jo Jones, Shooby Robert Simpson, Maddon Jay McShann, Burt Owen Billy Eckstine, Shanahan Gerry Mulligan, Background Oscar Pettiford, Moe Alvin of New Jersey Herman Lubinski of Savoy Records, Yordan Norman Granz etc.[63] Even Parker's music and the bars of the Village are recognizable: "Keke" is "Koko," "Invitation" is "Constellation," "Pow" is

61. The monkey descriptions of Johnny Carter are Bruno's not Cortázar's, but certain passages in *Rayuela* support the reading that Cortázar shares many views with Bruno. In terms of the story it remains open who is the pursuer, Johnny or Bruno.

62. Ross Russell, *The Sound*. New York: Dutton, 1961 was not available in West German libraries.

63. I was not able to identify Stephen Crane. Keel Robinson may owe certain traits to Ahmed Basheer; see Robert Reisner, ed., *Bird*, pp. 37-41.

"Wee." The Bohemia appears under its own name, but the Riviera is probably Louis' etc. The convention of the jazz novel building on an already existing body of legend about a jazz musician becomes the starting point for Williams' special technique of blending fact and fiction in *The Man Who Cried I Am* or *Captain Blackman*.

The indirect presentation of Charlie Parker through a white mono- or multiperspective has a long tradition going back at least to "Sparrow's Last Jump." So has the theme of exploitive relations: Moe Alvin in *Night Song* owes as much to Harry McNeil as the critic Stanley Crane to Cortázar's Bruno.[64] Hip talk, bohemia setting and interracial sex are also standard ingredients in the jazz novel. *Night Song* further depicts Parker in the tragic conventions of a Christ in black face (Cortázar) or ritual scapegoat (Holmes).[65] Williams' original contribution to the tradition lies in his foregrounding of the race question and in casting the "White Negro" or American beatnik in the Judas role. Thus *Night Song* appears as an implicit rejection and analysis of the beatnik's admiration for Charlie Parker and be bop life styles. The primitivism of his admirers is part of the same racism that destroyed Charlie Parker. Williams, however, still believes in the conversion of white liberals and — though far less optimistically than in *One for New York* — takes a cautious integrationist position. Integration cannot happen without white sacrifices. Della Madison has to obey Keel Robinson, and David Hillary fails Richie Stokes by not risking his position for him. This seemed a viable black statement in 1961 though it turned out to be the white students rather than the college professors or the beatniks who stood up to the challenge by joining the Civil Rights Movement.

There is another aspect in which *Night Song* might be considered representative of black fiction at the critical juncture between social-criticism traditions, Civil Rights Movement and Beat Generation. *Night Song* defines successful integration primarily in terms of interracial sex or, more precisely, in terms of the relation between a black man and a white woman. This motif had been firmly established by writers like Chester Himes and played an import-

64. I do not claim Williams read Cortázar.
65. Addison Gayle, Jr., *The Way of the New World: The Black Novel in America*. Garden City, N.Y.: Doubleday, 1976, pp. 185-201.

ant part in the discussion of racism.[66] But the conquest of the white woman was more than a powerful literary motif used by Williams, Baldwin, Jones or Styron to symbolize an attack on white supremacy in the United States. By 1964 seventeen Southern and border states still carried miscegenation laws, not to be struck down until 1967 by a Supreme Court decision. In 1961 the lynching of Emmett Till was still a fresh memory. And the increase of marriages between black men and white women was still a thing of the future.[67] What was safe in Greenwich village — as *Night Song* repeatedly makes clear — was far from being safe in Manhattan, though the state of New York had no miscegenation laws.

Thus the motif of interracial marriage seemed to serve various purposes at the same time: it helped black authors to work out problems of their own interracial marriages, it allowed for an intricate analysis of the psychodynamics of racism, and it challenged ruling literary conventions and marital legislation. To Williams in 1963 it was nothing short of a revolutionary act:

> When the black man, more often than not a visible symbol of the bottom income group, walks the street with the white woman, the whole complex structure of economic, sociological, and psychological barriers is threatened.[68]

Only a few years later under the influence of emerging black nationalism this limited definition of integration was challenged by Stokeley Carmichael:

> "Integration" is another current example of a word which has been defined according to the way white Americans see it. To many of them, it means black men wanting to marry white daughters; it means "race mixing" — implying bed or dance partners. To black people, it has meant a way to improve their lives — economically and politically. But the predom-

66. Calvin Hernton, *Sex and Racism*. London: Paladin, 1970, pp. 24-71 on the myth of sacred white womenhood and its castrating effect on the Negro male.

67. James E. Blackwell, "Social and Legal Dimensions of Interracial Liaisons," in Doris Y. Wilkinson and Ronald Taylor, eds., *The Black Male in America: Perspectives on his Status in Contemporary Society.* Chicago: Nelson Hall, 1977, pp. 219-243. See also Beth Day, *Sexual Life Between Blacks and Whites.* New York: Crowell, 1972, pp. 1-17.

68. John A. Williams, "Sex in Black and White," *Flashbacks*, p. 25.

inant white definition has stuck in the minds of too many people.[69]

The theme of interracial sex, so frequent in black fiction between 1947 and 1970 and in Williams' novels between 1960 and 1967, has become a minor one after 1970 because black writers have increasingly tried to define their own priorities and symbols instead of answering and undermining dominant white techniques or themes.

Night Song seems to reflect where John A. Williams — and with him Baldwin, Smith and other black writers — stood in the early sixties. But it is also an example of the limitations audience and publishers imposed on a black writers without any bargaining power. Social criticism, no longer marketable as "protest," had to be couched in literary conventions of "Anger," "Beat," and the well-made novel of the Henry James type to be acceptable. The contradictions in *Night Song* also reflect the uneasy compromise of a young writer with the exigencies of the publishing market which it may have helped to change a little.

BIOGRAPHY

Born 5 December 1925 in Jackson, Mississippi. Moved to Syracuse, New York, where he went to Central High School, an integrated school. He studied English Literature at Syracuse University (B.A. 1950), served in the United States Navy, 1943-1946. Married twice, he has three children. A professional writer, Williams has also worked for publishers, in an advertising agency, and has taught English at the City University of New York. Williams defines his stand as a writer as follows: "I think art has always been political and has served political ends more graciously than those of the muses. I consider myself to be a political novelist and writer to the extent that I am always aware of the social insufficiencies which are the result of political manipulation." (*Contemporary Novelists*, ed. James Vinson, London: St. James Press, New York: St. Martin's Press, 1972, p. 1495).

69. Stokely Carmichael and Charles Hamilton, *Black Power: The Politics of Liberation in America*. London: Cape, 1967, p. 17.

BIBLIOGRAPHY

NON-FICTION

Africa: Her History, Lands and People Told with Pictures. New York: Cooper Square, 1963.

Flashbacks: A Twenty-Years Diary of Article Writing. Garden City, N.Y.: Doubleday, 1973. (Includes material published in *Authors Guild Bulletin,* February/March 1972; *Cavalier,* September, November 1963; *Holiday,* August, September 1964; January, March, June 1967; *Nickel Review,* 1969; *Swank,* 1961; *Herald Tribune* Sunday Magazine, 25 April 1965; *Nugget,* December 1962; *Amistad 1,* edited by Williams and Harris; *The Immigrant Experience: The Anguish of Becoming an American,* edited by Thomas Wheeler; *Yardbird Reader,* 1.)

The King God Didn't Save: Reflections on the Life and Death of Martin Luther King. New York: Coward, McCaun & Geoghegan, 1970.

Minorities in the City. New York: Harper, 1975.

Romare Bearden. New York: Abrams, 1973.

The Most Native of Sons: A Biography of Richard Wright. Garden City, N.Y.: Doubleday, 1970.

This is My Country Too. New York: New American Library, 1964. (Portions first appeared in *Holiday* Magazine.)

(Anthology): Reed, Ishmail et al., (eds.), *Yardbird Reader,* vol. 1. Berkeley: Yardbird Publishing Cooperative, 1972.

(Periodicals): *Negro Digest,* September 1965; August 1967; November 1969.

NOVELS

The Angry Ones. New York: Ace, 1960.

Captain Blackman: A Novel. Garden City, N.Y.: Doubleday, 1972.

The Man Who Cried I Am. Boston: Little, Brown, 1967.

Mothersill and the Foxes. Garden City, N.Y.: Doubleday, 1975.

Night Song. New York: Farrar Straus & Cudaky, 1961.

Sissie. New York: Farrar, Straus & Cudaky, 1963.

Sons of Darkness, Sons of Light: A Novel of Some Probability. Boston: Little, Brown, 1969.

SHORT STORIES

(Anthologies):

Adoff, Arnold. *Brothers and Sisters: Modern Stories by Black Americans.* New York: Macmillan, 1970.

Baker, Houston A., Jr., (ed.). *Black Literature in America.* New York: Mc-Graw-Hill, 1971.

Emanuel, James A. and Theodore Gross, (eds.). *Dark Symphony: Negro*

Literature in America. New York: Free Press, 1968.

Hills, Penny Chapin and L. Rust Hills. *How We Live: Contemporary Fiction*, vols. 1 and 2. New York: Collier, 1968.

Hughes, Langston, (ed.). *The Best Short Stories by Negro Writers: An Anthology from 1899 to the Present.* Boston and Toronto: Little, Brown, 1967.

Kearns, Francis E., (ed.). *Black Identity.* New York: Holt, Rinehart & Winston, 1970.

King, Woodie, (ed.). *Black Short Story Anthology.* New York: Columbia University Press, 1972.

Margolies, Edward, (ed.). *A Native Sons Reader.* Philadelphia: Lippincott, 1970.

Patterson, Lindsay, (ed.). *An Introduction to Black Literature in America from 1746 to the Present.* New York: Publishers, 1968.

Simmons, Gloria M. and Helene D. Hutchinson, (eds.). *Black Culture: Reading and Writing Black.* New York: Holt, Rinehart & Winston, 1972.

Singh, Raman K. and Peter Fellowes, (eds.). *Black Literature in America: A Casebook.* New York: T.Y. Crowell, 1970.

Williams, John A., (ed.). *Beyond the Angry Black.* New York: Cooper Square, 1966.

POETRY

(Anthology):

Major, Clarence, (ed.). *The New Black Poetry.* New York: International, 1969.

(Periodical):

Partisan Review 35 (Spring 1968).

DRAMA

Reprieve for All God's Children.

EDITOR

With Charles F. Harris. *Amistad 1.* New York: Random House, 1970.
With Charles F. Harris. *Amistad 2.* New York: Random House, 1971.
The Angry Black. New York: Lancer, 1962.
Beyond the Anrgy Black. New York: Lancer, 1962; New York: Cooper Square, 1962.
Yardbird, 1, 2. Berkeley: Yardbird, 1978.

CRITICISM BY WILLIAMS

"Black Writer's Views of Literary Lions and Values." *Negro Digest*, 17

(January 1968), 46.

"The Harlem Renaissance: Its Artists, Its Impact, Its Meaning." *Black World*, 20 (November 1970), 17-18.

"The Literary Ghetto." In Hemenway, Robert, (ed.). *The Black Novelist.* Columbus: Charles E. Merrill, 1970. pp. 227-230.

"The Manipulation of History and Fact: An Ex-Southerner's Apologist Tract for Slavery and the Life of Nat Turner: or, William Styron's Faked Confessions." In Clarke, John Henrik, (ed.). *William Styron's Nat Turner.* Boston: Beacon, 1968, pp. 45-49.

"The Negro in Literature Today." *Ebony*. 8 (September 1963), 73-76.

"Problems of the Negro Writer." *Saturday Review*, 1963; reprinted in Bigsby, C.W.E., (ed.). *The Black American Writer*, vol. 1. Baltimore: Penguin, 1969, pp. 67-69.

PETER BRUCK

ROMANCE AS EPISTEMOLOGICAL DESIGN: WILLIAM MELVIN KELLEY'S *A DIFFERENT DRUMMER* (1962)

> If you know whence you came, there is really no limit to where you can go.
> James Baldwin, *The Fire Next Time.*

> We all came for something — else we woulda stayed where we was.
> W.M. Kelley, *A Drop of Patience.*

> The only obligation which I have a right to assume is to do at any time what I think right.
> Henry David Thoreau, *Civil Disobedience.*

From William Wells Brown's *Clotelle* (1853) to Alex Haley's *Roots* (1976) romance has been a widely used genre among those Afro-American writers of fiction who probe into black history. The continual use of this genre is not surprising, if one recalls its characteristics as delineated by Richard Chase. Such novels, as Chase pointed out, allow for astonishing events which usually have a symbolic or ideological rather than realistic significance, thus contributing to an aura of myth.[1] Translated into the context of Afro-American literary history, romance as genre has always been particularly germane whenever a black novelist employed the pattern of flight and revolt and sought to establish heroic modes of action either through the rejection of the state of slavery as in *Clotelle* or through the renunciation of racial oppression which is the principal concern of Sutton Grigg's political utopia *Imperium In Imperio* (1899). Here, the protagonist Bernard Belgrave, a "coming Moses," calls on the blacks to "emigrate in a body to the State of

1. Richard Chase, *The American Novel and its Tradition.* Garden City: Anchor, 1957, p. 13.

Texas" in order to "work out our destiny as a separate and distinct race."[2] The notion of the disappearance of the blacks has also been effectively dealt with in George Schuyler's *Black No More* (1931). Set in 1934, this romance centers around the fantastic glandular invention of a certain Dr. Crookman who can turn blacks into pure Caucasion whites. Central to the narrative action are the racial exodus of the blacks and the concomitant psychological reactions of the whites.

Both the idea of a mass exodus of the black population as well as its psychological effects upon the whites have been taken up by William Melvin Kelley in *A Different Drummer* (1962).[3] Indeed, Kelley not only forcefully synthesizes major notions of the earlier novels but expands upon them by linking the characteristics of romance with both a mythical frame of reference and such modernist concerns as the scepticism about rational explanations.

A Different Drummer is set in an imaginary southern state which is "bounded on the north by Tennessee; east by Alabama; south by the Gulf of Mexico; west by the Mississippi." (11) This state, as Kelley explains in the first chapter is "unique in being the only state in the union that cannot count even one member of the Negro race among its citizens." (12) The acting time of the novel begins on a Thursday in June 1957 when Tucker Caliban, great-great grandson of a former African chief, destroys his farm and leaves with his family never to return, and ends two days later with the lynching of the northern black militant church leader Bradshaw, who came south to study the cause of the mass departure of the black population which is triggered off by Tucker's act.

Similar to Ralph Ellison's *Invisible Man*, the story follows a circular plan. It begins at the end (late Saturday afternoon) and moves both backward and forward. Significantly, the action is not recorded by a central intelligence but is narrated rather by a group of white characters, all of whom are seeking to understand the reason that led Tucker to his enigmatic exploit. Each narrator, therefore, provides a different perspective for viewing Tucker's deed, depending greatly upon the degree to which his/her life was linked to Tucker's. The ensuing discontinuity of the narrative process,

2. Sutton Griggs, *Imperium In Imperio*. New York: Arno Press, 1969, pp. 109/245.
3. William Melvin Kelley, *A Different Drummer*. Garden City: Anchor, 1969 [All page numbers in brackets refer to this edition].

which clearly derives from romance, is thus marked by mystery and bewilderment and, in keeping with Richard Chase, makes for "uncontrolled experience."[4] Consequently, the reader cannot accept any narrative account as authoritative; rather he must bear in mind that each narrative explanation ultimately reflects the character's search for an epistemological design.

This strategy is introduced in the second chapter "The African." After all blacks have left Sutton, some of the white male population meet at Mr. Harper's place, trying "for the thousandth time in three days to discover how it ever began in the first place."(14) The following authorial comment makes it clear, however, that any attempt to unravel the enigma surrounding this event will be tentative: "They [the men] could not know it all, but what they did know might give them some part of an answer."(14) Authorial intrusion, which is otherwise rarely to be found in the novel, ironically undercuts here the first interpretative attempt about to follow and makes us aware from the very beginning that ambiguity is going to be the principal rhetoric device of the narration. This is made further apparent on the level of exchanges among the characters. The tall-tale about to be narrated by old Mr. Harper, front porch oracle of Sutton, is immediately questioned by the twenty year old Bobby Joe McCollum who considers the story to be "too fantastic, too simplistic" (15) to bear any relevance to the ongoing mass exodus. By having one of the characters initially challenge the validity of Harper's explanation, Kelley prevents the reader identifying with the narrative voice, inducting him, as it were, into a position of epistemological scepticism.

The tale which Harper recounts to his listeners minutely informs us of Tucker Caliban's genealogy, which is inexorably linked to that of the Willson family, a prominent dynasty of plantation owners who bought Tucker's great-great grandfather at a slave auction. Harper's rendition of Tucker's heritage follows the tradition of romance. He reports, for instance, that the African's "head was as large as one of them kettles you see in a cannibal movie" (21) and that in making his escape the African swung his chains, slicing off the auctioneer's head which "sailed like a cannon ball through the air a quarter mile, bounced another quarter mile and still had up enough steam to cripple a horse." (24) What is more, this colos-

4. Chase, op. cit., p. 25.

105

sal African eludes his captors for months and frees numerous slaves, notably those owned by the Willsons. Even though Dewitt Willson, founder of the Willson family line, proves unable to capture the African and can only shoot him, he manages to take the black's infant who is later named Caliban by General Willson, Dewitt Willson's son. Harper's story, then, provides a genealogical explanation, for, as he concludes, "the African's blood is running in Tucker Caliban's veins." (32)

At first glance, textual evidence would seem to support Harper's view. Just like the legendary African, Tucker has "a huge head" (143), and just as it is said of the African's eyes that they made "his head look like a gigantic black skull" (21), mention is repeatedly made of Tucker's eyes: "Behind the glasses there are great, hard brown eyes, with more in them than should be there". (119) The visionary qualities associated with Tucker are emphasized in the following recollection of Camille Willson, wife of the current farm owner David Willson. As she recalls the two year old Tucker:

> I remember once he'd built something even bigger than himself and had only one block left. He placed it on the very top and leaned back against the bars of the pen, looking at what he'd built, long and hard. Then he crawled back to it, balled up his fist and punched at it just once and destroyed it completely. He cut his hand doing it, but he didn't cry at all. You had the idea, the way he did it, that he wasn't playing. (143)

Similarly some years later, when Camille narrates a bedtime fairy tale to Tucker and her son Dewey, it is the black who grasps the analogy of the tale and offers her astute advice. The legendary, quasi mythic nature surrounding Tucker is also apparent on the level of the present action. When young Harold Leland, who together with the other white male figures of the town watches Tucker salting his land, shooting his livestock, shattering his grandfather's clock given to the Calibans as a symbol of faithful service to the Willsons, and finally setting fire to his house, asks the black: "But why'd you do all them evil, crazy things?", Tucker cryptically replies: "You young, ain't you ... and you ain't lost nothing, has you." (55) This answer would seem to indicate that Tucker is trying to recover his lost heritage and acts as a symbolic leader of the masses, liberating them from their state of bondage.

Such a political reading of the novel, which has been popular in recent criticism,[5] tends to disregard the narrative design of *A Different Drummer* and chooses to overlook the fact that six out of the novel's eleven chapters are told from the point of view of the various members of the Willson family. Indeed, as the successive modes of narration employed in these chapters shift from third person to first person narration and end with a first person narration in diary format, we witness an increasing degree of personal dismay on the part of the Willson family whose individual reminiscences reflect their intricate relationship to Tucker as well as their attempt to review their own lives in the light of Tucker's perplexing action. The Willson chapters thus furnish a different epistemological orientation, challenging the mythical interpretation of Mr Harper. This is not to suggest that the reader is being given the role of an arbiter, for the text clearly defies such a reading response. Rather, each chapter reminds us that *A Different Drummer*, whatever one's final interpretative response, foremost reflects Kelley's concern with the multilayered nature of meaning.

*

Kelley's generational history of the Willson family — David, Camille and their children, eighteen year old Dewey III and seventeen year old Dymphna — begins with an incident which occured at Dewey's tenth birthday when he learned to ride his new bicycle with the help of Tucker, then thirteen years old. The recollection of this experience still occupies Dewey's mind in the present, for when the two boys had returned late that evening, Dewey's father had seen to Tucker's being punished. The ensuing feeling of guilt on Dewey's part has pervaded his relationship with Tucker ever since and becomes even more troublesome in the present. Returning home from his first year at a northern college, Dewey carries with him a cryptic letter Tucker sent to him which alludes to the birthday incident without mentioning the punishment, however. As he is unable to understand the letter ("Tucker's message, written in a code he could not remember or had never known, evaded him"

5. See, for instance, Jill Weyant, "The Kelley Saga: Violence in America," *CLA Journal*, 19 (1975), 210-220; Noel Schraufnagel, *From Apology to Protest: The Black Novel in America*. Deland: Everett/Edwards, 1973, p. 174; Addison Gayle, *The Way of the New World: The Black Novel in America*. Garden City: Anchor, 1976, pp. 367-369.

(85)), as, moreover, Tucker is no longer available for comment, Dewey is forced to reexamine his relationship with his former boyhood companion.

This process is accompanied by a shift in the narrative perspective. Unlike the previous chapter which was recorded from the point of view of selective omniscience, the reminiscences following Tucker's departure make use of I-narration. The change in the focus of narration is indicative of the growing concern of Dewey to come to terms with his past as well as suggestive of the increasingly confessional mood that characterizes the Willson sections. Significantly, Dewey's attempt "to find some cause, some reason for Tucker doing what he did" (118) is preceded by a nightmarish dream he used to have as a child. The dream relates how he, his great-grandfather General Willson and a group of Confederate soldiers engage in a Civil War battle with a band of Yankees. The nightmare ends with his realization that he cannot move, for he is "paralyzed from the waist down." (117) The notion of paralysis not only echoes Dewey's guilt feelings but also reflects his incapability of finding a viable explanation for Tucker's action. This is clearly corroborated by the narrative structure and applies to most of the Willson chapters. By continually cutting up the process of explanation, by fragmenting it through the minds of multiple narrators, and by juxtaposing events of the past with Tucker's strange exploit, Kelley sets up each member of the Willson family as a quester searching for a point of orientation that will prove meaningful to them and unravel the inexplicable event.

This search is further dramatized by the reminiscences of Dymphna whose retrospective narration recalls the arrival of the new housemaid Bethrah, her falling in love with and marriage to Tucker, her leaving as well as returning to him. Even though Dymphna can only conclude, "maybe something happened yesterday, but I can't imagine what" (115), her recollections do provide us with a first insight into Tucker's motivations. Note the following utterance of Bethrah who is trying to explain to Dymphna why she and Tucker must leave the Willsons:

> ... maybe those of us who go to school, Dewey, myself, not so much your mother, I guess your father, maybe we lost something Tucker has. It may be we lost faith in ourselves. ... But Tucker, he just knows what he has to do. He doesn't think about it; he just knows. ... I'll be following him and

something inside him, but I think maybe some day I'll be following something inside me that I don't even know about. He'll teach me to listen. ... If you understand what's making me go, maybe it'll help you find something inside yourself that will make you survive whatever your parents decide to do. And helping yourself, your finding some comfort inside yourself, will be much better than any comfort I can ever give you. (114)

The implications inherent in Bethrah's advice escape Dymphna on account of her restricted consciousness. As she confesses: "That's all I know about everything; I guess it isn't much." (114) To the reader, however, Bethrah's advice opens up a new focus of orientation. In particular, the reference to Dymphna's parents is suggestive, for it links the younger generation's search for knowledge to the lives of the elder which, as the subsequent chapters make clear, have been crucially influenced by Tucker.

When Dewey returns home the day after Tucker's departure and is fetched at the railroad station by his parents, he notes to his surprise that his father "looked happier than [he] had ever remembered him, less oppressed." (89) Even more to his surprise, he finds his parents, who were on the verge of a divorce, "holding hands" (86) and he is completely bewildered when his father, with whom he has barely been on speaking terms, says to him: "I've been trying to get things going again. ... Maybe when we, you and I, get to know each other better, I can tell you what it was all about." (90) This sudden change in family relations has clearly been brought about by Tucker's leaving Sutton. Yet, once again narrative disconnectedness withholds further information and Dewey – as well as the reader – are perplexed by a cryptic statement of David Willson, who, when asked by his son if he believed in Tucker's setting fire to his own farm, remarks: "It's quite involved son, and I'd like to go into it when we have more time." (93)

The critical position Tucker has occupied in the lives of the older Willsons is given more emphasis in the chapter narrated by Camille. Here, Tucker's role as spiritual advisor and teacher is expanded in that he now becomes the savior of Camille's disintegrating marriage. Reviewing her courtship, her early happy years of married life to David as well as the infelicitous years spent at Sutton, Camille recalls a scene between her and the nine year old Tucker. One night she tells Dewey and Tucker a bed time story about a princess and a prince which reflects her own marital desperation. Asked by Camille to supply an ending to the story,

Tucker offers the following advice:

'I think the princess should wait. She shouldn't run away...' 'Why?' I wasn't playing. He looked straight at me, like an old friend who knew about David and me and was telling me what to do. 'Because the prince, he'll wake up one of these days and he'll make it all right.' (146/7)

Years later, when Tucker learns that Camille is about to start divorce proceedings, he repeats his advice almost verbatim: "I think the princess should wait, Missus Willson. Leastways, now when her waiting is almost over." (148) Even though Camille is aware that Tucker's counsel did indeed save her marriage, even though she realizes that his departure positively affected her husband's attitude toward her, she is unable to discover the reason for this change. As she acknowledges: "... nothing happened until yesterday. And then I'm not sure anything happened." (148) The redeeming qualities associated with Tucker finally culminate in the section recorded by David Willson. Unlike the previous retrospective reflections of Dewey, Dymphna and Camille, this chapter is presented in the form of diary entries which David began as a young man while attending Harvard. The various entries relate his close friendship with the black student Bennet Bradshaw, his commitment to socialist causes, his being blacklisted as a journalist as well as his moving to Sutton where he collected rents for his father. Chronologically, the entries begin at September 22, 1931 and, for the time being, end at September 1, 1938, the day David started to work for his father. For the following sixteen years, nothing of his life is revealed and it is not until October 20, 1954 that he resumes his entries with a newspaper clipping which reports the activities of his former friend Bradshaw, now a militant church leader. Significantly, his records of the past, which make no mention of Tucker at all, are framed by two entries directly related to the latter. The first, written the day after Tucker's departure, shows David to be spiritually reborn: "Today ... I feel almost as if I have a new start! as if all these years of waste ... have been given back to me to live over again." (149) He then goes on to note: "[Tucker] has freed himself; this had been very important to him. But somehow, he has freed me too. ... Yesterday, his act of renunciation was the first blow against my twenty misspent years, twenty years I have wasted feeling sorry for myself." (151) Tucker's act sharply contrasts with David's lack of courage who, despite a liberal stand in racial politics, could not bring himself to move to the North after he lost his position in journalism. It would hence appear that Tucker serves indeed, as one critic notes, as "a personification of the quest for freedom,"[6] liberating not only the blacks but also the white plantation owner from the genealogical guilt of his forefathers who bought and enslaved the Calibans.

Such a reading gains more weight if one compares the influence Bradshaw and Tucker have exercised on David. Bradshaw, his first black spiritual mentor who introduced him to socialist ideas and was largely responsible for David's anti-segregationist stance, tried in vain to persuade his friend to come to New York and continue to work for civil rights causes. As David noted in his diary: "I am afraid it is no use, Bennet. My rebuttals to you will not be adequate to convince you, or even myself. ... I have to do what I feel is my first responsibility." (173) Since David's misery coincides with the break of their friendship and his moving to Sutton with Camille, we come to realize that the complexity of southern racial relations is not to be solved by political programs but calls rather for the recognition of personal guilt. This aspect is emphasized in the longest of the diary entries which narrates an incident in 1956 when Tucker suddenly demanded to buy those seven acres of land where "the first Caliban worked." (179) By accepting Tucker's claim to the land, by returning an ancient white stone to him which is said to have been part of an altar the African chief had built prior to his being killed by Dewitt Willson, David admits his genealogical guilt. Note the confessional character of the following entry: "... I was doing something I had always wanted to do ..., it was almost like those things I wanted to see done twenty years ago." (179)

As much as this transaction restores the plantation owner to a feeling of self-respect, as much as it implies the recognition of historical guilt, it does not explain why David's spiritual rebirth comes about only *after* Tucker destroyed his farm. Similar to the previous sections narrated by the Willsons, David's diary entries do not provide us with an ultimately satisfying explanation of the event. Hence it is not surprising that the epistemological discon-

6. Gladys M. Williams, "Technique as Evaluation of Subject in *A Different Drummer*," *CLA Journal*, 19 (1975), 233.

tinuity which marks the characters' attempts to discern the final truth behind Tucker's act has greatly intrigued the critics. So far, two critical reactions stand out in particular. Whilst one critic has dismissed the epistemological complexity of the novel as "structural chaos,"[7] others have responded to this problem by largely disregarding the autobiographical narratives of the Willsons, adhering instead to an exclusively political interpretation of the text.[8] Strangely enough, both positions overlook the genealogical implications the text frequently alludes to.

One of the dominant features of Kelley's writings is the use of recurring figures and locales. The novel *A Drop of Patience*, for instance, establishes the origin of Bethrah and the short story "The Only Man on Liberty Street" introduces Josephine, mulatto offspring of General Willson. Similarly, Wallace Bedlow, a minor character in *A Different Drummer*, reappears in the story "Cry for Me." As Kelley has always carefully delineated the genealogy of such families as the Willsons, the Bedlows and the Dunfords, it is indeed astonishing that the genealogy of the Calibans is incomplete, for Tucker is fatherless, as a reconstruction of his family tree in the graph below indicates. Despite the fact that there are several textual references to his grandfather John and to his mother, Mrs. Caliban, mention is never made of his father. The mystery involving Tucker's immediate descent, which has been ignored by all but one critic,[9] lends itself to a tentative explanation, however, if viewed against specific references made by the different Willson narrators. Reconsider, for example, the omniscient advice of the nine year old Tucker to Camille, his regenerating influence on both Camille and David, and note the following dialogue between David and Tucker which concerns the sale of the seven acres:

'I have to know you can meet the payment on it.' 'I ain't making no payments. I got enough right now.' 'How do you know? I haven't told you

7. Gayle, op. cit., p. 370.

8. Notably Schraufnagel who reads the novel exclusively from the point of view of racial politics. See his *From Apology to Protest*, op. cit., p. 174 f., where he places *A Different Drummer* in the category "militant protest."

9. See Donald M. Weyl, "The Vision of Man in the Novels of William Melvin Kelley," *Critique*, 15 (1974), 18, who, however, interprets this as a symbolic rejection of "the Southern paternalistic attitude towards Negroes." Other criticism has simply disregarded the missing link in the genealogy or erroneously taken John Caliban to be Tucker's father.

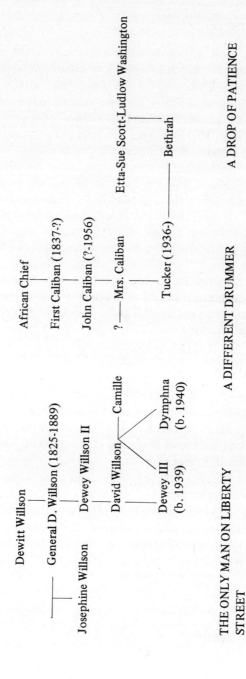

Family Tree of the Willsons and Calibans

Dewitt Willson
Josephine Willson
General D. Willson (1825-1889)
Dewey Willson II
David Willson — Camille
Dewey III (b. 1939)
Dymphna (b. 1940)

African Chief
First Caliban (1837-?)
John Caliban (?-1956)
? — Mrs. Caliban
Tucker (1936-)
Etta-Sue Scott-Ludlow Washington
Bethrah

THE ONLY MAN ON LIBERTY STREET

A DIFFERENT DRUMMER

A DROP OF PATIENCE

113

the price yet.' 'I have enough money to buy twenty acres, and besides, you know *whatever I got to offer is enough.*' We stared at each other for what seemed like a long time. (179)[10]

These as well as many other previously cited passages, which would remain undecipherable, lose their ambivalence only when one assumes Tucker to be the illegitimate son of David Willson. Such an interpretation is, to a necessary degree, conjectural. Yet, if we bear in mind that the Willson pedigree does include a mulatto line, if, moreover, we take into consideration that as early as Charles W. Chesnutt's "The Sheriff's Children" the complex relationship between white father and black son has been a common topos in Afro-American fiction, the conjectural reading in question will gain in plausibility. What separates *A Different Drummer* from this widely used constellation is the redeeming effect Tucker has on the white plantation owner. By thus transcending a traditionally violent encounter Kelley invests the historical connection between southern blacks and whites with a new meaning. From the point of view of southern history, Tucker's voluntary act of renunciation, which releases the southerner from his genealogical guilt, signals an end to the interracial plantation tradition.

*

The story of the Willson family is framed by the narrative accounts of Harry Leland and his son Mr. Leland, whose records of Tucker's act serve as an epistemological alternative, since they were eye witnesses of the event. Moreover, their observations, which include utterances of fellow townsmen, are not marked by the intimate degree of personal dismay that characterizes the narrative voices of the Willson section. Consequently, Kelley does here away with the mode of confessional I-narration and employs, rather, selective omniscience.

Within the overall design of the novel, the consciousness of Harry Leland and his eight year old son Harold contrast markedly with both the racial opinions held by the men on the porch as well as with the pseudo-liberal consciousness of the oral historian Mr. Harper, who can only interpret the ongoing exodus of the

10. My italics.

114

black population in mythical terms. Harry is thus clearly set apart from the other white figures by his humaneness which is free of any racial bias. Accordingly, his view of Tucker's act differs from that of the other witnesses. Asked by his son, "Is Mister Stewart telling the truth, Papa? Tucker gone crazy? Is that what happened?," Harry, though being unable to answer, is shown to be sympathetically understanding, which the following stream of consciousness reveals: "Craziness ain't driving him. I don't know what IS pushing at him, but it ain't craziness." (49) It is precisely this understanding attitude which makes Harry perceive the political idea behind the black's departure. As he tells Harold:

> I reckon they [the blacks] all heading for some place where they think they can get on better. ... I reckon they making what we called in the Army a STRATEGIC WITHDRAWAL. That's when you got thirty men and the other side got thirty thousand and you turn and run saying to yourself, 'Shucks, ain't no use in being brave and getting ourselves killed. We'll back up a ways and maybe fight some tomorrow.' I reckon them Negroes is backing up all the way. (64)

Harry Leland's interpretation of the mass exodus seems to have prompted a number of critics to discuss *A Different Drummer* in terms of the militant protest tradition of the 1960s. Thus critic Donald Weyl considers Tucker "a Moses figure who leads his people out of captivity"[11] and, according to Addison Gayle, Tucker Caliban "is the true revolutionary who ... has said 'enough' to oppression and vaulted outside of history."[12] These positions demand qualification, particularly since a polysemous text like *A Different Drummer* defies a one-sided approach. Moreover, such a selective reading negates both Kelley's political philosophy as well as the contrapuntal arrangement of the two major black figures in the novel. Characteristically, the northern Bennet Bradshaw, founder of the "Resurrected Church of the Black Jesus Christ of America, Inc.", which has "declared war on the white man! To the white world and all it stands for" (174), is depicted as an impotent militant organization man whose outlook is essentially intellectual. Tucker, by contrast, stands for the anti-intellectual, who opposes any form of political organization, even the moderate NAACP: "Ain't none of my battles being fought in

11. Weyl, op. cit., p. 21.
12. Gayle, op. cit., p. 369.

115

no courts. I'm fighting all my battles myself." (111) Tucker's individual stance clearly reflects Kelley's own view. As he once stated: "Each lone Negro must find something in himself that he feels is worthy of respect and decent treatment, and that ... can only be his unique quality as one lone human being."[13] Passages in *A Different Drummer* demonstrate this concern with regard to its political message. When Tucker and his mother are informed of old John Caliban's death and go into New Marsails to claim his body, they find him sitting in the colored section of a bus, the *Colored* sign hanging directly in front of him. Only two months later, Tucker buys those seven acres of land which he will later salt and destroy. If we relate the bus reference and Tucker's act to Mrs. Rosa Park's refusal to occupy a seat in the colored section of the bus, an incident which is generally said to have triggered off the Black Liberation movement, we may assume that Tucker's exploit echoes Kelley's belief that racial liberation is not arrived at by a liberal or even militant inspired movement but has to originate in a spontaneous act of the individual who is seeking to establish his own worth as a human being. This attitude becomes even more obvious when we take into consideration the novel's title which derives from Thoreau's *Walden*. Indeed, as *A Different Drummer* abounds with Thoreauvian notions, Tucker's act reads like a fictionalized black version of *Civil Disobedience*, which forcefully argued for a non-institutionalized, passive resistance, hence pleading for a change of individual lives rather than an organized change of society. The adaptation of Thoreau's defiant individualism is made further apparent if one juxtaposes the following phrase uttered by Tucker with a passage from the conclusion of *Walden*:

You only gets one change. That's when you can and when you feel like it. (182)
If one advances confidently in the direction of his dreams, and endeavors to live the life which he has imagined, he will meet with a success unexpected in common hours. He will put some things behind, will pass an invisible boundary; new, universal, and more liberal laws will begin to establish themselves around and within him.[14]

13. Statement by Kelley as quoted in "Talent's New Wave," *Negro Digest*, 11 (October 1962), 45.
14. Henry David Thoreau, *Walden*, in Owen Thomas, ed., *Henry David*

If viewed in this light, Tucker is not, as one critic has recently remarked, "a black Bartleby";[15] rather, he turns out to be the very epitome of the solitary Thoreauvian man who believes in individual action against society, who, in keeping with Thoreau's famous essay "Walking", instinctively follows his own "moral needle".

Earlier we saw that the use of old Mr. Harper as oral interpreter furnished the tall tale of the African with a mythic dimension. In the same manner, the rapt attention of the white observers during the black exodus as well as the following reason given by one of the blacks for leaving the South underscore the spectacular nature of the event:

> ... it seems like all the black folks up in Sutton got it into their heads they just won't stand for it no more. ... At least that's what Hilton told me this colored man up Sutton way said. He, Hilton that is, he says that there was this colored man up in Sutton who told the Negroes all about it, all about history and all that stuff, and that he said besides that the only way for things to be better was for all the colored folks to move out, to turn their backs on everything we knowed and started new. (131)

What emerges here is the legendary universe of romance with its inherent form of the oral tradition. From the point of view of genre, Tucker, whose very name refers to the first Afro-American born in the English North American colonies,[16] appears as the familiar romance hero who, to rephrase an earlier quote, "is building something even bigger than himself", i.e. leading the black population to a new destiny.

Significantly, the exodus of the black population has not only totally bewildered the white townspeople but also causes a complete disorientation of their racially determined frame of reference. Note the comment of Kelley as omniscient narrator: "None was able to think it through. It was like attempting to picture Nothing, something no one had ever considered. None of them had a reference point on which to fix the concept of a Negro-less world."

Thoreau: Walden and Civil Disobedience. New York: Norton Critical Edition, 1966, p. 214.

15. C.W.E. Bigsby, *The Second Black Renaissance: Essays in Black Literature.* Westport, Conn.: Greenwood Press, 1980, p. 171.

16. See Peter M. Bergman and Mort N. Bergman, *The Chronological History of the Negro in America.* New York: Mentor, 1969, p. 11.

(184) Desperate to have their orientation restored, the men on Mr. Harper's porch cling to Bobby Joe's interpretation of the event:

> ... you-all heard me when I said I didn't believe that blood business Mister Harper was trying to feed us. ... How the hell can something what happened a hundred fifty years ago — if it happened at all — how can that have something to do with what happened this week? That ain't nothing but tripe. No sir, it was that northern nigger, that ... agitator [who] ... got all the niggers to move off, go somewhere else instead of staying here where they belongs. (188)

The result of this explanation is devastating. Fatefully, Reverend Bradshaw, who is, at this moment, driving to the town square, is hauled from his car, humiliated, beaten and finally killed by some of the white men. Translated into the epistemological design of the novel, Bradshaw's lynching demonstrates the incapability of the white man to understand, let alone to accept the beginning change in race relations. Bradshaw, then, not only becomes "an agency for the working out of the meaning of Black-White relationships for a strata of the white community to whom Tucker Caliban's act of self-affirmation is meaningless,"[17] his accidental death also signals his mythic role as *pharmakos* who, in keeping with Northrop Frye, "has to be killed to strengthen the others."[18] Bradshaw's sacrificial death clearly recalls Frye's notion of tragic irony[19] in that it emphasizes the militant church leader's isolation from Afro-American society. If viewed against the grassroot movement triggered off by Tucker, the killing of Bradshaw illustrates perhaps best the ironic posture with which Kelley regards organized nationalistic black militancy.

The scene of violence is juxtaposed with a visionary dream of young Harold Leland. Misinterpreting the lynching mob's noises for "a party" (199) honoring Tucker's return, Harold envisions his reunion with Tucker who will joyously share with him the knowledge that he has found what he had lost. The optimistic notion with which the novel closes serves as a final pointer towards the redeeming qualities that Kelley associates with a

17. Williams, op. cit., p. 253.
18. Northrop Frye, *Anatomy of Criticism*. Princeton: Princeton University Press, 1971, p. 148.
19. *Ibid.*, p. 40f.

spontaneous, non-violent folk revolution. Consider the communal imagery of the last lines: "He [Tucker] would bring out large bowls of the leftover candy and popcorn and cracker-jack and chocolate drops. And they would eat until they were full. And all the while, they would be laughing." (200) The vision of this ceremony evokes here a sense of racial brotherhood. Given such a clue, it is not surprising that early critical commentary has considered Tucker to be Jesus-figure.[20] However, such interpretative analogy can only be substantiated, if one views *A Different Drummer* against the short story "Cry for Me".

As I have pointed out before, Kelley's fiction is characterized by the use of recurring figures which reappear in different geographical contexts. The very intertextuality of his oeuvre would seem to suggest that Kelley is working toward a fictional representation of the totality of black life in America. Within the cosmos of his writings, individual characters and situations thus depict only facets of the sum of the black's experience. The figure of Wallace Bedlow, the only character out of *A Different Drummer* to reappear in a later work, is here the case in point. "Cry for Me" is thus a sequel to *A Different Drummer*, providing, as it were, an alternative conclusion to the novel.

The story is set in New York in June 1957 and tells of the arrival of Wallace and other blacks at Pennsylvania Station where, as the narrator Carlyle Bedlow observes, "a whole bunch of colored people got off the train, all looking like somebody been keeping it a secret from them they had been free for a hundred years."[21] Immediately, Carlyle notices that his uncle has "the size of a black Grant's Tomb" (181). The reference to Wallace's size is highly allusive as it recalls Harper's description of the African chief and, at the same time, contrasts with those passages in the novel which make mention of Wallace. If we bear in mind that the novel's narrators never refer to his size, if, moreover, we realize that Wallace was the only person among the spectators

20. See Robert Nadeau, "Black Jesus: A Study of Kelley's *A Different Drummer*," *Studies in Black Literature*, 2 (1971), 13-15, and Howard Faulkner, "The Uses of Tradition: William Melvin Kelley's *A Different Drummer*," *Modern Fiction Studies*, 21 (1975), 535-542.

21. William Melvin Kelley, "Cry for Me", *Dancers on the Shore*. Chatham: The Chatham Bookseller, 1973. [All page numbers in brackets refer to this reprint edition].

watching Tucker's act to offer "help, whatever the hell you doing" (49), we may well consider him to be Tucker's disciple. From this point of view it would appear that Wallace has now symbolically grown into the position of a mythical figure who is about to continue the path outlined by Tucker's exemplary action.

In contradistinction to the familiar notion of Afro-American migration literature, "Cry for Me" does not depict the North as the "Promised Land" nor is it concerned with the shattered hopes of such a dream. Rather, the story centers around the redeeming qualities of Wallace Bedlow, the singer, who gives a performance in front of a black and white audience. Note the communal effect his singing has on the spectators, which echoes the vision of Harold Leland:

> Then the air changed. ... The people was rushing toward him. They was all crying and smiling too like people busting into a trance in church and it seemed like everybody in the place was on stage trying to get near enough to touch him, grab his hand and shake it and hug him and kiss him even. And then the singing stopped. ... Uncle Wallace was sitting in his chair, slumped over, his face in his lap ... he was dead all right. (199-200)

Within Kelley's fictional universe, "Cry for Me" is the only narrative to render a momentary scene of interracial consubstantiality. In this sense, the story expands upon the racial togetherness evoked by Tucker's ritual act in that it suggests a common bond of humanity. Yet, as this experience is interrupted by the sudden death of Wallace, the vision of an interracial brotherhood is revealed as utopian. This leads us back to Harold Leland's visionary dream which, if viewed against "Cry for Me", now stands corrected. By replacing Tucker's heroic deed with Wallace's sacrificial ritual Kelley makes us aware that Harold's dream is also utopian and will remain so as long as the white men on the porch as well as the Willsons are unable to transcend their racially determined views and discover themselves anew.

Significantly, Kelley was not to return to the idea of the black as sacrificial redeemer nor was he to turn to militant black nationalism. Unlike such novels as Ronald Fair's *Many Thousand Gone* (1965) and Sam Greelee's *The Spook Who Sat By The Door* (1969), which depict organized resistance to white oppression, *A Different Drummer* as well as his later novels *A Drop of Patience* (1965) and *Dunfords Travels Everywheres* (1970) demonstrate that

Kelley eschews black nationalist ideology. *A Different Drummer*, by contrast, explores, as we have seen, the intricate knotting of the white man's genealogy with that of the black. That recognition, as Alex Haley noted with regard to *Roots* in an interview in 1976, "reflects the real potential of harmonious relationships between blacks and whites in America."[22] Haley's philosophy clearly applies to *A Different Drummer*. To charge the novel with the "failure to take into consideration many of the practical aspects of the mass exodus"[23] is thus to misread a romance as a realistic novel, is to call for an instrumental role of literature. *A Different Drummer* not only eludes such a reading, it ultimately bears testimony to Kelley's belief that "a writer should ask questions" rather than present "solutions and answers to the Negro Problem."[24] What may amount to a negative statement to black nationalists, finally stands out as epistemological and, by implication, political scepticism with regard to organized and institutionalized actions. The result is not pessimism; rather it forces us to reconsider Kelley's concern with the destruction of illusions. This the reader is invited to share with the novelist.

BIOGRAPHY

William Melvin Kelley was born in New York City in 1937 and attended Harvard College where he studied under Archibald MacLeish and John Hawkes. He has taught at the New School, N.Y., and was author-in-residence at the State University of New York at Geneseo. He has received several literary awards from the Rosenthal Foundation, the National Institute of Arts and Letters, and the John Hay Whitney Award.

22. "A Talk with Alex Haley," *New York Times Book Review*, September 1976, 10.
23. Schraufnagel, op. cit., p. 176.
24. William Melvin Kelley, "Motto", *Dancers on the Shore*, op. cit.

BIBLIOGRAPHY

NOVELS

A Different Drummer. Garden City: Doubleday, 1962.
A Drop of Patience. Garden City: Doubleday, 1965; Chatham, N.J.: Chatham Booksellers, 1973.
dem. Garden City: Doubleday, 1967.
Dunfords Travels Everywheres. Garden City: Doubleday, 1969.

SHORT FICTION

Dancers on the Shore. Garden City: Doubleday, 1964; Chatham, N.J.: Chatham Booksellers, 1973.

SECONDARY SOURCES

The best bibliography to date is to be found in Carol Fairbanks/Eugene A. Engeldinger, *Black American Fiction: A Bibliography.* Metuchen, N.J.: The Scarecrow Press, 1978, pp. 182-185.

KLAUS P. HANSEN

WILLIAM DEMBY'S *THE CATACOMBS* (1965): A LATECOMER TO MODERNISM

Judged by the unanimity of criticism so far, William Demby's novels *Beetlecreek* (1950) and *The Catacombs* (1965) seem to offer no problems of understanding or classification. Conforming to the labels of black fiction put forward by Schraufnagel,[1] they are said to belong to the "accomodationist novel" of the post-Wright era, in so far as they approach the situation of the Afro-American in terms of what is regarded as the universal *condition humaine*. In the first novel, so critics maintain, a kind of "Christian existentialism"[2] defines that condition more or less pessimistically, whereas in the second a more hopeful outlook drawing mainly on the evolutionist theology of the French philosopher Pierre Teilhard de Chardin prevails.

As for the evaluation of Demby's novels as works of art, we find, however, a fundamental disagreement between the professional critics and the reading public in general. *Bettlecreek* occasioned praise from its reviewers, who spoke of the author as a promising young talent, and this first impression was later confirmed by extensive interpretations. Thus Herbert Hill writes in his anthology *Soon, One Morning*, "*Bettlecreek* is a highly imaginative work, rich with symbolic meaning and suggestion and concerned with questions of good and evil that go beyond race."[3] This verdict, Hill has to concede, clashes with the reaction of the larger public which took no notice of Demby's novel, so that it

1. Noel Schraufnagel, *From Apology to Protest: The Black American Novel.* Deland, Fl.: Everett/Edwards 1973.

2. Edward Margolies, *Native Sons: A Critical Study of the 20th Century Negro American Authors.* Philadelphia: Lippincott 1969.

3. Herbert Hill, ed., *Soon, One Morning: New Writing by American Negroes.* New York: Knopf 1963.

"soon passed out of print and into oblivion."[4] In the case of the second novel, the gap between the experts' appreciation and general neglect widens even more. *The Catacombs* met with no favorable reviews, and, as Robert Bone puts it metaphorically, "orbited briefly, encountered a thin cultural atmosphere, and parachuted soundlessly into a deserted sea."[5] According to the few critics who have analysed the novel thoroughly, its failure is entirely unmerited. Bone claims even that the novel succeeds in "expanding contemporary consciousness."[6] For him this verdict also accounts for the lack of popularity in so far as its unconventionality may well have put off the average reader.[7]

Hill's and Bone's enthusiasm about Demby's craft[8] would be more convincing if they showed fewer reservations in ranking him among those writers whom the critical establishment has canonized as the most important figures of black literature. Their high esteem would lead us to expect them to include Demby, together with Wright, Ellison and Baldwin, in this number. Perhaps their hesitancy provides sufficient reason for a re-consideration of Demby's achievement, particularly in his alleged masterpiece *The Catacombs*, and for a re-assessment of his place within Anglo-American literary history.

I

Before turning to the more important second novel, I would

4. Herbert Hill, "Afterword", in William Demby, *Beetlecreek*. New York: Avon Books 1969, 184.

5. Robert Bone "Introduction", in William Demby, *The Catacombs*. New York: Perennial Lib. 1970, vii.

6. Bone, "Introduction", vii.

7. As regards the general neglect of Demby, the survey of American authors offered by Jeffrey Helterman and Richard Layman, eds., *American Novelists Since World War II*. Detroit: Gale Research Company 1978 — is a case in point. Although a large number of better known white authors are mentioned, Demby's name is not to be found.

8. Hill writes in favor of *Beetlecreek*: "In its concern with questions relating to alienation, identity, and in the use of 'Negro' as a metaphor for all whose lives are denied dignity and meaning in modern society, Demby's book anticipates themes which were to significantly appear in the works of other writers after the publication of *Beetlecreek*." — "Afterword", 184.

like to correct a common misconception in critical commentary on *Beetlecreek*. The novel revolves around a fourteen-year-old boy who leaves his home town, Pittsburgh, to stay with his aunt and uncle in Beetlecreek, West Virginia. The characters who have the closest contact with Johnny are his uncle, David Diggs, a frustrated artist who seeks relief from the stifling provincial atmosphere by drinking and having an affair with Edith, his former sweetheart; his aunt Mary, who compensates for a loveless marriage by her activities in the Women's Missionary Guild; Bill Trapp, an old white recluse living at the edge of the black section of the community; and a gang of black youths, the "Nightriders", that Johnny eventually joins. It is the figure of Bill Trapp that arouses the pettiness of the residents of the town. By befriending Johnny and his uncle, he makes himself suspect, and by inviting a number of children of both races to his house he turns the village against him. Even his black friends desert him, and Johnny, although he does not believe the rumors about Bill's immorality, succumbs to the influence of the Nightriders and sets fire to the recluse's house as a part of the initiation rites that are necessary for acceptance by the gang.

Every reader of the novel would agree with Roger Whitlow's statement that *Beetlecreek* "probes a society gone dead."[9] Unexpectedly, however, it is not the racial conflict that accounts for the deadness, but the more general condition of provincialism which affects black and white alike. The special situation of the Afro-American is approached, as it were, by one of the many modification of environmental theory. In spite of Demby's own denial,[10] *Beetlecreek* must be regarded as a novel tending toward naturalism. Without being consciously indebted to Zola, Demby recalls the scheme of the *roman experimental* in so far as he uses environment as a basis for the structure of the novel. Milieu, in this case the repressions and inhibitions due to the provincial atmosphere of Beetlecreek, functions as a fundamental modality by setting up a frame of existence for every character. Consequently, the story concentrates on the different reactions to this

9. Roger Whitlow, *Black American Literature: A Critical History*. Chicago: Chicago Univ. Press 1976, 122.

10. Cf. John O'Brien, *Interviews with Black Writers*. New York: Liveright, 1973, 35 and 43.

modality, and by comparing and contrasting them offers a typology of possible human attitudes. Above all, this typology distinguishes the category of the insider who is fully absorbed by the environment from that of the outsider who more or less openly resists integration or, at least, cannot tolerate the limitations of convention. To the first category belong the members of the two centers of Beetlecreek's social life, the barbershop cronies with their formalized talk and the Women's Missionary Guild of the local church. Set apart from these centers and their subcommunities of clearly marked average people are two subdivisions of outsiders, the hard core who defy society openly, and the long suffering soft core who cannot adjust their emotional needs to meet the triviality of their surroundings.

Instead of accepting a conventional role and outlook, the hard core Nightriders contemptuously challenge society as is shown by their killing of a pigeon, the token of peace. This challenge, however, fails because it relapses into atavism, and therefore cannot offer a viable alternative. Similarly, Edith, another hard core outsider, has fallen victim to "good-timing", the easy distractions of big city life that includes sex and drinking, and has stifled the desire for seemingly unattainable freedom. Although the soft core outsiders, David, Johnny, and Bill Trapp, are in the same camp with their hard core counterparts — David elopes with Edith, Johnny joins the gang — they differ widely in their mental attitude. While Edith and the Nightriders reached a state of general callousness, the soft core group cannot give up their hope for a better existence. Their restlessness serves as an indicator of their humanity, and thus the novel drives home the point that a restricted cultural background — including the situation of the black — is liable to thwart any achievement adequate to the dignity of man.

This recapitulation of the novel's structure and theme will elucidate, I hope, its affinity with, in Carl van Doren's terminology, "the revolt from the village",[11] or with, what I will call, post-naturalistic American fiction. Naturalistic writers such as Zola, Hauptmann, Norris, Dreiser posited a deterministic universe and exposed man to the inevitable impact of environment. In their

11. Title of a series of articles by van Doren which were published in *Nation* in 1921.

positivistic concept the individual is deprived of freedom as well as of will-power, and, moreover, is unconscious of his lack of independence. This state of missing consciousness, to single out the decisive aspect, is overcome during the successive literary development, and replaced by a sensitive life of the mind in the fictional characters. Works like James Joyce's *Dubliners*, Edgar Lee Masters' *Spoon River Anthology*, and Sherwood Anderson's *Winesburg, Ohio* continue to stress the influence of milieu, although they shift the focus from the urban working class to provincialism, and introduce a cast of characters who consciously confront the choking grip of their surroundings.

As soon as these characters become aware of the inhibitions of conventional life, they strive to free themselves by running away or protesting openly, but the inflexibility of the majority proves to be more powerful than the individual's attempt to liberate himself. This futile protest against provincialism forms the theme of *Beetlecreek*. The more sensitive figures in the novel feel the danger they are in, as Johnny does for example, when he recognizes his position in the following description:

> "Often he would sit on the railing of the swinging bridge, looking down at the creek, watching the current. He would watch floating things – boxes, tin cans, bottles. He would watch how some of these things became trapped in the reeds alongside the shore. First there was a whirlpool to entice the floating object, then a slow-flowing pool, and finally, the deadly mud backwater in the reeds. In the reeds would be other objects already trapped.
> This was Beetlecreek, he thought. And he knew that, like the rusty cans, he was trapped, caught, unable to move again."[12]

Undoubtedly, this passage resembles Sherwood Anderson, whose figures experience their environment similarly and, like Johnny, try unsuccessfully to break away from it.

Apart from Hill who regards Beetlecreek as naturalistic – a classification which though nearer the truth is not delimiting enough – most critics persistently ascribe to it an existentialist approach.[13] While it is correct that the atmosphere of the depicted

---

12. *Beetlecreek*, 78.
13. Cf. Robert A. Bone, "William Demby's Dance of Life", *Tri-Quarterly* 15 (Spring 1969), 128: "The point of view is existentialist ..." (This article is identical with the above mentioned "Introduction"); Schraufnagel (p. 76)

town creates a "no exit" existential condition for the characters, such a fictional world contains little evidence of an indebtedness to the philosophy of existentialism. Whatever its various meanings — one critic speaks of "christian existentialism",[14] another of an "existentialist definition of evil"[15] — to apply the term to *Beetlecreek* is grounded either in a misreading of the novel or in an incorrect handling of the term which loses its relevance as a critical tool when it refers indiscriminately to a pessimistic outlook in general. Any comparison between Demby and the writers usually associated with existentialism, for instance Camus and Sartre, or as an early example in America, Hemingway, would surely conclude that the differences by far outweigh the elements shared. In fiction commonly labelled existentialist, to single out just one typical aspect, the apparent strangeness of the modern world is brought home to the reader by the application of two strategies. Either the protagonist encounters an unknown and mysterious world such as in *L'etranger*,[16] or he experiences a bewildering alienation from his usual surroundings which he no longer understands. Hemingway was among the first to introduce the latter strategy into American writing, and he did so by lacing his otherwise economic narrative with bits of apparently irrelevant information. For example, he describes non-functional scenery, names passers-by who never recur, relates what his protagonists eat and drink, mentions the tip given to the waiter, and so on. These meticulously rendered details seem to have little narrative function, at least for the understanding of the plot, but, taken as a whole, they convey a sense of the characters' dissociation from a world consisting of random bits of unrelated matter.[17] In contrast to such a realism of the redundant, Demby offers a closely knit referential structure where everything mentioned plays a part in the fictional whole. Thus, for instance, the "urine puddle" before

quotes Bone's statement approvingly; C.W.E. Bigsby, "From Protest to Paradox: The Black Writer at Mid Century", in Warren French, ed., *The Fifties: Fiction Poetry, Drama*. Deland, Fl.: Everett/ Edwards 1970, speaks of "implicit existentialism" (p. 234); cf. also note 14 and 15.

14. Margolies, 174.

15. Robert A Bone, *The Negro Novel in America*. New Haven: Yale University Press 1965, 89.

16. Otto Friedrich Bollnow, *Französischer Existentialismus*, Stuttgart: Kohlhammer 1965.

which Bill Trapp likes to stand, reflects his station as an outsider; the dirty river from which Beetlecreek takes its name signifies the snares of provincialism; and the struggle of the beetle lying on its back mirrors Johnny's vain efforts to free himself. Unlike the existentialist conception of a strange and enigmatic universe, the world of *Beetlecreek* has definite values although they are seen to be destructive. In this respect Demby's writing is more traditional, and to place him in the existentialist camp makes him appear more modern than he actually is.

II

Demby's ambitious second novel, *The Catacombs*, takes place in Rome against a background of newspaper reports telling of racial violence in the United States. The narrator, the black writer William Demby, recounts his life in Rome and inserts passages from a novel he is writing dealing with the black actress Doris and an Italian Count. As the writer appears in his novel himself and has an affair with Doris, the reader cannot distinguish fiction from reality. As a result of the two affairs, Doris becomes pregnant, presumably by the Italian. The baby is born dead and shortly afterwards the disenchanted Count informs his mistress that he is leaving the country. Doris somehow becomes lost in the Catacombs, and the narrator, given impetus by her disappearance, returns to the United States.

Fortunately, *The Catacombs* has been the subject of two excellent interpretations which trace the novel's manifold allusions and correspondence, so that it is unnecessary to do it here. Robert Bone and Nancy Y. Hoffman[18] have analysed the structure of *The Catacombs* which despite the novel's chaotic impression turns out to be quite straightforward. Adhering to the doctrine of the *new*

17. Cf. Helmut Papajewski, "Die Frage nach der Sinnhaftigkeit bei Hemingway", *Anglia* 70 (1951), 186-209; and John Killinger, *Hemingway and the Dead Gods: A study in Existentialism.* Lexington: U. of Kentucky Press 1960.

18. Bone, "Introduction"; Nancy Y. Hoffmann, "Technique in Demby's *The Catacombs*", *Studies in Black Literature* 2 (Summer 1971), 10-13; and "The Annunciation of William Demby", *Studies in Black Literature* 3 (Spring 1972), 8-13.

criticism, neither interpretation looks beyond the work, and although influences upon Demby are mentioned, as well as his affinities with other writers, the novel is not viewed in relation to literary history nor to its historic and cultural background. Moreover, though admirably demonstrating Demby's intentions, the two critics never question whether his experiment comes off well or whether he translates his purpose into an effective aesthetic whole. Perhaps Bone's and Hoffman's stopping short of explicit evaluation invites a further examination of Demby's craft.

Rather than praising *The Catacombs* as an "innovation", as Bone does,[19] it would be more useful to recognize its place in a well-established tradition of experimentation with the novel form. In fact, critics have noticed this, but in assessing it they have been liable either to misjudge its special place within the development of the tradition, or, when they have judged it correctly, they have failed to consider the resulting consequences. The first error has been committed by those who have regarded *The Catacombs* as a piece of post-modernist writing. Certainly, there are affinities with Dos Passos and James Joyce, but not with Barthelme or Nabokov. Those critics, however, who recognized the modernist quality of the novel, did not question what modernist narrative technique meant when taken up in 1965 by a black writer. To settle these problems, to reassess the novel's place in this tradition, and to consider the critical consequences, we need to look for a moment at the novel's structure.

One's first impression is that of a literary collage which blends heterogenous elements in a manner reminiscent of Dos Passos cinematographic technique in *Manhattan Transfer* (1925). The novel, so a further analysis will reveal, is a compound of three different narrative segments. The first of them, a kind of *künstler-roman,*[20] treats of the fictional black artist William Demby. The second unit is a novel written by this artist dealing with the black dancer Doris and an Italian count. The third segment comprises fragments of daily news, introduced in the form of headlines and passages from newspapers − recognizable by the use of capital letters and quotation marks − which are interspersed throughout the novel in seemingly haphazard order.

19. "Introduction", vii.
20. "Techniques in Demby's *The Catacombs*", 10.

Devoid of any traditional plot device, the *künstlerroman* segment is crammed with the daily experiences of the writer Demby, with his thoughts, associations, joys, and irritations. The reader is confronted by a mass of unspectacular and initially insignificant information. In contrast, the Doris-Count story certainly assumes the contours of a plot, but in the end does not meet the expectations associated with conventional narrative. First, it is unmasked as a product of an artist's imagination, and thus the illusion of realism is destroyed. Second, it is conceived as a novel in progress, i.e., it is being discussed, changed, and rewritten so that it fails to satisfy our yearnings for a definite narrative order. The third segment of the novel, introducing international politics, seems to be disconnected with the two other parts. It initially fails to constitute a macrocosm which encompasses the microcosm of the protagonist's life, as well as the microcosm of the Doris-Count story. Thus by combining three loosely connected units and by piling up a quantity of apparently incoherent narrative data, the novel imitates the way in which the mind of the individual receives impressions from the outside world. Hence Barbara Foley is right when she sees the novel employing a kind of "documentary mode."[21] In attempting to duplicate the process whereby the human intellect must organize the random bombardment of sense perception, Demby offers us a kind of realism devoid of all conventional indications of order.

Within the novel's scheme, the exposure of the reader to seemingly arbitrary detail represents only the surface narrative. Beneath it a deep structure exists which is marked by the occurrence of frequent repetitions. For instance, after introducing the "Algerian Diary", a report of the ongoing war between France and Algeria, the narrator quotes from Walt Whitman's "Civil War Diary"; when Doris thinks she is pregnant, the wife of the fictitious Demby believes the same; Laura's suicide occasions remarks on other selfdestructions, all paying homage to the fate of Marilyn Monroe which, linked with the sacrifice of Christ, gains the dimensions of an archetype. These repetitions and juxtapositions constitute the novel's deep structure in which Demby tries to demonstrate "simultaneity".[22] Events separated either in time or in space are brought into jarring proximity in order to hint at their

21. Barbara Foley, "The Uses of the Documentary Mode in Black Literature", *PMLA* 95, 3 (May 1980), 399.

— otherwise unproved — similarity, if not identity. Doing away with historic distance which implies the denial of historic differences the narrator sets the American civil war and the Algerian struggle for independence side by side, thus suggesting a correspondence never made explicit. Similarly distances in space are bridged by calling attention to things which, although far away from each other, happen at the same moment. Thus the real Demby interrupts the lovemaking between Doris and his fictional self with a headline announcing the joining in flight of two Russian space ships. Both events, the copulation of the lovers and the coupling of the space ships, so their juxtaposition suggests, mean the same in so far as they point forward to a force, or a tendency to become united. When Demby said to his interviewer, "The novelist must have this function of seeing connections."[23] we surely have an application of this function in *The Catacombs*.

By making use of simultaneous narration, which clearly adds to the chaotic complexity of the surface structure, *The Catacombs* tries to establish an equation between heterogenous facts, to stress their affinity, and to charge them with universal significance. The novel's structural device, therefore, must be twofold. Beneath a chaotic surface which reproduces the world as it is perceived by the senses, there exists a deep structure of ontological truth. Here the complexity of the phenomena is reduced to three sets of opposites: love and hate, war and peace, birth and death. Obviously the three pairs belong together, forming the existential unity of creation and destruction. This polarizing outlook brings all events, public as well as private, down to the same level, and, by flattening out differences and ignoring change,[24] sees life as an everlasting repetition of the same principle. The irrevocability of it makes legitimate everything that happens, and the result is a complete uncritical view which acknowledges, even welcomes, every item of existence because it exists.

Not sure who has caused her pregnancy, Doris exclaims: "What a mess."[25] This mess, so Demby seems to say, is no reason for

22. "Introduction", xii.
23. John O'Brien, 41.
24. Demby said during the interview: "In one period — at least the period I try to demonstrate in *The Catacombs* — there is no change. There is only the illusion of change."   O'Brien, 47.
25. *The Catacombs*, 115.

irritation, because only love and not the persons involved matters. When the narrator makes love to Doris, she serves as proxy for her mother who was his former mistress. Sometimes, during his sexual encounters with Doris, he invokes memories of her mother and combines them with fantasies involving his wife in an effort, so to say, to will her impregnation simultaneously with Doris'. On the ontological level of divine truths, no complication arises through this frenzied activity since all things are sacred. Such a creed, one must admit, is no tool qualified for the analysis of modern reality, and especially not for the situation of the black. If, after the first few pages, the reader had been inclined to join Doris' exclamation, What a mess, he might well, by the end of the book, change it to: What simplicity!

Because such a twofold structural device explaining reality through myth is not to be found in any post-modernist novel, Hofman's and Foley's view that Demby is among the outstanding writers of our day is not convincing. Hoffman maintains that "In Demby's dominant metaphorical title, *The Catacombs*, he demonstrates how much he is in the avant garde experimental forefront with Borges, Nabokov and now Barthelme ..."[26] She substantiates Demby's position at the very peak of postmodernism by citing his destruction of the novel's realistic illusion. Indeed, *The Catacombs* is interspersed with allusions to its fictional nature, but this attempt at self-reflexive fiction is not maintained at length and therefore has only a limited relevance to the work as a whole. To be sure, Demby asserts that the Doris-Count segment represents a development of this device, but the segment itself fails to realize Demby's objectives for reasons I will discuss below. Although the fictional Doris appears in it, the *künstlerroman* segment does not blur the borders between reality and imagination because it is conveyed as an autobiographical account of Demby's years in Rome. The impression of authenticity counteracts the attempts to destroy illusion. Moreover, by bringing in international politics, the third segment is strictly constituted as a reproduction of facts. What Demby alludes to here are provable items of history, and this is documented by the use of quotations.

But the observation that Demby unmasks the fictional status of his novel does not justify grouping him with postmodernist writers

26. "Technique", 10; Barbara Foley also stresses a relationship with John Barth (p. 399).

and evaluating his performance in relation to theirs. It was as early as Laurence Sterne's *Tristram Shandy*, one has to bear in mind, that novelists have given their readers insight into the internal mechanism of fiction. This feature is no peculiarity of postmodernism alone, but rather represents a long tradition, in the course of which it has served different functions. Consequently, we must ascertain Demby's purpose in applying this technique, and whether such a purpose is comparable with that of the postmodernists. Hoffman tries to answer, at least, the first part of the question: "For Demby, the technique of art as a process, the blurring of the lines between creator and created, between fact and fiction, asks the question about the nature of reality ..."[27] But this observation while arguably valid when applied to Demby is also true of Sterne and other writers who followed him. To assure Demby's specific place within the development, the analysis must look further and consider how Demby defines the nature of reality.

In *Tristram Shandy*, to set up a frame of reference where Demby can be placed, Sterne destroyed the conventional form of the novel, that is, the chronological narration of the plot. His novel does not represent a chaotic reality, but rather reproduces a well structured reality in a chaotic form.[28] Consequently, the author's irony was not directed at the nature of reality, but against the literary and philosophic conventions for rendering reality. Like Rousseau, Sterne mocked rigid, systematic rationalism as practiced by his contemporaries, and urged a more emotional engagement with the world. *Tristram Shandy* replaces formalistic chronological order with one based on the associative faculties of man, and this change of narrative technique advocates a more sensitive and intuitive epistemology. In contrast to recent American literature, Sterne was less interested in the imaginative nature of fiction. This problem, as the latest criticism has it, is the main concern of writers like Barth, Nabokov, and Barthelme, who by means of elaborate parody, even self-parody, create a totality of fictitiousness in order to raise the question whether reality is real or an invention of man's fancy.

Within this range of different intentions, Demby can be grouped

27. "Technique", 10.
28. Rainer Warning, *Illusion und Wirklichkeit in Tristram Shandy und Jacques le Fataliste*. München: Fink 1965.

neither with Sterne nor with the postmodernists, but lies somewhere in the middle. *The Catacombs* treats of the nature of fiction
and so goes beyond Sterne's irony. But it does so only marginally
and by not blurring the distinction between fiction and fact
effectively, it stops short of the postmodernists. The factual
quality of the news segment is never undercut, and the same is
true of the *künstlerroman* segment which maintains throughout an
impression of autobiographical realism. Hence Foley speaks of a
"documentary mode". The only segment that exposes its fictional
quality uncompromisingly, the Doris-Count story, may do so
because of its special status within the conception of the whole.
The protagonists in this segment are not without exact contours
as would be expected of people whose reality is not assured. On
the contrary, they are conventional flat characters fulfilling their
purpose with a vengeance. The count represents the decadence of
western civilization, and Doris the vitality of original woman.
Hence the story teaches the lesson that the possible rebirth of
decadent white man will be realized through the unspent strength
of the black race.

The simple message and the straightforwardness of rendering
it demonstrate what this segment really is, a parable. A parable,
of course, does not aim at realism, but is understood to be an
invented exemplum for the illustration of a certain point. Although
the reader never is in doubt as to its fictional quality, the parable
directly refers to reality by conveying a moral truth. In other
words, neither does the parable question the nature of reality nor
the function and effectiveness of literature. Although the Doris-
Count segment is accepted as fictitious by the reader, it does not
serve a purpose similar to that of self-reflective fiction because it
is a conventional parable. Since this segment is introduced as a
novel in the process of being written, since, in short, it calls itself
literature it sheds light upon the nature and function of literature
as Demby sees it. By forming this segment into a parable, Demby
seems to be saying that literature conveys truths by means of
fictional exempla. Such a notion of literature, it goes without
saying, is entirely different from the sceptical sophistication with
which the postmodernist writer handles his art.

As we have seen, Demby raises the question of the nature of
fiction in *The Catacombs*, but he does not translate it into an
aesthetic device informing his novel. Interjections such as "I am

beginning to have the strangest feelings that we are all nothing more than shadows, spirits, breathed into life by Pirandello's fertile mind",[29] are mere rhetoric because the representation of Demby's figures lacks the fanciful quality typical of Pirandello's offspring. In light of Demby's epistemological concept, his belief in the steadfastness of a reality firmly anchored in ontological patterns, we see that his characters do not possess such a quality. His creed, which finally determines his novel, does not entertain any doubts about the nature of reality. While the postmodernist writers articulated such doubts and thereby tried to analyse their world — a world re-created by man himself — Demby though displaying the contours of that world does not engage it on its own terms. He evades the necessary confrontation by evoking ontological deep structures which interpret history as being essentially just, even sacred.

Demby could easily have found his twofold structural device in the classic of modernism, James Joyce's *Ulysses*, but not in post-modernist fiction. In *Ulysses*, as T.S. Eliot was the first to notice,[30] a complex surface structure renders the labyrinth of subjective experience — the daily affairs, thoughts and feelings of the three main characters, that gain clarity and significance by Joyce's use of archetypal patterns in the deep structure. Stephen's wanderings through Dublin are depicted as a modern variation of those of Ulysses, and both are meant to contain the model of man's eternal destiny. The search for a father, or for a son, is another of these patterns which suggests the human urge for the protectiveness of home and claims universal and timeless validity.

Joyce's contemporary, Eliot, knew what he was saying, and his view of *Ulysses* interprets the novel in terms of an epoch that, facing the overwhelming complexity of the modern world, favored intellectual reduction through myth and archetype or by going back to biological foundations. When we think that Freud made the "Id" the basis for every human action, when we think of C.W. Jung's "collective unconscious", of Eliot's "Fisher King",[31]

29. *The Catacombs*, 45 and 49.

30. T.S. Eliot, "Ulysses: Order and Myth", The Dial (1923); repr. in: Seon Givens, ed., *James Joyce: Two Decades of Criticism*. New York: Knopf rev. ed. 1963, 198-202.

31. Cf. Eliot's "Notes on the Waste Land", in: Eliot, *The Waste Land and Other Poems*. London: Faber 1975, 50.

Hemingway's bullfighters[32] and D.H. Lawrence's sexual urge, we perceive this tendency towards reduction, towards roots which appeared to be the last resort of a lost generation. Being well accustomed to the modern world, Demby, however, does not share that feeling of being lost, and, accordingly his application of Joyce's twofold device serves a different function. From beginning to end *Ulysses* is dominated by the jungle of reality – which accounts for the vitality of narration – and the mythic foundations remain hidden below, shown only in hints and connotations. In *The Catacombs*, on the other hand, these foundations are stressed with a vengeance. While Joyce created a delicate tension between the dominating experience of disjunction and the traditional desire for existential unity, Demby let his simplistic creed overpower reality in the novel, so that the intended message ruins the quality of the narration.

The assertion maintained here that *The Catacombs* is modeled after Joyce's *Ulysses*, does not contradict Bone's statement that Demby derived his *weltanschauung* from the French Jesuit Pierre Teilhard de Chardin, as both of these men stood in the same tradition of thinking. Although Chardin wrote his works before and after the Second World War, his philosophy resembles that of the modernist thinkers and writers. The method and content of Chardin's reasoning shows clearly that he is a latecomer to a European group of thinkers who launched what was later called by their critics *Lebensphilosophie*.[33] Claiming Nietzsche as its mentor, this philosophic school became known, above all, through the writings of Henri Bergson, while its most gifted German supporters, Wilhelm Dilthey and Georg Simmel, never achieved international fame. Although the actual movement seems to have been ephemeral and short-lived – it had its climax between 1900 and 1920 – it nevertheless mirrors, as nothing else, the temper and intellectual climate of the modernist period. Similar to American pragmatism, the philosophy-of-life school heeds the warnings of epistemological scepticism, and rejects the traditional method of rational thinking and systematizing because of its inadequacy in grasping the phenomena of existence as these were re-defined.

32. Cf. Klaus P. Hansen, "Ernest Hemingway: Dialektik der Idylle", *Amerika Studien/American Studies* 23/1 (1978), 98-117.
33. Heinrich Rickert, *Die Philosophie des Lebens: Darstellung und Kritik der philosophischen Modeströmung Unserer Zeit.* Tübingen: Niemeyer 1920.

Since life, driven forward by the "élan vital" (Bergson), is regarded as a dynamic non-entity in perpetual flux, the tool of rationality is no longer a sufficient guide to knowledge because of its static nature. At the heart of this new philosophy, therefore, lies a new definition of life which not only accepts the condition of instability and flux, but rather values it because it is said to offer the potentialities of human fulfilment. Instead of deploring the rapid change as did the adherents of the archetype, the philosophy-of-life school embraces and affirms this state of affairs, and thus lays the foundation of modern historical thinking.

Demby's intellectual master, Teilhard de Chardin, also belongs to the context of this tradition. His special system, briefly stated, results from a combination of three concepts: the Christian idea of God, Darwin's theory of evolution, and the definition of existence as it was put forward by the *Lebensphilosophie*. Like Bergson, Teilhard rejects rationalism and empiricism, favoring instead an intuitive approach, and he, too, values life because of its perpetual motion. Hence his works, though written after the Second World War, owe a large debt to the late nineteenth and early twentieth century. If Teilhard is to be seen as a latecomer to the philosophy-of-life school, then his disciple's conversion must also be regarded as a late arrival. Demby draws on Joyce and Dos Passos in regard to form and structure, and borrows from Teilhard the central notion of "changeless change", as well as the belief in the holiness of existence. The unenthusiastic reception of *The Catacombs*, so one has to conclude, is a result of Demby's reliance upon formal and thematic concepts which were relevant about 1920, but which fifty years later were no longer compelling. Obviously, in 1965, it would have been difficult for such a late product of modernism to catch the imagination of readers.

III

What I have said so far would seem to confirm Margolies: "Demby's works reveal a thoroughly unself-conscious immersion in European modes of thinking, conditioned by a profoundly American outlook."[34] The vague influences Margolies names to substantiate his assertion, however, can now be replaced by more

34. Margolies, 174.

concrete and convincing ones. *Beetlecreek*, as I have tried to show, points back to the literature of post-naturalism. Borrowing from entirely different sources, *The Catacombs* emulates Dos Passos' technique of cinematographic collage, draws on Joyce's masterpiece *Ulysses*, and makes use of the philosophy of Teilhard de Chardin. Consequently, this variety of source material results in works differing radically from each other. So little does the second novel resemble the first that it seems impossible that they are by the same author. According to Demby, his third novel, *The Long Bearded Journey*, which has not appeared in print so far, conforms to this practice of departing from ways already taken.[35] Such a habit, however, is astonishing, as usually writers, after having

35. Although it is implied in Demby's statement, quoted above, that the novel, *The Long Bearded Journey*, has been completed, it has never appeared in print so far. Demby's latest work is a small novel called *Love Story Black* (New York: Reed, Cannon, and Johnson Co. 1978). In form this novel neither resembles *Beetlecreek* nor *The Catacombs*, although thematically there are links with the latter. The motive for writing a love story is expressed within the novel by one of the narrator's students — as in *The Catacombs*, the narrator is Demby in disguise:
"'Why don't Black writers ever write about real people — why do they always treat Black people like social problems ... Why don't Black writers write about love, for example?' 'I am sure there will be some most beautiful Black love stories in the future —'
'Written by you, Professor --?'" (p. 78/79)
This, of course, is a re-formulation of the time-worn universality concept of black literature. The plot of Demby's "beautiful Black love story" is as follows. The black novelist Mr. Edwards, a college professor, divorced and having random love affairs with black female journalists, has a series of interviews with the once famous Blues singer Mona Pariss, now past eighty. Mona's life story revolved around the problem that her first and only love, a handsome Pullman porter, had been castrated by the Ku Klux Klan. Because of this, Mona decided to remain a virgin, and although she did not marry him they have always been close to each other. Their constant quarreling makes their relationship seem to be that of any ordinary husband and wife. When Mr. Edwards comes back for the last interview — after a trip to Africa where he has lost his new sweetheart to a "Catholic-Marxist Revolutionary" of the African Liberation Movement — Mona's friend has died. In a kind of vision the old lady takes the interviewer to be her late lover and she imagines that the missed essentials "have grown back". In the moment of defloration by the interviewer, who understands where his duty lies, Mona Pariss dies. Although the story is related with irony, Demby, seeking connections as usual, created here another of his — in his own words — "strange journeys through time and reality and Myth".

found their individual style, adhere to it and thus establish their literary identity.

Demby is aware of this peculiarity: *"The Catacombs* is different from *Beetlecreek* and *The Long Bearded Journey* is different from *The Catacombs.* I shall never allow myself to become iceberged into a style. There is much I want to say and I am convinced that the American negro's experience is historically unique."[36] This statement, of course, is open to criticism. If the black's experience is unique, then an adequately unique style would be indispensable for the manifestation of that experience. Demby's conclusion does not follow from his premise, but what he says seems to betray a meaning he may not consciously hold. The fact is that Demby has employed styles and thematic patterns taken out of various English and American traditions and has created novels as far removed from each other as the movements that supplied the models. This unusual method of producing literature cannot be justified by pointing to an "immersion in European thinking" as Margolies does. Immersion implies that one becomes a part of something, and for a writer it means that he finds his identity by coming to terms with a certain literary development. Such a description, however, is inadequate in dealing with Demby, for in his case we must speak of eclecticism. He has not found his place in the literary tradition, and all he did so far is to experiment with ready made concepts and to arrive at predictable ends. Neither the pessimistic outlook of *Beetlecreek* nor the hopeful one of *The Catacombs*, seems to have expressed Demby's true self or provided him with material out of which he could form his identity as an artist.

The failure of Demby's novels, however, implies more than an individual destiny caused by lack of talent. Demby's talent is undeniable, but in extreme form his misfortune is symptomatic of that black writer who, discarding the Afro-American cultural and literary tradition, seeks to elaborate his art on white models. Not only does he reject the Wright school of naturalistic protest, but also denies the ethnicity of art. Demby certainly is right when he calls the experience of the American black unique. This ethnic, cultural and social uniqueness, however, cannot be expressed aesthetically by practicing an eclecticism which draws entirely on

36. Quoted by Hill in his "Afterword", p. 186.

the white tradition.[37]

To illuminate the situation of blacks, *Beetlecreek* is cast in post-naturalistic conventions of white authors such as Anderson that describe emotional deprivation as the outcome of a provincial milieu, namely that of the rural white lowers-middle class. Though neither rich nor influential, the members of this class can at least be sure of their acceptance by the rural community. Certainly Anderson's protagonists are mediocre and their lives are trivial, but in the midst of mediocrity and triviality they maintain their place in society. Social acceptance, therefore, serves as a necessary condition of the figures' emotional needs. Accordingly, leaving the community and the renunciation of social acceptance is the first step towards liberation. These post-naturalistic conventions, however, are not appropriate for defining the special problems of blacks in America and their unique emotional deprivation. Although some have reached the middle class economically, they can, in contrast to Anderson's protagonists, never be sure of complete social integration: that is, their acceptance by middle class whites, even in a rural community. It is not integration, therefore, but their lack of assurance about their position that lies at the centre of their desolation. Consequently, the most urgent need of these blacks is not emotional liberation, as Anderson's characters achieve through the vision of the artist dissociating himself from society, but rather is recognition as an American citizen with equal rights.

Beetlecreek, viewed in this light, demonstrates how ideological models suitable for the description of the socio-historic circumstance of white writers in a white society lose their validity when applied to the situation of blacks. A too-direct link, therefore, between white and black literature might be detrimental to the latter. Thus critics should not consider it selfevident that "... all black fiction of significance in America is modern fiction, and what we expect of modernism in general, we expect of this literature as well: complexity of expression, elusiveness of meaning, opposition to established and traditional systems ..."[38] Such a view implies that in order to master his craft the black novelist

37. Although Demby would not agree with the influences maintained here, he himself only named white novelists and artists when asked about persons who had some impact on his development as a writer (cf. O'Brien).
38. Roger Rosenblatt, *Black Fiction*. Cambridge, Mass.: Harvard Uni-

can profit only from the achievements of white modernism. But in drawing on the style and the formal structure of white literature the black artist must adopt ideological patterns as well. For Rosenblatt this is no impediment because he sees a kind of mental concordance between the black and the white intellectual who expresses himself in the modern novel. According to Rosenblatt, "all modern heroes are losers", and this deplorable state he takes as a link between the races. He forgets, however, that there are different ways of being and becoming a loser and that these may be rooted in various conditions.[39] First of all, there are voluntary losers, or as I would prefer, voluntary outsiders and involuntary outsiders. The protagonists of the white novel, of course, belong to the first category. Either they disdain society from a superior intellectual or emotional stance, or they play the fool or rogue whose blunders reveal the inhumanity of social institutions rather than his own clumsiness. In both cases the door to assimilation stands wide open, but the protagonist refuses to enter. Not so for the black counterpart in the novel as well as in real life. He still sits in the antechamber waiting for his admission, and when he articulates a contempt for society from this position, his motivation and circumstance are entirely different. What for white artists may be an intellectual luxury by which they guarantee elitism is for blacks a vital and urgent human need.

The danger of perpetuating detrimental ideological patterns surfaces also in cases of pro-black outlooks promoted by white writers. Analyses of famous examples of this kind, *Uncle Tom's Cabin* and Anderson's *Dark Laughter*, have revealed that the expressed appreciation of the black race, nevertheless, rests on prejudicial notions about it.[40] The same is true of Demby's *The Catacombs*. The thematic structure of this novel – simplification through archetype and affirmation of existence as formulated by

versity Press, 1974, 7.

39. Cf. Ihab Hassan, *Radical Innocence: The Contemporary American Novel.* Princeton: Princeton Univ. Press 1973; "Part I: The Hero and the World", 9-96; and David D. Galloway, *The Absurd Hero in American Fiction.* Austin: University of Texas Press 1966.

40. James Baldwin, *Notes on a Native Son.* London: Transworld Publishers 1964, "Everybody's Protest Novel", 9-17; Theodore L. Gross, "The Negro in the Literature of the Reconstruction", in: Saymour L. Gross and John Edward Hardy, eds., *Images of the Negro in American Literature.* Chicago: Univ. of Chicago Press 1966, 71-83.

the *Lebensphilosophie* – provides a description and evaluation of the tension between the races. By turning blacks into the holders of the "élan vital", Demby picks up the old racist concept that blacks teem with vitality. Re-formulating this conventional concept, Demby expresses the hope that, as the modern world stands, blacks will bring back health, sex, fertility, and a natural affirmation of existence in order to achieve the overdue rebirth of man. As usual, to be black is defined by means of an alleged affinity with nature and this quality functions as the condition of his worth. Such an argument seems unhappily reminiscent of the *topos* of the "noble savage". This *topos* and all its different manifestations work through a fundamental contradiction of, as Hieatt puts it in describing ancient pastoral poetry, "ideality and inferiority".[41] The ancient shepherd, Cooper's Leatherstocking, Hemingway's bull-fighter, and the exotic, vital black man or woman represent idealized figures whose very naturalness, in itself virtuous and attractive, nevertheless excludes them from social acceptance because they lack refinement and intelligence. Thus their affinity with nature, the very basis on which the appreciation rests, also contributes to depreciation, even if not expressed explicitly. Unwittingly, Demby pays tribute to this paradox in the presentation of his model black, Doris. She is a second rate dancer, and she is a mistress who sells her beauty to a white master. In introducing these minor details Demby is most realistic and paints the true picture of the black's situation. Leaving untouched the problem of whether Demby is right in favoring integration, we see that he will never achieve it by means of this alleged pro-black concept. Doris' virtues, vigor, beauty, and sex underscore the difference between black and white, a difference which at face value favors blacks but which ultimately depreciates them by robbing them of one half of their humanity. As long as Demby only makes his protagonist excel in naturalness, he cannot argue for the fitness of blacks to be integrated into a society demanding complex abilities.

41. Charles W. Hieatt, "The Integrity of Pastoral: A Basis for Definition", *Genre* 5 (1972), 11.

BIOGRAPHY

William Demby was born in Pittsburg, Pa., in 1922. In 1947 he graduated from Fisk University in Nashville, Tennessee. After initial visits to Italy during his two years in the Army, where he wrote for the Army newspaper, he returned to Rome to study painting and to work as a jazz musician. Later he wrote screen treatments for the film director Roberto Rosellini and did commercial work for TV programs. Demby married an Italian woman and had a son by her. Around 1964, after having stayed in Rome for fifteen years, he went back to New York and was divorced. There, he first worked as a writer in a New York advertising agency, then became Associate Professor of English at Staten Island Community College, New York, where he still teaches.

BIBLIOGRAPHY

Beetlecreek 1950.
The Catacombs 1965.
Love Story Black 1978.

EBERHARD KREUTZER

DARK GHETTO FANTASY AND THE GREAT SOCIETY: CHARLES WRIGHT'S *THE WIG* (1966)

Although Charles Wright is a writer with only a modest output of prose, his work justifies our interest because it brings together some of the most prominent literary tendencies of the sixties within a black context. Thematically as well as technically it reflects a period stirring with the revived awareness of the social environment and set on new approaches in dealing with it. His first novel, *The Messenger* (1963), presents a neo-realistic slice-of-life by focusing on a shabby New York segment and giving glimpses of the city's other milieus through the eyes of a young black drifter from the South. *Absolutely Nothing to Get Alarmed About* (1973) collects Wright's *Village Voice* chronicle of the sub-cultures from the East Village to Harlem in a black version of the New Journalism, which evokes the fantasy element in the contemporary scene. Between these two, not only chronologically, comes *The Wig* (1966), a farcical novel blending reality and fantasy in the story of a young Harlemite's vain attempt at economic and personal self-realization during the Johnson era.[1] It is mainly for this novel that Wright has caught the critics' attention as one of the first black writers to turn to black humor. His frontline position of the "black black humorist" implies a dissatisfaction with the realistic tradition of the black protest novel. Rather than confronting the reader with a fictional picture, however stylized, of authentic reality, he decides to counter reality with the fantastic distortions of satire.[2] More directly, the book dramatizes the disillusionment

1. Charles Wright, *The Wig* (1966; rpt. New York: Ballantine Books, 1968). Subsequent page references are incorporated in the text.
2. The best analysis of the novel to date is Max F. Schulz, *Black Humor Fiction of the Sixties: A Pluralistic Definition of Man and His World* (Athens, Ohio: Ohio Univ. Press, 1973), pp. 91-123, discussing the hero's anxiety of personal incompleteness and racial ostracism, the farce of his endlessly shift-

with the Great Society, which confirmed the suspicions of those blacks who criticized it as yet another mirage of liberal rhetoric. The black community's thwarted hopes for a substantial improvement in their situation, most manifest wherever this belated version of the American Dream would be put to the test, makes up the theme of the novel. *The Wig* exemplifies this theme in the episodic plot of the hero's quest and its interwoven parallels drawn from America's archetypal "dark ghetto."

The hero is Lester Jefferson, a 21-year-old tenant in a run-down, overcrowded Harlem rooming house who has failed to make it even trying the job of an Arab waiter and street entertaining. At the beginning of the novel he is bent on one more gimmick to change his fortune and get his share of the common goal — the Great Society. Since he looks acceptable, apart from his kinky hair, he hopes to gain access to WASP America by removing this blemish: with the panacea of a hair relaxer he turns his hair into a miracle of silky curls (a later touch-up even gives him a reddish-golden shine). Now certain to have unlimited possibilities he sets out to take his new future in his hands. He is joined by his friend Jimmy Wishbone, a Hollywood has-been with still something of a name, yet mentally disturbed ever since the movie industry dropped him because of a shift in racial policy. Together they bank on the musical youth culture and, after getting high on pot, they offer themselves as Rhythm and Blues singers to a record company in its Tin Pan Alley empire. However, belying one of the most cherished black stereotypes, Lester cannot even carry a tune. He seems to score more of a success with The Deb, a Harlem prostitute, who is impressed by his foreign airs. Ironically, his private life comes to grief the moment he manages to secure a job. The Deb, herself keen on joining white society, falls out with Lester when she discovers that he is only another "nigger." Meanwhile, Lester has succumbed to the time-honored American principle of working one's way up from rags to riches by accepting the job of a chicken impersonator in the streets of New York, a

ing and failing impersonation of stereotypes and the narrative style of Pop Art fragmentation and ironic antithesis. Frances S. Foster, "Charles Wright: Black Black Humorist," *CLA Journal*, 15.1 (1971), 44-53, distinguishes Wright as a twofold avantgardist who satirizes the role-playing protagonist in a succession of largely unrelated images and blurs reality and fantasy in various degress.

larger-than-life advertising gag for The King of Southern Fried Chicken, if not exactly a man-size occupation. Inside and outside his new masquerade he is more lonely than ever. He even consults the Harlem sorceress Madam X to be cured of the frustrating "love habit." When he picks up a strange girl in the street who is just as frantically hungering for love he strikes up an immediate rapport but is all the more disgusted to find her offering money for a more permanent relationship. As many incidents before, this encounter seems to suggest a connection with Mr. Fishback, the uncanny undertaker, a quasi-allegorical power-figure in the background of the novel, until he makes a climactic appearance in the final scene where he shears off Lester's hair, cauterizes his penis, and thus relieves him of the strain of being more than what he is — a kinky, impotent "nigger."

If this summary suggests a sparse plot, it should be added that the novel is as much a sequence of scenes, ranging from the atmospheric to the dramatic, each confronting the hero with a situation that calls for typical role-behavior and the whole suffused with a mixture of stark realism and madcap fantasy. In an early review which has some authority because Wright later endorsed it, C. Knickerbocker pointed out the main characteristics of the novel: the sardonic suggestion that the black man's greatest burden is his self-hatred; the denouncement of the black man who accepts the roles imposed upon him, as unsparing as that of the white man who imposes them; the carnival-like parade of people demonstrating the escapist, fraudulent or evil disguises blacks assume in order to survive; the depiction of a nightmarish Harlem inhabited by "inmates"; the mean and vicious style as an appropriate vehicle for the author's zany pessimism; the fierce satire which exposes the sores no Great Society will ever heal.[3] Wright's wholehearted approval of this critique indirectly provides a set of clues for a closer reading of the novel. More directly, if less explicitly, we are given a frame of reference in the book itself. The subtitle ("a mirror image") signifies the ironic theme of

3. Conrad Knickerbocker, "Laughing on the Outside," *The New York Times*, 5 March 1966, p. 25. For Wright's approval of this review and his own comments on the novel see John O'Brien, "Charles Wright," in *Interviews with Black Writers* (New York: Liveright, 1973), pp. 245-257, especially 250 ff.

reflection in reverse; an author's note explains the title (black slang for 'hair') and the setting ("an America of tomorrow"), thus suggesting the fetishist folklore of the central symbol and the dystopian atmosphere of the whole; and the mottos of the three parts taken from Joyce, Fitzgerald, and the Blues tradition imply major influences on the author. Putting these aspects together and bringing them into focus I shall analyze, first, the hero's quest and his self-defeating masquerade, second, the social context and the urban environment, third, the reflected ghetto pathology and the envisaged prospect of the Great Society, and fourth, the book's technique and its place in contemporary American fiction.

Lester's quest for his admission into the Great Society is from the start beset with the psychodynamics of despair and delusion, pursued with the doggedness of one who will not admit the contradictions of his behavior, and finally given up in utter resignation to the dehumanizing forces around him. When he expects from his changed Wig the subsequent miracle of a "new life," he is led by the forced optimism of a destitute man who seeks refuge from past failures in attacking his future. At first, glances at himself in the mirror and reactions of the people he meets seem to confirm that he is "reborn," a different person altogether. But the most flattering compliments about his appearance ironically come from those who share his identity problem in one way or another: his neighbor Sandra Hanover, a queen in high drag, and The Deb, a girl extremely self-conscious about her kinky hair. He gets the impression that he literally blinds people in the street and with the additional help of a British accent, an elegant suit, a forged credit card and similar aids from the conman's bag of tricks, he brings off an even more elaborate façade. But he cannot deceive anyone for long and, more poignantly, as a fraud he alienates most strongly those who are his closest friends. He suffers his first great setback when he bungles the audition and makes Jimmy go it alone. He upsets his godfather Tom Lacy to such a degree that he physically attacks him. And in exceeding The Deb's worst suspicions about his identity he drives away the one person with whom he has felt an occasional moment of happiness.

But most of all he deceives and alienates himself. If he intends to develop his personality and, more basically, ensure his humanity his efforts are misguided and they push him into the worst of black stereotypes and conformist attitudes — a living parody of the invisible man made visible. Wright uses his eager, yet ludicrous hero-narrator as a *persona* to play the fool in a racist, capitalist society and to demonstrate the catch that only the economically successful may "become human," yet to be eligible for such an advancement they have to have learned the "art of being human," that is "the art of being white" (18, 39). The psychological and social terms of this absurd notion inevitably lead the black man into self-destruction, especially since they are constantly reinforced by the media: Lester's mind is flooded by their delusory images of a consumer's good life (3 ff.) and disturbed by the message in their weird job descriptions (107 ff.). Like everybody else he does try to "make it," dreaming of fame and fortune or, more plainly, money and girls. Not surprisingly, however, even the modest successes within his reach abound with ironies. When he eventually becomes a minor TV celebrity it is as the Chicken Man cackling and crawling through the streets, the anonymous innards of an artificial animal. When he first meets The Deb he draws on his appeal as a "foreigner" wittily pleading for free love, only to be rebuffed by this cash-and-carry girl's trade union slogan "No finance, no romance" (37). When he later takes his revenge it is in a typical shift of roles: as soon as he has proved himself to her as a sexual performer he acts the mean *macho*.

The lesson he is supposed to draw from one encounter after another is spelled out in an oracular manner by his two magician-guides, Madam X and Mr. Fishback. Madam X gives him to understand that as long as his people do not enjoy a naturalized status their only worthwhile passion will be hard cash — as opposed to love — and she interprets the Wig as a sign of his fearful, self-destructive vanity, a flaw in his "portrait" he will be lucky to get rid of (119ff.). This forebodes the final scene as much as Mr. Fishback's obscurer and earlier piece of advice: "you're almost a man. It's time you learned something. That Harlem skyline is the outline of your life. There is very little to discover by looking at the pavement." By way of explaining this unenlightening eye-opener he tells Lester that he is "on his own for now" and that his guide's *"presence won't be required until ..."* (129). It is not until the final scene with its perverse rite of passage, performed in the acts of unmasking and castration, that the ominous meaning of the image becomes clear. Only superficially could it have been taken as an encouragement to widen one's horizon and look up to a dynamic life;

rather, it must be understood as a warning not to transcend the enclosed world of the ghetto, whether in the capacity of the charming foreigner or the talked-about Chicken Man. Fishback himself symbolizes the ambivalent relation of the white downtown world toward the uptown ghetto. Indeed, early on it is implied that Lester may leave Harlem only with Fishback's permission (7). And although he has received from him the gift of a credit card — apparently forged and thus a limited open-sesame anyway — he knows perfectly well that some day he will have to pay for such favors (22). When this day comes it will come with a vengeance: the price he has to pay is the humiliating acquiescence in the brutal fact of his "nigger" status. Rather than continue to strive for his naturalization as an American he yields to the release from his neutralization as a lover.

The immediate context of the climactic scene stresses the exemplary character of Lester's development and reveals the author's apocalyptic undertone. Shortly before the final encounter Lester receives a telepathic message from Fishback: "when love waxes cold, said Paul in 'The Third Coming ...' " (141f.) On the face of it a corny joke about the weakening of sexual prowess, this travesty alludes to Christ's prophecy of his Second Coming at a time when "iniquity shall abound" and hence "the love of many shall wax cold" (St. Matthew 24:12). The context of the source, applied to the black man's situation, suggests a dystopian significance. Lester, of course, does not see more in it than a foreboding of his aggravated misery when he hears from Fishback about The Deb's death in a traffic accident. Ironically, The Deb provides the most obvious mirror image of his own life, thus reinforcing the representative quality of his case: in a way, she is more successful when she becomes café society's darling — her greatest asset being precisely her "natural" hair according to a new vogue — but she is also more completely undone; and at least in her death both Madam X and Mr. Fishback once more seem to have conspired. When Lester first experiences the separation from The Deb as "the death of a bright dream" and puts the blame on his wretched impersonation (116), he speaks only half the truth because he has known for some time that Fishback is the "prime mover of people"always hovering over him and that he alone would have the authority to decide whether his pursuit of happiness is an unalienable right or a crime and a sin (128f.). In the final scene Fishback clearly assumes the role of a *deus-ex-machina* in an upside-down world where the guide gives misleading counsel, the sponsor takes more than he gives, the doctor mutilates the healthy. Above all, both Mr. Fishback and Madam X allegorize the death-and-money principle. They make an odd pair of unholy "saints" obstructing natural instincts and creative purpose. It is as typical of Madam X to have wanted to be "the mad bomber" and then an efficient city planner and to oppose any increase in population (118, 145) as it is of Fishback to indulge in necrophilia on a big scale. The sorceress specializes in deadening love as a painful habit, the undertaker in loving the dead in their irresponsive availability, and both of them teach the capitalist gospel while combining business with pleasure. More specifically, they play mother and father to Lester's inverted initiation, turning him back into the bare existence of the black boy.

This ironically brings him full circle since his strongest motivation for self-improvement derives from an unhappy childhood. While watching his new self in the mirror, he dreams the old dream of succeeding where his parents have miserably failed (17f). He also remembers how as a child, sniffing someone's opium, he had sensed for the first time what it must mean to fly and be free, and he now seems on the brink of following countless Americans who with confidence and diverse strategies have liberated and fulfilled themselves: "American until the last breath, a true believer in The Great Society, I'd turn the other cheek, cheat, steal, take the fifth amendment, walk bareassed up Mr. Jones's ladder, and state firmly that I was too human" (41). Meek religion, criminal competition, legal insistence, unashamed social slimbing make an odd mixture to ensure success but, again, the "land of hope" is out of reach for blacks anyway despite the ever renewed promise of endless opportunities.

If Lester realizes some crucial limitation and even admits to a touch of schizophrenia he plays this down coquettishly, as when he first confesses to be an ambitious lunatic, then makes the point that an impersonator must be courageous, skilled, and aware of his limitations and in a final turnabout exempts himself from any limitations whatsoever (71). Not before his Chicken Man days does it dawn upon him that he has overestimated his own capacity and taken a wrong course from the start:

Following my own shadow, it seemed that I was taking a step in *some* direction and that The Wig was my guide. Progress is our most important product, General Electric says, and I had progressed to the front door of hell when all I had actually been striving for was a quiet purgatory. And I did not find it strange that hell had a soft blue sky, a springlike air, music, dust, laughter, curses. (137)

Pursuing his dark mirror image, misguided by his own impersonation, and unaware of its incompatibilities, he suffers from the delusion that to move on is to move forward. But this pilgrim's progress has advanced from bad to worse: no purgatorial prospects for him. The ghetto ambience, even at its best, seems hell.

Through most of the book, however, Lester sees the make-believe in everybody else without recognizing it in himself, a typical case of the old satirical mirror reflecting everybody's face except one's own. In emphasizing this contrast Wright provides multiple reflections of his hero's behavior in the social environment. The catchphrase "Everybody's got *something* working for them" (16) rules most people's lives in a society propagating the possibilities of the individual, but the Harlem environment makes it a dubious magic formula driving people into behavior based on fantasies. Everybody in the ghetto adheres to some sort of role-playing in order to survive psychologically. In one encounter after another Lester meets a carnival of impersonators. Beginning with his fellow tenants, there are Nonnie Swift, a part-time prostitute who claims Creole extraction and suffers in her frequent drunkenness from an hysterical pregnancy; old Mrs. Tucker who pretends even to a background of southern white aristocracy and keeps voicing her disgust at the Harlem riffraff; Sandra Hanover, the drag queen and lady with class, who mimicks in every detail of looks, gesture, and talk the models of film and fashion and works as personal maid for a Sutton Place call-girl, which later brings him to Europe. Like Lester, his neighbors — and the minor characters to follow — strain after a white appearance, project themselves into a better class and get most of their inspiration from the media. Inasmuch as these fantasies serve an escapist purpose, it is ironic that those who have actually crossed the ghetto's borders find themselves only in a more complex predicament. Such cases, again, provide a commentary on Lester's development and enlarge its import. Although these characters are more experienced and may easily detect Lester's fallacies, they are themselves hardly safe from self-inflicted deceptions. Jimmy Wishbone deflates Lester's enthusiasm about his promising "American" Wig (26) while Lester considers Jimmy's fall from grace and utter confusion (28); yet when they turn up for their audition Jimmy feels just as reborn as Lester and sees a real chance to recapture his public image, only to retire after further failures to the mental institution where he had been before and where he now expects his friend to join him (128 f.). The Duke, a dope-dealer living in luxury at Harlem's "gilt edge" and collecting southern curiosa, criticizes the two for their paradoxical scheme to become "colored" rock 'n' roll singers because he expects genuine soul music with its harmonizing effect on racial tension to be the big future hit, but as it turns out, he is himself a belated would-be Ellington and an infantile addict smoking pot from a baby saxophone (51 ff.). A grotesque intertwining of role-playing takes place when Lester visits his godfather Tom, a servant in an upper class midtown apartment. Tom has perfected the eye-rolling, shuffling sambo routine to such a degree that it has become second nature and spoils the communication with his own people while it is meant to camouflage his —somewhat ineffectual — militancy as a statistician of white casualties culled from the news reports. When he takes Lester with his conked hair severely to task Lester protests commitment to the cause and explains the Wig away as his camouflage for alleged sit-ins. As soon as Lester is in the street again, he resumes the role of the cosmopolitan Manhattanite, but when he puts down an approaching black beggar for another cheat he is, for once, confronted with a runaway "real slave" (73 ff.). The tactical maneuvres in such face-to-face relations, typical of the book's central theme, take on further significance here in historical and utopian terms: the nineteenth century runaway slave carrying a chastity belt with his proprietor's inscription highlights the continued struggle for freedom in times of "unchained slavery" (10) and presents a foreshadowing image of Lester's final enslavement while Tom's statistical charts express the untimely hope for a future when blacks will by sheer population numbers supersede the white majority.

In addition to the temporal reference, the slave episode contains some spatial significance. It is one of the few scenes away from Harlem evoking in Lester the contradictory feelings that his roots are really deep in the countryside but that he is as determined as ever to "shake up this town." To make it in the big city has always been a special attraction for the young man from the hinterland

— for no one more than for the southern black — and the disillusioning process in getting about the city makes up the oldest device of American city fiction. Wright is, however, not concerned with this kind of character development and urban portrayal but with the situation of the ghetto-dweller who has no scope for development, finding the enormous fascinations of the larger metropolis a constant source of irritation. What Wright does, in a way, is to play off against each other two of New York's most conspicuous images, Naked City and Fun City, exposing the harsh reality in one of its seediest slums and exploiting the fantasy element in its atmosphere to counter it through hyperbolic distortion. The portrait of the young Harlemite who tries to get his share of what the metropolis seems to offer is put in perspective as a series of pot dreams: quite literally so when Lester views his new life on the way down from the Duke's place to Manhattan's famous Tin Pan Alley. The cabride which takes him and Jimmy to Paradise Records on 52nd Street is a significant episode in the urban context (55 ff.). The white taxi driver, who has fitted his car with the sado-masochistic equipment of leather straps and steel rods, adjusts his behavior to the changing territories. When he picks the two up in the Harlem border land he puts on a perversely submissive act but as soon as he reaches his own "turf" on the Upper East Side he switches to an equally aggressive manner. Only by posing as pop stars — enlarging, as it were, their turf to the entertainment scene and underlining their importance for the national economy — do Lester and Jimmy bring him back to his sycophant bearing. All this happens against the background of similarly heterogeneous street impressions — from the car Lester glimpses an atmosphere of bleakness and hilarity, the angry unemployed in the street and the snug apartment wives above — until they reach their destination, one of those quasi-surreal New York pyramids and a Tower of Babel tootling with muzak from the record company's program.

As in this scene, the city's socio-topography is patterned by strictly observed demarcation lines between territories and their subdivisions. In particular, Harlem is a city-within-the-city with its "frontier gate" at 96th Street opening into the uptown "Badlands" (82). There is a characteristic uptown-downtown axis: Harlemites like Lester, Jimmy, and The Deb try to get into the downtown entertainment business and, vice versa, whites come up to the colorful ghetto for kicks of a special variety (27 f.). Commuters between Harlem and the white world are ridiculed as leading a double life which makes them put kinky-bur false wigs over their conked hair on their daily home journey (21). The subway is a particularly potent — and traditional — symbol in this context. The A-Train connects Harlem and downtown Manhattan as a subversive vehicle in both directions: providing access to an enclave of hidden pleasures as well as an escape route from the dark ghetto. When the invitation to take the A-train is transmogrified into a sarcasm about the "A-men train to success" it undermines a black accomodationist attitude (45). It is significant that Lester should return on the A-train to Harlem, receive Fishback's telepathic message among a crowd of indifferent passengers and emerge to the symbolic completion of his failure when the story takes its final nightmarish turn (141 f.).

Lester's movement through New York is limited and concentric. Only his Chicken Man job brings him to all parts of the city but it also reduces him to a street spectacle whose main interest lies in the subjective interpretation it elicits from curious bystanders (113 f.). Apart from that he does not venture beyond Sutton Place and sooner or later he finds his own level in central Harlem. Consequently, the "heart of Harlem" along 125th Street is the recurring setting which receives the most detailed description. The novel opens in Lester's rooming house, a place infested with fungus, cockroaches, and rats and equipped with a single bathroom for seventy-five blacks of all shades (4 f.). It is typically a suffocating environment which drives him out into the street where he may hope to find some stimulation or, at least, distraction, especially in the magical mood of a Saturday night (27). The Harlem ambience, however, is far from being as picturesque and vital as a widespread cliché will have it. For one thing, most of the time in his wanderings through the ghetto Lester remains as lonely as ever: in this respect he hardly differs from people like Mr. Sunflower Ashley-Smithe, the smart black impresario who has devoted his life to "colored" music and thereby completely isolated himself (63 ff.), or the love-starved girl from the Upper West Side, the well-to-do single who is oppressed by the urban wasteland around her with its masses of people (137 f.). What is more, Wright dramatizes some of the very real grievances of Harlem housing and Harlem street life in the grotesqueries of an all-out farce.

Lester's extermination of the rats in Nonnie's room includes a specimen of the notorious Harlem super-rat and the description turns the scene into a mock-heroic battle complete with the traditional devices of the lady-love, the field of honor, the passage at arms and its rituals of speech and action.[4] The omnipresence of the police is conjured up in the street scenes. Cops appear as knightly protectors on 125th Street where nevertheless passers-by have to run the gauntlet sprinting toward the "right side" of Eighth Avenue, a good exercise for the Run-Nigger-Run Games (30 ff.). A cop gives a mother a helping hand who beats her boy to death because he refuses to attend a segregated school (130 ff.). The picture, though, is not uniformly depressing and does allow for some ambivalence. Lester has glimpses of a happier Harlem surviving and renewing itself: children playing games on the fire escapes or blues, jazz, gospel songs, and Latin music filling the air (100 f.). The experience he gains varies: the pleasure he derives from the playful streetcorner rap with the whores and his easy rapport with The Deb suffers a setback when she suddenly begins to talk business; and later on he is shocked by the fatal heart attack of a civil servant in the street who has suffered from racial nightmares and is watched with little sympathy by the crowd (32 ff.). The ambivalence of the Harlem scene is perhaps best, though hardly originally, symbolized in the mandarin tree which miraculously grows on a garbage dump in the backyard of Lester's rooming house (114).

Wright's novel reads in many respects like a fictional counterpart to Kenneth B. Clark's *Dark Ghetto* (1965), a remarkably factual and committed analysis of the social dilemmas concerning the black community. Drawing on his experience with a Harlem youth opportunity project Clark underlines the social dynamics and the psychopathological symptoms of life in the archetypal black ghetto. He develops a very similar picture with a wealth of documentary detail and an analytical sharpness that may serve to illuminate our text. Apart from the phenomena of poor health, inadequate education, family instability, drug addiction, and early delinquency the ghetto society is marked by the double trauma of rejection in terms of class and race, the housing decay and

---

4. The various mock-heroic devices are listed in R.P. Sedlack, "Jousting with Rats: Charles Wright," *Satire Newsletter*, 7 (Fall 1969), 37-39.

overcrowding, the deteriorating employment situation (despite the civil rights movement and the increasing prosperity of the nation as a whole), and the lack of social mobility apparent in the failure to overcome stereotypes and to leave the ghetto. The ghetto psychology shows most pertinently in the widespread apathy and despair as well as the self- and group-hatred arising from an inferiority complex and leading to assimilative manipulations (hair straightening, skin bleaching) or self-aggrandizing fantasies (posturing, verbal bombast). The compensatory mechanism appears most strikingly perhaps in the historical emasculation of the black man by the white man and the ensuing importance attached to sexual prowess.

The dark ghetto is determined by a self-perpetuating pathology, an emotional disturbance ranging from a relatively normal anxiety to a criminal psychosis and often feeding upon the projections of the mass media and expressing itself in the fantasies of acceptance or denial. Clark makes the point that the "social schizophrenia" rampant in the dark ghetto might seem comic, if it were not tragic.[5] This is precisely what Wright makes his point of departure bringing into play some of the fictional resources of tragicomedy: a highly serious criticism in low farce, an exposure of the accomodationist's fantasies through the *persona* of a young Harlemite whose dream of success blurs into the ultimate nightmare, all presented in a mixture of realistic slices and hyperbolic fabulation. The novel reveals basically the same Harlem syndrom of naivete, shiftlessness, desperate activity, obsession with sex, drug addiction, aggressiveness and swaggering as Clark's study but from an utterly pessimistic point-of-view and in the irritating manner of a spun-out alienation effect.

Both Clark and Wright hint at the historical and circumstantial

5. Kenneth B. Clark, *Dark Ghetto: Dilemmas of Social Power* (1965; rpt. New York: Harper & Row, 1967), p. 67. The above summary is based on chapters 3-5. Although Clark persuasively speaks for the realities behind the figures he includes some telling statistics about Harlem as compared with the rest of New York in the early sixties: Harlem has more people in fewer rooms and in a greater percentage of decaying houses (30), it is a particularly young community with twice as many jobless youths (34), it has the highest rate of admission to mental hospitals (82), its juvenile delinquency is more than twice the normal rate (87), and its rate of narcotic use has been ten times as high for years (90).

forces behind such behavior but concentrate on the situation in the early sixties. The period when the reactivated social conscience and the urge for reform during the Kennedy years merged into Johnson's vision of the Great Society held both its special promises and latent fallacies. It is true that Johnson took the most advanced position on the racial problem of any American president but, apart from the paralyzing impact of the Vietnam involvement, he failed to realize the obstacles inherent in the dynamics of economic power and the persistence of habit and tradition. His programs for the relief of poverty, assistance in education, organization of social work etc. took up the New Deal model but went beyond the aim of a just distribution of wealth. The idea of the Great Society, as first outlined in his Ann Arbor Address (1964), proclaimed the chance to develop a higher quality of society out of improved living conditions: "We have the opportunity to move not only toward the rich society and the powerful society but upward to the Great Society," a society based on "abundance and liberty for all" and demanding "an end to poverty and racial injustice". The specific "task" of the racial issue he formulated a year later in the Howard University Address: "to give 20 million Negroes the same chance as every other American to learn and grow, to work and share in society, to develop their abilities – physical, mental and spiritual, and to pursue their individual happiness." It was a sweeping reform program, which for all its vagaries had practical consequences. First and foremost came the War on Poverty with such legislation as the Economic Opportunity Act of 1964. Intended to set the Great Society on its course, it only revealed the agony of progress, if it did bring progress at all. As a matter of fact, the economic conditions of the black minority further deteriorated in comparison with the white majority. Though the program's delusions did not become widely apparent before 1966 it provoked the skepticism of the more radical social critics and heightened the tension between expectation and frustration among the black poor, a contributing factor to the development of black militancy and the anger ventilated in the urban riots of the mid-sixties.[6]

6. Lyndon B. Johnson's Ann Arbor Speech, May 22, 1964, and his Commencement Address at Howard University, June 4, 1965, are reprinted in *The Great Society Reader: The Failure of American Liberalism*, ed. Marvin

When Wright sends his hero "studying the map of the Great Society" after the maxim "One is not defeated until one is defeated" (68) he makes him the quixotic dupe of precisely the delusion in the Dream rhetoric, the tragicomic victim acting out the brutal consequences of the accomodationist's incentives. By ridiculing the fallacy of such ready belief and unbroken optimism it does not, however, advocate black militancy: a side glance at Black Muslims in front of the Theresa Hotel hawking chances on an armored tank which is supposed to make a round trip to Georgia on a gallon of gas satirizes what Clark calls the fantasy of militancy. In contrast to Clark and other social critics Wright does not provide an alternative: his perspective remains that of the debunking satirist as he explodes the myth of the Great Society and deflates the delusions of the black man in a mirror image of distorted realities without allowing for much insight or future policy on the part of the hero or any other character. Rather, the novel's dystopian illustrations function as a future warning for America and its farcical treatment of contemporary ghetto life is all fixed upon destroying the various fantasies. Given this intention and accepting it as a feasible objective of fiction, the impact of the book depends to a considerable degree on the author's satirical imagination and stylistic execution. It is here, unfortunately, that Wright largely fails: some of his targets are too worn-out to yield more than hackneyed reflections or they are simply shortlived (the concept of physical beauty would soon change and give rise to black pride). Too often

E. Gettleman and David Mermelstein (New York: Random House, 1967), pp. 15-23, 253-260 (see especially pp. 15f., 254). The editorial introductions to the book as a whole and to Part V on "The Black Man in the Great Society" in particular (pp.3-11, 243-250) give critical overviews of the major issues from a socialist point-of-view. Typical of the controversy about political strategies are Bayard Rustin, "From Protest to Coalition Politics" (pp. 263-277) and Ronald Radosh, "From Protest to Black Power: The Failure of Coalition Politics" (pp. 278-293). For equally opposed views compare Ralph Ellison, "The Myth of the Flawed White Southerner," in *To Heal and to Build: The Programs of President Lyndon B. Johnson*, ed. James Mac Gregor Burns (New York: McGraw, 1968), pp. 207-216, a pleading for Johnson's legislative achievement, and Malcolm X,"Prospects for Freedom in 1965," in *Malcolm X Speaks: Selected Speeches and Statements*, ed. George Breitman (1965; rpt. New York: Grove Press, 1966), pp. 147-156, a denunciation of the delusion of the Great Society. A moderate insider's view is provided by Doris Kearns, *Lyndon Johnson and the American Dream* (London: Deutsch, 1976), see especially chapter 8.

his use of ironic contrasts seems predictable, whereas his efforts to impress us with the extraordinary usually results in either strained or crude effects. Not that one expects much character development, a subtle point-of-view or a complex structure from a book that uses for its main device the caricature of a quester who gets involved in a series of episodes and encounters with other characters as typified as himself (see the name symbolism). And the piecemeal experiences of the hero delivered in a fast nervous style may be seen to convey his disorientation among the flood of images in the hectic urban environment.[7] But the intended tragicomedy cannot convince us because the comedy boils down to cheap jokes and the tragedy never makes itself felt for the sheer inadequacy of expression. That the flashiness and the shallowness is essentially the author's and not the narrator's idiom could be shown by a comparison with his other books. Weaknesses of this kind abound in *The Wig* from the opening with its excessive use of evocative compounds ("waferthin stomach", "butterscotch-colored dreams", etc.) to the final scene spoiled by its trite castration symbolism and its uninventive presentation in terms of a dystopian climax. Awkward imagery and sloppy language come in all varieties: the overworked significant detail ("I keep a dozen milk bottles filled with lice so I won't be lonely," 64 f.); inflated Pop style at its worst ("her Texas-cowboy sadist's boots morse-coded a lament," 14); the pseudocryptic impromptu ("extrasensory and paranoic ice-cream bars," 57); mangled imagery ("you wanted to take the mood home and sleep with it," 28); plain silly hyperbole ("ice-cube-sized window," 7); and thoughtless labeling ("Fascisti silk fans," 57). There is a half-hearted attempt at imitating Joyce when the atmosphere at Paradise Records is suggested in musical metaphors (61 f.) or the more frequent, if equally derivative, association of blacks with athletic imagery to suggest a common mechanism of stereotyping – like similar devices these do not amount to much.

The third part of the novel is set on April Fool's Day and indeed the whole book has something of a series of practical jokes

7. A. Robert Lee, "Making New: Styles of Innovation in the Contemporary Black American Novel," in *Black Fiction: New Studies in the Afro-American Novel Since 1945*, ed. A. Robert Lee (London: Vision Press, 1980), pp. 222-250, emphasizes Wright's dreamlike "accelerated" style prompted by the urban environment (239 ff.).

with everybody trying to fool everybody else. It contains a lot of slapstick situation comedy in a structure resembling that of vaudeville acts. It also employs the more strictly literary methods of satirical inversion, exaggerating or diminishing distortion, ironical juxtaposition and word-play. Since the hero is essentially a satirical *persona* – gullible, contradictory, and vacillating – who attempts to fool his way into the Great Society in one impersonation after another and rebounds from each rebuff the episodic structure lends itself to a pattern of parallelisms. Keywords and catchphrases recur and bring their connotations into play, especially the main theme of the "Wig" in its manifold contexts and the associated leitmotif of "making it," or they assume an ambiguous undertone as in the use of "slave" and "progress:" Lester, originally willing to "work like a slave" in order to overcome the obstacles on "the road to progress" (3, 12), maneuvres himself in his repeated autosuggestion into his final enslavement and regress. There are also the complementary motifs of (re)birth and death, crucial in Lester's hope for a new lease on life that is thwarted by the various forms of death toward the end of the book, and the concomitant rise-and-fall pattern, which is demonstrated with some consistency and a diversity ranging from slapstick instances to a macabre symbolism: Nonnie collapses in the hall (8), queen Sandra topples from the sofa (19), the civil servant drops dead in the street (39), Jimmy Wishbone is a fallen star; and Lester himself, getting high on pot and playing haughty roles, proves himself a flop (Paradise Records), is knocked down (Tom), turned down (The Deb), and finally, as it were, cut down to size (Fishback). Since the book is conceived as a "mirror image" one can see in these motif patterns a method of narrative and linguistic reflection, yet again, the parallels are often obtrusive and the overall structure is largely repetitive.

Wright's division of the book into three parts seems equally superficial although it gains some importance from the mottos attached. Part I is prefixed by a quotation from *Ulysses*: "Every phenomenon has its natural cause," a statement significantly picked out of the phantasmagoric Circe episode and implying the context of Bloom's first encounter with the 'madam' of nighttown whose fan ensures his subservience while he attributes his present predicament to the fact that he parted with his talisman. The motto, thus, introduces the novel's cause-and-effect pattern and the trauma of slavery. More immediately, it signals Lester's departure as he resorts to the magic hood of his Wig and tries to free himself from racial history's nightmare conjured up in a cluster of memories toward the end of the first part. Among these, the recollection of an obscene New York happening which led to the murder of a black youth absurdly foreshadows Lester's own fate (40 f.). Part III has an equally ironic motto quoting a phrase from the ambivalent ending of *The Great Gatsby* where Nick Carraway's outlook suggests a pursuit of one's dream against the currents carrying one back in the vague expectation: "And one fine morning —." This hope against hope, which makes the pursuer run faster and faster, is a recurring reference in Wright's books and receives in the ending of *The Wig* its most pessimistic interpretation. Another quotation of similar significance from another of Wright's favorite authors occurs toward the end of the central, ninth chapter. When Lester is startled by the runaway slave and tries to make his escape, he suddenly finds himself in front of a plaque commemorating Nathaniel West with a quotation from *Miss Lonelyhearts*: "Life is worthwhile for it is full of dreams and peace, gentleness and ecstasy, and faith that burns like a clear white flame on a grim dark altar" (81). It is a consoling wisdom belied by the development of both West's hero and Wright's, two unmasked impersonators. A closer parallel even suggests itself between Lester and Lemuel Pitkin in *A Cool Million* as both heroes are naive young men who try to make it in the surreal metropolis and suffer a brutal dismantlement. The integration of these references seems to set Wright firmly in the modern tradition but the models referred to also reveal the wide gap in artistic achievement.[8]

He may be on safer ground with the oral tradition of black America. The largest section of the book, Part II, takes as its motto a line from "How Long Blues," a classic in its own genre: "If I could holler like a mountain jack ... ." For one thing, the implied context of the song, expressing the lament for lost love in the code

8. See James Joyce, *Ulysses* (1922; rpt. New York: Random House, 1961) p. 529; F. Scott Fitzgerald, *The Great Gatsby* (1925; rpt. New York: Scribner's, 1953), p. 182 ("Tomorrow we will run faster," from the same passage, turns up in *The Messenger* (1963; rpt. New York: Manor Books, 1974), p. 209, and *Absolutely Nothing to Get Alarmed About* (New York: Farrar, Straus & Giroux, 1973), p. 191); *The Complete Works of Nathaniel West* (New York: Farrar, Straus & Cudahy, 1957), p. 66.

of black folklore, sets the tone for the increasingly blue mood in this section which leads up to the visit with Madam X, a kind of voodoo priestess treating the love habit.[9] If one can generalize from here, Wright's style seems most promising where he tries to combine the traditions of black folklore and literature within the modes of fantasy and comedy. There is a considerable thematic and technical range reflecting such a background. In particular, he draws on the rich resources of indigenous humor: the street culture ingenuity of the shoeshine boys' tricks of the trade (132 f.); the rapping rituals of swaggering and insult (32 f., 56 f.); the ridiculed stereotype of food tastes in Lester's sudden dislike for watermelon (6) and his later change into a walking reminder of the inordinate love for chicken; the standard joke about the black passenger and the white taxi driver; and, above all, the many varieties of disguise and roleplaying in Tomming it, including the recourse to cosmetic and magical panaceas. The remarkable capability of black America to create laughter out of a depressing situation goes back to the early days of slavery and has proved psychologically the most effective mechanism by exposing the paradoxes of a racist society and releasing the pent-up aggression toward it. The humor of absurdity undermining racism by playing up to it usually involves some form of inversion and often employs the rhetoric of exaggeration. Wright obviously stands in this tradition and may even remind one of the once popular form of the animal trickster tale since the Chicken Man episode has something of the fable about the trickster getting himself entrapped.[10]

In the more literary tradition of the black novel Wright takes up where the Harlem Renaissance satirists left off with such assimilationist fantasies as George Schuyler's *Black No More* (1931).[11] The difference lies, among other things, in the fact that Wright's

9. Leroy Carr's "How Long Blues" as sung by Joe Williams in the Jimmy Rushing/Count Basie version laments the situation of the stood up lover and the passage in question reads: "I could holler like a mountain jack / way upon the mountain and call my baby back / how long ..." (Quoted from taped recording made available by Wolfgang Karrer).

10. On the folklore of "Black Laughter" see Lawrence W. Levine, *Black Culture and Black Consciousness: Afro American Folk Thought from Slavery to Freedom* (1977; rpt. New York: Oxford Univ. Press, 1978), chapter 5; on the animal trickster tale, pp. 102 ff.

11. On the Harlem School satirists see Robert A. Bone, *The Negro Novel in America*, rev. ed. (New Haven: Yale Univ. Press, 1965), pp. 89 ff.

fantasy develops out of a realism pushed to its limits and tipping over into hallucination and farce, a process which can be traced back to the atmospheric touches in *The Messenger*, an otherwise blatantly realistic — and largely autobiographical — novel in the tradition of Richard Wright. It is directly related to the fantasy element in the all too real city which constantly catches up with one's wildest imagination.[12] *The Wig* takes its essential material from the physical, psychological and social realities of the dark ghetto and, in a way, blows them up into grotesque fantasy. Perhaps the most interesting example in this respect is the episode of the rat fight recalling the opening scene of *Native Son* (1940), a *locus classicus* of black realism turned into a mock-heroic feat: it keeps in view the ghetto reality and ironizes the scope it allows for black heroism. The episode also clearly indicates Wright's departure from the traditional protest literature, his revival of the black folklore tradition and his alignment with the parodist-fantasists among such modern classics as Joyce and West. Whether the rat episode deserves a whole chapter is another question and shows once more a lack of artistic economy.

The novel sets off with some of the stock features of environmental realism, such as the tenement microcosm, and displays a considerable variety of fantasy elements — day-dreaming, roleplaying, drug hallucination, nightmarish allegory. It ridicules the latest version of the old American Dream bringing in some of the oldest stereotypes of American literature, the conman and Uncle Tom, presenting, as it were, a black Horatio Alger in whiteface. If this seems to be a new attempt to make black laughter serve its old regulative purpose, it is undercut by the author's scathing pessimism which aims at a more radical response in the reader. The accomplishment of his purpose is, however, limited by the inadequacy of the style. As an author who made his name in a transitional period of postwar (black) American literature he is symptomatic in the recapitulating and anticipating aspects of his work, but never comes near a major achievement. His fantasy will appear rather coarse compared with Ellison's subtle symbolism and rather uninventive compared with Ishmael Reed's verbal dexterity.[13] He wrote, of

12. See O'Brien, pp. 245, 252.
13. In all fairness it should be added that Wright has received generous praise from some writers and critics sharing his predilection for fantasy: Ish-

course, at a time when many writers felt that writing in balanced fictional structures had become obsolete and when the new writing of the various American movements were still in their experimental stage. Asked about his literary approach, he has pointed to the interpenetration, and even interchangeability, of realism and fantasy and the thin line between fiction and journalism.[14] This associates him with the contemporary neo-realism and New Journalism as well as the emerging fantasists. Such an open approach must have proved too much for his limited capabilities. He may also have been constrained by the fact that the public was not quite ready yet for the special blend of "black black humor."

BIOGRAPHY

Charles Stevenson Wright was born in New Franklin, Mo., 4 June 1932. He attended public schools in New Franklin and Sedalia, Mo., and was a parttime student at Lowney Handy Writers Colony in Marshall, Ill. From 1952 to 1954 he served in the Army in Korea. He went to New York doing odd jobs and working as a free-lance writer, later supporting himself as columnist ("Wright's World") for the *Village Voice*, 1967-1973. In 1972 he made his 'escape' from New York to Veracruz, Mexico, where he stayed for an unspecified period.

BIBLIOGRAPHY

Books by Wright:
The Messenger (New York: Farrar, Straus & Giroux, 1963).
The Wig (New York: Farrar, Straus & Giroux, 1966).
Absolutely Nothing to Get Alarmed About (New York: Farrar, Straus & Giroux, 1973). A comprehensive primary and secondary bibliography including Wright's uncollected short stories and the criticism on Wright up to 1976 is provided by:
Carol Fairbanks and Eugene A. Engeldinger, *Black American Fiction: A Bibliography* (Metuchen, N.J.: The Scarecrow Press, 1978), pp. 300-301.

mael Reed, *19 Necromancers from Now* (Garden City, N.Y.: Doubleday, 1970), p. 329; Jerome Klinkowitz, "The New Black Writer and the Old Black Art," *Fiction International*, 1 (1973), 123-127; Clarence Major, "Traditional and Presence," *American Poetry Review*, 5 (May/June 1976), 33-34.
    14. See O'Brien, pp. 250 f., 256 f.

A more recent article containing a discussion of Wright is:

A. Robert Lee, "Making New: Styles of Innovation in the Contemporary Black American Novel, in *Black Fiction: New Studies in the Afro-American Novel Since 1945,* ed. A. Robert Lee (London: Vision Press, 1980), pp. 222-250.

MICHEL FABRE

POSTMODERNIST RHETORIC IN ISHMAEL REED'S
YELLOW BACK RADIO BROKE DOWN (1969)

Whereas the fantasy of Ishmael Reed's first novel, *The Freelance Pallbearers* (1967) was carried along, rather than structured, by the sprawling form of the *Bildungsroman*, the framework of *Yellow Back Radio Broke Down* (1969), his second novel, is a multi-dimensional Western, re-enacting the ancient struggle of conflicting world views. Here, Reed strikes at the heart of American history's most mythical dimension — the winning of a continent. Frontier life and the conquest of the open lands, wagon trains, powerful owners and boisterous cowboys, cattle migrating along the Chrisholm Trail, shotgun towns complete with outlaws and their saloon and main street battling places — all are described colorfully. The expected clichés accompany the myth of Eldorado and the Rocky Candy Mountains (the seven cities of Cibola), while ghost towns evoke encounters between legendary heroes like Billy the Kid or Kit Carson. He casts as villains not only land capitalist Drag Gibson and his gang of thugs and cowpokes but also all the powers that be, whether state or federal, religious or military. He sets up as hero a black super cowboy, Loop Garoo Kid, who can wield curses as efficiently as he can the bullwhip, being an inventive Voodoo *houngan* as well as a somewhat apocryphal twin of Christ. Loop busies himself avenging a group of circus performers and "flower power" children who have been butchered by the villains on their way to the techno-anarchical paradise of Cibola. Chief Showcase, the good redskin, comes to the rescue of the hero who is also seconded by the eternal feminine, diversely embodied by voodoo priestess Marie Laveau alias Zozo Labrique, by Haitian *loa* Erzulie/Yemaja, or by the Virgin Mary alias Black Diane. The bad guys are legion: a couple of Negro Judases with Greek names; outlaw and killer John Wesley Hardin, summoned for the occasion;

Bo Shmo, chief of the neo-realist gang; masochist Reverend Boyd; several doubledealing prostitutes and a dozen disreputable historical characters handed down to posterity as Founding Fathers or brave explorers by primary school textbooks; not to mention Royal Flush Gooseman, the unscrupulous fur trapper, and Mighty Dyke, the bulldyker octoroon. Since none of them prove able to beat Loop, Pope Innocent himself is sent for to help Drag restore law and order, but he only manages to compromise with the black cowboy for whom God the Father has a strong liking and the Blessed Mary a definite crush.

The myriad episodes in this comic strip struggle are truly hilarious, but they also function quite logically according to the genre of the Western, with its set antagonistic parties and its stereotypical roles, out of which Loop's creative spiritual technology — namely hoodoo — emerges triumphantly.

The widening of the space and time categories in *Yellow Back Radio*, which greatly expands the scope of the plot as cosmic drama, closely corresponds to the development of the part played by voodoo. In the first novel, Booka Doopeyduck had been turned into a werewolf through the spells cast by his wife's grandmother while Lenore, convicted of witchcraft by the court, was a reincarnation of beneficent occult powers. In the second novel, Loop Garoo (i.e., werewolf, from the French *loup garou*) is endowed with superhuman stature because he is a *houngan*, while New Orleans voodoo priestess Marie (whichever alias she may assume) also plays a major part.

Although the links between the parodic strategies of *The Freelance Pallbearers* and *Yellow Back Radio* are patent, the second novel represents a significant departure from Reed's *Bildungsroman* whose anti-hero failed to debunk an obscene, Nixon-like potentate. *Yellow Back Radio* ranges over at least three telescoping centuries and the whole of the North American scene, even drawing upon ancient European and African religions in order to portray this "local" conflict as the mere avatar of long-standing cultural warfare.

As for power, here defined as the power of private property dictating governmental and papal policies, it remains akin to the dictatorship of Harry Sam, whom Drag embodies in new ways. Like Sam, Drag is characterized by lust, violence, greed and treachery; like Sam, he is surrounded by a team of ruthless, sycophantic and uncivilized ruffians. Sam was literally a heap of constipated "shit"; in spite of his deodorant, Drag also stinks, if only of formal de- hyde, offending even his own cowpokes' noses. Like Sam, he is a hopeless homosexual who marries only in the hope of bequeathing his noxious genes to his scions. Although he is introduced at first as a "ladykiller" and brags about his sexual appetites, he is only a murderer of women: like Bluebeard, he has done away with six wives and will dispose of the seventh in the course of the novel. His sexual games remain largely verbal, or oral: he is mostly seen French-kissing his green horse (which the mares avoid, thinking that "since green he was a queer horse" (p. 19)), or reading the life story of Catherine the Great on a velvet sofa in his negligee, or else "sticking a pudgy hand in the pocket of his monogramed silkrobe" (p.44), when not spreading mascara on his eyelashes to pose as a Mexican dancer. He explains that "Drag is not only the name for the horseman who rides to the rear of the cattle but ... also the shorthand for something scaly, slimy and huge with dirt" (p. 47). Since Gibson etymologically means the offspring of a gelded cat, the man is a contradiction in terms.

It is significant that two other embodiments of power in the novel, military chief Theda Doompussy Blackwell and politician Pete the Peke, should also be notorious "fairies." Aristocratic The- da, as his name suggests, finds satisfaction in the hands of his black masseur in a late eighteenth century club which strongly evokes a male harem. The fact that he is a white field marshall implies no small criticism of American army brass and of the so-called master race. As a result, power and abnormal sexuality are pictured as e- quivalent in obscenity. It is significant, not only of the literary genre chosen but also of Reed's own aims and prepossessions, that sexuality and culture should be so tightly linked. Three main stere- otypes are thus defined and exploited: the female, the homosexual and the supermale. Next to the prostitutes and Hurdy Gurdy girls in Big Lizzie's Rabid Cougar Saloon, Drag's bride, Mustache Sal, is an interesting representative of the liberated woman who selects her partners and uses them for her own enjoyment and profit. The homosexual ranchman allows her to indulge in frenzied nympho- mania with his employees and guests, but contemporary society begrudges her orgastic gratification, especially when she breaks racial taboos by trying Chief Showcase's "little-man-in-the-canoe" erotic technique.

169

Such triumphant, if overriding, female sexuality contributes to Reed's definition of a heroic protagonist, even though, later in the novel, the cult of the female initiated by the Blessed Mary is satirized as a Women's Lib fad. In contradistinction, as we have seen, the villains are pictured as "fairies." To the ridiculous figure of the white pseudo-male, Reeds contrasts that of the somewhat stereotyped phallic man of color, under the dual guise of the Black and the Red.

Although he appears first as a dandy and a bizarre "paraphysical" neo-surrealist, Chief Showcase (Cochise) soon develops into a fundamental embodiment of a positive cultural essence. Through allusion to Sitting Bull and nineteenth century battles, Reed starts with the traditional, derisive image of the Indian massacred in the name of religion and dispossessed for economic purposes: children dress as Indians, cowboys exhibit their scalps, tourists weep over a bygone past, the head of an Indian appears on the nickel, and his artifacts are embalmed in the Smithsonian Institute or the Metropolitan Museum. From genocide to ethnocide, Indian culture barely survives on reservations, exemplified by Showcase's teepee. Himself a "showcase" for the bland display of picturesque ethnicity, the New Indian is doomed to read militant poetry for the entertainment of people whose forebears were responsible for the massacre of his ancestors. Thus, Showcase performs as a buffoon to Drag and his henchmen. However, he soon appears to be outwitting his more powerful adversary: Showcase's flattery is steeped in irony, when he emphasizes white honesty concerning Indian treaties, for instance. Showcase thus performs as the mythological trickster through his use of double entendre. He dissembles and plays several parts, employing language as a tool against white power. His elegant Beau Brummel accoutrement is contrasted with the raggedy appearance of his white "superiors." The Indian is also cast as the superior technologist, the inventor of a flying craft which the white man has appropriated, a wielder of words whose phrases survive in American usage. He is an embodiment of the Promethean spirit and also of Apollinian forces, a harmonious blend of mind and body, superior even to the black superlover.

Loop is something of a braggart, yet the passion which the Virgin Mary feels for him and his irresistible attraction for Sal are evident proofs of his abilities as a lover. It is even doubtful that Reed is deriding the myth of the black supermale, among other, when he makes Showcase the outright winner in the field of dalliance, since he never divorces manliness from manhood or even machismo. Although male chauvinism triumphs, it appears that the novel mostly advocates naturally free and uninhibited sex, which admits of license but not of deviation from "healthy" heterosexuality.

However, Loop is less a sexual superman than a spiritual high priest, and it is significant that he should resort to a black mass instead of a shootout in the streets of Yellow Back Radio or Video Junction in order to achieve his ends as an avenger. Thanks to magic spells and the supernatural help of the African python-god, Loop triumphs over the hydralike embodiments of white greed and racism. This role of the hero a *houngan* is remarkable in two ways: first, it establishes voodoo as a viable countertradition to the officially recognized beliefs of the Judeo-Christian faith; second, it defines the artist as a maker of spells ("ouangas" or "wangols"). This is reiterated in the lines of Reed's poem "catechism":

D YR ART D WAY U WANT
ANY WAY YOU WANT
ANY WANGOL U WANT

and in his definition of the Afro-American artist as "a conjurer who works Juju upon his oppressors; a witch doctor who frees his fellow victims from the psychic attack launched by demons."[1]

Critics have occasionally found that the Pope's long lectures about Christianity and voodoo were a disservice to the book, turning it into a book about noodoo instead of a hoodoo novel.[2] It is true that they slow down the narrative considerably, but they perform the important function of helping the average American reader to acquaint himself not only with voodoo as a syncretic religion but also with the cultural/ideological warfare which has been waged for centuries in the name of religion. Above all, they allow Reed to bring together Christianity and voodoo in a larger spiritual framework in which Innocent and Loop are not only intimates,

1. "Introduction," *19 Necromancers from Now*, New York: Doubleday, 1970, p. xvii.
2. See, for instance, Neil Schmitz in "Neo-Hoodoo: The Experimental Fiction of Ishmael Reed," *Twentieth Century Literature*, 20 (April 1974), 135.

rivals and friends but also equivalents: the leader of the Catholic Church supports the institutions ensuring white supremacy while his black counterpart undermines them. In that respect, one of Loop's accusations is illuminating: "You and your crowd are the devils. The way you massacred the Gnostics, not to mention the Bogomils, Albigenses and Waldenses!" On the contrary, the principle he represents has "always been harmless" and such popular rituals as Christmas were destined to make him appear "foolish, the scapegoat of all history" (p. 165).

More interesting than Loop's claim that he is a twin brother of Jesus or that Mary (or Black Diane) fell in love with him the day after Jesus was crucified and is eager to make up their quarrel is the reinsertion of the Judeo-Christian tradition into the wider context of earth goddess cults, depicting Christianity as an outgrowth, or pseudo-rationalization, of authentic primeval faiths. This was to be more elaborately developed by Reed in *Mumbo Jumbo* (1972), a novel in which the white Cartesian tradition of the Atonists is challenged by Egyptian lore of the partisans of Osiris, Dionysian champions of "soul," physical exhilaration, vitality and creative impulses.

For the traditional opposition of races, an opposition of cultures is substituted, the sophisticated civilization of the Reds and the vital force of the Blacks being vindicated against the violent acquisitiveness of the Whites. The three major protagonists, Chief Showcase (the red Indian), Drag Gibson (the white lord of the land) and Loop Garoo Kid (the black cowboy), and the lesser characters who side with each of them, all can be analyzed as embodiments of opposed or complementary principles in this "chrestomachy" which, as the narrative develops, can be read as a triumph of "soul" (black) over materialism (white) which had overpowered the spirit (red). Thus, when Pope Innocent defines voodoo as "an American version of the Ju-Ju religion that originated in Africa — you know, that strange continent which serves as the subconscious of our planet — where we've found the earliest remains of man" (p. 152), not only does he imply the anteriority of the African "soul" principle but also its deeper roots in man's original being.

Loop's own brand of voodoo is defined as a "syncretistic American version" with potentially revolutionary undertones, hence the danger he represents for the supporters of Western culture. What is more, the neo-hoodoo artist (whom Reed portrayed at a greater

172

length as a "necromancer" in his introduction to the anthology, *19 Necromancer from Now* (1970)) is said to be:

> scatting arbitrarily, using forms of this and adding his own. He's blowing like that celebrated musician Charles Yardbird Parker — improvising as he goes along. He's throwing clusters of demon chords at you and you don't know the changes. (p. 154)

The artist, here the black American novelist-cum-wizard, innovates only within the ancient but vital cultural tradition of voodoo, projected as a liberating consciousness which whites find hard to share. The structuring of the novel, both on the spatial/temporal and the metaphysical levels (a kind of "before and beyond" which explains and inspires Loop's behavior), represents a major innovation from *The Freelance Pallbearers* which was only a satire on Nowhere, i.e. Now/here, the American *hic et nunc*. *Yellow Back Radio* is to be decoded simultaneously on several wavelengths which range from B.C. to the present and pertain to a variety of modes, from carnival to morality play. This qualitative jump reflects a definite improvement which could be illustrated by a comparable development in textual and linguistic achievement. In the first novel, for instance, Bukka says of Sam's mother, "Dead as a doornail, she died, mean and hard" (p. 1) — the idiom being made only slightly more striking through alliteration. In the second novel, a cowboy exclaims, "Bingo, poof, and my man is in doornail country." We could say that the same qualitative gap exists between the two novels as that between the metaphoric connotations of "doornail country" and the cliché "dead as a doornail."

Reed has said in an interview that he was extremely aware of form when he wrote *Yellow Back Radio*, and that he tended to consider the Western genre as an example of fiction legitimately getting the better of reality:

> Yellow Back writers were really dudes from the East like me. The cowboys would read their books and begin to ape the exaggerations of themselves they read. A case of life imitating art.[3]

These "Yellow Backs" were popular Western novels, a genre which confers some stature to John Wesley Hardin, the killer hired by Gibson — "the famous gunslinger I've read in da lurid yellow kivered books" (p. 128). Another reference to "Yellow Back" could be

3. "Ishmael Reed: A Self Interview," *Black World*, June 1974, p. 25.

found on the shelves of Drag's library: "The shelves were full of yellow kivered books and volumes on the life of the benevolent despotess Catherine the Great" (p. 114). The "Radio" element in the title and in the name of the city of Yellow Back Radio, which is located about fifty miles from Video Junction, is surprising; although this reference to the mass media seems satisfying, as Loop Garoo's magic could be understood to account for the breakdown in the station. In the interview quoted above Reed brings all these elements together in his explanation of the title's meaning:

> The title ... was based upon a poem by Lorenzo Thomas called "Modern Plumbing Illustrated" ... I based the book on old radio scripts in which the listener constructed the sets with his imagination; that's why "radio"; also because it's an oral book, a talking book ... There's more dialogue than scenery or description. "Yellow back" because that's what they used to call Old West books about cowboy heroes, they were "yellow covered books and were usually lurid and sensation," so the lurid scenes are in the book because that is what the form calls for. They're not in there to shock. "Broke-down" is a take off on Lorenzo Thomas's "Illustrated." When people say "Break it down," they mean to strip something down to its basic components. So *Yellow Back Radio Broke Down* is the dismantling of a genre done in an oral way like radio.[4]

This last remark points to the novelty of Reed's attempt in his second novel. Fiction, stripped of its defenses, with its back to the wall, is thus dismantled, reduced from a complex whole to the sum total of its discrete elements. In *The Freelance Pallbearers* Reed's narrative was essentially exuberant, full of proliferations and excrescences, or whirling upon linguistic merry-go-rounds whose spirals were hard to arrest. Here, Reed himself undertakes to break things down, to slow the narrative movement in order to designate its processes and to catalogue the elements and conventions of which he makes use not without derision. From paranoid, Reed's style becomes schizoid in the disjunctive mode of Nathanael West whom he admires. *Yellow Back Radio* thus owes much to comic strips, not only because each sequence can work forward and backward in time and space but also because even the typographical arrangement juxtaposes description and dialogue in blocks (units might be a better term) separated by wide blanks. *Yellow Back Radio* is visually characterized by its discontinuity,

4. *Ibidem*.

the basic elements being rather long sentences, remarkable for their lack of relief. Similarly, each character speaks his (or her) lines, then is silent, seldom angry or excited enough to shout in capitals. Each narrative block seems to repudiate narration in order to become a set of stage directions rather than a description. In brief, the novel assumes the function of a film script.

Stripped down to such minimalness, fiction is offered almost defenseless to the reader's manipulating appetites. He can slow down or speed up its course, which implies an increased participation on his part. This is a characteristic of what Reed calls "an oral book, a talking book. People say they read it aloud: that is, it speaks through them, which makes it a *loa*."[5] For Reed, the spirit which moves the participant in a voodoo ceremony is synonymous with inspiration, and he speaks of his works as being dictated to him by the *loas*. Here, voice alone can animate what would otherwise remain a flat comic strip. The narrator's status is affected by this; at the opening, he is an omniscient author/raconteur:

> Folks. This here is the story of the Loop Garoo Kid. A cowboy so bad he made a working posse of spells phone in sick. A bullwhacker so unfeeling he left the print of winged mice on the hides of crawling women. A desperado so ornery he made the Pope cry and the most powerful of cattlemen shed his head to the Executioner' swine. (p. 1)

We thus launch right into a "tall tale" with its unbelievable hyperboles. The first stage in a rhetorical strategy aimed at creating the mythical character of Loop also presents a rather accurate summary of the plot; it is programmatic and invites the reader to leave things in the narrator's hands, or rather in his mouth. When read aloud, the narrative is sustained and given credibility by the narrator/reader, whose audience is much wider than the part of himself which listens to him reading. The reader thus becomes actor/narrator while remaining necessarily part of the audience.

As an accomplice vindicating the "tall tale" and a "do-it-yourself" maker of fiction from the separate parts of the "broke-down" fictional kit, the reader refers to the directions for use provided by the author and adopts the latter's perspectives concerning genre and form, even when disagreeing with his ideological outlook. In *Yellow Back Radio* more than in any other novel Reed alludes to

5. *Ibidem*, p. 24.

texts and books, developing a network of intertextuality in order to confront his aesthetics with conflicting stance and to clearly differentiate himself from other schools. All of this takes place within the very genre of the comic strip Western which sets up character, background and scene according to their appropriate canonic function and status.

First of all, Reed aims at repudiating the sort of mimetic fiction which has been revered by "the great tradition"; this is expressed by the cultural revolution of the Flower Power children who have driven the adults out of town:

> For three hours a day we went to school to hear teachers praise the old. Made us learn facts by rote. Lies really bent upon making us behave. *We decided to create our own fiction.* (p. 10; emphasis mine)

As the circus for whom Loop is employed arrives, what assuages the children's suspicion (together with the travellers' costumes) is Jack the Barker's allusion to the Seven Cities of Gibola, which significantly symbolize, not an Eldorado of wealth, but a "magnificent legendary American paradise where ... man could be free to dream" (p. 24). When the surviving children participate in the "jigsaw of a last minute rescue" in the final chapter (here fiction is explicitly called a "puzzle," i.e. a playful putting together of irregular, imbricating parts), they have actually discovered Cibola and it is, as could be expected, "a really garish super schmaltzy super technological anarcho-paradise" (p. 170), which smacks of Marcusian utopia. Moreover, at the last moment, the children leave Loop alone on stage, forsaking the "broke-down" to turn to a different performance, this time an audio-visual one: "Let's go, the late late show is about to begin on the boob toob and we can watch eating Pooped Out Soggies" (p. 173).

In his vignette-like advertisement for the circus, Jack comments:

> Stupid historians who are hired by cattlemen to promote reason, law and order — toad men who adore facts -- say that such an anarchotechnological paradise ... is as real as a green horse's nightmare. Shucks, I've always been a fool, eros appeals to me more than logos. I'm just silly enough to strike out for it tomorrow ... (p. 25)

As should be expected, the narrative will apply itself to realizing the prophecy thus evoked. Jake is, in fact, the mouthpiece of Loop, who represents the Artist (he later defines himself as "the

176

comic jester"), and Reed himself is his twin, born, like Jake, in Tennessee.

In Chapter Two, the writer is defined *a contrario*, in a dazzling exchange between Loop and Bo Shmo. The latter, whose only talent was playing Hoagland Howard Carmichael's "Buttermilk" backwards in the 1930's, has acquired the reputation of being a charismatic leader among fellow citizens who yearn to be duped. He is at the head of the socio-realist gang and declares, "All art must be for the end of liberating the masses. A landscape is good only when it sees the oppressor hanging from a tree" (p. 37). This pronouncement of the "part time autocrat monarchist and guru" does not apply exclusively to a CP commissar, but satirizes whoever would dictate what the writer ought to write, including black nationalist critics.[6] In fact, Bo's literary specialty is "those suffering books I wrote about my old neighborhood and how hard it was." Ideological rivalry as well as fear of economic competition lead Bo's men to hasten the death which awaits Loop in the desert:

> If he makes it across the desert he might land a typewriter and do a book on his trials. He'll corner the misery market and pound out one of those Christian confessionals to which we are so much endeared. (p. 26)

Lacking originality, as might be expected, the socio-realists thus bury Loop up to his neck in the sand and smear his face with jam.

The criticism leveled at Loop by Bo interestingly recalls that heaped on Reed's first fictional attempt by a number of American critics: Loop is "an alienated individualist," making "deliberate attempts at being obscure," a "buffoon, an outsider and frequentor of sideshows." Bo ends up calling him:

> Crazy dada nigger, that's what you are. You are given to fantasy and are off in matters of detail. Far out esoteric bullshit is where you're at. In those suffering books that I write ... every gundrop machine is in place while your work is a blur and a doodle. I bet you can't create the difference between a German and a Redskin. (pp. 35-36)

---

6. One may wonder whether this plea does not reflect, culturally speaking, a return to traditional stances, such as art vs. commitment. Reed's position, however, has to be judged globally and his activities in the publishing field provide enough evidence of his effort to serve the needs of cultural minorities by providing alternate outlets to the monopoly of New York publishing houses.

One can note in passing the allusion to Amiri Baraka's "black dada nihilismus," with which Reed did side, and the definition of his own fiction as "a blur and a doodle," but one should emphasize Loop's statement of his novelistic aims: "What if I write circusses. No one says a novel has to be one thing. It can be anything it wants to be, a vaudeville show, the six o'clock news, the mumblings of wild men saddled by demons" (p. 36). All those are fair descriptions of Reed's fiction, and the novel's declaration of independence vis-à-vis its author is even more striking: the novel is said to become anything *it* wants to (not anything its author wants it to), as if it were gifted with a sort of autonomy.This is a distinctly post-modernistic position.

Endowed as it is with the power of generating itself, and with its tendency to give precedence to comedy and dreams, it is logical that such fiction should take off on the least suggestion or challenge from pseudo-realism. A fine example of this is to be found in Chapter Three, entitled "Loop Garoo Comes Back Mad." Pages 59 -65 are devoted to Loop's elaborate do-it-yourself voodoo ceremony aimed at providing the Avenger with a panoply of spells to be unleashed against the villains. The following episode begins, as could be expected, with a violent outbreak against the cattlemen:

> The Germans attacked the next day. There had always been skirmishes to the north between these dauntless, hearty warriors and the cattlemen who taxed them heavily, rode off with their women, rustled their cattle, stole their best grazing areas and burned their corn.
> A warrior blew a signal from the top of Blackfoot Mountain. (p. 66)

Caught up in a whirlwind of battle axes, naked bodies and horned helmets, the reader, as accustomed as he is to repeated skirmishes against Red Indians and to Reed's frequent puns and surface games, first believes that there is an error in the text, if he has not actually misread "Indian" for "German." Yet, "German" is repeated, and one realizes that Germans and Indians have the same battle tactics. Is Reed confused? Certainly not. Only then does the attentive reader remember that, on page 36, Bo Shmo had told Loop, "I bet you can't create the difference between a German and a Redskin ..." At that time, the phrase was supposed a gratuitous insult, yet it acted as a challenge which the fiction has later taken up. Although the present passage seems to vindicate Bo Shmo's accusation, subtle differences in detail do appear (between

178

horned helmets and feather headgear, or tomahawks and battle-axes, for instance); even if, referentially, there is indeed little difference between "Germans" and "Redskins" as far as warfare is concerned.

The fictional challenge becomes compounded as violence increases and one fears that all the villains, Drag included, will be slain, bringing the novel to a premature end. Indeed, the battle scene (which is printed in italics) stops abruptly by being defined as a story within the story, the significance of which appears to lie less in the tale itself than in its telling:

The warriors obediently walked over to the horse's stall and were about to chop off its head when it awoke — wringing wet and snorting from the effects of its recurrent nightmare. (p. 68)

The episode now defines itself as a dream; fiction thus explicitly appears to be the narration of tales, which repudiates the claim for its truth or verisimilitude made by socio- or neo-realism. This fictional episode clearly picks up the gauntlet thrown by Bo Shmo but it also disproves the contention of the "rationalists and law givers" who, earlier in the book, asserted that the anarcho-technological paradise Cibola was "no more real than a green horse's nightmare" (p. 25). From a current metaphor, here taken literally, a fictional episode has sprung whole. One could even say that Drag Gibson's green horse has a nightmare in the novel *because* a linguistic expression had challenged the possibility of such an occurrence. Likewise, the German (and not the Indian) raid on Drag's farm occurs because Bo Shmo, some forty pages earlier, had accused Loop in an aesthetic exchange of being unable to create the difference between the two. At the same time, the reality of fiction as such (not as a reflection, or mimesis, of any referential world) is vindicated, since there does indeed exist little discernible difference between the two groups in the attack episode and since the attack itself has just as much reality as the ugly dream of a fictional green horse, although this nightmare has been motivated in the plot by Loop's casting spells upon the ranch.

In this perspective, the reader must always be ready to consider that any potentiality enunciated in the narrative, be it on a trite linguistic or purely metaphoric level, can be realized later in the novel. For instance, when we hear that Drag Gibson keeps Chief Showcase around "in case the Pope wants to visit or something"

(p. 126), this is not just a figure of speech; sure enough, the Pope will actually (and we might say, because of the phrase) pay a visit to Drag. This does not mean that anything can happen: rather, an eventuality evoked by the narrative can only become actualized according to certain rules (even if these are opposed to traditional novelistic processes) which contain the genre of the "broke down."

References to other literary or narrative genres are quite frequent in the book. Probably with the aim of emphasizing less the fictive character of artistic expression than the fact that it should not attempt reflection or mimesis, the narrator comments in the desert episode:

> Loop Garoo had to shoot his hoss... You ever see a horse shot in the movies? So that gives you an idea of the fluke of luck Loop was reeling in on this queer fish of a day. (p. 34)

Each character knows the limits of his role and the rules of the genre, with the result that telescoping narrative codes not only produces comedy but questions the rules which have heretofore prevailed. When left alone, a character acts and thinks according to the requirements of his role or of the given situation according to the genre. Thus Drag ponders upon his marital problems, "alone with his thoughts which is a spooky situation since Drag ... is also shorthand for something scaly, slimy and huge with dirt" (p. 47). He is contemplating getting rid of his wife when she appears:

> It was like a monster flickah drammer — the confrontation. Horrible Hybrid meets Spooky Situation. Horrible Hybrid was dripping wet... In a quivering voice the Various Arrangement of Dead Parts said: What happened Drag dear husband you were supposed to bring me a towel? (p. 49)

Or, upon hearing Showcase's helicopter in the desert, Bo Shmo exclaims: "Gads! the arch-nemesis of villains like me. The Flying Brush Beeve Monster. Let's get out of here" (p. 37). Here, the character (as opposed to the protagonist) remains a prisoner of the definition imposed upon him by fiction and of the part he is cast in: the villain, the monster perform accordingly, just as the Sheriff, the Banker, and the Reverend fulfill their social roles in Yellow Back Radio City. Horrible Hybrid herself, who is a symbol of the "broke down" since she is a "Various Arrangement of Dead Parts," can only literally fall to pieces when she dies. Conversely, the good guys, the positive protagonists, are defined by their capacity for

180

change, for conceiving other shapes and assuming several roles. Crossing the boundaries and limits of genre, Loop finds no difficulty in turning to another narrative type in order to describe his situation: "Not only would he be desert carrion but now something right out of Science Fiction was descending upon him from the heavens, Loop thought" (p. 37). As a consequence, the character/ role tends to be petrified in stereotyped discourse whereas the protagonist /author generates dynamic and eclectic fiction. Drag fears Loop's revenge because it is made inevitable by the literature he is found in: "He'll come after me... You know the revenge motif" (p. 48). Similarly, the Sheriff believes he can escape by taking shelter behind the clichés of the genre — "Now Kid, the Marshall said, what is a Western without tall tales and gaudy romance. Have a drink!" (p. 101) - when Loop arrives, Zoro-like, with whip in hand. Of course, this is not enough to save the Sheriff. As Loop later tells Drag: "No amount of romantic dosage is going to save your neck, dead man, Heroes given to hyperbole — I even chased the Marshall out of town!" (p. 117).

Intelligence versus violence, imagination versus rhetoric, fantasy versus sentimentalism, such is Reed's aesthetic, forcibly outlined by Chief Showcase as he swoops down in his helicopter to rescue Loop from Bo Shmo:

Those mediocre bandits ... Deserts are for visions not for materialists. Read any American narrative about crossing — apparitions, ravens walking about as tall as men, the whole golden phantasmagoria ... I'm a kind of patarealist Indian going around inventing do dads. This machine comes in better than nags and creaky stagecoaches. Stupid shmucks and boobs around here think it's some kind of flying ghost cow... Bo Shmo and the cattlemen are in the same routine. Afraid of anything that can get off the ground, materialists that they are — anything capable of groovy up up and aways strikes terror in their hearts. (p. 38).

Along these lines, the narrative continually opposes conflicting aesthetics. For Showcase, functionalism and fun are more important than harmony and beauty. He reminisces:

the Indian names Toohoolhoolzote, Looking Glass and Man-Afraid-Of-His-Horse which opened up new possibilities of being named after phobias, objects and even words which didn't mean anything but sounded like music... Chief Showcase is a kind of letdown. I assure you it works though. You see I'm Chief Cochise's cousin which makes me Chief Showcase. Yuk, yuk, yuk, yuk. (p. 41)

181

Even between well-intentioned cowboys, the so-called logic of grammatical rules easily leads to joking:

You mean moose, don't you bartender? the Marshal asked.

No Marshal meese. Goose is to geese what moose is to meese. I know we're out in the old frontier but everything can't be in a state of anarchy, I mean how will we communicate?

You got a point there, Skinny added, but we cowpokes make up language as we go along. Compare our names for landscape, towns, industry, with those of tenderfoots back East — Syracuse, Troy, Ithaca... Seem to worship Europe. Why there's a whole school in New York of poets writing like Frenchmen. But when you get out here, except for those names given by injuns and Spaniards, cowpoke genius takes over — Milk River, Hangtown, Poker Flats, Tombstone, Boot Hill. (pp. 53-54)

Similarly, every speechmaker or poet in the book has an original style, perceived differently by others. The tortured lyricism of the masochist Reverend who declares, "Stomp me o lord!!/i am the theoretical mother of all insects!!/ mash my 21 or so body segments!!" (p. 101), is applauded by the cowboys as "poetic allegory." The vengeful lyrics of Chief Showcase hurling maledictions at his people's tyrants in "Wolf Ticket" meet with the approval of a lone hurdy-gurdy girl ("What bitter and tortured Americana. Hey Indjun come over here and loop up my dress" (p. 79)), while an obscure academic, "a Japanese semanticist" out of the curtains, is dissatisfied with the ethnic tendency of the "child of nature" to overuse the word "like." Last but not least, Loop's wild lyricism lends scope to his voodoo invocation which culminates in:

O Black Hawk American Indian houngan of Hoo-Doo please do open up some of these prissy orthodox minds so that they will no longer call Black People's American experience "corrupt" "perverse" and "decadent" ... Teach them that anywhere people go they have experience and that all experience is art. (p. 64)

And the two black traitors, Alcibiades and Jeff, who listen to him are only able to laugh and remark that "with gossip columnists invading our skulls you should not be surprised that we should ridicule anything we can't understand" (p. 65).

There could be no better plea for cultural tolerance.[7] In fact,

7. Most Black Aestheticians either overlooked Reed's writings or else did not know how to deal with them. In *The Way of the New World* (1975), Ad-

an open-minded approach is rare indeed for, to the average character, a stroke of originality is worse than the plague. As soon as he leaves his prescribed role, he loses his head, and he is quick to notice that he is literally out of character. For instance, when Reverend Boyd, having drunk himself to a state of delirium tremens, says "something about a Gila monster who was God," Drag retorts, "Those Protestants, so lazy with allegory." The cowpokes immediately react with, "What did you say, boss? " And Drag is forced to apologize, "Nothing boys, just a blue streak inflaming my mind. It'll go away." (p. 46). A far-fetched aesthetic comparison made by Skinny, the uncultured overseer, brings about a similar self-correction:

This place is really getting eerie... there's a disproportionate amount of shadows in reference to the sun we get — its like a pen and ink drawing by Edward Munch or some of them Expressionist fellows.
Huh?
See, got me talking out of my noodle. (p. 97)

Fiction cannot treat a specific character worse than by putting in his mouth someone else's text, a text he is not supposed to generate according to the rules of realism. When he discovers he can utter such discourse, he has to admit he is mad.

Is the point, then, just to achieve striking effects, clever staging and theatricality, when, for example, John Wesley Hardin, the gunman, finds good excuses to appear too late on stage ("Sorry I missed your cue, Drag, but I was looking for your copy of the good book" (p. 115))? Maybe, but there exists a fundamental difference between traditional forms and Reed's innovations: traditional aesthetics are expressed in the grand show of Crucifixion which, Loop believes, exploited gaudy effects like striking *deus ex machina*, lightning and thunder techniques on Golgotha. When he envisions his capture and possible martyrdom, Loop does not want to "set up his own happening," as Pope Innocent accuses, but to emphasize through parody the emptiness of Christian ritual.

dison Gayle acknowledges Reed's definition of the novel as "anything it wants to be" yet only mentions him as a superior satirist whose novels verge on the surrealistic. In *Black World* (June 1975), Houston Baker is rather severe in his review of *The Last Days of Louisiana Red* because of its satire of Blacks. *Negro Digest / Black World*, however, devoted much space to reviews of Reed's books and articles by him.

Loop's strength consists in never taking anything too seriously, including himself. He thus defines himself as "the cosmic jester" (p. 165), more harmless than any kind of sacrificial scapegoat in the tragic mode. He stakes his claim for a type of aesthetics characterized, through laughter, as "monkey business":

> What's your point?
> Horse opera. Clever, don't you think? And the Hoo-Doo cult of North America. A much richer art form than preaching to fishermen and riding into a town on the back of an ass. (p. 163)

As a result, when the black cowboy on Drag's green horse crashes in upon the scene of his second wedding, Drag accurately defines him as a "BLACK MAGICIAN TO END THEM ALL PSYCHING UP A BAD LOONED SPEECH OF GRAFFITI THAT WOULD ESTRANGE POPEYE" (p. 81). As an avant-garde artist who seuloysly works to liberate language without mistaking his role as a writer for a mission, Loop remains conscious of the critical establishment he derides. Chief Showcase also admits of taking his audience into consideration:

> I don't even want to get into how Moses sneaked around the Pharaoh's court abusing his hospitality by swiping all the magic he could get his clutches around. If I run down that shit, Loop, the book won't be reviewed in Manhattan. (p. 39)

Loop retorts, "If I ever sell this mind sauna to Hollywood I'll give you all of Gene Autry's bicycles" (p. 43).

This fictional type, which had initially been defined as a "brokedown," is finally that of the "horse opera" taken to its (il)logical extremes. It abolished space and time conventions as well as linguistic ones, mocking in turn each of its successive avatars. Reed never apologizes and hardly explains his aim when he mixes centuries or superimposed settings; thus, gigantic prehistoric sloths coexist with futuristic technology, Germans with Red Indians, Revolutionary War generals with late nineteenth-century cowboys, fiery dragons with the Pope; and Loop can be rescued by a group of Amazons from being beheaded on the day when the annexation of Texas is decreed, with the Seven Cities of Cibola looming on the horizon. All the elements of this gigantic jigsaw puzzle already existed or, when need be, are invented on the spot. As a result, anachronism becomes impossible, and character can allude simultaneously to the guillotine as a device from the "recent" (1789) French Revolution and to the crosses marking American graves at Omaha Beach. Like time, space is distorted and becomes distended; the American East and West coalesce in the same quest for power. Fiction itself can jump unexpectedly ahead, reverse and backtrack in low gear, or take off for the heavens like Showcase's Brush Beeve Monster or the Pope's ship.

Linguistic dexterity, linked with a coherent, if often far-fetched, use of lexical resources, gives Reed's fiction the impulse necessary to bring the pieces of the puzzle together nicely in the end. Meaning is impacted from one term to another, from one episode to the next like a ball in a pinball machine, ringing bells, lighting markers, bumping back and forth and ascoring again and again. As in *The Freelance Pallbearers*, Reed's language is characterized by the blending of many styles and levels to which an often near-phonetic transcription gives a degree of homogeneity. But syntax and use are less strictly Afro-American than in the earlier novel, and hardly realistic; rather than ethnic speech, they reconstruct the parlance of the media as befits the genre. The vocabulary ranges from pseudo-scientific terms like "oviposit" to words disfigured by common usage like "stifficate." There is definitely more invention through semantic combination than through word coinage; however, Reed resurrects a number of obsolete terms, particularly black slang of the 1920's and specific agricultural vocabulary. An example of this is "woodshed" (an improvised solo in jazz circles), which is superbly fitted to Loop's improvisation of a voodoo ritual in his cave. Another is "mitt man," which seems to spring from some Teutonic dream and has a touch of the pimp as Sal Mustache exstatically applies it to Loop. The term takes on its full meaning when it is applied to a religious charlatan by association with Christ: it seems to be a Reedian transciption of "myth man" though it was coined half a century ago.

The abundant similes are just as hilarious as they are appropriate. Drag, for instance, has "an ego as wide as the Grand Canyon"; the guillotine invented by the French is "a device said to be as rational as their recent revolution." An utterance may even lose track of itself, as when Drag says, "I'm a big man in these parts, fish fill my fill I mean full fish my swim" (p. 74); and stops short without even bothering to correct his sentence, yet gets an appropriate response from Sal. Or noises simply become language, such as Showcase's "yuk, yuk, yuk" or the Marshal's "har, har har," not to mention the "va-va-voom" of engines and other sounds which belong to comic strip captions.

Comedy often arises simply from the accumulation, or agglomeration, of terms, as in the sentence, "We've braved alkali, coyotes, wolves, rattlesnakes, catamounts, hunters" (p. 115). Sometimes, this is coupled with grotesque descriptions:

> The street was a dumpheap of Brueghel faces, of Hogarth faces, of Coney Island hot-dog kissers, ugly pusses and sinking mugs, whole precincts of flat peepers and silly lookers. The sun's wise broad lips smiled making the goats horny with cosmic seed as monstrous shapes who could never unbend their hands all looked as the Marshal ripped off his badge, boarded his horse and rode out of town. (p. 104)

Here accumulation is less important than the juxtaposition of connotations hinting at widely different fields of reference (lurid "cultured" caricature; popular imagery; mythological pan-eroticism), all in the context of stereotyped behavior, and surface baroque becomes the mark of surrealism. In fact, if one compares the triumphant parade of Eclair Porshop in Soulville (in *The Freelance Pallbearers*) with Pope Innocent's ride into Yellow Back Radio on a bull, one quickly perceives that, although they are picturesque and pertinent in both cases, the symbols refer mostly to an invented, synthetic system in the first case and mostly to a corpus of beliefs rooted in Western ideological tradition in the latter. The brief apparition of Reverend Boyd as a winged and electrified imp (whom a papal squirt incapacitates at once) is a response to Drag's mockery of Protestants for their lack of an allegorical sense. Yet, on the semantic level, this apparition serves to turn the scene into an extended metaphor or to locate the discourse on the level of a "morality play" — which actually happens in the final dialogue between Pope Innocent and the Loop Garoo Kid.

Without this opposition and mythical complementarity in which the conflict between diverse avatars of the static and the dynamic, of good and evil, functions, the whole narrative would be reduced to a comic strip, a cleverly structured but one-dimensional series of syntagmatic sequences proliferating in all spatio-temporal directions but devoid of paradigmatic depth. In fact, above the appropriate creation of a "broke down" technique, the success of *Yellow Back Radio* is due to the ability of Reed's fiction to reach beyond thematic developments and manicheistic chrestomachy, not so much in the direction of parallel fantasies as towards the deeper areas of our subconscious imagination, to fly "up up and aways" in order to reconcile our dreams and our beliefs.

In later novels, such as *Mumbo Jumbo* and *Flight to Canada* (1976), Reed makes more refined use, respectively, of the clash between antithetic cultures as expressed in gang warfare and of the interplay between history and fiction in the South and the continuing racial and Civil War. In those two novels he exploits each direction more fully and, possibly, more artistically than he did in *Yellow Back Radio*. However, the balanced blend of challenging thematic development and "deconstructed" form is unique here; possibly making his second novel his richest attempt to date at exploring new verbal techniques as well as at reflecting critically upon the possibilities of fiction in the post-modern age.

ISHMAEL REED: BIOGRAPHICAL NOTE

Ishmael Reed was born at Chattanooga, Tennessee, on February 22, 1938. He was very active with the *Umbra* workshop of poets in the mid-1960's and with a group of black experimental fiction writers, such as Steve Cannon, Clarence Major, Cecil Brown, etc. He initiated *The East Village Other* magazine in 1965. In 1967, he moved to the West Coast, where he taught black studies at Berkeley University for a while. He is a poet, novelist, dramatist, screenwriter (his script of *Yellow Back Radio* was reportedly stolen and used as the basis for Mel Brooks's *Blazing Saddles*) and essayist, as can be gathered from the bibliography of his works. He has published several magazines in which white and non-white minority writers are represented, *Yardbird Reader* (1972 -1976) and *Y'bird* (1978 to date), as well as anthologies like *Yardbird Lives*, which he co-edited with Al Young (Grove Press, 1978), and *Calafia, The California Poetry* (Y'bird Books, Berkeley, 1979). One of the owners of Reed, Johnson and Cannon Publications, later Ishmael Reed Books, he has made available new works by William Demby, Bill Gunn, Mei-Mei Bressenburge, etc., in an attempt to fight the quasi-monopoly of New York publishing houses and to reveal vigorous ethnic writing.

BIBLIOGRAPHY

Fiction

The Freelance Pallbearers. Garden City, N.Y.: Doubleday, 1967.
Yellow Back Radio Broke Down. Garden City, N.Y.:Doubelday, 1969.
Mumbo Jumbo. Garden City, N.Y.: Doubleday, 1972.
The Last Days of Louisiana Red. New York: Random House, 1974.
Flight to Canada. New York: Random House, 1976.
Ed., *19 Necromancers from Now.* An Anthology of original American writing for the 1970s. Garden City, N.Y.: Doubleday, 1970. Includes Reed's short fiction piece "Cab Calloway Stands in for the Moon" and an important introduction.

Non-fiction.

Shrovetide in Old New Orleans. Garden City, N.Y.: Doubleday, 1978.
A collection of articles, mostly on black fiction and art, most of them already published.

Poetry

catechism of d neoamerican hoodoo church. London: Paul Breman (Heritage Series), 1970.
conjure; Selected Poems, 1963-1970. University of Massachusetts Press, 1972.
Chattanooga. New York: Random House, 1973.
A Secretary to the Spirits. New York: NOK Publishers, 1978.

KLAUS ENSSLEN

COLLECTIVE EXPERIENCE AND INDIVIDUAL
RESPONSIBILITY: ALICE WALKER'S
THE THIRD LIFE OF GRANGE COPELAND

Alice Walker (born in 1944) started her writing career with a book
of poems (*Once*) in 1968, and saw it go through a second printing
the same year. As she testified herself, the poems had been written
in rapid succession as an act of reaffirmation of her will to live
during a sharp crisis caused by threatening pregnancy, plans for
suicide, and then abortion, all of which eventually brought a clearer awareness to the college student of her situation as a woman.[1]
The poems of her first book are concerned with Africa and Civil
Rights, with love and death, thus reflecting basic experiences of
the young writer. Born in Eatonton, Georgia, the youngest of
eight children of a sharecropper (who was beginning to move away
from the land although remaining a poor peasant laborer "exploited by the rural middle-class rich"[2]), Alice Walker had spent two
years each at Spelman College in Atlanta and at Sarah Lawrence
College in Bronxville, N.Y., had then travelled in Africa and Europe and participated in the drive for black voters' registration in

1. Alice Walker has herself provided a succinct and graphic description of
the crisis in her interview with John O'Brien (in *Interviews with Black Writers*
ed. by John O'Brien, New York, 1973, pp. 185-211, esp. 186-191).
2. V.A. Walker, "My Father's Country is the Poor." *The New York Times*,
March 21, 1977, p. 27. Although Alice Walker often mentions structural
characteristics of the lives of her parents and of her own experience,
she is quite reticent about detailed biographical information which therefore has to be deduced from poetic as well as discursive statements. One
of the poems in the first section of *Revolutionary Petunias*, "Three Dollars
Cash," allows such a sudden glimpse when the poet's mother says "We
wasn't so country then ..." "You being the last one —" [of the children]. As
a consequence, the midwife this time is not paid in produce (a pig from the
pen) but is given three dollars cash.

Georgia and other Civil Rights activities.[3] Her novel *The Third Life of Grange Copeland*, published in 1970, in a first draft had concentrated on the Civil Rights decade and on the perspective of a militant female activist; in the final version the author added historical dimension by including exemplary experience of Southern rural blacks almost from the beginning of the century. In 1973 a second volume of poetry, *Revolutionary Petunias*, articulated a growing interest in personal and group history in the sharpened focus of representative autobiographical and public moments of experience. Still the same year a collection of short stories appeared, *In Love and Trouble: Stories of Black Women*, probing a wide spectrum in the perceptions and actions of individual women (some of the stories prepublished in magazines). Beside the author's continuing engagement in welfare and political issues (leading among other things to her marriage with the Jewish Civil Rights attorney Mel Leventhal), she found work as a teacher and writer-in-residence at various universities.[4] Her second novel, *Meridian*, published in 1976, reflects some of the private and public tension of this phase by focusing on the state of mind of a young woman torn between absorbing sociopolitical commitment and the necessary search for a more personal form of self-realization. In addition to a biography for young readers (*Langston Hughes*, 1974) and a growing number of essays and articles in magazines, Alice Walker's work to date includes a third volume of poetry (*Good Night, Willie Lee, I'll See You in the Morning*, 1979), a thematically diversified range of poems articulated by a more self-confident lyrical voice, and a second collection of short stories (*You Can't Keep a Good Woman Down*, 1981) which shows women no longer in suffering and dependent roles, but as articulating their own vital demands and imaginative space (whether in love or sex, social relations or professional and artistic ambitions).

3. Alice Walker " has worked in voter registration in Georgia, in welfare rights and Head Start in Mississippi, and in the New York City Welfare Department. She was Consultant in Black History for Friends of the Children of Mississippi in 1967." (Quoted from the cover flap of *The Third Life of Grange Copeland*, New York, 1970).

4. Writer-in-residence and teacher of Black Studies at Jackson State College 1968-69; Writer-in-residence at Tougaloo College, Mississippi, in 1970. (*Ibid.*)

In synopsis, Alice Walker's literary production shows a preponderance of poetic discourse and its concomitant strategies of expression. This comes through even in her prose, both fictional and non-fictional, either as a preference for concrete moments of sensory or imaginative empathy over more analytical modes of observation (v. "Lulls," "In Search of Our Mothers' Gardens," "In Search of Zora Neale Hurston"), or in the emphasis on personal moments of experience as yet unresolved by authorial or delegated interpretation (*Meridian*), leading to an immediacy of condensed feeling and situation in the short prose fiction which combines Tchekhov's thematic concentration with an experimental variability in formal properties. If Walker's first novel has been chosen here for a detailed analysis over her more experimental and modernist second novel, this can be justified by the wider social and historical range of that book pointing towards central problems of the collective experience and self-projection of the group, and moving closer in its narrative mode to a collective oral tradition, while at the same time putting emphasis on personal ethos no less than the author's second novel.

The Third Life of Grange Copeland takes the adult life of its title character as the historical delimitation of its fictional action, roughly comprising three generations from the 1920's to the peak of the Civil Rights movement in the early 1960's (as marked by systematic black voters' registration, freedom marches and the first struggles for school integration). Half a century of family history is the narrative material used by the novel to dramatize essential changes in the conditions of black people in the rural South of the United States, beginning in total economic and psychological dependence and moving towards a certain measure of self-awareness as the ground for new self-concepts and the social roles or life-plans based on them. Grange Copeland as a young man sets out, like millions of black men before him, with the socially propagated illusion that he will be able to provide a home and the necessary subsistence for himself and his attractive wife Margaret via his labor as a sharecropper in the heart of Georgia. Quite soon the efficient system of exploitation by manipulation of debt and wage cutting (which the white South developed since Reconstruction as a practical means of securing the continuation of slavery under legal guise) begins to close its grip on Grange Copeland. He stops fighting the decay of delapidated cabins unworthy of human habitation, he seeks escape from the total drain of physical energy and an overwhelming sense of helplesness in the arms of Josie, a prostitute he has known from before his marriage. He totally neglects his wife who after an initial phase of apathy begins to protest against this treatment by craving dissipation for herself, not disdaining even the white boss Shipley, and ends up giving birth to a second son obviously fathered by a white man, half-brother to her first child Brownfield (whose name graphically reflects the hopelessness of his parents). Inspite of his basically unchanged affection for his wife, Grange under the burden of his psychological humiliation and economic defeat goes through the inevitable escalation of violent quarreling and withdrawal and finally resorts to the classical escape of the black man denied any options for responsible action. Grange disappears, Margaret a few weeks later poisons herself and her younger child, leaving the 15-year-old Brownfield who under constant neglect has become so hard-boiled that he instinctively evades Shipley's effort to tie him to the soil and sets out on his own.

Brownfield is marked by lack of parental love and by the ignorance of the sharecropper's world. Correctly assuming that his father must have gone to the mythical North, he chooses the same destination, but is unable to even find the next railroad line. So it is not surprising, though ironic, that Brownfield ends up in the same Dew Drop Inn of the next little town run by his father's friend, voluptuous lightskinned Josie, and her muscular daughter Lorene. Josie is a countertype to Brownfield's mother, with an antithetical way of life: Seduced and made pregnant when sixteen, cursed and expelled by her father, sexually exploited by the male world around her, Josie has forged her weakness into a weapon for gaining economic independence. The lucrative métier of prostitution has added to her biological and emotional largesse the edge of a good business sense. By way of compensation she continues to dream of her great love for Grange Copeland, and so his son comes in quite handy as a security. Brownfield hires out his sexual energy to both mother and daughter. His animal-like state of saturation becomes irksome only when Brownfield falls in love with Josie's adopted daughter Mem. The illegitimate child of Josie's sister and a Black minister up North, Mem goes to school in Atlanta and wants to become a teacher. She speaks correct English and is untouched by moral corruption. After a short courtship Brownfield marries her and starts working on a farm – as a sharecropper.

Lack of imagination and of practical alternatives thus lead Brownfield back into the same vicious circle his father managed to escape only at the price of abandoning his family. For a short time Mem and Brownfield due to their love remain unaffected by their material condition; but when discouragement sets in, the erosion of their partnership and individual sense of value becomes far more destructive than in the case of Brownfield's parents. Mem has given up teaching with her marriage; through childbirth and heavy work she rapidly loses her vitality, grows ugly and emaciated. Brownfield is incapable of acknowledging the real causes of his situation and vents his frustration on Mem and the children, growing vicious, brutal and cynical, with special contempt for her education. On the brink of total collapse Mem one day summons up her last resources and actively resists Brownfield's power: Armed with a gun she dictates the conditions of their future relations to a demoralized husband and takes things in her own hands. She finds work in town, at considerably better pay than Brownfield's, rents a house for the family and sends her children to school. Brownfield bides his time, planfully weakening Mem through pregnancies, and eventually takes back control over the family, cancelling many of Mem's material achievements. When he loses his job as a final ratification of personal weakness and economic conditions, his accumulated frustration spills over in his deliberately killing Mem one Christmas eve with the same gun she had used to suddue him.

This point of the action of the novel marks the final shift, foreshadowed by Grange's sudden reappearance, to the dominant thematic materical indicated by the title: After some years spent in Harlem as hustler and rebel against conventional norms (comprising his second life), Grange has returned to Georgia, deliberately married Josie and bought himself a farm with her money from the sale of the Dew Drop Inn. From his return Grange dates the beginning of his third life: Made confident by the stronghold of his own land he has started out by helping Mem and her children, leaving no doubt about his contempt for the character and actions of his son. After Brownfield's ten year prison sentence Grange takes his youngest daughter Ruth into his house (her two older sisters have been brought North by Mem's father). Ruth, ever since he assisted at her birth, has been Grange's favorite grandchild, and to ensure a meaningful future to her has become the main purpose of his remaining life ("Survival was not everything. *He* had survived. But to survive *whole* was what he wanted for Ruth.")[5] Grange tries to pass on to Ruth all he can from his accumulated life experience, including his late insight into the history and culture of his group (with one of his conclusions being that a black person might have to leave America if things didn't change for the better). When the first Civil Rights workers reach the forsaken county, agitating for the political rights of Black people, Grange sees the dawn of a new age in their courage and joie-de-vivre. They represent a new chance for constructive living, such as Grange has hoped to make possible for Ruth. To prevent such a development from being thwarted, Grange eventually decides to fend off his son Brownfield by force: Released from prison after seven years, Brownfield tries to get his daughter back through the courts, even though Josie (who out of resentment about Grange's indifference towards her has shacked up with his son) advises Brownfield aginst this plan. When the white judge (in recognition of the work done for him by Brownfield as inmate) gives Ruth to her father, Grange shoots his son before leaving court, and dies with gun in hand on his own land under the bullets of his white hunters.

Grange Copeland as the explicit central character of the novel dramatizes essential parts of the collective experience of his group. His answer to the total subjugation and discouragement on the economic level by an overpowering, cynical and hypocritical white world is an unshakable moral judgment — expressed at the beginning of the novel by Grange's avoiding to meet the eyes of his oppressor Chipley — a symbolic gesture of non-cooperation and masked contempt of long standing in Afro-American literature (frequently to be met with in the fugitive slave narratives of the 19th century). Grange's calm contempt for the white man's norms — interrupted only temporarily by his rebellious rage in the Harlem phase of his second life — contrasts sharply with Brownfield's attitude whose self-destructive hatred stamps him as a total victim of white domination. Grange and Brownfield are set up as contrasting figures embodying diametrically opposed options for the black man under white supremacy. Grange's flight from the sharecropper's condition is destructive towards his family, but not with

5. *The Third Life of Grange Copeland*, p. 214.

regard to his own person: It turns self-aggression into the more constructive act of resistance against the norms of the South and initiates a learning process as prerequisite for a positive self-concept.

In New York Grange gets to know extensively the form of discrimination specific to the urban North, i.e. the exclusion of black people through ignoring them — Ellison's metaphor of invisibility is pointedly taken up by the text.[6] A scene presented with particular completeness of detail and expanded narrative time illuminates drastically the fusion of Northern and Southern stereotypes of the Negro: Involuntarily Grange becomes a witness in Central Park of how a pregnant white woman is abandoned by her lover who offers her money as a recompense. In spontaneous sympathy Grange addresses the woman, triggering a tidal wave of hate and contempt against himself, as overwhelming evidence of the fact that she has not been humanized by her own suffering. In response Grange watches the hysterical woman run out on an ice-covered pond where she breaks in and disappears. Looking back on this incident, Grange cannot help but see himself as momentarily infected by white hatred and robbed of his own humaneness, while at the same time going through a necessary therapeutic act of mobilizing his will to resist (somewhat in the same way Bigger Thomas in Wright's *Native Son* unwittingly creates a new self through a murderous act of self-protection)[7]:

> The death of the woman was simple murder, he thought, and soul condemning; but in a strange way, a bizarre way, it liberated him. He felt in some way repaid for his own unfortunate life. It was the taking of that white woman's life — and the denying of the life of her child — the taking of her life, not the taking of her money, that forced him to want to try to live again. He believed that, against his will, he had stumbled on the necessary act that black men must commit to regain, or to manufacture their manhood, their self-respect. They must kill their oppressors.

6. *Op.cit.*, pp. 144-145: ... to the people he met and passed daily he was not even in existence! The South had made him miserable, with nerve endings raw from continual surveillance from contemptuous eyes, but they *knew he was there*. Their very disdain proved it. The North put him in solitary confinement where he had to manufacture his own hostile stares in order to see himself. For why were they pretending he was not there? .. Only the term 'invisibility' is avoided as being too obvious an echo of Ellison's title.

7. *Op. cit.*, p. 153.

He never ceased to believe this, adding only to this belief, in later years, that if one kills, he must not shun death in his turn. And this, he had found, was the hardest part, since after freeing your suppressed manhood by killing whatever suppressed it you were then taken with the most passionate desire to live.

This crucial experience, added to years of symptomatic self-alienation in the criminalizing conditions of the urban ghetto, finally moves Grange to return to the South where racial antagonism seems more honest to him in its personal virulence than in the impersonal undermining of self-esteem up North. His aloof retirement to his own land (even at the price of purposeful exploitation of a black woman) and his full dedication to Ruth's education are signal acts of individual independence from the dominant culture. It is true that Grange Copeland tends to view his social and moral separatism as a relic of past times, as soon as he is faced with the moral enthusiasm of black and white Civil Rights workers. But from the perspective of post-Civil Rights developments (both as seen in 1970 or in 1980) Grange's independent stance and tough scepticism as to possible changes in the minds of America's white citizens gains new relevance as part of the symbolic action of the novel.

At the same time, however, Grange Copeland as an heroic individual embodying the will to resist and to claim an autonomous base of living must raise serious problems with regard to representative group experience. Both his positive enhancement and its counterpart, Brownfield's negative demonization, result from a reduction of their fictional motivation to individual moral traits. Grange's unlimited ability for individual growth and accumulated insight, the same as Brownfield's progressive moral and practical disintegration, serve as contrasting foils to explicate individual worth or unworthiness. Brownfield in particular is a fictional character totally determined by his function as thematic contrast: The author moves him close to the stock figure of the gothic villain, when Brownfield finds pleasure in pouring poison into streams, or when he gloats (in an account to Josie) over the memory of how he deliberately exposed his last-born child in midwinter to freeze to death while he himself enjoyed a particularly good night's sleep. Just as Brownfield's moral fiber seems unaffected by the collective suffering surrounding him, Grange's individual strength and improved self-image is largely unconnected to any collective culture

196

or experience, neither deriving from them its sustenance nor flowing back into them as a reinvigorating force. Grange is always shown in terms of an individual consciousness struggling for self-assertion, never as part of a community of people with common aspirations. Yet he participates in group-specific networks — the rural and urban "tenderloin," i.e. amusement district, in his first and second life; the sale of moonshine whisky and cardplaying in his third life, used as a means of getting money towards a dowry for Ruth — collective areas of experience with a wealth of black folklore and the implications belonging to such cultural substrata. In contrast, however, to a view of cultural milieus as shaping and maintaining group cohesion which we get in texts like *The Autobiography of Malcolm X* (1965) or even in Wright's late novel written in exile *The Long Dream* (1958), Alice Walker's novel does not try to bring those factors to the fore of its fictional world. Similarly, when Grange is said to delve into the history of his people by reading all he can in New York, this remains clearly an ascription of an educationally or intellectually enlightening experience — it never gains the status of a revolutionizing reorientation from the survival strategy of a hustler to the collectively meaningful perspective of conscious dedication to a common goal that reading and understanding history had for Malcolm. Not that Malcolm should have been taken as matrix for a fictional character — but the comparison helps to underline that Grange uses collective experience mainly for strengthening his individual moral fiber, without any repercussions on his view on community, a concept which continues to be practically nonexistent for him.

Fictionally dramatized collective experience not subordinated to heroic individual traits can be found in Walker's novel more readily in some of the female characters. Brownfield on leaving his parental place runs into a woman by the roadside who in her situation and way of speaking about it represents a biographical sum of the lives of many black women in the rural South. Doing her washing the old style, she generously feeds Brownfield, is openly curious about him and talks frankly about her own situation: Five children have already gone up North; three small ones are playing about her in the yard. When Brownfield ventures to remark that the North maybe itsn't all it is supposed to be, she replies:[8]

8. *Op. cit.*, p. 30.

"Maybe not, maybe 'tis," she said, stirring her pot, spitting snuff juice into the fire. "I wouldn't be saying I knows. But I *declare* it so out of fashion round here you'd think most any other place would be better."

Asked about the father of her little children she unabashedly reveals the social conditions of her life:

"Well, I tell you," she said, standing up from putting more rubber around the pot and resting her back by swaying it, "one of they daddies is dead from being in the war, although he only got as far as Fort Bennet. The other one of they daddies is now married to the woman that lives in the next house down the road. If you stands up on your tippy toes you can jest about see her roof, sort of green colored. I thought she was helpin' me get another husband and all the time she was lookin' out for herself. But I am still her friend. The other one of they daddies was my last husband, by common law, but he dead too now, shot by the old man he was working for for taking the chitlins out of a hog they kill." She looked at the children and frowned. "But they is so much alike, just to look at; they git along right well together."

In less than four pages of text the author in this episode provides a condensed vignette of a woman's existence (a sujet easily to be imagined in more extended form as one of the stories in Walker's collection *In Love and Trouble*). In the novel the passage is given the function of an inconspicuous prelude to Brownfield's encounter with Josie whose situation and expectations are presented in much fuller detail.

Josie is a complex and in some ways contradictory character, and as such embedded in considerably more social context than the male figures of the novel. In retrospect she is first shown in her role as young girl and victim of male sexism, drastically exemplified in a scene where her father refuses to help up his pregnant daughter from the floor, leaving her exposed to the eyes of several men "like an exhausted, overturned pregnant turtle" or like a "spider, deformed and grotesque beneath the panicked stares of the gathered men," with "the big thrusting stomach that none of them owned."[9] Pushed into her new part, Josie soon learns to play it "with a gusto that denied shame,"[10] acquires the Dew Drop Inn, a businesslike 'madame' with plenty of mother wit and yet not devoid of her inborn sensual and emotional generosity, capable of

9. *Op. cit.*, p. 40.
10. *Op. cit.*, p. 41.

wishful dreaming and of a companionable though rivalizing stance towards her daughter. Still later, as Grange's wife, new facets are added to her composite portrait, Josie becoming sensitive and self-pitying by turns, naive or tactically shrewd, — adaptive or demanding aspects of her nature which undergo further pragmatic modifications when she finally joins Brownfield. Thus Josie is always seen in her social ambience, taking into account or reacting to the people surrounding her, profiting or suffering from them. Despite the occasional authorial allegation of innate corruption (introduced to justify Grange's unscrupulous use of her, among other things), Josie remains the most complex female character of the novel, free of the programmatic enhancement of others.

Alice Walker has repeatedly made clear her feminist convictions, most explicitly perhaps at a symposium held at Radcliffe:[11]

I am a thoroughgoing feminist — although I know a lot of Black women don't believe in it. I get very angry with Black women for taking all the stuff they take, but at the same time they are the only people that I respect collectively and with no reservations. I believe in them.

In her view the ideologically buttressed disrespect for women, regarded as "the mules of the world" in the 19th century, carries over into the 20th century and has been aggravated if anything for black women in the face of therapeutic demands by the black man claiming that his ego needed boosting and reconstructing first and foremost by way of compensation for the historical undermining of his role in the family. As a result, black women find themselves "suspended," economically and psychologically, carrying the burden of a twofold repression as black persons and as women.[12]

11. Alice Walker, "In Search of Our Mothers' Gardens," *Ms.* 2 (May 1974) p. 65 (also quoted by Mary Helen Washington, "In Love and Trouble," *Black World* 23, No. 12 (October 1974), p. 51).

12. "In Search of Our Mothers' Gardens," p. 64 ff. Cp. also Mary Helen Washington, "An Essay on Alice Walker," in *Sturdy Black Bridges: Visions of Black Women in Literature*, Garden City, N.Y., 1979, pp. 133-156, where the author quotes Alice Walker from an interview with herself (pp. 137-8):
They were suspended in a time in history when the options for Black women were severely limited ... And they either kill themselves or they are used up by the man, or by the children, or by ... whatever the pressures against them. And they cannot go anywhere. I mean, you can't, you just can't move, until there is room for you to move *into*. And that's the way I see many of the women I have created in fiction. They are closer to my mother's generation than to mine. They had few choices.

In the novel, Grange's wife Margaret drastically exemplifies this state of suspension without creative outlet, devoid of real options, when we see her driven into the radical moral resignation of suicide. On the other hand, Margaret's spontaneous reaction to her husband's desertion already contains the seed for an as yet unseized opportunity for self-definition equaling or even transcending Grange's self-estimate at that point: while he goes through the accelerating motion of flight, she seems to be able to discover — even if only fleetingly — a positive form of self-directed joy in living, in sexual self-assertion — comparable to what Alice Walker has described in other women when they take recourse to flower gardens or the knitting of quilts.[13] Margaret thus embodies a kind of germinal unconscious attempt at feminine self-realization.

Brownfield's wife Mem, a woman of the next generation, is given a heavier programmatic burden in the novel with regard to feminist concepts. Her brutalization by her husband is more radical, threatening the total destruction of her physical and psychic makeup. This process is underlined by the equally radical alienation between Mem and Brownfield which shows up the loss of moral substance in both as a consequence of their succumbing to the destructive forces of hate and contempt (while Margaret and Grange managed to keep intact the core of their moral character, including a remnant of mutual respect). Similar to the act of unconditioned resistance at the very moment of threatened annihilation described by Frederick Douglass in his slave narrative as the birth of a new self and positive self-image, antithetical to the norms of the oppressor,[14] Mem (in stark contrast to Brownfield) inadvertently discovers the constructive will to resist in herself, fanning the last embers of her vitality. Mem has to carry a double burden in the novel: Her brutalization is more unalleviated than any other character's deterioration under the pressure of dehum-

13. Cp. "In Search of Our Mothers' Gardens," p. 105; Interview with John O'Brien, p. 208 (in explanation for the title *Revolutionary Petunias*); in fictional form feminine creativity is dramatized in the quilt made by the country-bound mother and appropriated by a citified daughter in "Everyday Use" (*In Love and Trouble*).

14. Frederick Douglass, *Narrative of the Life of F.D.*, N.Y. (Signet), 1968, p. 83: It was a glorious resurrection, from the tomb of slavery, to the heaven of freedom. My long-crushed spirit rose, cowardice departed, bold defiance took its place ..." etc.

anizing conditions, so that her initial efforts towards self-expression via education and vocation are almost completely effaced. To make her sudden resurgence, her bold gesture of defiance more dramatic, the author saw fit first to intensify her dehumanization. In a sense, this is an overdrawn dramatization of the historically documented tough resilience of black women contained in the concept of the suspended woman (vividly illustrated by Walker in her own mother's sustained though repressed vitality) – a concept given up in the novel for the sake of didactically polarized contrasts. Mem rises like a phoenix of feminist theory from the ashes of her environmental abasement: With a cocked gun Mem forcibly presents a ten-point catalogue of demands to a Brownfield stretched out in his own vomit, her militant stance having less to do with psychological plausibility than with an emblematic act of feminine revolt against the joint forces of an unconscionable *machismo* and the mediated pressure of white exploitation. If Mem for a while manages to maintain her practical and moral ascendancy over Brownfield, this goes to confirm the symbolic adequacy of her position. On the level of plot, however, Mem's again falling victim to Brownfield's strategy of biological subversion amounts to a denial of Mem's capacity to learn and to know her opponent, thereby robbing her of the status of a truly emancipatory woman and in a sense reducing her to a figure in the overwhelming culture of poverty.

Even more than Mem's dropping back to a level of victimization which she might be expected to have left behind in her act of heroic self-assertion, it is the grounding of this act in her fictionally ascribed innocence or moral purity that must weaken her function as a vehicle for feminist options. It is one thing to attribute to Mem "the expectation of a less destructive or inhumane future" in an initial stage of the deteriorating marriage than to Brownfield[15] – it is another matter to absolve Mem and Ruth from the destruction of their souls by virtue of their inherent "innocence" and "freshness" (two concepts used emphatically to justify Grange's decision for Ruth and against Josie),[16] while at the same time

15. *The Third Life of Grange Copeland*, p. 103.
16. *Op. cit.*, p. 156: Ruth, who needed him and who was completely fresh and irresistibly innocent, as alas, Josie was not. Also p. 47: Their lives infinitely lacked freshness. They were as stale as the two-dollar rooms upstairs. Inno-

Brownfield under very comparable conditions is damned to play an unalleviatedly contemptible part. The author here introduces categorical simplifications by ascribing heroic or demonic traits to individual characters, presumably for didactic contrast.

Sensitized to such fictional strategies, the reader will discover certain ideological presuppositions in the author's conception of moral character. Brownfield's moral deterioration, for example, is closely associated with animalism. Passively brutalized by Josie's sexuality (underlined by the limited role Josie's daughter is given as her mother's *double* in embodying sexuality sheer and simple — which helps to explain her complete disappearance from the later parts of the novel!), Brownfield later acts out his animal nature in brutalizing Mem. Sexuality, moral corruption and hostility toward education form one semantic axis for Brownfield, juxtaposed to oppositional qualities such as indestructible freshness of soul, aspiration towards education and knowledge, and the absence of sexuality — as embodied in different admixtures in Grange, Mem and Ruth. (In this spectrum, sexuality gains a particularly symptomatic stature, its absence for the three fictional characters being practically outside their moral volition, for reasons of age or exhaustion.) Grange, among the character on his semantic axis, is privileged in being the only one capable of accumulating wisdom and self-assurance — traits of his moral character he hopes to see brought to an as yet unheard of flowering in Ruth. The solidarity between Grange and Ruth (somewhat onesided and precarious, as it must appear) might be taken as at least partly overcoming the repression of black men and black women. Yet for its continuation it would depend on the dream of individual moral perfectibility in a restored or healed society — a dream that circumvents the central fact of sexuality in the relationship of black men and women. Thus the symbolic action of the novel can be said to release male-female solidarity as a model only on a plane of dream fantasy sharply removed from social options. When Grange experiences a kind of Rip-van-Winkle sensation in his confrontation with the vision of the Civil Rights workers[17] — shown as resplen-

cence continued to exist in him for them ... (referring to Josie and Lorene vs the young Brownfield, cp. below pp. 211-212 for context).

17. *Op. cit.* p. 240: "Well, I be damned," said Grange. He felt he had been caught sleeping and that his nap had lasted twenty or forty years.

dent apparitions of a new age and society — this motif makes explicit Grange's instinctive groping for a concrete utopia similar to the expectations of the Civil Rights era — the only context in which Ruth might be imagined as coming into her own, both as a person and a woman.

Such a vision (implied in Grange's individual attempt at autonomy, and made explicit in Civil Rights optimism) tends to exclude the majority of rural blacks in Grange's world who cannot afford personal intellectual and moral growth the way he does as the sum of a lifetime. With Mem, the mass of black people in the fictional world of *The Third Life of Grange Copeland* are kept prisoners in the anonymous culture of poverty, a community of stigmatized victims reinforcing their socially dictated dependence by holding back individual members via the classical crab-basket effect (group cohesion to prevent the escape of privileged individuals). These are the assumptions behind Bownfield's and Josie's patterns of action, and at some points in the text they become tangible in key situations (e.g. Josie and Mem not fighting their being pushed back into dependence). Grange, on the other hand, accumulates strength by escaping the conditions of his group rather than by an act of reinterpretation of a collective situation. This can be demonstrated in the way he puts to use inalienable parts of the cultural heritage of his group: In his angry Harlem phase Grange absorbs Uncle Remus folklore and collective history by reading, not via an oral tradition which would imply participation in rituals of collective memory and communicative reenactment.[17a] This group lore is then handed on to Ruth in a personal relationship excluding group

17a. This separation from all forms of oral enactment in the novel of such collective traditions is particularly surprising in view of the fact that Alice Walker has herself repeatedly acknowledged the importance of collective memory and oral tradition. V. her tribute to her mother's storytelling as a source of her own art ("In Search of Our Mothers' Gardens," pp. 70 and 105): And so our mothers and grandmothers have, more often than not anonymously, handed on the creative spark, the seed of the flower they themselves never hoped to see: or like a sealed letter they could not plainly read .... Unlike "Ma" Rainey's songs ... no song or poem will bear my mother's name. Yet so many of the stories that I write, that we all write, are my mother's stories. Only recently did I fully realize this: that through years of listening to my mother's stories of her life, I have absorbed not only the stories themselves, but something of the manner in which she spoke, something of the urgency that involves the knowledge that her stories — like her life — must be

participation — one could say in an ethically justified private space which while teaching a member of the young generation conclusions from the group experience, at the same time guarantees a splendid isolation of grandchild and grandfather. The 'lifting' of group lore to a morally purified realm is even more apparent in Grange's teaching Ruth to dance at home — the context of the black "tenderloin" as a communication subsystem of the group including its counter-white-protestant-ethic standards and sexual implications has been bowdlerized into a domesticated and respectable family realm and constellation. By extension, folk culture and experience through Grange's example is awarded an enlightening and constructive function only after being filtered by the reflected and consciously political appropriation of a militant individual consciousness — a function it apparently is not granted in its original context of group enactment.

The underlying point of reference for such a perspective is the axiomatic concept of an "inviolate sanctuary" of the individual soul, i.e. of an inherent worth or unworth of the individual and his moral substance ("You got to hold tight a place in you where they can't come" obviously appeals to individual responsibility, not to a group culture as a reservoir of oppositional self-definition).[18] The ignoring and underrating of group culture and community results in attributing collective insights into the norms of the white world, or the defensive code of the black group, to individual perception (mostly that of Grange as over-life-size impersonator of group experience). On the aphoristic level this comes through in Grange's aside " 'Course the rumor is that they *is* people, but the funny part is why they don't act human' " (where Grange adopts

recorded... ... the telling of these stories, which came from my mother's lips as naturally as breathing ...
V. also her programmatic statement on the importance of group memory in her essay "The Unglamorous but Worthwhile Duties of the Black Revolutionary Artist, or of the Black Writer Who Simply Works and Writes" (*The Black Collegian*, September/October 1971), p. 43:
And if, some gray rushing day, all our black books are burned, it must be in my head and I must be able to drag it out and recite it, though it be bitter to the tongue and painful to the ears. For that is also the role of the black Revolutionary artist. He must be a walking filing cabinet of poems and songs and stories, of people, of places, of deeds and misdeeds.

18. *The Third Life of Grange Copeland*, pp. 155 and 209.

the moral judgment and verbal stance of an unmistakably collective way of perception).[19] With more fictional emphasis a reaction of racial group pride is attributed to Ruth at school: Shocked by a racist school book adorned with the murderous comments of a white fellow student, she challenges her teacher, gets en evasive reaction and storms out of class cursing teacher, class and school system.[20] This incident is presented as further proof for Ruth's moral courage and individual substance (she had already called her father a "son-a-bitch" when a small child), and she is shown as being completely alone in her class in mobilizing this sort of resistance, the rest of the students and the teacher remaining passive and subdued. Ruth's hatred in conjunction with her moral character automatically assumes moral worth and is seen as a token of strength — while Brownfield's hatred, lacking the required individual substance, is programmatically stigmatized by Grange and subsumed under his moral weakness:[21]

> "By George, I *know* the danger of putting all the blame on somebody else for the mess you make out of your life. I fell into the trap myself! And I'm bound to believe that that's the way the white folks can corrupt you even when you done held up before. 'Cause when they got you thinking that they're to blame for *everything* they have you thinking they's some kind of gods! You can't do nothing wrong without them being behind it. You gits just as weak as water, no feeling of doing *nothing* yourself. Then you begins to think up evil and begins to destroy everybody around you, and you blames it on the crackers. *Shit!* Nobody's as powerful as we make them out to be. We got our own *souls*, don't we?

The vernacular ease of Grange's words here (as in the whole extended discussion with his son and Josie from which the passage is taken) succeeds in veiling, without completely obscuring, the fact that Grange uses individual moral responsibility as a measure for achieving, or falling short of, human stature. As a consequence, his using the word "soul" points more to the Christian concepts reinforced by a Protestant ethic than to the communal implications of the term within the black group. Judging by Grange's capacity for self-reflexion and self-analysis (including the risky business of self-accusation with regard to his treatment of Josie), he stands be-

19. *Op. cit.*, p. 182.
20. *Op. cit.*, pp. 184-187.
21. *Op. cit.* p. 207.

fore us over-life-size and heroic, directly articulating some of the author's reflexion and and judgment of her fictional characters.

Grange's violent end serves to complement the novel's central normative axis of individual moral worth: It springs from his manichean battle against the abject moral worthlessness of Brownfield, a demonic and destructive force which merely summons forth the additional support of the judicial system of the American South at the novel's end. Grange's main enemy, however, is the threat of thwarted moral growth, in himself as in others. While Brownfield uses white racism as an excuse for his individual moral decay, Grange has used it as crystallizing point for his moral rebirth — both processes, however, are seen in the context of the fictional world of *The Third Life* as options the individual is responsible for. Group cohesion, group culture or group knowledge remain at best at the periphery of this struggle for heroic self-realization or pathetic self-destruction — they are not seen as constituting factors in the individual's search for identity. Individual responsibility is so prominent in the novel's moral scheme that one of the few extensive critical evaluations of *The Third Life* to date almost exclusively focusses on the opposition in moral character between Grange and Brownfield.[22] The overburdening of fictional characters with moral valuation described here points towards a didactic streamlining of the narrative material of the novel which can in part be explained by the author's political perspective and biography. In an extended interview (given by correspondence) Alice Walker has herself described the dominant thematic thrust of the novel in its initial draft, inadvertently laying bare the political orientation of her fictional vision as it persists in the published version:[23]

> But my first draft (which was never used, not even one line, in the final version) began with Ruth as a civil-rights lawyer in Georgia going to rescue her father, Brownfield Copeland, from a drunken accident, and to have a confrontation with him. In that version she is married — also to a lawyer — and they are both committed to insuring freedom for black people in the South. In Georgia, specifically. There was lots of love-making and courage in that version. But it was too recent, too superficial — everything seemed a product of the immediate present. And I believe nothing ever is.

22. Trudier Harris, "Violence in *The Third Life of Grange Copeland*," *CLA Journal* 19, No. 2 (Dec. 1975), pp. 238-247.
23. Interview with John O'Brien, p. 197.

The historical depth given the narrative plot in the final version adds a great deal of collectively grounded social experience, but this experience as exemplified in the individualized drama of one family's history through three generations remains very closely tied to the culminating point of the Civil Rights phase implicit in the plot from the beginning. Grange's initial lack of orientation — due to a world seen as "almost entirely menacing"[24] to which he reacts with spontaneous protest and fury, a kind of undirected Sturm-und-Drang-rebellion against the status quo — turns into a stabilizing and coherent view of society and his position in it only through the hopeful projection of Ruth's chances over and beyond defensive individual protection into a constructive future for her generation in a reconstructed body politic. Grange's defensive stance of moral self-preservation (which prevents a deterioration similar to that of his son) is sublimated and given its ultimate value in Ruth's expectation of a self-healing process for American society. The symbolic action of the novel does not envisage an alternative to this moral recovery of the whole society as embodied in Civil Rights postulates — unless one wishes to attribute a great deal of antithetical weight to Grange's rhetorical reservation that in the face of an unredeemable state of the nation he would see emigration a a last recourse.[25]

The basic opposition between moral resignation (fall) and moral self-discovery (rise), between moral loss or rebirth as represented by Brownfield and Grange, is emphatically underlined by the constellation of other fictional characters in the novel: Grange's first

24. Interview with John O'Brien, p. 204.
25. Grange's reservation remains rhetorical despite the concrete form the author endeavors to endow it with (*The Third Life*, p. 214):
He spent evenings examining maps, wondering about the places in the world he would never see, and gradually what he was groping for became almost tangible. Believing unshakably that his granddaughter's purity and open-eyedness and humor and compassion were more important than any country, people or place, he must prepare her to protect them. Assured, by his own life, that America would kill her innocence and eventually put out the two big eyes that searched for the seed of truth in everything, he must make her unhesitant to leave it.
On one level, however, this proposition is plausible and helps to bring out the categorical assumptions of the novel: The salvation of Ruth's individual soul and moral substance is more important than the collective fate of the group.

wife Margaret and Josie represent passive adaptation to the conditions of the closed world of the American South — lives of quiet desperation (to use Thoreau's words), in Josie's case ironically underlined by the contradiction between her economic autonomy and her helplessly remaining bound within traditional female roles. Mem and Ruth, on the other hand, signalize the possibility of resistance to the social pressure reducing women to passive victims — Mem by way of a desperate rebellion still falling short of attaining a viable form of self-realization, Ruth as privileged heiress of Grange's accumulated experience in the role of the one fictional character with a real chance for self-fulfilment, making her in the deep structure of the novel the fairy-tale princess on the point of being translated (or awakened) to a higher plane of living. In support of the criterion of moral self-realization the novel introduces the motif of hatred towards white supremacy: Brownfield's hate of everything white is destructive for himself as well as others, thus ratifying his insufficient moral substance; Grange's hate, in contrast, is seen as turning into constructive anger and after a long learning process finally setting free Grange's capacity for self-forgetfulness, for love of something beyond his own person.[26] By paradigmatic extension Grange recognizes this moral quality in other historical persons, most explicitly in Martin Luther King ("The thing about him that stands in my mind is that even with crackers spitting all over him, he gentle with his wife and childrens")[27] — a claiming of moral kinship which is particularly telling for the moral structure of the novel in view of the fact that Grange is completely free of any hankering for the consolations of Christianity and independent of the community of the Christian church. Overcoming moral egotism in the sense ascribed to Grange and King places the title character of Alice Walker's novel in one genealogy with historical advocates of the same vision of what would make for a more humane life — a genealogy which while including political figures like Che Guevara, Malcolm X or Medgar Evers, at the same time tends to disperse their specific political goals by

26. Interview with John O'Brien, p. 194: So Grange Copeland was *expected* to change. He was fortunate enough to be touched by love of something beyond himself. Brownfield did not change, because he was not prepared to give his life for anything, or *to* anything. He was the kind of man who could never understand Jesus (or Ch è or King or Malcolm or Medgar)...

27. *The Third Life of Grange Copeland*, p. 232.

placing them next and subordinate to Jesus.[28] The didactic deep structure of Walker's novel eventually releases a tripartite model of moral options inviting moral imitation or rejection: destructive self-abandonment (the first life; conclusively enacted by Margaret); defensive escape as a prerequisite for self-preservation and therapy (Grange in his second life); and finally self-transcendence and constructive service for others (Grange's third life, the Civil Rights workers).

With regard to narrative technique, *The Third Life of Grange Copeland* remains on traditional ground. Alice Walker has expressed her belief in the collective subconscious of a culture as an important criterion for the relevance of that culture's literature — a quality she recognized in the work of Zora Neale Hurston and Jean Toomer for her own group, and more manifestly even in some African writers.[29] In her search for this collective reference she has instinctively moved the narrative structure of her novel close to autobiographical patterns (one of the oldest and most telling narrative vehicles of Afro-American literature).[30] Narrative mediation in Walker's novel, although providing room for unobtrusive authorial valuation and implicit comment, on the surface of the narrative action remains bound to the perspective of individual characters. It sets in with Brownfield as a naive center of consciousness (following him from the age of ten in irregular steps into manhood), changes over temporarily to Josie (in Chapters 7 to 9), only to return again to Brownfield whose dramatized perspective remains dominant, giving way briefly at certain moments to Mem's perceptions as indicators of her ascendancy, until the incisive act of Brownfield murdering Mem. Here, about halfway through the novel, the perspective in Chapter 30 changes over to Ruth, at first in a somewhat diffuse way (which still allows for a sort of collect-

28. See footnote 26.
29. Interview with John O'Brien, pp. 202-203.
30. Cp. more recent studies on black autobiography and fiction, such as Sidonie Smith, *Where I'm Bound*. Patterns of Slavery and Freedom in Black American Autobiography, Westport, Conn., 1974; Robert B. Stepto, *From Behind the Veil*. A Study of Afro-American Narrative, Chicago 1979; and the general theses in Klaus Ensslen, "Schwarze Autobiographie in den USA seit 1960", *gulliver* 3 (1978). 96-116, and in Barbara Foley, "History, Fiction, and the Ground Between: The Uses of the Documentary Mode in Black Literature," *PMLA* 95, No. 2 (May 1980), 389-404.

ive perspective of Brownfield's daughters in Chapter 30), then definitely settling on Ruth with Chapter 31 (or Part VII in the loose subdivision of the novel into eleven parts of unequal length): "When Ruth struggled sleepily to open her eyes the morning of her first day at Grange's house, the big grandfather clock on the mantel made a last clinking echo across the chilly bed and sitting room"[31] — from this point on Ruth's perspective dominates the rest of the novel.

In general, narrative perspective can be said to be mobile in *The Third Life*, allowing for intermittent changes from one character to another when the author sees fit. Thus in Chapter 30, the very last paragraph is given to Mem ("Mem's grief over losing the "decent house" was not a sign around her neck. She recovered from the illness that had caused her to lose it and with grim determination attended to roof leaks and rat holes in this house" etc.)[32], expanding the community of Brownfield's daughters (mentioned above) to include the mother, thus giving them the status of a collective group of victimized women. Ruth's perspective, dominant in the second half of the novel, does not preclude abrupt changes to Brownfield or Josie, whenever the author wants to emphasize their state of consciousness at pronounced moments of the plot, and it gives way for longer stretches of the text to Grange's perceptions in Chapter 37 (the flashback on Grange's second life, the longest chapter of the novel) and in a sort of interior monologue of Grange's in Chapter 41 which carries Grange back to his first life.[33]

The high degree of flexibility in changing personalized perspectives indicates the veiled dominance of authorial control over distribution of action and the dramatized perception of that action through individual characters. Though the author strives to hide behind the perspective of fictional characters, she maintains a broad license on widening or narrowing the focus, on letting the characters speak for themselves (e.g. through extended dialogue and action) or on explaining them succinctly to themselves and to the reader. One example should suffice to demonstrate the coexistence of these different layers of presentation and valuation to

31. *The Third Life of Grange Copeland*, p. 115.
32. *Op. cit.*, p. 112.
33. *Op. cit.*, pp. 177-179.

be found throughout the text of the novel, measurable in the implicit or explicit presence of the authorial intelligence: When Brownfield begins to notice Mem as a countertype to Josie and her daughter, the author sets out by presenting Brownfield's divided feelings precisely enough, then suddenly uses the situation for a handy formula to make plausible Josie and Lorene ("He was a pawn in a game that Josie and Lorence enjoyed ... They existed for the simple pleasure of flirting with each other's men ...") – a formula which reduces their human substance and makes them subservient to a didactic moral argument –, and finally sharpens the foreshortened constellation into an axiomatic judgment on the two women ("Their lives infinitely lacked freshness"), with the basic assumption about human character indicated above that result from it. In the final short paragraph of Chapter 11 (from which chapter the quotes are taken) the axiomatic judgment on Josie and Lorene is then applied to them in another situation (churchgoing) which provides the author with material to introduce a categorical moral comment hardly veiled any longer by the alleged dramatic perception of a fictional character (as can be gathered from the authorial signals of words such as "if", "perhaps," "minimal" and "momentary," "pleasurable passion of repentance," "inflamed readings," "paroxysms," "hardly," all adding up to authorial irony).[34]

...Besides, Mem had never told him she cared for him.
But what really began to bother Brownfield was that since he became the man of the establishment, he had never felt it necessary to draw a salary. He was constantly dependent on Josie or Lorene for money, which they gave him readily enough, but with the understanding that he must work for his living and in exactly the ways they specified. And so he stood it around the house as long as he could, screwing Josie and Lorene like the animal he felt himself to be, especially when he stood next day in the same room with Mem, whose heart, pained, was becoming readable in her eyes. There was no longer any joy in his conquest of the two women, for he had long since realized that *he* wasn't using them, *they* were using him. He was a pawn in a game that Josie and Lorene enjoyed. Sometimes he felt he was the link they used to prove themselves mother and daughter. Otherwise they might have been strangers. They existed for the simple pleasure of flirting with each other's men, and then of fighting it out in the street in

34. *Op. cit.*, pp. 47-48.

front of the lounge, where every man in the district soon learned that if you wanted a piece of pussy you only had to make up to one of them to have the other fall in your lap.

For a while it was grand being prize pawn; for both women, fast breaking from the strain of liquor, whoredom, money-making and battle, thought they truly loved him — but as a clean young animal they had not finished soiling. Their lives infinitely lacked freshness. They were as stale as the two-dollar rooms upstairs. Innocence continued to exist in him for them, since they were not able to see anything wrong in what they did with him. He enjoyed it and after all he was nobody's husband.

And if guilt feeling did exist, as perhaps it did on Sunday mornings in the Baptist church, when they outdressed all the women in town and out-shouted half of them, it was a minimal and momentary uneasiness, fanned into a pleasurable passion of repentance by inflamed readings from the Scripture. They shouted out their sins in paroxysms of enjoyable grief. The righteous cleanliness of their souls harldy outlasted the service.

Whether one wants to read the traces of authorial comment as condensations of action and character, or as the tendency of the authorial stance to maintain the option of a conclusive valuation of the narrative material, it should be obvious in both cases that Alice Walker manages to exert considerable influence on the normative level on her fictional characters and on their reception by the reader. She claims for herself more or less explicitly tne role of a reliable narrator, even though in disembodied form.

If *The Third Life of Grange Copeland* can claim a distinct and original narrative tone, this results neither from narrative structure nor from the described mixture of presenting, telling and judging. It is to be found in a general approximation of the language of the novel to the oral code of the vernacular. The idiom of the rural Southern black is most manifest, of course, in the dialogue of un-educated characters like Brownfield, Josie, Lorene and other minor figures of comparable cultural background.

"How you figure that?" Brownfield asked, scowling.
" 'Cause he know which side he on. And it ain't your side and it ain't even just his own. He *bigger* than us, Brownfield. We going to die and go to hell and ain't nobody going to give a damn one way or the other, 'cause we ain't made no kind of plan for what happens after we gone ... "[35]

35. *Op. cit.*, p. 223.

As here delivered by Josie, this idiom is direct and sober, devoid of poetic or stylized features (in the sense, e.g., in which Ernest Gaines uses it in his fiction as a kind of unchanging medium of expression), fluid in moving closer or further away from Standard English (and thus showing the basic openness of black English towards standard speech varying in degree depending on the individual speaker). In contrast to the idiom of the black urban ghetto, the language of the Southern sharecropper does not tend to virtuoso performance or deliberate, playfully heightened verbal and situational richness of allusion and role playing, but rather towards drastic and condensed speech. It is laconic and reductive rather than exuberant and cumulative. This tendency towards sparse and economic expression informs the language of *The Third Life* beyond mimetically rendered direct or indirect speech passages. It shapes descriptive parts of the text as well, and is carried over from the dramatized perspective of fictional characters into authorial comment and evaluation:

> Often they came home together, still bright, flushed from fighting or from good times, but with the glow gradually dying out of their eyes as they faced the creaking floorboards of their unpainted house. Depression always gave way to fighting, as if fighting preserved some part of the feeling of being alive. It was confusing to realize but not hard to know that they loved each other.[36]

> In prison, condemned for ten years to cut lawns and plant trees for jailers, judges, and prominent citizens of Baker County (though he was to be paroled after seven years), he realized an extraordinary emotion. He loved the South. And he knew he loved it because he had never seriously considered leaving it. He felt he had a real understanding of it. Its ways did not mystify him in the least. It was a sweet, violent, peculiarly accomodating land. It bent itself to fit its own laws. One's life, underneath the rigidity of caste, was essentially one of invisibility and luck. One did not feel alone in one's guilt. Guilt dripped and moved all over and around and about one like the moss that clung to the trees.[37]

Even where the text gropes for mythic dimensions reminiscent of Faulkner's adumbrations (as in the last quote), it shares to some degree the concrete, laconic way of perception and expression of its fictional characters, and thus over long stretches contributes to the

36. *Op. cit.*, p. 20.
37. *Op. cit.*, p. 163.

dramatization of their way of life and mentality. (Only in the concluding chapters of the novel, the presence of both Civil Rights pioneers and of Ruth's as yet unsettled perspective conjoin in creating a different plane of articulation, barely held down by Grange's undiminished tough-and-earthy diction.)

Alice Walker can be said to have attempted a kind of encompassing imaginative empathy with the world of the Southern black sharecropper giving due weight to the ubiquitous presence of physical and psychic violence and its burdening effect on the human capacity for self-expression. The deterioration of Mem's educated language under the onslaught of a brutal husband and situation is only the most explicit illustration of a perspective of hopelessness and its concomitant threat of inarticulateness, just as Grange's capacity for cumulative learning is meant to buttress Ruth's claim to more self-realization including self-articulation. (Compared to her, Margaret remains inarticulate, Mem gains only a desperate spurt of self-expression, and Josie illustrates the attrition of a latent vague yearning for self-projection). But here again, whether for reasons of didactic emphasis or because of a more bitter vision of life resting on personal experience and temperament, Alice Walker chose to present a stark contrast in her novel between the general conditions of living of rural blacks as a collective group and the concrete utopia of an unusually privileged individual among them.[38] While the author may claim that her first novel represents (as the gift of lonely exploration) "a radical vision of society or one's people that has not previously been taken into account," and is not necessarily fit "to second the masses' motions, whatever they are" [i.e. to encourage temporarily dominant aspirations of a given group], Alice Walker in *The Third Life* without doubt still falls short of

38. Interview with Mary Helen Washington (quoted in M.H. Washington, "An Essay on Alice Walker," *op. cit.*, p. 143):
I have this theory that Black women in the '50's, in the '40's — the late 40's and early 50's — got away from their roots much more than they will probably ever do again, because that was the time of greatest striving to get into White Society, and to erase all of the backgrounds of poverty. It was a time when you could be the Exception, could be the One, and my sister was the One. But I think she's not unique — so many, many, many Black families have a daughter or sister who was the one who escaped because, you see, that was what was set up for her; she was going to be the one who escaped, and the rest of us weren't supposed to escape, because we had given our One.

what she has herself indicated as her over-all goal: "I am trying to arrive at that place where black music already is; to arrive at that unselfconscious sense of collective oneness; that naturalness, that (even when anguished) grace."[39] In Alice Walker's eyes, only Zora Neale Hurston among her predecessors can be said to have captured this quality in the medium of narrative prose, being "so at ease with her blackness" that she could "capture the beauty of rural black expression" and saw "poetry" where others merely saw incorrect English.[40] Of Hurston's major novel *Their Eyes Were Watching God* (1937) Alice Walker said: "There is enough self-love in that one book — love of community, culture, traditions — to restore a world. Or create a new one."[41]

Measured by this criterion, Walker's first novel only adumbrates the creation of a new world for black men and women on the basis of the destruction of an outlived, insupportable old world in which violence and hate dominated in external conditions as well as in the consiousness of black people. Stopping the self-destruction of black men and women and beginning a process of constructive self-renewal, on a personal as well as a family level, is the novel's thematic proposal. In Ruth's burgeoning expectations the tentatively reconstructed black family would of course call for complementation of the precarious partnership of grandfather and granddaughter by a new relationship of black men and women in general.[42] How this new black family based on new black men and women might become reintegrated into the culture and community of the black group, remains elusive in Alice Walker's first novel, despite the claim raised by Mary Helen Washington in *Sturdy Black Bridges.*[43] The "sense of collective oneness" inherent in black music — and this must be said with due respect to the novel's creative achievement — is barely yet in sight, let alone within

39. Interview with John O'Brien, p. 204.

40. *Op. cit.*, p. 202.

41. Alice Walker, "Dedication" in *I Love Myself When I Am Laughing. A Zora Neal Hurston Reader*, ed. by Alice Walker, N.Y. 1979, p. 2.

42. "How the novel makes the leap from the pattern of destructive family relationships to the positive image of family at the end" (p. 73) is the basic hypothesis for a reading of Alice Walker's first and second novel in Peter Erickson's article " 'Cast Out Alone / To Heal / And Re-Create / Ourselves': Family-Based Identity in the Work of Alice Walker," *CLA JOurnal* 23, No. 1 (Sept. 1979), 71-94.

43. Mary Helen Washington, "An Essay on Alice Walker," *op. cit.*, p. 148.

reach of attainment at the close of the symbolic action of *The Third Life of Grange Copeland.*

BIBLIOGRAPHY

Primary sources

1) Poetry.
   Once. New York: Harcourt, Brace & World, 1968.
   Revolutionary Petunias and Other Poems. New York: Harcourt Brace Jovanovich, 1973.
   Good Night, Willie Lee, I'll See You in the Morning. New York: Dial Press, 1979.
2) Fiction
   The Third Life of Grange Copeland. New York: Harcourt Brace Jovanovich, 1970.
   In Love and Trouble: Stories of Black Women. New York: Harcourt Brace Jovanovich, 1973.
   Meridian. New York: Harcourt Brace Jovanovich, 1976.
   You Can't Keep a Good Woman Down. New York: Harcourt Brace Jovanovich, 1981.

Uncollected Stories
"A Sudden Trip Home in the Spring," *Essence, Spetember 1971. (Also in Black-Eyed Susans.* Classic Stories By and About Black Women, ed. by Mary Helen Washington, Garden City, N.Y.: Anchor Books, 1975, 141-154).
"The First Day (A Fable After Brown)," *Freedomways* 14 (Fourth Quarter 1974).

3) Nonfictional prose
   "But Yet and Still, the Cotton Gin Kept on Working," *The Black Scholar*, 1, January-February 1970, 17-21.
   "The Black Writer and the Southern Experience," *New South* 25 (Fall 1970), 23-26.
   "The Unglamorous but Worthwhile Duties of the Black Revolutionary Artist, or of the Black Writer Who Simply Works and Writes," *The Black Collegian*, (Sept/Oct. 1971).
   "Women on Women," panel discussion with Lillian Hellman et al., *The American Scholar* (Fall 1972).
   "Eudora Welty: An Interview," *Harvard Advocate* 106 (Winter 1973), 68-72.
   "Interview" in *Interviews with Black Writers*, ed. by John O'Brien, New York: Liveright, 1973, 186-211.

"Staying at Home in Mississippi," *New York Times Magazine*, Aug. 26, 1973.

Langston Hughes. New York: Thomas Y Crowell Co., 1974.

"In Search of Our Mothers' Gardens," *Ms.* 2 (May 1974), 64-70, 105.

"In Search of Zora Neale Hurston," *Ms.* 3 (March 1975), 74-79, 85-89.

"Saving the Life that is Your Own: The Importance of Models in the Artist's Life." The Women's Center Reid Lectureship. New York, N.Y., November 11, 1955.

"Beyond the Peacock: The Reconstruction of Flannery O'Connor," *Ms.* 4 (December 1975).

"Lulls," *Black Scholar* 7 (May 1976), 3-12 (also *Ms.* 5, January 1977).

"My Father's Country is the Poor," *The New York Times*, March 21, 1977, 27.

"Anais Nin: 1903-1977," *Ms.* 5 (April 1977).

"Advancing Luna — and Ida B. Wells," *Ms.* 6 (July 1977).

"Secrets of the New Cuba," *Ms.* 6 (September 1977).

"Dedication," in *I Love Myself When I am Laughing.* A Zora Neale Hurston Reader, ed. by Alice Walker, New York: Feminist Press, 1979.

Secondary Sources
(For *The Third Life of Grange Copeland*)

Christian, Barbara, *Black Women Novelists: The Beginning of a Tradition, 1892-1976.* Westport, Conn., London: Greenwood Pr., 1980, esp. pp. 181-204, 234-238).

Coles, Robert, "To Try Men's Souls," *The New Yorker*, February 27, 1971, 104-106.

Erickson, Peter, " 'Cast Out Alone / To Heal / and Re-Create / Ourselves: Family-Based Identity in the Work of Alice Walker," *CLA Journal* 23, No. 1 (Sept. 1979), 71 94.

Fowler, Carolyn, "Solid at the Core," *Freedomways* 14 (1st Quarter, 1974), 59-62.

Gaston, Karen C., "Women in the Lives of Grange Copeland," *CLA Journal* 24, No. 3 (March 1981), 276-286.

Halio, Jay L., "First and Last Things," *The Southern Review* 9 (New Series), No. 1 (Jan. 1973), 455 467.

Harris, Trudier, "Violence in *The Third Life of Grange Copeland,*" *CLA Journal* 19, (Dec. 1975), 238 47.

— — —, — — —, "Folklore in the Fiction of Alice Walker: A Perpetuation of Historical and Literary Traditions," *Black American Literature Forum* 2 (Spring 1977), 3-8.

Smith, Barbara, "The Souls of Black Women," *Ms.* 2 (Febr. 1974), 42-43, 78.

Schorer, Mark, "Novels and Nothingness," *American Scholar*, Winter 1970/71

169-70.

Washington, Mary Helen, "An Essay on Alice Walker," in *Sturdy Black Bridges: Visions of Black Women in Literature*, ed. by Roseann P. Bell et al., Garden City, N.Y.: Anchor Press / Doubleday, 1979, 133-49.

ALBERT WERTHEIM

JOURNEY TO FREEDOM: ERNEST GAINES'
THE AUTOBIOGRAPHY OF MISS JANE PITTMAN (1971)

Many readers, deceived by the title of *The Autobiography of Miss Jane Pittman* and deceived as well by Ernest Gaines' historian persona in the Introduction in the novel, feel certain that they are reading an authentic, edited autobiography and are shocked when they learn the *The Autobiography of Miss Jane Pittman* is a work of fiction. The confusion on the part of the reader is precisely what Gaines wants, for in *The Autobiography of Miss Jane Pittman* he successfully attempts to integrate the development of a vital, idiosyncratic, unforgettable fictional character with an objective history of blacks in the American South from their emancipation to the 1950s. On one occasion, Gaines said that he has wished through *Miss Jane* to write "a folk autobiography."[1] On another occasion, Gaines playfully and slyly pointed to the doubleness of his novel:

Who is Miss Jane — what does she represent? I've heard all kinds of interpretations. More than one reviewer has said that she is a capsule history of black people of the rural South during the last hundred years. I must disagree, and I'm sure Miss Jane would, too. Miss Jane is Miss Jane."[2]

Even in this statement, with Miss Jane defying the reviewers, the line between fiction and non-fiction beomes hopelessly blurred.

The Autobiography of Miss Jane Pittman is divided into four books. The first of these begins by suggesting that the novel will chart what appears to be the epic journey of Ticey, a freed slave girl, to the North and to freedom at the close of the American

1. Ruth Laney, "A Conversation with Ernest Gaines," *The Southern Review*, N.S. 10 (1974), 7.
2. Ernest J. Gaines, "Miss Jane and I," *Callaloo*, I, ii (1978), 37.

Civil War. The archetype of *Uncle Tom's Cabin* comes immediately to mind, an archetype that Gaines consciously invokes in order to forego it, since the geographic journey of Ticey, renamed Jane, to Ohio and freedon is soon aborted. Geographically, Miss Jane will never in the course of her 110 year life span travel beyond the borders of her native Louisiana; but *The Autobiography of Miss Jane Pittman* records an epic jouney of the spirit from slavery and the fact of freedom to the first struggle for integration in the late 1950s and an initial understanding of what freedom actually means. The travels in Gaines's novel are epic but they are spiritual and sociological, and played against the changing landscape of race relations in the deep South. Like the classical epic, like *The Aeneid*, the novel is at once the history and development of a people. That the novel is divided into Books rather than Parts is reminiscent of the epic; and that the number of Books falls short of the requisite Homeric twenty-four seems a gentle reminder that the epic journey of black people in America is far from over.

In the Introduction to this novel, Ernest Gaines presents the supposed author of the work that follows as an historian, who, like the epic poets, works in an oral tradition taping and setting down the essence of Jane Pittman's narrative. What is consciously not being written is either white history, in which the emancipation of the slaves and the life of blacks in American thereafter is only of relatively minor interest, or black history, which dwells on major figures and notable events. The oral history of Miss Jane Pittman becomes the appropriate medium for conveying a folk autobiography,[3] not the history of great men and events but a combined history of the generations of black people who remained in the rural South to work on the plantations where they had once been in bondage. As such, the events of the novel are important occasions in the life of Miss Jane but frequently function as well as symbolic events in a journey from *de facto* liberation to a recognition of what freedom actually entails.

The novel begins with just such a simultaneously biographical and symbolic occasion. Late in the Civil War, Corporal Brown and the Yankee soldiers under his command come to the plantation on

3. See Barry Beckham, "Jane Pittman and the Oral Tradition," *Callaloo*, I, ii (1978), 102-109.

which Ticey is enslaved. The young corporal grandly and benevolently tries to explain to Ticey that he has come to Louisiana "to beat them Rebs and set y'all free"(8).[4] He then endows Ticey with the new name of her freedom explaining, "Ticey is a slave name, and I don't like slavery. I'm go'n call you Jane... Well, from now on your name is Jane. Not Ticey no more." (8). And before he departs, Corporal Brown tells Jane, "And if any of them ever hit you again, you catch up with me and let me know ... I'll come back here and I'll burn down this place" (8). Certainly Corporal Brown means well, but his relationship with the ignorant, trusting young black girl exemplifies the role the Yankees played in black history. They abrogated the system of slavery; they gave the slaves a new name, freed men; and they rode off into the sunset saying, "Call us if you need us."[5] The Union troops left the blacks, as Brown leaves Jane, to deal with their masters or erstwhile masters unaided. When Brown rides off, Jane defiantly refuses to answer to the name of Ticey when her mistress calls: "You called me Ticey. My name ain't no Ticey no more, it's Miss Jane Brown. And Mr. Brown say catch him and tell him if you don't like it" (9). For her self-assertion, the ten or eleven year old Jane is badly beaten and sent to labor in the fields. It is, further, this beating that may well have caused the physical injury making it impossible for her to bear children in later life. The pattern here established in the novel's first chapter is the pattern reiterated throughout *Jane Pittman*: every impulse by blacks towards self-assertion or acting upon the freedom technically given them by the Civil War leads to their bodily harm or murder by whites. The novel begins with freedom for the slaves and at the end of the novel, set in the 1950s, blacks are still struggling to find that freedom (236). *The Autobiography of Miss Jane Pittman* recalls an arduous, painful, slow 100 year journey in search of the freedom promised by Corporal Brown and white American society by the Emancipation Proclamation of 1863.

4. Ernest J. Gaines, *The Autobiography of Miss Jane Pittman* (New York: Bantam Books, 1971). Parentheses following references indicate page numbers in this edition.

5. See James R. Giles, "Revolution and Myth: Kelley's *A Different Drummer* and Gaines' *The Autobiography of Miss Jane Pittman*," *Minority Voices*, I, ii (1977), 46 and Jerry H. Bryant, "From Death to Life: The Fiction of Ernest J. Gaines," *Iowa Review*, 3 (1972), 114.

The Negro spiritual "Let My People Go," recounting the bond-age of the Israelites and Moses's pleas to Pharaoh described in Exodus, clearly refers as well to black slavery. With one chapter of his novel even entitled "Exodus," Gaines reiterates the analogy. As with the Israelites in Exodus 12:39, freedom catches Miss Jane and her fellow slaves unprepared:

> We didn't know a thing. We didn't know where we was going, we didn't know what we was go'n eat when the apples and potatoes ran out, we didn't know where we was go'n sleep that night ... We had never thought a-bout nothing like that, because we had never thought we was go'n ever be free. Yes, we had heard about freedom, we had even talked about free-dom, but we never thought we was go'n ever see that day ... That's why we hadn't got ourself ready. When the word came down that we was free, we dropped everything and started out. (15-16)

The newly freed blacks, like the Israelites before them, are brought forth from slavery by a Moses figure: Big Laura. Like her biblical archetype, Big Laura brings moral laws, when for example, she prevents the half-wit from raping Jane and then turns to the others commanding, "You free, then you go'n act like did on that planta-tion, turn around now and go back to that plantation" (19). Like Moses, too, Big Laura, following the North Star, resolutely leads her sometimes disgruntled flock:

> We walked and walked and walked and walked. Lord, we walked. I got so tired I wanted to drop. Some of the people started grumbling and hanging back ... Big Laura never stopped ... she moved through them trees like she knowed exactly where she was going and wasn't go'n let nothing in the world get in her way. (19-20)

Killed by vicious members of the disbanded Confederate army, Laura dies before she sees the Promised Land. She never, then, comes to realize that for the freed slaves freedom, the Promised Land, is not the state of Ohio but a state of mind. In her death, however, Big Laura leaves behind a legacy: her son Ned and the flint and iron she had used to light a fire. As other readers have realized, Laura's flint rocks are the flame and Ned becomes the keeper of that flame.[6] Big Laura, Ned and other figures in *The Autobiography of Miss Jane Pittman* become, moreover, a series of leaders and martyrs of almost biblical stature.

6. Giles, 45 and Bryant, 115.

A double pulse that is deftly controlled by Ernest Gaines gives structure and meaning to *The Autobiography of Miss Jane Pittman*. On the one hand, the novel is highly episodic and anecdotal with a succession of powerful characters and events shaping the narrative; on the other hand, the novel maintains a continuous flow, provided by Miss Jane's longevity and her autobiographical, single narrative voice. The episodes recount radical events, but these are played off against Miss Jane's abiding conservatism. The sassy Ticey still exists, but for her own survival, Miss Jane learns to repress her. The episodes of the novel, by contrast, portray acts of defiance by courageous and, consequently, short-lived heroes.

When, on her abortive journey North, the young Miss Jane cannot manage to travel beyond the confines of Louisiana, she exclaims in frustration, "Lazana must be the whole wide world" (33). In many ways it is, for the lessons Miss Jane learns in Louisiana are the lessons blacks everywhere learned. In Book I, she learns dramatically the lesson essential for survival in a white world. For speaking out and defying her mistress, the feisty Jane is made barren. On the march to freedom, Miss Jane, Big Laura and the other wandering ex-slaves are massacred by the defeated Confederate patrollers. The scene is significant in a number of ways, for it describes the race hatred of whites for blacks and its most primal level. The reader learns as well of Big Laura, a heroic female Samson, defying and killing a number of patrollers before they manage finally to murder her. Miss Jane and Ned survive because they are well hidden and silent:

> I kept one hand on my bundle and one on the side of Ned's face holding him down. I was go'n stay there till I thought they had spotted me, then I was getting out of there fast. I told Ned be ready to run, but stay till I gived him the sign. I was pressing so hard on his face I doubt if he even heard me, but all my pressing he never made a sound. Small as he was he knowed death was only a few feet away. (22)

The lesson is clear: silence and obscurity are the means for survival; courageous defiance and obtrusiveness bring injury or death. The double pulse of the novel is, then, part of the tragic pattern that underlies Gaines's folk autobiography. Blacks are shown as caught in an impossible dilemma, a "no-win" situation. If they openly declare their freedom and their rights, they are beaten like Ticey or gunned down like Big Laura, Ned and Jimmy; if they are silent and compliant, they are reduced to a life only just short of slavery, a living death in which they must hold back or kill a part of themselves, their outrage. And there is a third and most reprehensible category: those who have neither open nor suppressed defiance but willingly, unquestioningly, accept a slave mentality and the idea of their natural inferiority. These, like the scornful black Union soldiers, are what Miss Jane calls "nigger." As she explains to Ned, "Not all colored is niggers, but them niggers back there" (38).

The polemics of defiance and perseverance that inform *The Autobiography of Miss Jane Pittman* become increasingly pronounced as Gaines's novel takes shape. In Book II, they are present in the portrayal of the special, nonverbal heroism of Jane's husband, Joe Pittman. A ranch hand and an expert tamer of wild horses, Joe Pittman experiences the unique frustration of the black man, who is like an amateur player contending against a professional on the professional's home court, with a set of rules that is always changing and that is controlled by the professional. The situation is an "Alice in Wonderland" nightmare. When Joe wishes to leave Colonel Dye's ranch for a better position near the Texas-Louisiana border, Dye first tries to convince him to stay, then demands repayment of a supposed debt of one hundred and fifty dollars, a minor fortune to any black during the Reconstruction period. And when Joe does manage to amass the sum, Dye demands an additional thirty dollars in interest. Joe and Jane, though they suffer the angry caprice of Dye, do manage to win the game and experience the exultation of triumph:

> ... every time we looked at each other we had to grin. We tried to keep from looking at each other. I looked at the firehalf, Joe looked at the door; then I looked at the door, Joe looked at the firehalf. When we couldn't find nowhere else to look we looked at each other and grinned. No touching, no patting each other on the knee, just grinning. (84)

But such moments of achievement and success winning despite the white man's manipulation of the rules, are far outnumbered by the defeats and martyrdom the autobiography recounts.

Joe Pittman's philosophy, embodied in both his words and his actions, goes a long way in conveying what the novel holds out as a model of the staunch perseverance of blacks in rural America. For Joe, a man must make his mark by doing what he is best able to do and doing it as best he can. When Jane is beset by fears that her husband will meet an untimely death breaking horses, he philosophically replies:

Now, little mama, man come here to die, didn't he?
That's the contract he signed when he was born — 'I hereby degree that one of these days I'm go'n lay down these old bones.' Now, all he can do while he's here is do something and do that thing good. The best thing I can do in this world is ride horses ... Maybe one day one of them'll come along and get me ... But till that day get here I got to keep going. That's what life's about, doing it good as you can. When the time come for them to lay you down in that long black hole, they can say one thing: 'He did it good as he could.' That's the best thing you can say for a man. Horse breaker or yard sweeper, let them say the poor boy did it good as he could. (89-90)

Shortly thereafter Joe does meet his death trying to break an unusually savage, black, wild stallion, who is perceived as a devil or an evil, destructive spirit (91). Joe's encounter with the black stallion is a moving and a symbolic one, for the horse clearly comes to represent the incarnation of hostile forces that try the strength of and, in this case, defeat the black man. The episode illustrates as well an important aspect of *Miss Jane* as a thoughtful, provocative, significant novel. Gaines does not yield to a simplistic allegory that depicts Whitey as the devil, something he could easily have done by making the satanic stallion a white one. Instead, Gaines recognizes that the obstacles confronting and defeating the black man are not reducible to the whole white race. And in Gaines's ability to see the history of blacks after the Civil War as more than racial armageddon lies the source of his unusual power as a writer. Joe "did it good as he could" and, as Gaines shows, he dies struggling, entangled in the stallion's ropes, but he dies *a man*, without racial adjective.

Much of what *The Autobiography of Miss Jane Pittman* has to say surfaces at the very center of the novel, at one of its unquestionable high points: the death and the sermon of Ned. Inheriting the strength and spiritual stature of his mother, Ned, like a biblical patriarch or prophet returns to Louisiana in 1899 as an educated man and as a civil rights leader far ahead of his time. From the outset, Gaines consciously eschews suspense, having Miss Jane state, "That war [the Spanish-American] ended in 1898. He came here the next summer. And a year later, almost to the day, Albert

225

Cluveau shot him down" (98). Instead, Gaines focuses on Miss Jane's reaction to the inevitability of Ned's death and on Ned's brilliant, moving sermon at the river's edge.

As a part of the repeated pattern in the novel, Ned's outspokenness brings his violent demise. Miss Jane, learning that Albert Cluveau has been hired to kill Ned, wishes to scream out her rage, as Ticey would have, at Cluveau; but she has, despite the unusual pain it brings, learned to suppress the Ticey within her. Silence and suppresssion have become a painful and not unheroic instinct, so that when Cluveau admits he will kill Ned, Jane's narrative records:

> I looked at Albert Cluveau a moment, then I felt my head spinning. I made one step toward the house, then I was down on the ground. I heard somebody way off saying, "Jane, Jane, what's the matter, Jane?" I opened my eyes and I saw Albert Cluveau with his ugly face kneeling over me. And I thought I was in hell, and he was the devil. I started screaming: "Get away from me, devil. Get away from me, devil. Get away from me, devil." But all my screaming was inside, and not a sound was coming out. I heard from way off: "You sick, Jane? You sick?" I was screaming, but I wasn't making any noise. (105-106)

Racked by silent screams, Miss Jane becomes a symbol here of the horrifying long, *silent* suffering of her people. Cluveau, like the black stallion, becomes another incarnation of the whole range of antagonisms, evil spirits against which blacks have striven. Jane's description here is that of a waking nightmare, a term with some aptness for describing black life in the white Southern world.

As the novel's most articulate and commanding figure, Ned serves to deliver Gaines's most moving and eloquent formulation of the role of the black man in America. Like Christ's "Sermon on the Mount," Ned's "Sermon at the River" is meant to outline a new testament, a new vision for his listeners. The point of view of Ned's sermon very much captures the spirit of the novel as a whole, for although he sees whites as antagonists hoping to retard the progress of blacks by turning them against one another, Ned sees that it is more to the point for blacks to see some whites as friends, some blacks as enemies. They then must necessarily recognize that the most important thing blacks can do is to stand together as Americans, for the land belongs to those who cultivated it, regardless of color. Ned, then, asks for a breadth of vision that may not as yet have been achieved even in our day, a breadth of vision that transcends racial antagonism. He first gives a double view of whites, stating, "If it wasn't for some white men, none of us would be a-live here today. I myself probably'll be killed by a white man" (108). His view of blacks is equally double-edged, as he argues that blacks became slaves because their own people sold them to the white slave traders and because the blacks in Africa were tribes divided against each other (108-109). Then, developing Miss Jane's earlier insight (38), Ned distinguishes between a nigger and a black American:

> "Do you know what a nigger is?" he asked us. "First a nigger feels below anybody else on earth. He's been beaten so much by the white man, he don't care for himself, for nobody else, and for nothing else ... But there's a big difference between a nigger and a black American. A black American cares, and will always struggle. Every day that he get up he hopes that this day will be better. The nigger knows it won't ..." (110)

In essence, freedom for Ned is standing up and being counted an American, for "America is for red, white, and black men ... America is for all of us ... and all of America is for all of us" (109). Significantly, Gaines's vision, projected through Ned, is of an America that is the product of a shared dream, shared *equally* by all the races that served to build it. Coming from Ned, a man marked for death, as he, his listeners and the reader already know, the sermon serves almost as a prognostication of the future, of the end of the black man's journey. In this respect, not only is Ned's sermon reminiscent of Christ's, but also brings to mind Odysseus' descent into Hades (*The Odyssey*, Book XI) and Aeneas' encounter with the Cumaean Sibyl (*The Aeneid*, Book VI) in which the dead project and prophesy of vision of the distant future. The death of Ned and its immediate aftermath, however, italicize his identity with Christ and the Christian martyrs. Ned dies staunchly facing the bullets of his enemies and in his death galvanizes even those who had no use for him alive into adoration and faith in the future of black Americans:

> They didn't want to go near him when he was living, but when they heard he was dead they cried like children. They ran up to the wagon when it stopped at the gate. They wanted to touch his body. When they couldn't touch his body they took lumber from the wagon. They wanted a piece of lumber with his blood on it. (116)

And Ned's death is seen as significant not merely for blacks but for all Americans. His school became, as Miss Jane explains, a Louisiana state monument, "It is for children of this parish and this State. Black and white, we don't care. We want them to know a black man died many years ago for them" (113). The "them," true to the spirit of Ned's sermon, does not refer to blacks but to all Americans.

Ernest Gaines is a writer who has the ability to probe the human spirit, yet it is important to see as well that he is a writer able to use the Louisiana landscape he knows so well,[7] to serve at once as a realistic and a symbolic landscape. In this regard, Gaines stands in the tradition of George Eliot, and Gaines's treatment of the river and the land around it brings to mind *The Mill on the Floss*. The river in *Miss Jane*, as in George Eliot's novel, comes to mean the flow of life itself. It is fitting that Ned's sermon be given at the river's edge with the white assassins sitting in their boats hostilely listening. It is fitting because the blacks are not yet ready to cross that river to freedom. In Book II, Ned brings them to the shore but cannot make them forge the water. In Book III, however, as part of the journey motif of *Miss Jane Pittman*, the reader is presented with a chapter entitled "The Travels of Miss Jane Pittman," wherein Jane's spiritual journey, her religious experience, is narrated. Importantly, Miss Jane's visionary experience is a kind of pilgrim's progress wherein Jane must carry her heavy load across the river. Both Ned and Joe appear to her, offering to relieve her of her burden but she declines their aid, for she recognizes that there can be no proxies. Each person must cross the river himself. The river itself is beset by satanic creatures, snakes and alligators, and by a conflation of the devil figures Miss Jane has known. Jane relates, "When it came up to my neck I looked up to see how far I had to go -- and there was Albert Cluveau. He was sitting on the horse that had killed Joe Pittman, he was holding the gun that had killed Ned" (137). Jane is frightened but undaunted, crossing the river to meet her Saviour, who tells her she has been reborn (138). Jane's religious experience brings rebirth of the spirit and her travel across the river suggests that spiritual freedom in a non-religious sense must also be achieved by crossing a river made treach-

7. An excellent sense of Gaines's landscape can be derived from his photographs in "Home: A Photo-Essay," *Callaloo*, I, iii (1978), 52-67.

erous by the Albert Cluveaus and by the ways men have attempted to control the flow of the river.

Deftly, Gaines follows the narration of Miss Jane's religious travels with a chapter that will introduce the main story and idea of Book III of the *Autobiography of Miss Jane Pittman*, a rebellion against the traditional racist social rules of the South, the color line. And then Gaines interrupts that narrative by juxtaposing to it a seemingly unrelated, abstract chapter entitled "Of Men and Rivers." By placing the beginning of his narrative about Tee Bob's tragic rebellion against the racial proscriptions of his society between the chapter on Miss Jane's spiritual travel across a river and her speculations about the nature of rivers, Gaines creates a symbolic context for the Tee Bob episode and for Book III of the novel. The tragedy of Tee Bob and Mary Agnes serves as a poignant, specific illustration of the abstractions in "Of Men and Rivers."

For Miss Jane, the river dominates her landscape and its floods are one important way she measures time. Explaining the periodic floods, Jane asserts, "high water was caused by man, because man wanted to control the rivers, and you cannot control water"(147). The Indians, moreover, lived at peace, worshipping the rivers "till the white people came here and conquered them and tried to conquer the rivers, too" (147). The first levee, according to Miss Jane, was built during slavery and is seen by her as an act against the natural order of things. The system of levees was the brainchild of a Frenchman, who said:

> "This here water got to be confined ... We got to get that water to running where it's suppose to run. Suppose to run in the river, and we got to keep it there." (148-149)

Miss Jane sarcastically rejoins, "Like you can tell water where to go." The dikes create a situation that forces the river periodically to have so strong a current that it overflows, leaving great devastation in its wake. And even when people thought the flood tides had passed, and then offered that the waters had subsided, they suddenly turned around, horror-stricken, to find a whole sea coming toward them (149-150). Rather than learn the lesson of the river, men, Miss Jane narrates, only made matters worse by replacing the old levees with modern spillways, and she concludes the chapter with a meaningful prophecy:

But one day the water will break down his spillways just like it broke through the levee. That little Frenchman was long dead when the water broke his levee in '27, and these that built the spillways will be long dead, too, but the water will never die. That same water the Indian used to believe in will run free again. You just wait and see. (150)

The white man's doomed attempt to control the natural flow of the waters is clearly a symbolic analogy for his doomed attempt to control the flow of human life by slavery, segregation and the whole range of modern unnatural restrictions, like the river's spillways, that seek to make human relations flow against their natural direction. The proscriptions of Southerners, like their levees, have brought and will bring periodic, destructive floods; but, as the analogy implies, natural relations among the races "will run free again. You just wait and see." Miss Jane's religious travels take her across the river to freedom of the soul. Social freedom has yet to come but is, like the freedom of the river, inevitable.

Book III of *The Autobiography of Miss Jane Pittman* surveys the restrictions, the dikes, that restrain justice and passion, and recounts the devastation that ensues when the rules give way. Reminiscent of Joe Pittman's hardship through the irrational and patently unfair rules set down by Colonel Dye, Book III recounts how the black farmworker Katie is fired by the plantation owner, Robert Samson, when she runs afoul of her redneck overseer Tom Joe, and how, likewise, Samson must send away his own half-caste (and therefore black), illegitimate son, Timmy, when the boy defies Tom Joe. Katie and Timmy are both morally in the right but, since they are also both black, they cannot be allowed to claim a victory over the vicious, despicable, *white* overseer. Blacks must play by the house rules, and the house is white. Samson's wife argues that the overseer must be fired or jailed, but her husband explains, "You pinned medals on white man when he beat a nigger for drawing back his hand" (146). The unfair house rules enforced by whites are understood by Miss Jane and the other blacks. Only Robert Samson's legitimate son, Tee Bob, is unable to live by the rules:

Robert thought he didn't have to tell Tee Bob about these things. They was part of life, like the sun and the rain was part of life, and Tee Bob would learn them for himself when he got older. But Tee Bob never did. He killed himself before he learned how he was supposed to live in this world. (147)

230

The passions Tee Bob will feel for the Creole teacher, Mary Agnes, will place such pressure upon the rules meant to direct his behavior that his overflowing passions cause him to break the inflexible rules, the social taboos of the South, and bring his consequent demise.[8]

Tee Bob's attraction to Mary Agnes is, in his society, an acceptable, understandable attraction and may find an approved outlet were he to sow his wild oats with the Creole teacher. But, as Miss Jane recognizes, Tee Bob's is more than a mere lustful attraction, for "He looked at her with love, and I mean the kind that's way deep inside of you." And Jane recognizes, too, that "he was ready to go against his family, this whole world, for Mary Agnes" (171). Confiding his love for Mary Agnes in his friend Jimmy Caya, Tee Bob hears only a recitation of the rules: he may have Mary Agnes sexually but anything beyond that would be impossible, unthinkable, too. After Tee Bob commits suicide, Jimmy Caya earnestly weeps, "I didn't tell him no more than what my daddy told me ... What my daddy's daddy told him. What your daddy told you. No more than the rules we been living by ever since we been here" (190). Tee Bob's inability to abide by the taboos leads not only to his destruction but to a more general devastation within the Samson household. The very Samson house is physically shaken and damaged as Robert Samson attempts to discover the meaning of his son's actions by breaking down the door to the room into which Tee Bob has fled:

> He wasn't aiming to break the door in, he wanted to chop it down now. Every time he hit the door the water from the axe sprayed the people in front and they had to move further back. The sound of the axe against the door went like thunder through that old house. Pictures of the old people shook on every wall. A looking-glass fell and scattered all over the floor. Women screamed. That gal, Judy Major, almost knocked her daddy over getting in his arms. (185)

Society is shaken. The white generations tremble within their picture frames. And Robert Samson finds his only legitimate son and heir dead, a suicide.

In a way that stressed the breadth of vision Gaines has throughout his novel, the significance of Tee Bob's death is given by Tee Bob's white godfather, Jules Raynard. The tragic death, Raynard

8. See Giles, 47.

philosophically argues, has been brought about by society, by the society that includes blacks, whites and Creoles. "We all killed him," Raynard exclaims, "We tried to make him follow a set of rules our people gived to us long ago. But these rules just ain't old enough, Jane ... But Tee Bob couldn't obey. That why we got rid of him. All us. Me, you, the girl — all us" (193). Separation of races may have been a white concept, but, as in the "The LeFabre Family" chapter, it is endorsed by the Creoles and blacks as well. On the closing page of Book III, Jane laments, "Poor Tee Bob," to which Raynard astutely replies, "No. Poor us" (196). Book III, then, records the devastation rendered by a crack in the social levees. The rent grows larger in Book IV, which brings the novel to the 1950s and which heralds a new era.

Throughout *The Autobiography of Miss Jane Pittman*, strength and resistance of the black people first evidenced by Big Laura and the sassy Ticey gains momentum. And it is a momentum that marks not merely the growing dignity and power of blacks on their long journey to freedom but the concomitant breakdown of the old, constricting ways as well. Ned carries the spark his mother hands down but the resistance of Tee Bob, a white, is also a forerunner of things to come. Increasingly in the novel, the games and rules are no longer completely in the white man's hands; and Jane's admiration for the emergent breed of black sports figures — Jackie Robinson, Joe Louis, Sonny Liston — underscores the growing adeptness of blacks at hitherto white games. As Miss Jane ends her autobiography, the folk autobiography of her people, in Book IV of Gaines's novel, a new, perhaps penultimate stage on the epic journey to true freedom is reached; the civil rights movement.

In the last section of the novel, Gaines once again posits a leader, a new young man to follow, nearly a half-century later, in the footsteps of Ned. If Ned is a voice crying in the Southern wilderness, Miss Jane and her friends know early on that Jimmy is "the One." In part, Jimmy is formed by what he sees and hears in the quarters where Miss Jane lives. He sees the life of Southern blacks changing and he hears from Jane and others the history of what has come before:

Now he hears this: heard us on that gallery talking about slavery, talking about the high water, talking about Long. He heard me talk about Cluveau and Ned. He heard us all talk about Black Harriet and Katie; Tom Joe and Timmy ... Jimmy hears all this before he was twelve, by the time he was twelve he was definitely the One. (207-208)

What Jimmy hears and sees to make him the One, is precisely what the reader hears and sees in the process of reading *Miss Jane*; thus Gaines's fiction itself serves to stimulate the reader to become one of Jimmy's followers. Book IV, moreover, indicates a widening resistance to white control and a widening, brave refusal to acquiesce to white rule and white rules.

In the face of a new black vitality, the old white South seems increasingly decadent. Scarred by the suicide of Tee Bob, Robert Samson seems a broken man anachronistic though still curmudgeonly in his insistence that the blacks on his land not take part in civil rights demonstrations lest he summarily evict them from his property, "there ain't go'n be no demonstrating on my place. Anybody 'round here think he needs more freedom than he already got is free to pack up and leave now" (220).

When one of the young men on Samson's land does take part in a demonstration, he and his mother are evicted. That action crystallizes for Jane and for the reader the fragility of black life and to what extent the white landowner still controls the rules. The evicted family poignantly hang signs on their wagon reading, "AFTER FIFTY YEARS, ROBERT SAMSON KICKED US OFF. BLACK PEOPLE FATE" (221). In a symbolic moment, Gaines brilliantly radiates this message to Miss Jane, to all the blacks, and quite specifically to all his readers. As the evicted Yoko and her son pass in their wagons and with their signs through the blacks quarters, Yoko's chiffonier of "chifforobe" reflects everywhere:

Yoko hadn't covered that chifforobe glass and the glass was flashing all over the place. From the time they brought it out the house till they left the quarters it flashed all over the place. All over the empty places where houses used to be and where the Cajuns got their fields now. It flashed on all these old houses and all these old fences. It flashed on you, too, if you didn't get out the way. (221-222)

The "you" in the last sentence clearly embraces the reader as well as the people who populate Miss Jane's world. The light from Yoko's mirror and the message on her wagon spread everywhere in the pages that draw *Miss Jane Pittman* to its conclusion.

Following the pattern set by the novel's other martyr figures,

233

Jimmy, the One, is assassinated. Active in Martin Luther King's movement and like Dr. King, (who met his death just three years prior to the publication of *The Autobiography of Miss Jane Pittman*) Jimmy is a teacher whose teachings survive his death and survive partially because of his death. On the last page of the novel, the murder of Jimmy is directly responsible for the 110 year-old Miss Jane's taking her stand, showing her courage and defiance, travelling across the river that separates her from dignity, and finding the meaning of the freedom toward which she has journeyed since the initial pages of the novel. Gaines end *The Autobiography of Miss Jane Pittman* with a powerful sentence as the aged Jane defiantly disobeys Robert Samson: "Me and Robert looked at each other there a long time, then I went by him" (246). It is a line of triumph: one that marks a new beginning rather than an end.

BIOGRAPHY

Ernest J. Gaines was born on January 15, 1933 in Oscar, Louisiana. He was raised there by a crippled aunt able to move about only by crawling on the floor. In 1948, Gaines left Louisiana and the South so he could join his mother and stepfather, and so he could attend junior high school and high school in California. Gaines began his secondary school education in Vallejo, California, where his mother and stepfather, who was in the merchant marines, resided. In the years that followed, the family moved frequently within California.

After service in the U.S. Army from 1943 to 1955, Gaines enrolled at San Francisco State College, from which he received a B.A. degree in 1957. A recipient of the Wallace Stegner Fellowship, Gaines then spent a year, 1958-1959, in the Stanford University writing program. In the years that followed, Gaines published several short stories, some of which appeared in his two short story collections: *Bloodline* (1968) and *A Long Day in November* (1971). In addition to the much acclaimed *The Autobiography of Miss Jane Pittman* (1971), and *In My Father's House* (1978). Gaines's fiction deals mostly with black Americans and Creoles in the American South. Although he continues to reside in California, Gaines spends extensive periods of time in Louisiana gathering material for his writing and creating the bases for a fictive world that has often been compared to Faulkner's.

234

SECONDARY SOURCES

A number of fine essays on Ernest Gaines and *The Autobiography of Miss Jane Pittman* appear in the special number of *Callaloo* devoted to Gaines, Volume I, iii (1978). Among these essays are:

Barry Beckman, "Jane Pittman and Oral Tradition," 102-109.

Michel Fabre, "Bayonne or the Yoknapatawpha of Ernest Gaines," 110-124 [a translation of an article originally published in *Recherches Anglaises et Américaines*, 9, 208-222.]

Ernest J. Gaines, "Home: A Photo-Essay," 52-67.

"Miss Jane and I," 23-38.

Charles H. Rowell, "Ernest J. Gaines: A Checklist, 1964-1978, 125-131.

Among useful articles published elsewhere are:

Jerry H. Bryant, "From Death to Life: The Fiction of Ernest J. Gaines," *Iowa Review*, 3 (1973), 106-120.

Jerry H. Bryant, "Ernest J. Gaines: Change, Growth and History," *Southern Review*, N.S. 10 (1974), 851-864.

John Callahan, "Image-Making: Tradition and the Two Versions of The Autobiography of Miss Jane Pittman," *Chicago Review*, 29, ii (1977), 45-62.

James R. Giles, "Revolution and Myth: Kelley's *A Different Drummer* and Gaines' *The Autobiography of Miss Jane Pittman*," *Minority Voices*, I, ii (1977), 39-48.

Ruth Laney, "Conversation with Ernest Gaines," *The Southern Review*, N.S. 10 (1974), 1-14.

WOLFGANG KARRER

THE NOVEL AS BLUES: ALBERT MURRAY'S
TRAIN WHISTLE GUITAR (1974)

Albert Murray's only attempt at a novel so far[1] deals with young Scooter's way into manhood by imitation of adult role models, or as psychologists would say, the construction of an ego ideal.[2] Gasoline Point, Mobile, Alabama between 1926 and 1930[3] becomes the specific scene for such well-known themes of American fiction like initiation and quest for identity. The plot characteristically is one of revelation rather than resolution,[4] i.e. the various seemingly unconnected episodes repeatedly show Scooter having some meaningful experience or epiphany[5] which generally centers around an adult hero or mentor. Between the tenth and the fourteenth year of his life Scooter encounters the heroes he tries to build his identity on. He finds them by direct experience or in

1. Theresa Gunnels Rush, Carol Fairbanks Myers, and Esther Spring Aratha, *Black American Writers. Past and Present: A Biographical and Bibliographical Dictionary*. Metuchen, N.J.: Scarecrow Press, 1975, v.II, p. 562 report a work in progress "The Story Teller as Blues Singer" about a young man who interrupts his college education to play bass fiddle in a jazz band. It has not appeared so far.

2. Edith Jacobson's *The Self and the Object World*. New York: International Universities Press, 1964 provides an excellent theoretical framework for an understanding of Scooter's quest for identity in psychoanalytic terms.

3. Popular songs and the baseball seasons allow a dating of the events.

4. Seymour Chatman, *Story and Discourse. Narrative Structure in Fiction and Film*. Ithaca: Cornell University Press 1978, p. 48. This plot structure, also called the "ideological story" (Todorov) seems to have a strong affinity to the story of identity. See Manfred Pütz, *The Story of Identity. American Fiction of the Sixties*. Stuttgart: Metzler, 1979, pp. 6-13.

5. Northrop Frye, *The Anatomy of Criticism. Four Essays*. Princeton: Princeton University Press 1957, pp. 60-62. In Frye's scheme this plot belongs to the ironic thematic mode.

the oral and written traditions of his community, and he tries out their lessons in adventures of his own.

The nine episodes of the novel, leaving aside for the moment four short interludes and the introduction, accordingly fall into three different groups: encounters with heroes, past and present, and adventures.

In the first episode Scooter and his friend Little Buddy Marshall return home after their attempt to follow their idol Luzana Cholly, a local bluesplayer and hobo, about to board a northbound freight train. Luzana Cholly has sent them back to school. In the second episode the two boys, flunking school, find a decaying corpse in the swamp. In the third Scooter learns about American history, both black and white, John Henry and George Washington, at the fireside of his home. In episode four Scooter learns about the African past of Unka JoJo whose proud black nationalism he finally rejects for the philosophy of his favorite "auntee" Miss Tee, who holds that no ancestral bloodlines of identity were likely to stand him in better stead than "the background you could create for yourself by always doing best in school" (86f.).[6] Episode five turns to the two dominant and conflicting oral traditions of the black community in Gasoline Point: church on Sunday, blues on Monday. Scooter has to choose between the Amen-Corner respectability of Lucinda Wiggins or the attractive sinfulness of such blues singers and badmen as Luzana Cholly and Stagolee Dupas. In episode six Scooter and his friend Little Buddy Marshall witness the murder of Beau Beau Weaver by the hands of Bea "Red" Ella Thornton who kills him because as the blues ballad goes "He was her man, and he done her wrong."[7] In episode seven the two boys observe how their secret hero Stagolee Dupas defends the piano he has been playing in a juke joint against the white sheriff trying to kick the keys off the piano. They are not surprised when the body of Deputy Sheriff Earl Joseph Brantley Timberlake is found next day under mysterious circumstances, never to be cleared up. In episode eight Scooter manages to lose his virginity to Deljean Mc-Cray in the house of Miss Tee, somehow keeping his fingers cross-

6. Albert Murray, *Train Whistle Guitar*. New York: McGraw-Hill, 1975 [1974]. All page references in the article refer to this edition.
7. "Frankie and Johnnie" is one of the most often performed and best known blues ballads.

ed all the time. And the final goodbye to childhood comes when Scooter learns at a wake that Miss Tee is his real mother and that those whom he called Mama and Papa have adopted him, a revelation or *cognitio*[8] that has been foreshadowed since episode one.

Scooter and Little Buddy Marshall who owe more to Ralph Ellison's Buster and Riley than to Tom Sawyer and Huckleberry Finn, confront reality by imitating the walk, voice, or stance of their two main heroes, to which could be added Gator Gus the baseball pitcher, Jack Johnson the heavyweight champion, Natchez Trace bandits, millwrights, railroad porters (33, 31, 53, 54, 66, 38) and numerous others.[9] They try out their new roles in adventurous encounters with love and death. This thematic structure of the plot can be represented thus:[10]

1. *Hero*: Luzana Cholly	2. *Adventure*: Death in the Swamp	3. *Past*: John Henry and George Washington
4. *Hero*: Unka JoJo (rejected)	5. *Past*: The church and the blues	6. *Adventure*: Death on the Street
7. *Hero*: Stagolee Dupas (*fils*)	8. *Adventure*: Love with Deljean McCray	9. *Past*: "Mama" and Miss Tee.

What can be thus decribed as an identity quest in the ironic mode and in the comedy plot (which ends by including its hero into the larger society)[11] on quite a different level also turns out to

8. Typical of the comedy in Frye's anatomy: Northrop Frye, *The Anatomy of Criticism*, pp. 169-171.

9. The main heroes are linked by simile to each other (12, 31, 124, 135). Compare the contrast between the sporty limp of Luzana Cholly (15) with the stiff walk of Unka JoJo (80).

10. The graph reveals thematic relationships beyond the obvious ones (episodes 1, 4, 7 or 2, 6, 8): Compare the relation between 4 and 9 (the rejection of ancestral lineage for achievement, the ironic contrast between 7 and 3, the central position of 5 which mediates between 1 and 7 on the one, and 3 and 9 on the other side. 5 also mediates between past and present.

11. Again, characteristic of the comedy plot in Frye's system; Northrop Frye, *The Anatomy of Criticism*, pp. 43-52.

be a classic oedipal romance.[12] Scooter is obviously looking for a father figure to build his ego ideal and super ego on, an ideal which "Papa," also called "Unka Whit," cannot provide (60f.). Ironically his quest ends in finding his real mother, whose values (in direct opposition to those of the blues) finally carry the victory: Scooter becomes the best pupil in school and finally leaves Gasoline Point to go to college, leaving his friends, loves and hero models behind.[13] That Scooter really wants to prove his manhood with his mother comes out beautifully in the hilarious sex-encounters with Deljean McCray and the other girls. Miss Tee and Mama had nicknamed Scooter "My Mister" and "Little Man," or sometimes "Mister Man" (9). Not only does Scooter's seduction take place in Miss Tee's house with Miss Tee's husband's niece, but also does Deljean McCray incite Scooter with such incendiary words like "little old mister boy" (141), "you mannish rascal you," "little old mannish pisstail boy," and finally the relieving "Well come on then little old mannish boy, she said. Since you think you already such a mister big man." (144). During the sex play and in later recollections Deljean gleefully and excitingly reminds Scooter of Miss Tee and of what she would say if she found out about them (160 f., 162 f., 164). The other school girls remind Scooter of another mother-figure, his favorite teacher, Miss Lexine Metcalf (150, 154) who is explicitly associated with Miss Tee (160). Nor are the menace of castration and the jealous father figure absent (141 f., 88 f., 145). The "manhood" of Scooter is thus thoroughly tested by his girlfriends and the two encounters with death. Albert Murray invites the reader to share irony and nostalgic pleasure in looking back at Scooter's mockheroic boyhood adventures and fervent hero worship. But, as Northrop Frye has pointed out, the modern ironic mode, in which the hero is inferior in insight or power to the narrator and his audience,[14] tends to return to the mythical mode. This aspect of *Train Whistle Guitar* deserves a closer look.

12. Murray rejects Freud as violently as he does Marx in his writings, e.g. *The Hero and the Blues.* Columbia: University of Missouri Press 1973, pp. 17, 44, 100 f.

13. As Luzana Cholly himself has already prophesied: *"Make old Luze glad to take his hat off to you some of these days. You going further than old Luze ever dreamed of."* (30).

14. Northrop Frye, *The Anatomy of Criticism*, p. 34.

If it is true that all literary genres are based on "inferior (sub-literary) genres" and that these genres are in constant need of "re-barbarization"[15] then the specific foundations of American fiction, as Constance Rourke and Daniel Hoffman have shown, lie in the American folktales and their heroes, in the Yankee, frontiersman, and the Negro, in the tall tales, witchcraft lore and providences.[16] If, on the other hand, folk culture since Johann Gottfried Herder has been used to establish a national culture against foreign cultural hegemony[17] then Afro-American fiction could not simply adopt the dominant white folk culture which had served to define the American character against Europe but it had to go back to the rich black oral traditions. This old and central problem of a black aesthetic[18] had found an important answer in Ralph Ellison's work which makes extensive use of black folklore.[19] But, as Ellison was careful to point out against a white critic:

> I use folklore in my work not because I am a Negro, but because writers like Eliot and Joyce made me conscious of the literary value of my folk inheritance.[20]

If Ellison seems to have discovered the uses of folklore as underlying myth via Joyce and Eliot, Murray seems to have made his discoveries via Ellison and Thomas Mann.[21] In *The Omni-Americans*

15. René Wellek and Austin Warren, *Theory of Literature*. repr. New York: Harcourt, Brace & World 1961, pp. 226.

16. Constance Rourke, *American Humor. A Study of the National Character*. repr. Garden City: Doubleday, 1971 [1939]; Daniel Hoffman, *Form and Fable in American Fiction*. New York: Norton 1965.

17. Gene Bluestein, *The Voice of the Folk. Folklore and American Literary Theory*. Amherst: University of Massachusetts Press, 1972, p. 4.

18. Robert Felgar, "Black Content, White Form," *Studies in Black Literature* 5 (1975), 28-30. Melvin Wade and Margaret Wade, "The Black Aesthetic in the Black Novel," *Journal of Black Studies 2* (1971), 391-408.

19. *Not Without Laughter* (1930) by Langston Hughes may also have left a trace on Albert Murray's work. For the uses of the blues in the twenties see Irvin Nathan Huggins, *Harlem Renaissance*. Oxford: Oxford University Press, 1971, pp. 72-83, 190-243.

20. Ralph Ellison, "Change the Joke and Slip the Yoke," in Alan Dundes, ed., *Mother Wit from the Laughing Barrel. Readings in the Interpretation of Afro-American Folklore*. Englewood Cliffs: Prentice-Hall, 1973, p. 64.

21. Albert Murray, *The Hero and the Blues*, pp. 51-63; Albert Murray, *The Omni-American. New Perspectives on Black Experience and American*

Murray revises the minstrel traits of Rourke's third representative of the American character, the Negro, to make the black blues singer a cultural hero.[22] He praises *Invisible Man* as

> *par excellence* the literary extension of the blues. It was as if Ellison had taken an everyday twelve bar blues tune (by a man from down South sitting in a manhole up North in New York singing and signifying about how he got there) and scored it for full orchestra.[23]

And Murray adds in a characteristic turn

> Both Baldwin and Wright seem to have overlooked the rich possibilities available to them in the blues tradition ... *it is the product of the most complicated culture, and therefore the most complicated sensibility in the modern world.*[24]

Murray's assessment of the blues and his literary aesthetic owe quite a lot to Ellison's essays in *Shadow and Act*. Indeed, the main propositions outlined in *The Omni-Americans* (1970) and *The Hero and the Blues* (1973) are firmly rooted in the aesthetic thought of the fifties when concepts like "the end of ideology" and "the search for a new myth" were common.[25]

For Murray art has a primarily cognitive function, it changes and enhances our world comprehension.[26] Like Ellison, Murray bases his art on myth and ritual:

> The aboriginal source of fiction ... is the song and dance ritual or *molpê* ... The story teller works with language, but even so he is a song and dance man (a maker of *molpês*) whose fundamental objectives are extensions of those of the bard, the minstrel, and the ballad maker which incidentally, are also those of the contemporary American bluessinger.[27]

Culture. New York: Outbridge & Dienstfrey, 1970, pp. 142-169. As Ellison points out in *The Massachusetts Review* 18 (1977), 428 he has known Murray since their days at Tuskegee.

22. *Ibid.*, p. 17. Albert Murray, *Stomping the Blues*. repr. New York: Quartet Books, 1978, pp. 67, 163, 193 shows clearly the tendency to write jazz history as a history of black culture heroes.

23. Albert Murray, *The Omni-Americans*, p. 167.

24. *Ibid.*, p. 166.

25. Murray is quite at home with the work of Susanne K. Langer, Thomas Mann, Northrop Frye, Constance Rourke, David Riesman, etc.

26. Albert Murray, *The Hero and the Blues*, p. 9.

27. *Ibid.*, p. 21.

The blues tradition represents best what Murray calls the principle of antagonistic cooperation:

> Heroism, which like the sword is nothing if not steadfast, is measured in terms of the stress and strain it can endure and the magnitude and complexity of the obstacles it overcomes.[28]

In this conception the author, like the bluessinger, takes the place of the hero:

> It is the storyteller working on his own terms as mythmaker (and by implication, as value maker), who dignifies the conflict, identifies the hero (which is to say the good man – perhaps better the adequate man), and decides the outcome; and in doing so he not only evokes the image of possibility, but also prefigures the contingencies of a happily balanced humanity and of the Great Good Place.[29]

This proposition rather neatly describes what is happening in *Train Whistle Guitar*. The blues tradition, accepted and imitated by a white audience and white singers more readily than any black folk tradition, can be used as an integrative strategy by the black author:

> Precisely as white musicians who work in the blues idiom have been simulating the tribulations of U.S. Negroes for years ... so in fiction must readers, through their desire to imitate and emulate black story book heroes, come to identify themselves with the disjunctures as well as the continuities of black experience as if to the idiom born.[30]

Murray sees a basis for this new audience in the young white activists of the Civil Rights Movement. As a logical correlate Murray takes a universalist stand in the universalism/nationalism debate: "All stories are examples of some essential aspect of human experience in general ..."[31] This aesthetic position, as Murray repeatedly makes perfectly clear, is also a political one: the ubiquitous dragon in his heroic scheme is the Marx/Freud school of "social science

28. *Ibid.*, pp. 38, 58.
29. *Ibid.*, p. 11.
30. *Ibid.*, 50. For the tradition of this approach see Gunnar Myrdal, *An American Dilemma. The Negro Problem and Modern Democracy*. repr. New York: Harper, 1969, vol. II, pp. 753 f. and Gene Bluestein, *The Voice of the Folk*, pp. 110f.
31. Albert Murray, *The Hero and the Blues*, p. 93.

fiction" or the so called "protest novel."[32] This coherent though hardly original position, which develops certain implications in Ralph Ellison's work, leads to *Train Whistle Guitar* which, however, in some ways goes much beyond *Invisible Man* in developing a black fictional approach based on black folklore and the blues.[33]

The folklore material or the myth *Train Whistle Guitar* is based on, comes from the Brer Rabbit cycle of stories, as collected and retold by Joel Chandler Harris in his *Uncle Remus* tales. If the analogy between Brer Bear and the narrator of *Invisible Man*, between Brer Rabbit and his various mentors is rather unspecific and only hinted at,[34] *Train Whistle Guitar* links Scooter's education as firmly to Brer Rabbit as Luzana Cholly to Uncle Remus (29). In the well-known Tar-Baby story the trickster Brer Rabbit, of an old West African heritage,[35] for once falls into the hands of his usual victim Brer Fox. But Brer Rabbit escapes again by asking his enemy to do with him as he pleases but not, please, to throw him into the briarpatch. Which, of course, is exactly what Brer Fox does, only to hear to his dismay Brer Rabbit shout: "Bred and bawn in a briar patch, Brer Fox — bred and bawn in a briarpatch! en wid dat he skip out des ez lively ez a cricket in de embers."[36] This becomes the key fantasy for Scooter who calls himself Jack the Rabbit and his home the briarpatch (4).

32. *Ibid.*, pp. 15, 16, 44: "American protest fiction of the current Marx/ Freud - oriented variety is essentially anti-adventure and, in effect, nonheroic."

33. For an interpretation of the blues qualities of *Invisible Man* see Edward Margolies, *Native Sons. A Critical Study of Twentieth Century Negro American Authors*. Philadelphia: Lippincott, 1968, pp. 127-148; Gene Bluestein, *The Voice of the Folk*, pp128-140; Sherley Anne Williams, *Give Birth to Brightness. A Thematic Study in Neo-Black Literature*. New York: The Dial Press 1972, pp. 87-96.

34. Floyd R. Horowitz, "Ralph Ellison's Modern Version of Brer Bear and Brer Rabbit in *Invisible Man*," *Midcontinent American Studies Journal* 4 (1963), 21-27 tries to build an ingenuous and rather farfetched interpretation of *Invisible Man* on a few, partly misread, references to the story cycle.

35. Bernard Wolfe, "Uncle Remus and the Malevolent Rabbit," in Alan Dundes, ed., *Motherwit from the Laughing Barrel*, pp. 524-540. For an interpretation of the Tar-Baby and the briarpatch see Lawrence W. Levine, *Black Culture and Black Consciousness. Afro-American Folk Thought from Slavery to Freedom*. Oxford: Oxford University Press 1977, pp. 106f.

36. Joel Chandler Harris, *The Complete Tales of Uncle Remus*. compiled Richard Chase, Boston: Houghton Mifflin 1955 pp. 6-9, 12-14, 14.

In this particular adaptation of the myth Brer Rabbit undergoes several important transformations. He becomes Jack the Rabbit which makes him assimilable to Jack the Bear, Jack and the Bean-stalk, Jack be Nimble and Jack Frost (4, 3, 31, 52), and on the other hand changes the focus from being a brother to being a Jack of all trades.[37] Secondly, and more important, Brer Rabbit loses his mythical trickster qualities. Scooter is closer to the innocence of the American Adam than to the trickster tradition. The briar-patch, of rather subordinate and incidental function in the story cycle, becomes in *Train Whistle Guitar* the central metaphor for protection at home and in the community.

The introduction, which on a different level turns out to be the "theme" of the novel, will serve as an illustration. From the china-berrytree in his front yard Scooter (the boy) surveys and Scooter (the adult narrator) recreates Gasoline Point as his briarpatch: in a clockwise movement the eyes take in — like in a slow camera's pan — the sights from the East to the North, and the imagination transcends the limitations of the horizon:

> All you could see due north up Dodge Mill Road beyond Buckshaw Corner and the crawfish pond that was once part of a Civil War artillery embank-ment was the sky above Bay Poplar Woods fading away into the marco po-lo blue horizon mist on the other side of which were such express train destinations as Birmingham, Alabama and Nashville, Tennessee, and Cincinnati, Ohio, and Detroit, Michigan, plus the snowbound Klondike of Canada plus the icebound tundras of Alaska plus the North Pole. (3)[38]

The opposition between the briarpatch and the marco polo blue, both imaginary, but one limited, the other transcendent, introdu-ces one important thematic strand of the novel: the rhythm of centrifugality and centripetality, of the hero's sally and return. The briarpatch is as much starting point as refuge from the distant dreamy sky blue of boyhood (6) and the future steel blue of man-hood (7) which run as a sort of *leitmotif* through the novel[39] : The

37. Other fantasies clearly come from white folklore traditions (Cinderella, Robin Hood, 54), or books (Buster Brown, 54, cowboys and explorers, 37).

38. This imaginary spatial expansion recurs in the novel (15, 16, 20, 32, etc.), often associated with the color blue which thus tends to stand for the exotic and the imaginative world.

39. Compare: 9, 15, 16, 17, 23, 25, 37, 40, etc. The motif slowly fades out like the corresponding image of the briarpatch.

specific ambiguity between sky blue and steel blue is repeated in the briarpatch which is not only the place of home and protection but has ambiguities and dangers of its own:

> blues music was mostly about ... the blue steel train whistle blueness of the briarpatch (the habitat not only of the booger bear whose job was to frighten naughty children into obedience but also of that most grizzly and terrifying of all bears, the one who according to fireside and barbershop accounts put the mug on you, ripped out the seat of your pants and made you a tramp ...) (97 f.)

Scooter and his buddy also call themselves Jack the Bear (whose home is nowhere and anywhere and everywhere) (4). Localism and universalism, past and present, quickness and strength, safety and danger are equally represented in Scooter's briarpatch "which is perhaps even more of a location in time than an intersection on a map" (3).

The use of blues tradition in *Train Whistle Guitar* parallels and complements in many aspects the use Murray made of the Brer Rabbit tales. The blues permeate the novel from its title on down. As Murray repeatedly points out in his novel and in *Stomping the Blues*, it is an old blues technique to imitate the sound of trains and of train whistles on instruments like the guitar or the piano.[40] Significantly the title compounds and transcribes this practice not as "Guitar Train Whistles" but as *Train Whistle Guitar*: the medium seems to be the message. Because the problem of oral vs. written culture is at the root of the problem of how to use the blues in fiction. This is, of course, no problem as long as one restricts the use of blues to titles, mottoes or direct speech in the novel. The use of blues quotes for implications like *If Beale Street Could Talk* (married men would have to take their beds and walk) or "Sometimes I wonder ..." as a poignant motto or commentary to *American Hunger* can be found quite often, but the relation to the blues tradition remains superficial. Nor does the insertion of a blues quote as a background event like the brief appearance of "Casey Jones" in *This Side of Paradise* make a blues novel. The relation

---

40. Compare: 8, 15, 56, 97. For a description of the technique see Albert Murray, *Stomping the Blues*, p. 118 where Murray suggests that railroad onomatopoeia may have replaced West African drum talk. A fine example of train whistle guitar can be heard on Blind Willie McTell's "Travelin' Blues."

becomes more intimate if you assign such quotes to real or imaginary bluessingers who appear in the novel. Ellison, for instance, introduces the real and very popular bluessinger Peetie Wheatstraw (his real name was William Bunch) in *Invisible Man* and has him sing a jump blues, also sung by Jimmy Rushing with the title "I may be wrong, but I won't be wrong always."[41] Another more allusive relation to Jimmy Rushing's "Harvard Blues" exists in the name and character of Rhinehart ("Rhinehart, Rhinehart, I'm a most indifferent guy").[42] From here on it is only one more step to expand the allusions to several characters and their relations in a blues, in other words, to base a whole story on a blues ballad, much in the same way James Joyce used Homer, T.S. Eliot the Grail myth, or Thomas Mann the Old Testament. Hollywood has done so in *Her Man* (1930) by Tay Garnett or *She done Him Wrong* (1933) by Lowell Sherman, a serious or a funny version of the old blues ballad "Frankie and Johnnie." The fact that Murray uses quote, allusion, blues characters and implied mythical parallel and several other techniques makes *Train Whistle Guitar* an innovative and important approach of how to use the blues in the novel.

Murray himself clearly points at the problem underlying the novel when he describes how Luzana Cholly

was forever turning guitar strings into train whistles which were not only the once-upon-a-time voices of storytellers but of all the voices saying what was being said in the stories as well (15).[43]

The bluesplayer's artistry in imitating the real sounds of train whistles becomes the novelist's concern of not only imitating the voices of real characters in the novel's dialogue but also of finding a voice for the narrator.[44]

41. Ralph Ellison, *Invisible Man.* repr. New York: New American Library, 1960, pp. 152-158. The description of this blues may have suggested the title for *Train Whistle Guitar*: "... in its flutter and swoop I heard the sound of a railroad train highballing it, lonely across the lonely night. He was the Devil's son-in-law, all right, and he was a man who could whistle a three-toned chord ..." (156).
42. Ellison himself had to point out this reference which critics missed; Gene Bluestein, *The Voice of the Folk*, p. 138.
43. Narrator's discourse and the characters' speech do not only belong to different levels, but the first seems to frame and subordinate the second.
44. One assumption shared by many black novelists in the sixties and

The dialogue in the novel is permeated with blues language. It also shares some of the basic structures and devices with the blues. Consider the exchange between Scooter and Little Buddy Marshall as they are about to follow Luzana Cholly up North:

Hey, Lebo.
Hey, Skebo.
Skipping city.
Man, you tell em.
Getting further.
Man ain't no lie.
Getting long gone.
Main, ain't no dooky.(22 f.)

After the opening exchange of nicknames the classic call and response pattern underlying the sermon, the blues, and so much of blues-based jazz[45] emerges quite clearly: in a moment of doubt Scooter turns to a series of reaffirming and almost ritualized formula the last one of which alludes to a well known traditional blues ("Long gone, like a turkey through the corn"), while Little Buddy Marshall warmly supports and echoes Scooter's phrases. Even the three part structure of the blues (after the address) is observed. This call- and- response structure permeates the dialogues in the novel, whether the two boys do a little parody of the sermon (39), school children answer their teacher (52), Miss Sister Lucinda Wiggins shouts support from the Amen Corner in church (91 f.) or trades gossip with Miss Libby Lee Tyler like "two trombone players begin trading blues choruses on an up-tempo dance arrangement" (96), or the adults share their sorrow at the wake (180 f.).

Signifying or woofing is another technique which found its way from everyday dialogue into the blues. Here is an example where the two boys try to get some spending money from Luzana Cholly by signifying at him:

seventies seems to be that black writers have to find a new verbal stance based not only on Standard English but also on Black English.

45. Charles Edward Smith, "New Orleans and Traditions in Jazz," in Nat Hentoff and Albert J. McCarthy, eds., *Jazz*. London: Cassell, 1960, pp. 23-41 deals with the West African origins of this pattern. LeRoi Jones, *Blues People. Negro Music in White America*. New York: William Morrow 1963, pp. 50-80 describes the connections between sermon, blues, and early jazz.

Say now hey now Mister Luzana Cholly.
Mister Luzana Cholly one time.
...
Mister Luzana Cholly all night long.
Yeah me, ain't nobody else but.
The one and only Mister Luzana Cholly from Bogaluzana bolly.
...
Got the world in a jug.
And the stopper in your hand.
A man among men.
And Lord God among women!
Well tell the dy ya. (11)

Again the dialogue is sprinkled with formulas ("all night long") and quotations from blues ("Got the world in a jug and the stopper in your hand" comes from Bessie Smith's "Down Hearted Blues") and sermon ("A man among men"). Again these allusions reaffirm a common cultural heritage between the boys. *"Signifying*, however, also refers to a way of encoding messages or meanings which involves, in most cases, an element of indirection."[46]

The indirection is partly carried by the boys' pretense of talking to each other, once they have caught Luzana Cholly's attention, partly by the allusions themselves: "All night long" usually refers to drinking, gambling or sex[47], Bessie Smith continues her line with "I-m gonna hold it until you been come under my command.", and both the boys and Luzana Cholly share the knowledge that the bluessinger does not rate very highly with the church community. There is even more involved: the boys perform an improvised piece of verbal art, they turn the tables on their master who sometimes "would sneak our names into some very well known ballad just to signify at us about something." (10). So they boys make their pitch:

Can't tell no more though.
How come, little sooner, how the goddamn hell come?
B'cause money talks.
Well shut my mouth. Shut my big wide mouth and call me suitcase.

46. Claudia Mitchell-Kernan, "Signifying," in Alan Dundes, *Motherwit from the Laughing Barrel*, p. 311.
47. Compare: "I've been drinking bad whiskey all night long" in the erotic blues " 'Bout a Spoonful," as sung by Mance Lipscombe.

Ain't nobody can do that.
Not nobody that got to eat and sleep. (12)

Unlike the examples quoted by Mitchell-Kernan who emphasizes the aggressive aspects of signifying, most of the examples in *Train Whistle Guitar* are good-humored and friendly. Mama signifies at Scooter about the dangers of the dirty dozens (85): the game might reveal to Scooter Miss Tee's secret. Stagolee Dupas, "the king of the signifying monkeys" (99), and his friend the barrelhouse piano player Claiborne Williams lace their blues playing with wicked winks or heavy signifying at the dancing women (133). The old men in the barbershop talk for the benefit of the boys, pretending not to notice their presence (111 f.) or duel in signifying with Beau Beau Weaver about his money, clothes, and success with women (116, 118). A final example is Deljean McCray's affectionate attempt to signify at Scooter who his real mother is (160 f.).[48]

A third technique to be found in black speech, blues, sermon and jazz is called riffing. Here is Soldier Boy Crawford's answer to those blacks like Unka JoJo who are proud of their African origins:

You know what I tell them? This is what I always tell them. I tell them don't make no goddamn difference to me. And I mean it. What the goddamn hell I care? You know what I tell them? The same thing I told them goddamn Germans. Fuck that shit. Let's go. Them som'iches over there talking about Nigger where your tail at. I said up your mama's ass, motherfucker, and this goddamn cold steel bayonet right here up yours. Because that's what I say. Don't make a goddamn bit of difference to be if my goddamn granddaddy was a goddamn tadpole, LET'S GO. Because I'm the som'ich right here ready to go up side your head. Don't care if my poor old grandmammy wasn't nothing but a stomp hole, LET'S GO. And that's exactly the same thing I say when another one of the Hill Africans come trying to make out like his granddaddy used to be sitting on a solid gold diamond studded stool somewhere on the left-handed side of the Zulu River with his own niggers waiting on him. I say that's all right with me. LET'S GO. I say, Man, my old granddaddy was so dumb Old Marster wouldn't even trust him to pick cotton. Old Marster used to say the only

---

48. About the signifying monkey toast see Roger D. Abrahams, *Deep down in the Jungle.* Hatboro, Pa: Folklore Associates, 1964, pp. 97-172. The final revelation at the wake is curiously close to the other signifying scenes in *Train Whistle Guitar.*

my poor old granddaddy was good for was mixing cowshit and horseshit on the compost pile, so maybe that's how come I'm so full of bullshit. BUT THAT'S ALL RIGHT WITH ME, LET'S GO. (83 f.)

The emphatic phrase "Let's go." accompanies Crawford's growing excitement and the amplification of his theme resembles the way a big band like that of Count Basie supports an instrumental soloist during his improvisation by riffs. Again, Crawford is not only saying something. His playful use of formulas in "running it down"[49] and the self ironic ending make it clear that he has also performed a little piece of verbal art very much like Stagolee Dupas who "was not singing lyrics but humming all the instrumental fills, riffs and solo take-off to him himself as if he were a one man band." (123) The comic sermon becomes indeed one of the main vehicles of verbal artistry in the novel: Uncle Jerome's numerous sermons in the family circle (59 f., 67, 71, 85), Old Sawmill Turner's Dollar Bill History of the United States (73f.), Uncle Jim Bob on Emancipation (174f.), and even Claiborne Williams and Stagolee Dupas seem two pastors warming up their congregation (132).[50]

The blues references in the novel and *Stomping the Blues* make abundantly clear that Murray very often thinks of instrumental and big band jazz when he talks about the blues,[51] and the guitar in *Train Whistle Guitar* — like the novel — is not only a solo instrument but also an instrument of many strings[52] which reproduces "*all* the voices saying what was being said in the stories." (15). So the blues and its rhythms affect the "once-upon-a-time storytellers," too (106 f.). Though the narrator's voice sounds different from the other voices in the novel, the adult narrator owes much to the rich oral culture of church, school, fireside, barbershop, and

49. Thomas Kochman, "Toward an Ethnography of Black American Speech Behavior," in David G. Bromley and Charles F. Longino, eds., *White Racism and Black Americans*. Cambridge, Mass.: Schenkman, 1972, p. 638. For the importance of riffs and their relation to the sermon see Albert Murray, *Stomping the Blues*, pp. 96-98.

50. Charles Keil, *Urban Blues*. Chicago: University of Chicago Press 1966, pp. 143-152 analyzes the preacher roles in many blues performances.

51. Compare the jazz titles by Jelly Roll Morton, Louis Armstrong, Fletcher Henderson, King Oliver mentioned in *Train Whistle Guitar* (159,160, 102, 168).

52. Luzana Cholly plays a twelve-string guitar like Huddie Ledbetter or Leadbelly to whom he is compared (11).

juke joint. The narrator does not separate his voice from the other voices by putting them between quotation marks. This allows him to shift rather freely from direct speech into indirect speech and — as most of the characters' speech remains untagged[53] — into indirect free speech, narrated monologue, reported speech and other forms of neutralizing the difference between the narrator's and the characters' voices. One example will make the point:

> *Luzana Cholly who was the one who used to walk his trochaic-sporty stomping-ground limp-walk picking and plucking and knuckle knocking and strumming (like an anapestic locomotive) while singsongsaying Anywhere I hang my hat anywhere I prop my feet. Who could drink muddy water who could sleep in a hollow log.* (4f.)

"Anywhere I hang my hat anywhere I prop my feet" is tagged and therewith clearly identified as speech and blues phrase of Luzana Cholly. The comparison "like an anapestic locomotive" obviously belongs to the narrator. But the voices of Luzana Cholly and the narrator easily blend in the last sentence: blues phrase and character description at the same time. Thus blues talk is almost as frequent in the narrator's voice as in voices of the characters of the book.

The narrator has no dialogue partner other than the implied reader. The call-and-response structure cannot be used on this level. But the three part blues structure, the AAB of the blues stanza has found its way into the narrator's voice. Using repetition of the first line for tension, and the third line as release the bluessinger will subtly vary tone, speed and pitch when he repeats the first line, something almost impossible to transcribe.[54] The variation open to the writer who wants to make use of the blues structure of

53. Seymour Chatman, *Story and Discourse*, pp. 198-209.

54. Here Ernest Borneman's generalizations about African language and music seem helpful; Ernest Borneman, "The Roots of Jazz," in Nat Hentoff and Albert J. McCarthy, eds., *Jazz*, p. 17: "While the whole European tradition strives for regularity — of pitch, of time, of timbre and of vibrato — the African tradition strives precisely for the negation of these elements. In language, the African tradition aims at circumlocution rather than exact definition. The direct statement is considered crude and unimaginative; the veiling of all content in ever-changing paraphrases is considered the criterion of intelligence and personality. In music, the same tendency toward obliquity and ellipsis is noticeable: no note is attacked straight; the voice or instrument al-

tension and release lies in the length of phrases, vocabulary and —
when read aloud — rhythm and speed. Here is an example, again
taken from the introduction:

> You couldn't see the post office flag from the chinaberry tree because it
> was down in Buckshaw Flat at the L & N whistlestop. You couldn't see
> the switch sidings for the sawmills along that part of Mobile River either,
> because all that was on the other side of the tank yard of the Gulf Refin-
> ing Company. All you could see beyond the kite pasture were the tele-
> graph poles and the sky above the pine ridge overlooking Chickasabogue
> Creek and Hog Bayou. (2)

This is more than rhetorical parallelism. The structure of "You
couldn't see ... You couldn't see ... All you could see ..." is musical: like in the blues stanza repetition matches variation, here in vocabulary and speed changes through compounding the nouns and
making the rest of the words monosyllabic while maintaining the
syntactical structure, and then the release through semantic
change. Even the "Gulf Refining Company" becomes for a moment part of a larger melody.[55] Looking at the other paragraphs
of the introduction a similar pattern appears. After the first introductory paragraph, patterned on a "Then ... Then... when" structure and after a bridge in the second paragraph the following paragraphs begin with "You couldn't see ... You couldn't see ... South-
east of all ... Nor could you see... All you could see." The blues
form is extented to a triple repetition plus one variation and the
concluding paragraph brings in the surprise and the imaginary expansion of the horizon to the North Pole. A final outchorus (a variation of the first paragraph) concludes the statement. The music-

ways approaches it from above or below, plays around the implied pitch without ever remaining on it for any length of time, and departs from it without
ever having committed itself to a single meaning. The timbre is veiled and
paraphrased by constant changing vibrato, tremolo and overtone effects. The
timing and accentuation, finally, are not *stated*, but *implied* or *suggested*.
The musician challenges himself to find and hold his orientation while denying or withholding all signposts." This quote describes large parts of *Train
Whistle Guitar*.

55. Compounding in *Train Whistle Guitar* is very frequent and goes to the
length of fourteen words (100, 172). It slows down reading speed and creates
tension. Longer compounds are often reserved for references to clothes which
hold a characteristic fascination for the narrator (7, 17, 35, 53, 90, 99, 131,
135, 136).

al structure of the introduction can be represented as A_1 B CCC_1 CD A_2. It is an extended orchestral blues structure dealing with such old blues favorites like the M&O, L&N, and the Southern, railroad lines so many bluessingers have used and sung about.[56] In other words, Murray uses the musical structures and themes of the blues much in the same way James Joyce use the fugue structure in his "Sirens" chapter.

The use of the blues structure does not only appear in the introduction. Triple (and sometimes extended) structures permeate all episodes on the phrase, sentence, and paragraph levels. Formulas like "Sometimes ... Sometimes ... But sometimes ..." (7, 10, 31, 33 f., 50-54, 123 f.), "I used to think ... I used to think... I knew ..." (76 f., 80 f.), or "You remember ... You remember ... I can remember ..." (6 f.) are particular close to the blues, but many others occur as well.[57] In describing Scooter's love adventures Murray transfers the blues structures to the subsections (divided by astericks) of that episode.[58] Even when there is no clear three part blues structure, formulas like "I remember when I remember" or simply "I remember" underline the narrator's affinity to the blues and to oral story telling. Formulas in the oral tradition serve to facilitate improvisation[59], and it is indeed tempting to interpret the nine episodes and four interludes as a series of blues improvisa-

---

56. The L&N (Louisville-Nashville) was sung about by Sleepy John Estes in his "Hobo Blues" and in "L&N" collected from an unknown black migrant by Howard W. Odum around 1911. The M&O (Mobile-Ohio) has been sung about by Walter Davis, Willie Brown and Blind Boy Fuller. The Southern, finally has become the subject matter of W.C. Handy's "Yellow Dog Blues" and Big Bill Broonzy's "Southern Blues." A map of the most important migratory routes and blues trains can be found in Paul Oliver, *The Story of the Blues* repr. London: Barrie & Jenkins 1970, back inside cover. About their significance for the bluessingers see Paul Oliver, *The Meaning of the Blues*. New York: Collier, 1963, pp. 84-95 (originally published as *Blues Fell This Morning*).

57. Compare 34 f., 36, 95, 98, 111, 124f., 137f., etc.

58. "That was the first time (144) ... The next time (145) ... The time after that (146)" and "The one (148) ... One somebody else (152) ... On the other hand there also was (156)" and "The one I remember when I remember (157) ... The Gins Alley victrola music I remember when I remember (159) ... When I came back for Christmas that time (161) ... The last time (164)."

59. Robert Scholes and Robert Kellog, *The Nature of Narrative*. Oxford University Press, 1966, p. 21.

tions, not in the sense of nine stanzas of a certain blues[60], but in the jazz sense of a given theme, the phrases and harmonies of which are a starting point for a series of choruses. For the application of the triple blues structure to the three chapter blocks fails. But a closer look at the beginning of each chapter reveals that each selects a phrase from the introduction which, now, I would like to call the blues theme of the novel, to extend this phrase into a long improvisation.[61] In other words, the mental map of Gasoline Point is gradually filled out by Scooter's experiences or memories. The nine solo improvisations are interrupted by four orchestral interludes which develop the theme of the introduction further.[62]

Signifying is another technique adopted by bluessingers and narrator alike. Again, the narrator does not have any partner other than the implied reader to talk to. But just as Chee Cholly Middleton and Decatur Callahan signified at Beau Beau Weaver pretending not to notice his presence, the narrator gets into some heavy signifying at the reader. He assumes and creates a common frame of reference for himself and the reader by alluding to blues and popular songs, folk traditions[63] and nostalgia items from the twenties. He foreshadows the revelation at the end, signifying at the reader in almost all the episodes.[64] And he bases several episodes on blues ballads. The reader's understanding and enjoyment of Beau Beau Weaver is definitely enhanced by knowing "Frankie and Johnnie." Recognizing that Stagolee Dupas (fils) derives from

60. This rather unconvincing claim has been made for the chapters in *Invisible Man*; Edward Margolies, *Native Sons*, p. 133.

61. There is no space to go into details, but here are the phrases from the theme each episode is built on: "the marco polo horizon mist" (episode 1), "Chichasabogue Creek and Hog Bayou" (2), "night whistles" (3), "the L&N whistlestop" (4). "school bell mornings" (5), episodes 6 and 7 are linked to each other but not to the introductory theme, 8 starts from "dog fennels" in the introduction, 9 from "the front porch .. and chinaberry shade all the way from the steps to the gate."

62. These interludes are in italics (so is the introduction to episode 6) and expand the theme of naming (briarpatch, Jack the Rabbit, Mobile, Miss Tee) and identity.

63. The folk traditions in Mobile are omni-American: Spanish, French, Indian, African, and English, but Afro-American traditions are foregrounded throughout.

64. Miss Tee appears as a balancing counter-force in all episodes, except 6 and 7. In 7 her anti-blues values are represented by Miss Pauline.

that famous badman who killed Billy Lyon because he touched his Stetson hat adds to the mythic dimension of the confrontation in episode seven.[65] Luzana Cholly's adventures are based on numerous blues songs about hoboing north though it is hard to come up with one specific example.[66] And Deljean McCray's love lessons to Scooter owe a lot to barrelhouse and brothel blues like "Do the Bobo," "Doing the messaround," and "Nobody in town can bake sweet jelly roll like mine."[67] As with Eliot, Joyce and Thomas Mann this indirect and oblique use of myth to structure the contemporary story raises questions about the relationship between past and present, tradition and innovation.

And here it is necessary to go beyond the blues tradition. If Scooter, the boy, indiscriminately mixes folk blues and Tin Pan Alley songs like "Three Little Words," "My Blue Heaven," or "Little White Lies,"[68] bluessinger and Uncle Remus, the adult narrator freely blends blues traditions with what I would like to call "the syntax of nostalgia." The first person, quasiautobiographical mode of narration[69] plus the theme of childhood recollections has of course become a long romantic tradition and has produced such different works as *The Prelude, Snow Bound*, the first volume of *A la recherche du temps perdu* or José Lezama Lima's *Paradiso*. The tendency to emotionalize childhood experiences leads in *Train Whistle Guitar* to a choice of syntactical devices which have nothing to do with the blues, which, indeed, are in almost exact opposition to it.[70] There is the sentimental split between the "I" of the narrator and the "you" of the former self as in:

65. "Stagolee" again is one of the best known blues ballads and has been recorded in numerous versions.

66. Bukka White's "Atlanta Special" and Wesley Wallace's "Number 29" come very close to episode 1.

67. Paul Oliver, *The Meaning of the Blues*, pp. 131-153.

68. The chapter on the twenties in David Ewen, *The Life and Death of Tin Pan Alley*. New York: Harper 1974 is helpful.

69. Franz K. Stanzel, *Theorie des Erzählens*. Goettingen: Vandenhoeck & Ruprecht, 1979, pp. 267-284.

70. Murray seems to have taken many years of these devices from William Faulkner's *Absalom, Absalom!* and *Intruder in the Dust*, where Faulkner uses a characteristic technique of enchaining paragraphs through recurrence of keywords. For the Southern context of Murray's novel see Richard Gray, *The Literature of Memory. Modern Writers of the South*. London: Arnold 1977.

You could smell the mid-May woods up the slope behind *us* then ... Waiting and watching, you were also aware of how damp and cool the sandy soft ground was ... (19)

There is a continuous interplay of adult and adolescent point of views by means of the names given to other characters: if "mama" and "papa" are necessary deceits to preserve "Miss Tee's" secret, there are other reasons for appellations like "Uncle Jerome" or "Unka JoJo." There is the frequent use of "as if" for imaginative enrichment of the past. There is the preference for the iterative form, sentences liberally sprinkled with "would," "always," and "used to."[71] There is the associative concatenation of sentences by "and" or "also" and a marked tendency to link sentences to their predecessors by retrospective conjunctions.[72] And there is finally the generalizing commentary in the present tense which tries to lift the tendency of nostalgia to take the past for a better present into a rationalizing philosophy:

For the moment involves anticipation as well as memory, and action itself is of its very nature nothing if not the most obvious commitment to the future. But if like me and Little Buddy you had been as profoundly conditioned by the twelve-string guitar insinuations of Luzana Cholly and the honky-tonk piano of Stagolee Dupas as by anything you had ever heard or overheard in church at school by the fireside of from any other listening post, you knew very well that anything, whether strange or ordinary, happening in Gasoline Point was, in the very nature of things, also part and parcel of the same old briarpatch, which was the same old blue steel network of endlessly engaging and frequently enraging mysteries and riddling ambiguities which encompass all the possibilities and determine all the probabilities in the world. But you also knew something else:
no matter how accurate your historical data, no matter how impressive your statistics, the application of experience to flesh-and-blood behavior must always leave something to chance and circumstance. (106 f.)

"Chance and circumstance" but not human agency may interfere

71. Seymour Chatman, *Story and Discourse*, pp. 78f.
72. Out of the 132 sentences in episode 7 72 have a conjunction or particle that links the sentence to its predecessor. Out of the 72 sentences 42 begin with "But," "Because," or "And." "Also" sometimes refers to the guitar riddles of Luzana Cholly (4) but more often to nostalgic association. "Also" appears more than 200 times in *Train Whistle Guitar*, mainly in the interludes and the beginnings of the episodes.

with the murder of Beau Beau Weaver which otherwise becomes as inevitable as that of its mythic parallels or that of any *pharmakos* in any know culture and society. The encounter between Stagolee and the sheriff becomes a ritual between badman and the law, not a specific example of Southern racism. This ritualization of black folklore is irreconcilable with everything the blues stands for:

> Ritualization of black folklore applies the implications of ritual to the specific social conflict between black people and an institution of slavery and Jim Crow. It implies that this conflict is part of a general, eternal and inescapable conflict between human beings and their limitations. It transforms the social conflict at the heart of the folk expression into the metaphysical conflict of the framing myth, thus denying the social conflict any importance of its own. But the relationship between an oppressed people and an oppressive society *is* social. It is the result of human action and can be changed by human agency. To imply otherwise is in Ellison's own words, to rationalize.[73]

Nor the are essentially reactionary psychodynamics of nostalgia underlying this rationalization compatible with the blues:

> Looking back on his past life the blues singer brushes quickly over his childhood with but a passing, perfunctory reference to where he was born and raised. He neither yearns for the idle days of his childhood with the sentimental nostalgia of a fictitious Stephen Foster plantation Negro, nor does he reminisce with self-pity on childhood unhappiness.[74]

The conservative implications of Murray's specific adaptation of the blues tradition become apparent now.

"In a general sense perhaps all statements are also counter-statements." With this dialectic insight into the specific historicity of texts Albert Murray introduces his essays in *The Omni-Americans*, "an affirmative rebuttal to negative allegations and conclusions about some aspects of Negro life in the United States."[75] *Train Whistle Guitar* is not only a (probably largely autobiographical) statement of what it meant to grow up black in the twenties in the South, but also a deliberate counterstatement to what Murray calls "the fakelore of pathology" and the "Social science fiction" about

---

73. Susan L. Blake, "Ritual and Rationalization: Black Folklore in the Works of Ralph Ellison" *PMLA* 94 (1979), 134.
74. Paul Oliver, *The Meaning of the Blues*, pp. 329 f.
75. Albert Murray, *The Omni-Americans*, pp. 1, 3.

the ghettoes.[76] It is indeed difficult for the reader to recognize Gasoline Point as a ghetto, the saw mill quarters, the riverside Bottom of a Southern town.[77] It is equally difficult to realize that the Great Depression set in somewhere during the novel, and that somewhere else in Alabama the Scotsboro trial began. As *The Omni-Americans* implies *Train Whistle Guitar* is also a specific counter-statement to Richard Wright's *Black Boy* which Ralph Ellison had reviewed as a blues autobiography:

> As a form, the blues is an autobiographical chronicle of personal catastrophe expressed lyrically ... Black Boy is filled with blues-tempered echoes of railroad trains, the names of Southern towns and cities, estrangements, fights and flights, deaths and disappointments, charged with physical and spiritual hungers and pain.[78]

Here it becomes clear why Murray had to introduce Jack the Rabbit and the briarpatch into the novel: the blues reflects trouble, the suffering of Southern black people under a racist system, the trouble of family disintegration, enforced mobility, and poverty. The blues tries to overcome this trouble by art:

> The blues is an impulse to keep the painful details and episodes of a brutal experience in one's aching consciousness, to finger its jagged grain, and to transcend it, not by the consolation of philosophy but by squeezing from it a near-tragic, near comic lyricism.[79]

Take the trouble and the black experience out of the blues, and "Muddy Waters" becomes "My Blue Haven." By relegating trouble and the bluessingers to a subordinate position, by placing blues language within a framework of nostalgia, by ritualizing the blues experience Murray emasculates the blues tradition. He presents the ghetto and the South as an idyl.

With his careful distinction between middle-class "whitefolks" and ignorant and racist "peckerwoods" in *Train Whistle Guitar*,[80] between brown and black people,[81] Murray tries to capture a mixed audience of whites and blacks who have interiorized white

76. Ibid., pp. 38, 97-112.
77. Mobile was 44 percent black in 1910, 57 in 1970. Compare LeRoi Jones' description of a Southern Bottoms in *The System of Dante's Hell*.
78. Quoted in *The Omni-Americans*, p. 162.
79. Ibid., p. 162 (again, Ellison speaking).
80. Compare 29 f., 12, 13, 64, 69, 88 to 18, 21, 30, 45, 78, 113.

middle class values. *Train Whistle Guitar* carefully selects those aspects of blues and folklore that are easily assimilated into the dominant white culture and its favorite myth: the American Dream and the Horatio Alger myth. Scooter who is continuously encouraged and admonished[82] to advance by a college career into a middle-class position, has to overcome and control his yearnings for the blues heroes of his childhood. The novel's basic conflict between blues and church, barrelhouse and school, working class foster-parents and middle-class Miss Tee, between the antagonistic cooperation with trouble in blues artistry and romantic nostalgia for childhood innocence, between "Stagolee" and "Little White Lies" is finally resolved in favor of the latter.

At a decisive turning point of the black struggle for more power and self determination *Train Whistle Guitar* (1974) turns to nostalgia and the rural folklore of the past, and thus implicitly rejects not only the "fakelore of pathology" but also black nationalism and the Left.[83] It is precisely this use of blues and black folklore that was rejected by Eldridge Cleaver[84] and — in indirect allusion to *Invisible Man* — by Maulana Ron Karenga:

> Therefore, we say the blues are invalid; for they teach resignation, in a word acceptance of reality — and we have come to change reality. We will not submit to the resignation of our fathers who lost their money, their women, and their lives and sat around wondering "what did they do to be so black and blue." ... And whatever we do, we cannot remain in the past, for we have too much at stake in the present.[85]

To call *Train Whistle Guitar* "an updated version of Uncle Tomism", as one critic did[86], would be equally unfair to Harriet Beecher Stowe, who wrote socalled "protest fiction," and Albert Murray

81. Scooter is and prefers honey brown (60, 87, 156; 34, 53, 87, 124, 139, 158). The narrator avoids the word "black" for Afro-Americans: the only reference comes from Soldier Boy Crawford (84).
82. Compare 12, 29, 69, 74, 75, etc. Scooter is continuously told to imi-. tate whitefolks.
83. See pp. ???? of the introduction to his book.
84. In Alan Dundes, ed., *Motherwit from the Laughing Barrel*, pp. 1-45.
85. Maulana Ron Karenga, "Black Art: Mute Matter Given Force and Function," in Abraham Chapman, ed., *New Black Voices. An Anthology of Contemporary Afro-American Literature*. New York: New American Library, 1972, p. 482.
86. Vivian Mercier, "Gasoline Point Blues," *Saturday Review/World*, May

who objects to such fiction. In *Train Whistle Guitar* Murray finds a new voice for the narrator in contemporary black fiction, an alternative to the jive talk in Ishmael Reed and Cecil Brown, a voice equally rooted in black oral culture. But *Train Whistle Guitar* takes, transforms and finally sacrifices blues and folk values for such middle class ideals as education and social mobility. Murray's attempt to find a new heroic stance for the black writer by modeling himself on the bluessinger as a culture hero means conforming that hero to the dominant culture, to assimilate his traits to the expectations of a white middle-class audience reared on Stephen Foster, Joel Chandler Harris and William Faulkner. *Train Whistle Guitar* does little or no justice to the tough and unsentimental blues tradition running from Charlie Patton to Louisiana Red.[87]

BIOGRAPHY

Born 12 May 1916 in Nokomis, Alabama. He grew up in Mobile, Alabama, studied at Tuskegee Institute (B.S. in Education, 1939; M.A.in English 1948), where he met Ralph Ellison. During World War II he served as Training Officer, conducting cultural orientation programs for Americans overseas and briefings in psychological warfare; present status Major, USAF, retired. He taught Literature at Tuskegee, Columbia University, Colgate University, University of Massachusetts, and the University of Missouri. He also served as consultant to local radio programs on jazz. For Murray the political engagement of a novelist must fail; instead of "racist notions of *negritude*" the serious novelist maintains ambivalence (*The Omni-Americans. New Perspectives on Black Experience and American Culture.* New York: Outerbridge & Dienstfrey, 1970, p. 151-153).

4, 1974, 51.

87. Compare Bernhard Ostendorf, "Black Poetry, Blues and Folklore: Double Consciousness in Afro-American Oral Culture" *Amerikastudien / American Studies* 20 (1975), 209-259.

BIBLIOGRAPHY

NON-FICTION

The Hero and the Blues. The Paul Anthony Lectures, Ninth Series. Columbia: University of Missouri Press, 1973.

The Omni-Americans: New Perspectives on Black Experience and American Culture. New York: Outerbridge, 1970.

South to a Very Old Place. New York: Mc Grow-Hill, 1972.

Stomping the Blues. New York: Quartet Books 1978.

NOVEL

Train Wistle Guitar. New York: Mc Grow-Hill, 1974.

SHORT STORIES

(Anthologies)

Bambara, Toni Cade, (ed.). *Tales and Stories for Black Folks.* Garden City, N.Y.: Doubleday, 1971.

Clarke, John Hendrik, (ed.). *American Negro Short Stories.* New York: Hill & Wang, 1966. (Anthology).

Emanuel, James A. and Theodore Gross, (eds.). *Dark Symphony: Negro Literature in America.* New York: Free Press, 1968. pp. 376-391 (early version of chapter II in *Train Whistle Guitar*).

Margolies, Edward, (ed.). *A Native Sons Reader.* Philadelphia: Lippincott, 1970.

CRITICISM

"Something Different, Something More." In Hill, Herbert, (ed.). *Anger, and Beyond: The Negro Writer in the United States.* New York: Harper & Row, 1966.

262

ELIZABETH SCHULTZ

SEARCH FOR "SOUL SPACE":
A STUDY OF AL YOUNG'S *WHO IS ANGELINA?* (1975)
AND THE DIMENSIONS OF FREEDOM

As students of Afro-American literature have frequently observed, one of the literature's dominant themes has always been the search for freedom, what poet Robert Hayden calls, "the beautiful, necessary thing."[1] From William Wells Brown's *Clotelle* (1864) to Ernest Gaines' *The Autobiography of Miss Jane Pittman* (1971), the individual black American's attempt to achieve liberation has been associated with the liberation of the Afro-American people as a group. Ralph Ellison's narrator in *Invisible Man* (1952) however, expresses a conviction that underscores the personal, existential nature of the Afro-American's yearning to be free: "When I discover who I am, I'll be free."[2] The struggle to achieve self-knowledge and hence personal freedom characterizes the lives of several of Afro-American literature's most memorable characters: Kabnis of Jean Toomer's *Cane* (1923), Janie Woods of Zora Neale Hurston's *Their Eyes Were Watching God* (1937), Bigger Thomas of Richard Wright's *Native Son*, (1941), John Grimes of James Baldwin's *Go Tell It on the Mountain* (1953), and Sula Peace of Toni Morrison's *Sula* (1973). The heroine of Al Young's *Who Is Angelina?* (1975), by contrast with other black protagonists is startingly free at the beginning of the novel; yet her story is also her struggle to understand herself and the meaning of her freedom.

1. Stephen Henderson, for example, argues persuasively that "the great theme of Black poetry, and, indeed of Black life in the United States is liberation." In *Understanding The New Black Poetry* (New York: William Morrow & Co., 1973), p. 20. Hayden's phrase occurs in the last line of "Frederick Douglass," *Angel of Ascent* (New York: Liveright, 1975), p. 131.
2. Ralph Ellison, *Invisible Man* (New York: Vintage Books, 1972), p. 237.

In *Who Is Angelina?* Young has written his *Portrait of a Lady*, with the center of consciousness being Angelina Green, who, like Isabel Archer, begins her travels into life alone and independent. Unlike the protagonists of other Afro-American novels, Angelina is not enslaved because of her race. Her color has not barred her from acting according to her will, from obtaining the jobs she wishes, from traveling as she wishes; nor has her color caused her to view either herself or her people as other than complex human beings. In this, as in other respects, Angelina resembles the three, all male, protagonists of Young's other novels: MC of *Snakes* (1970), Sidney J. Prettymon of *Sitting Pretty* (1976), and Durwood Knight of *Ask Me Now* (1980). As others readily acknowledge Isabel's beauty, so do they Angelina's, and hence, like James' heroine, like Gaines' Miss Jane, Morrison's Sula, Paule Marshall's Merle Kinbona of *The Chosen Place, The Timeless People* (1969), Corregidora of Gayl Jones' *Corregidora* (1975), or Cora Green of Alice Childress' *A Short Walk* (1979), Angelina never evaluates her appearance.[3] Although Angelina does not become an heiress as does Isabel — indeed in the novel's third chapter, she is robbed of all her worldy possessions — she has friends who provide, unpredictably and extravagantly. She is not, consequently, enslaved by either toil or poverty. Discussing his heroine and his novel in an interview, Young has said, "I tried to make Angelina anything but a stereotype of any kind. That book is really about ... Uprootedness, in general."[4] Angelina's "uprootedness," her very freedom, however, prevents her from discovering her identity and answering the questions which haunt her from the beginning of the novel: "Who am I? Who is Angelina?"[5]

In the course of *The Portrait of a Lady*, Isabel learns the limits of her freedom; in the course of *Who Is Angelina?* , Angelina

3. Wallace Thurman's Emma Lou Brown in *The Blacker the Berry* (1929), Chester Himes' Mrs. Taylor in *The Third Generation* (1954), and Toni Morrison's Pecola Breedlove in *The Bluest Eye* (1970) exemplify the tragedy of those Afro-American women who are condemned by racist standards of beauty to evaluate their appearance and themselves negatively.

4. Nathaniel Mackey, "Interview with Al Young," *Melus*, 5, IV (1978), p 46.

5. Al Young, *Who Is Angelina?* (New York: Holt, Rinehart and Winston 1975), p. 17. Subsequent references to this work will be noted parenthetically in the text

learns to recognize both the limitations and the possibilities of freedom. She progresses from a terrifying state of independence to an exhilarating state of independence, from a condition of "uprootedness" to a condition in which she is deeply and firmly rooted in herself. Initially adrift in the chaos of the present time and the chaos of shifting relationships, she is, finally, able to convert chaos to opportunity and to find her place, her "soul space," in the continuity of time and the continuity of evolving relationships. Initially vulnerable to unpredictable, chance circumstances, she is, finally, able to make conscious choices. Both James and Young bring their heroines to knowledge of self as they come to define themselves in relation to others and to circumstances and limitations beyond their control and as they learn to make their choices in terms of these conditions. To follow the process by which Angelina discovers the joys of being herself, a free Afro-American woman, a free soul, we must examine the "changes" she goes through — Young's frequently used, Afro-American idiom for describing any series of experiences an individual may encounter in the course of time.

Young's carefully structured novel is divided into four books. In Books I and II, Angelina travels from California to Mexico and on to Michigan; changes happen to her. In Books III and IV, she travels from Michigan back to California; here she makes the changes happen. Thus Young brings his heroine full cycle geographically. Her journeying also forces her to time-travel — to look backward into her past and to dream ahead into the future; her cycle becomes a spiral, and she learns to play the changes on it. With audacious and delightful simplicity, Young lays out the plot of his novel in the second chapter when Angelina visits a fortune teller who spells out her character as well as her past, present, and future for her. Quite predictable the gypsy predicts that Angelina will meet " 'a man — very tall, very dark ... And very handsome' " and that she is going to take a trip. She is also told, however, that her journeying will be along

"... a special path, call it what you will — the path of righteousness, the spiritual path. In your heart you like adventure. You want to know the truth about yourself, the real truth, because by finding that you feel that then you'll know all there is to know about everything under the sun ... It's nothing to be afraid of. We all got to go down secret paths sooner or later." (16-18)

265

In her traveling, Angelina becomes associated with the theme which Morrison has identified as that ussually characteristic of male characters in Afro-American literature:

> The big scene is the traveling Ulysses scene, for black men. They are moving ... And, boy, you know, they spread their seed all over the world. They are really moving! Perhaps it's because they don't have dominion. You can trace that historically, and one never knows what would have been the case if we'd never been tampered with at all. But that looking out and over and beyond and changing and so on — that, it seems to me, is one of the monumental themes in black literature about men. That's what they do. It is the Ulysses theme, the leaving home ... Curiosity, what's around the corner, what's across the hill, what's in the valley, what's down the track. Go find out what that is, you know! And in the process of finding, they are also making themselves.[6]

With Morrison's own Sula and Pilate Dead of *Song of Solomon* (1977), Young's heroine seems an anomaly among Afro-American women characters, for she is a true Ulysses, making a cyclical journey in time and space and making herself "strong in will / To strive, to seek, to find, and not to yield."

In discussing *Who Is Angelina?* , Young indicates that his novel emphatically reflects a particular period in our recent history: "... during that particular period I guess a lot of things were newly crystallizing that I felt a need to get out. That book was written in the early 70s."[7] Angelina's existence in Books I and II of the novel exemplify this period of the late sixties and early seventies; in her actions and her associations, her life epitomizes the excesses, the vagueries, the irresponsibilities of that time, especially as Young saw them flourishing in California. Later, in Book III, Angelina is able to observe about this time and place:

> "It's kind of crazy, I mean, it's more than kind of crazy. You've got all these people and all that mild weather and no seasons really and your brain operates funny. You go around trying to figure out where you fit in and come to find out there're all these other people wandering around trying to figure out where *they* fit in." (142)

---

6. "A Conversation with Toni Morrison," *Chant of Saints*, ed. Michael S. Harper and Robert B. Stepto (Urbana: University of Illinois Press, 1979), p. 226.

7. *Melus* interview, p. 46.

8. *Ibid.*

In the same book, she further comments on the pretentiousness of the time and place: " ' Berkeley's a state of mind, an attitude, a pose, a style, a way of dealing with the real world by not dealing with it' " (197).

In the first chapter of the novel, Young describes Angelina's life as "crazy" indeed; it has no center. For five nights she has been partying, ending up each night in bed with a different man; she pictures herself in different worlds — a quiet gallery in New York or "in Paris with talented Africans ... or at sea in Barcelona" (11). She is without a job, a lover, a purpose or a direction; she has recently attempted suicide. She is alone, and unconnected to place, time, people, or plan, she is unconnected to herself; she claims to be "sick of time and the world" (4). But she is free, terrifyingly so.

When she is robbed of her household possessions in the novel's third chapter, her loss frees her further. Young, however, unlike William Faulkner and Morrison, whose Ike McCaslin and Milkman Dead must relinquish their material possessions in order to gain the wilderness and themselves, does not suggest that, paradoxically, loss equals gain. Angelina's robbery, the first of several which occur or are referred to in the course of the novel, contributes to her sense of purposelessness and helplessness; in losing her possessions, she exercises no choice of her own. Although Angelina's gypsy had told her, " 'You see, we all have a certain amount of control over our lives. We have free will. We're born with that — the freedom to choose between this and that' " (18), Angelina, not knowing herself and hence not knowing how to exercise her free will, is at the mercy of arbitrary, external circumstances. Her friend, Margo Tanaka, decides how Angelina should act in this instance; she pays for Angelina to fly to Mexico. Unlike Bigger Thomas, who yearned to fly, unlike the other caged birds of Afro-American literature for whom flight was synonymous with freedom, Young's heroine flies, not because of her own choice, with no plans and with exhilarating ease: "Suspended this way, between heaven and earth, she felt happy to be free and uncommitted for the time being, at least until the plane set down again" (30). Although Morrison in *Song of Solomon*, a novel which makes flight its central image, recognizes that plane travel may be the equivalent of escape, Young's description of Angelina's condition at the beginning of *Who Is Angelina?* and his description of her flight to Mexico represent a unique expression in Afro-American literature of a character's sense of absolute freedom. Angelina neither yearns nor struggles for freedom; it is a given in her life, and as such, Young insists that she must understand its value; she must, therefore, learn to exercise her free will, choosing carefully and consciously between this and that.

In Mexico, away from the chaos of California, Angelina begins to work through the gypsy's predictions. She begins her journeying, and she meets that tall, dark, and handsome stranger. Although she does not direct the changes and the choices during her Mexican sojourn, and although, consequently, her identity remains obscure to her, in this section of the novel, Young reveals the qualities in her character which prove to be the basis for her choices and her identity. These qualities, which she shares with the protagonists of Young's other novels, reflect his constant values. Like MC, Sitting Pretty, Woody, Angelina grows, and her growth is the product of a questing, questioning mind; yet she, like them, is also characterized by certain constant traits: an appreciation of Afro-American style, especially as its is expressed in language and music; an abhorrence of all forms of hypocrisy and a corresponding concern for honesty in all matters; a delight in the diversity of human beings and a corresponding delight in the integrity and independence of one's self; an ease with sex; and a devotion to the members of one's family.

In defining the time in which he had set *Who Is Angelina?* , Young comments that

> ... during that time I was affected deeply by a lot of the phony Black literature that was getting attention in America. I've always felt that a writer should project his or her visions from where they happen to find themselves, and if other people disapprove of it that's all well and good but you've at least tried your shot. So I might have been trying in [*Who Is Angelina?*] to compensate, subconsciously, for things that weren't being said and types of people that weren't being written about.

Who Is Angelina? seems the fulfillment of a statement Young had made in 1972 in which he aligned himself with other writers,

> ... original men & women striving to express & give shape to the unthinkable variety of feeling & thought in the black communities we weren't allowed to share in the 1960s say, when Black Anger was all the rage & media made a killing.[9]

Thus we find in *Who Is Angelina?* that Young creates a black woman who represents the unrepresented black community, in particular those who are middle-class, educated, and free, in particular those who, uprooted as they may be, know their "roots" and accept their blackness unself-consciously, naturally, and jubilantly. "Everybody nowadays is busy digging for roots. Well, I know my roots," explains Angelina. "I know them well and it doesn't make a damn bit of difference when it comes to making sense of who I am and why I make the kinds of mistakes I do" (164-65). Angelina's search is neither to understand nor to accept her race; steeped in its ways, she both appreciates and revels in them.

In Mexico City, she is consequently drawn to one Sylvester Poindexter Buchanan, a.k.a., Watusi, a black man, "who seemed to Angelina to be all of seven and a half feet tall ... and had a broad, cheerful Toltec-looking face" (44), who reminded her "of her father and her father's father, both big flat-nosed, barrel-chested men with willpower to spare and sense of humor as sharp and shiny as machetes" (49). She it literally seduced by "the way he moved, the way he spoke, switching out of and back into his sly Niggerese" (92). Watusi's "sly Niggerese" is shared by her Aunt Jujie, her Uncle Roscoe, and her high school friend, Louetta Mae Barnes, all of whom she returns to love in Book III. With her homefolks, she realizes that "withing a day or two her whole way of speaking would change. Strange. It had almost happened while she was off goofing and taking chances with Watusi with his flatout agrammatical self" (109).

Perry Lentz has noted that Angelina has several different modes of speech, and that through her speech, she like Huck Finn, "undercuts the 'tears and flapdoodle' of the shore; herein the rhythms and patterns — the vivid imagery, the tangetial overstatement, the superbly vitalized synecdoche — the rhythms and patterns of black American speech differentiate the true from the false."[10] Significantly, we do not hear Angelina speak in pure "Niggerese" until

9. Al Young, "Statement on Aesthetics, Poetics, Kinetics," *New Black Voices*, ed. Abraham Chapman (New York: New American Library, 1972), p. 554.

10. Perry Lentz, "A Lovable Novel," *Michigan Quarterly Review*, 15 (spring 1976), p. 238. According to Mackey, Wallace Stegner has also noted

the wonderful scene in Book IV in which she not only defends her decision to catch a thief, but she also attacks the white hippie who categorizes her as an " 'Uncle Tom collaborationist' ":

"I'm sicka you refugees from suburbia jumping up in my face with that Uncle Tom shit! There's a whole lotta people around here who work hard to stay poor and just because youre mad at your mommy and daddy because they gave you everything in the world except themselves now youre gonna move to Berkeley and talk all that ignorant horseshit and get a whole lotta black people's backs busted and heads split open in the name of the revolution — whatever the fuck that is! — so you can get your sick rocks off and score your expensive dope and then straighten up when you feel like it and take a bath and trim your mangy hair and put on a suit and go get some high-paying executive job or get your law degree and run for congress on the Peace and Love ticket, naturally. You put on a suit and you just another nice white boy. I dress up and get a fucking Ph.D. and win the goddam Nobel Prize and I'm still a nigger, you square motherfucker, you ... corny scavenger creep!" (217)

Although Angelina claims that she tries "to stay outta situations that cause me to use such *language* ... [because] I'm really an easy-going all-American girl [,] ... every now and then I have to get my nigger up' " (218); when she does, she proclaims her own and her people's integrity.

Young, who has maintained that "all of [his] writings proceeds from a tradition of the spoken word rather than the written,"[11] says, in addition, that "I found out early that speech is characterization."[12] In all of his novels, his characters reveal themselves by the language they use, with his protagonists readily puncturing the pretentious language of the pretentious Afro-American. Thus Angelina has an ear for "jive" and deflates the facile signifying of the aggressive black administrator she meets early in the novel at a Berkeley party, the pedantry of the black geography professor she meets in Mexico, and the revolutionary hype of her friend Louetta's husband. Very quietly, she plays the dozens on him after listening to his long diatribe which reveals that, in spite of his dog

the resemblance of Young's use of language to Twain's, having remarked that *Sitting Pretty* is " 'the *Huckleberry Finn* of Black English,' " p. 38 in the *Melus* interview.

11. *Interviews with Black Writers*, ed. John O'Brien (New York: Liveright 1973), p. 266.

12. *Melus* interview, p. 37.

named Black Pride, his children named Jomo and Ahmed, and his claim to know " 'just about every kinda nigger allowable by now' " (179), he'd just as soon be white.

Young's statements about his craft as a writer repeatedly express his desire to reflect "true experience" rather than a trend or an ideology; *Who Is Angelina?* is, consequently, a protest against the "attitudinizing" of "the phony Black literature" of the 70s.[13] It is not surprising, therefore, that for Angelina, "a fancy dashiki and an ascot" (7) do not make a soul brother. Nor can she believe that a meal of "chitlins, hamhocks, hog maws, pigsfeet, spareribs and cooking with lard − soulfood so-called − [which leads] more toward bringing about black genocide, as the phrasemongers would have it, than Sickle Cell Anemia" (165) is necessarily good for either body or soul. In Mexico, watching peasant through her train window, she recalls her "old orthodox Berkeley-style rhetoric" (66) and wonders whether her views have become romantic, simplistic, capitalistic. She thus questions the categorizing of humanity by *ersatz* ethnic trends or ideologies, and as the train moves along, she focuses her attention on "The gorgeous unphotographable light shining down on the whole world, dirt and loveliness, that astounded her at this moment" (66).

Watusi, whose role in Book II is to challenge Angelina to express her basic characteristics, reinforces several of these traits including hers and Young's antipathy for trends and ideologies. In his introduction to Angelina, Watusi makes it clear that he belongs to the same culture that claims her:

> "If you from outta someplace like Berkeley then you kinda like me − in the sense we share certain unarguable affinities and similarities, dig it. I'm from all them outta the way places too − them offbeat settins where niggers do all right for themselves living by they wits between the cracks ... if it's one thing I know about it's this shadowy AA." (49)

His "sly Niggerese" above all confirms his knowledge of the "AA," the Afro-American, and his kinship with Angelina. Like Angelina, he is independent; fulfilling Morrison's criteria for the black Ulysses, he has women and children in Queens, Brussels, and Veracruz, and his business and curiosity continue to take him around the

---

13. *Ibid.*, 43.

world. However, like Angelina, the traveling he enjoys most is a-
long inner paths: " 'I like to wander around through countries and
cities and towns and mountains and valleys and various settings,
especially those situated on the surface of that vast ocean the
human mind as it's commonly called' " (45). Thus he joins Angelina in rejecting a self-conscious "negritude," recognizing that it can
be exploitative of others:

> "Bullshit revolution done played out. Hippies done played out, and look
> here, I'll tell you somethin — nigger shit done just about played out too!
> That's how come I dont spend too much time hustlin round the States no
> more. All them psychotic Negroes. All them dangerous-ass Americans!
> You cant win. If the white folks dont get you, the niggers sure will!" (80)

His rejection of categories leads him to vigorously assert his individuality:

> "The Nation's all right with me, ... but where matters of religion're con-
> cerned I take the ultimate fifth. I'm strictly me. Hear people talking bout
> 'I'm a Freudian, I'm a Marxist, I'm a Christian' and all that, not necessari-
> ly in that order, historically speaking, y'understand, and all I got to say is
> I'm me, a stone Watusian if there ever was one." (68-69)

As "a stone Watusian," Watusi, and ultimately Angelina, embody
Young's conviction that the individual and changes in the individual are more important than ideologies: "I've always believed the
individual human heart to be more revolutionary than any political party or platform."[14]

A dismay with "Black Rage" and the "Black Aesthetic" have
lead to Young's being accused of writing "White";[15] yet *Who Is
Angelina?* as well as his other three novels provide us with a reflection of Afro-American consciousness similar to Angelina's response to the accusation of being an " 'Uncle Tom collaborationist' ": " 'I'm still a nigger.' " Knowing her "roots" and at ease with
them, Angelina does not have to define herself against a racial enemy. As a rule of thumb, "She didn't hate white people; she simply
was careful in her personal associations with them" (60). In Mexico, she is distressed initially in a taxi-cab to think that she should
have to define herself racially and debates passing as a Latin: "As

14. "Statement on Aesthetics, Poetics, Kinetics," p. 554.
15. *Melus* interview, p. 43.

was often the case in the States, everybody's racism and her own skin was going in her favor. She could come on anyway she wanted because, no matter what she did, no one would really take her seriously, the way they would a regular universal individual, a white person" (39). Defensive for a moment in this foreign context, prepared to be cynical and deceptive, Angelina nevertheless risks the truth, "always more confusing than sarcasm" (39). Angelina, like the protagonists of Young's other novel, simply does not judge others by that most superficial means, by that most common means in American life: the color of one's skin. Through the novel, Angelina's closest friend is Margo Tanaka, a Southern white woman, who "in many unofficial ways, was blacker in expressing herself than Angelina was or would ever become. Margo had soul, and soul, like blood, went way beyond pop ideas of sisterhood or brotherhood" (26). Saddened momentarily in Book IV by Margo's confessions of her racial consciousness —

All this time she'd been knowing Margo, all this time they'd been hanging out together, leaning on one another, and they still had to go through these changes. The American Racial Problem. Wouldn't they be better off talking about men or menstrual periods and letting old blood feuds run their course? (261-62)

— Angelina sleeps at the end of this episode with her head in Margo's lap, both of them exhausted by their conversation and by their witnessing the human experience of death. Thus, the color of one's soul — one's capacity for compassion, for generosity, for wonder — is the basis for Angelina's judgment of others rather than their skin color. Thus, Angelina in the course of the novel chooses her "personal associations" with all people, including white people, "carefully." In Book III she can denounce "'... rich white people ... That's my one big prejudice. Ive been to school with em, Ive worked with em, Ive even been in their homes. Theyre really hung up on being rich and a lot of em never get over it'" (190), but she can appreciate the white Baxter family, who with their 17 children have remained in her family's neighborhood as it became predominantly black, for, as her Aunt Jujie says, "'They quality white folks too and right in tune with the community'" (191). She can also simultaneously denounce her former white high school friend, Renee Appel Heinz, whom she discovers at a New Year's party ensconced with her boyfriend, her ex-husband,

273

and his mistress sharing cocaine and sex, and leave the party with a former white college friend to meditate quietly as the old year passes. In Book IV, she will exert herself to catch a black thief in order to retrieve a white friend's purse and then berate the white hippie who would deny both her moral and racial integrity.

But Angelina chooses her friendships from among the many ethnic groups in the United States and the world. Early in the novel she projects an image of herself, of people sniggling behind her back, " 'There go old Angelina Green with her little stuck-up black hincty self. Broad hang out with spooks, japs, chinamens, mexicans, honkies, jews and aint tellin' what all!' " (6). Valuing "open-heartedness" (176) above all in people, she is herself open-hearted in the relationships she has, for each individual and each ethnic group presents the possibility for discovery of humanity's diverse possibilities. In Mexico, Angelina's fundamental open-heartedness is made apparent in her relationships with Watusi and with Senora Ruiz, "A Latin-looking lady, a portly beauty-parlor blonde in elegant middle-aged dress" (39). Sra. Ruiz, a Montvideoan visiting Mexico City, takes pleasure in her American connections while Watusi revels in the possibilities of combinations. Not only do we learn that his children are Afro-American, Afro-American French, and Afro-American-Mexican, but we hear him laud the "Afro-Gypsy-Hispanic" culture of Moorish Spain and long for " 'an American Cheese Sandwich with a taste of refried beans on the side and a Coke' " (69). To Young, racial and ethnic mergings represent enhanced possibilities.

Discussing his own life, he explains that he lived "in the South for the first third of my life, moved to Detroit, and then to California, with brief intervals in New Orleans, Pennsylvania, and Chicago,"[16] moving, thus, very much as Angelina does. The advantage to such geographical rootlessness he claims is "that having had to make so many different friends at schools has made me mobile in being able to live in a wide variety of different-styled communities."[17] His editorial work with Ishmael Reed on the *Yardbird Reader* and *Y'Bird*, publications committed to the possibilities of ethnic diversity in American culture, is underscored by his belief

16. *Interviews with Black Writers*, p. 262.
17. *Ibid*.

that "dynamism in American culture has depended on diversity."[18] He testifies further that "What I've learned from reading different kinds of writers of America — Chicano, Appalachian, Asian-American, Native American, Black, whatever — is that America is and always will be, always has been many things to a lot of different people."[19] However, he also asserts that a study of ethnicity reveals our general humanity: "... that we all really suffer and we all are going though some process of growth or process of self-realization."[20] San Francisco and its environs, the locale for *Who Is Angelina?* and his subsequent novels and his own present home, as an area of great ethnic diversity and hence human possibility, can be seen to represent for Young the hopes for fulfilling the American Dream of *e pluribus unum.*

Thus Young implies that in the variety of Angelina's relationships with others, she transcends the constrictions of racist behavior and moves toward fulfilling this dream. She resembles Sitting Pretty, who, living in a run-down Oakland hotel, is the confidant of its occupants who represent a variety of ethnic backgrounds; she resembles Woody Knight, former professional basketball player for the San Francisco Beanstalks, who remains the friend of his team-mates, who together comprise the spectrum of American ethnic possibilities. Angelina's early friendship with Renee, her continuing friendship with Margo, and her spontaneous friendship with Sra. Ruiz are remarkable in American literature which has been characterized by an ideal relationship between a dark-skinned man and a white man; this pattern, which appears prominently in literature written by white males, does not, with few exceptions,[21] have its counterpart in a relationship between two women of different ethnic backgrounds. Toward the novel's conclusion, Young gives Angelina a dream. She is initially surrounded by music resonating with the sounds of various cultures and harmonizing them all:

---

18. *Melus* interview, p. 49.
19. *Ibid.*, p. 50.
20. *Ibid.*
21. An exception is the Lesbian relationship between a black woman and a white woman in Ann Allen Shockley's *Loving Her* (1975).

... – a giddying mix of Roland Kirk, West African high-life, Bessie Smith blues, the Holiness Church choir; Japanese koto music, Django Rhinehart gypsy/jazz guitar crammed with intermittent surprises; a solo piano ripe with ragtime, drumbeats invoking the Spirit, the precious rattling of wind chimes to accompany tree leaves in their trembling. (254)

In this ambience, the major personages in Angelina's life appear to her, each in gorgeous costume, each giving her his or her own wisdom spoken in language true to character. The vision is one of the possibilities to be discovered and mysteries to be revealed, of peace on earth and good will amongst people. She is awakened from her dream by a desperate call from Margo; choosing to respond to her friend, Angelina at this point in the novel proves herself not only able to convert chaos to possibility but also to recognize that human life continues to demand painful choices.

In Mexico, Angelina's sexual independence is also challenged. A lyrical love letter from Curtis Benton, a man in San Francisco with whom she'd had a one-night stand, and the constant presence of Watusi lead her to question herself as a woman. To Curtis' tantalizing and seductive letter, she replies with a straight-forward description of herself and her life:

My life to date's has been a series of misses and near-misses. I never get a bargain, it seems, I always have to pay the full going price and then some. For years now I've lived in self-imposed exile from my family and all the people I grew up with. You could say, I imagine, that I'm something of a recluse and misfit who wants desperately to be a part of something bigger than this stifling little cocoon of flesh and nerve endings that we so glibly call Self. (55).

Her words convey her confusion, her yearning to discover her relationship with others and to assert herself as an individual, her honest recognition of her past errors and her hopes for the future, but in relation to Curtis she retains her sense of Self, stifling as she feels it to be in Book II. To Watusi's bigness, however, she succumbs. When he graciously offers her Kahlua, she accepts although she would have preferred brandy. Gradually she finds herself overwhelmed by his ways. On her first night in Mexico City, Angelina, wishing for her accustomed independence, regrets that she is not a man who, at 2:00 A.M., would "simply get into some clothes and go out into the night to forage for food" (35). She envies the freedom to which Watusi's masculinity seems to entitle him: "I should hate this bastard but I dont. I like the way he lives on the run. I'd probably do it myself it I were a devilish man" (77). First meeting him, she is sceptical of his advances, his fabulous generosity, his frequent affairs with other women, his shady business dealings, his "jiving and shucking." Although Young makes it clear that his open-heartedness, his delight in diversity, and his ease with himself as a unique individual and an Afro-American reinforce Angelina's commitment to these qualities in herself, it is also clear that in Book II she readily loses herself in the drugs, sex, and immensity of experience which he lavishes upon her. Her physical independence in Mexico City is sacrificed for a dependence on his unknown plans for traveling into the Mexican interior, her sexual independence for a dependence on the pleasure of his sexual favors, her intellectual independence for a dependence on his knowledge of Mexico. Not until Book III does Angelina realize that she has sacrificed her independence in being absorbed by Watusi: "she ... loved being left to the privacy of her thoughts and emotions. That was the way she'd thought Mexico was going to be − a chance to lose herself in a whole lot of unpressured soul space − before Watusi turned up to charm her away from herself" (123).

Book III is the pivotal section of *Who Is Angelina?* . In Books I and II, we see Angelina committed to defining herself as an individual, a woman, an Afro-American, a human being against the shifting trends, systems, ideologies, and events of her particular time. However, she struggles to do so, unable either to control or to accept the changes which happen to her. Book II concludes with Angelina's receiving word of her beloved father's hospitalization and with her reluctant departure from Mexico and Watusi for Detroit. Book III begins with her learning that her father, like herself, had been robbed, but had barely escaped death in defending himself and the sanctity of his home. The circumstances of the "particular period," which Young initially associates with California and Berkeley, thus come to seem ubiquitous. In the course of her Detroit sojourn, Angelina verifies her Aunt Jujie's description of her hometown:

> "It's a whole lotsa thievin *and* killin go on round this Detroit now. It aint never been no Garden of Eden, you wanna know the truth, but it's done got so here lately where you cant even walk down the street in broad daylight without worryin bout whether some dope fiend gon snatch your purse or knock you in the head." (119)

She sees the physical deterioration of her neighborhood and hears stories of the moral deterioration of black people into "crazy niggers"; she is saddened by " 'a respectable ex-soldier colored man,'" who accosts her selling stolen produce; depressed by guards and bars and signs threatening thieves; outraged by the orgy of drugs and sex in which her wealthy white friends engage. Young implies, however, that both the ubiquity and the intensity of external changes, of the elements of chaos, cause Angelina to determine to make her own changes. In Detroit, she recognizes the essential contribution of three factors — time, solitude, and her own free will — to the making of herself and her "soul space."

Coming back to Detroit, Angelina returns to the past. In Mexico, she had said to Watusi, " 'Never look back,' " and he had reinforced her imperative, " 'Never look back — somethin might be gainin on you. That's my philosophy ... I try to live every day like it might be the last' " (71-72). But Angelina must look back, not to understand her roots, but to understand herself. Her initial response on returning was that "For the first time in years she felt connection to something real again, to something from the past that had more than immediate meaning" (108). Yet Young also indicates from the outset of this stage of her journey that she cannot retreat into the past. She cannot linger over the pleasures of childhood:

> What happy times she remembered from those days! Why do people have to grow up and spoil everything? It'd been so nice being a child and feeling that adults knew what they were doing and what the world was all about. Now that she was one of them, the truth was out, and the truth was breaking her heart by the hour. (111)

Nor can she any longer sentimentalize with self-pity upon her attempted suicide. Nor can she become mired in the guilt generated by having struck for independence from her family.

Separated by death from her mother, she constantly seeks her approval for her liberated ways. Separated geographically from her father, she thinks lovingly about him. Watusi instantly reminds her of him, in appearance and in wit, and on the night they first make love, he plays music her father had taught her to appreciate and describes her father to her as if he had known him. As they make love, the past seems recreacted as if

> Suddenly it was raining moments, moments that stretched into soft, fleshy years. Some ancient tune was sweetening the silence inside her head, some song that conveyed without words just how her mother might have felt the instant her father's seed entered her womb and — (93)

Young's description here prompts not a snap Freudian judgment, but rather a recognition of his conviction that an individual, to be fulfilled, must be able to reconcile the past with the present. For a moment, Angelina is able to do this in Mexico.

With her father during the days of his recuperation in Detroit, she ponders her present identity, however, by examining the familiar, taunting questions through the medium of the past:

> Daddy, what was the weather like the day I was born? Why did you and Mama have me? What was it that first attracted you to Mama? Why did you give up playing music? What possessed you to move from Georgia to Michigan and why that little racist town Milan and all that farming stuff? Why'd you pick the post office to work at for the rest of your life? Was I strange as a little girl? Do you love me as much as Mama did? Do you still love Mama? Do you still love me now that Ive been away for so long? Why'd you name me what you did? Did my name have any special significance to you and Mama? What was it? Who is Angelina? (129)

In her long talks and walks with her father, he reveals himself to her and implicitly herself to herself. He speaks to her of his enduring love for her mother, who he watched over while she was dying of cancer even as Angelina is watching over him; he speaks to her of his subsequent belief:

> "... in a high power, some kinda God or spirit or whatever you wanna call it that's bigger and more beautiful than anything we know in this world ... Going to church is a style the same as just eating vegetables or not wearing a hat. Later for that! I'm for the real thing which is being for real, if you get me, like, religion is for real — you can feel it from the minute you wake up till the minute you lie down at night and all through your dreams if youre living right — ... That secret little thing that gives you the power to go on living when everything else says 'Forget it and die!' — that's what I'm talking about." (154)

His statement of belief becomes his legacy to Angelina. It releases her from the tormented past, from "the dusty corner of herself that was nothing but guilt and shadow" (157) through her knowledge that her father will be able to continue to live a full and vigorous life; it also releases her into the present and the future, into the continuity of time, far bigger than herself, but her own "secret little thing," her secret path the gypsy had predicted she would find.

In Detroit, face-to-face with her past, with the presence of her father and memories of her mother, with her old high school friends and memories of their days together, she realizes that "Time was her drug really":

> All her life she'd been rummaging around in time looking for some version of this bliss she'd heard and read so much about ... Call it whatever you wanted. She called it ecstasy — a joyous feeling of total release. She wanted to rise up out of herself and go zooming above the stupid-ass world like some giggly old saint who knew that nothing short of ecstasy mattered anyway. Was this what she sought in a man? Was this the kind of freedom she was looking for when she drifted away from this very town to become a wanderer like so many of her old friends had done? (128)

"The beautiful thing about time, she was coming to believe, was that it never stands still" (149). In Mexico, there were brief moments when, as it were, she had time, when she felt at one with the peasants moving slowly across the land as her ancestors might have done, when she reenacted her parents' experience as she made love to Watusi, when she found a day for "unscheduled and imaginative loafing [such as] she never seemd to have time for in the States anymore ... Most of all she loved being on top of time as it flowed on and passed by and simply slipped away" (56). To lose time, as she does taking drugs with Renee is, for Angelina, to lose contact with life's possibilities. Young seems to suggest that to be unaware of time's flow or to be unable to accept is is to be trapped by time. Thus Angelina's time in Detroit, by forcing her to confront the past, frees her to accept certain changes which time brings: in particular, her father's near death and his recovery. She writes to Curtis, again defining herself in a letter, "Time's the biggest problem (or asset) I've got. What used to take months to make itself clear now only takes weeks. I feel older than old, and if the world ended tonight I'd feel that I died a merciful death" (165).

Angelina's ability to accept the changes which time brings coincides with her study of meditation and her realization of her need for solitude. She recognizes the anomaly of the fact that her interest should have flowered in Detroit rather than in San Francisco: "It amused her that she'd avoided mystical literature ... the whole time she'd been in California, and now, stranded in hardbop do-or-die Detroit, she found herself gobbling up yoga, Zen and occult books as if by doctor's prescription" (152). "In hardbop do-or-die Detroit," however, Angelina is alone. In the house where she had been raised, with the memories of the past surrounding her, she finds that there is wonder in silence and solitude. The fear that solitude might sour into loneliness, the fear that she realizes has been partially responsible for her dependence on men, is absolved. As she learns how to meditate, time flows through her, bringing images of past, present and future, but gradually, she seems to transcend her own personal involvement with time to make contact with time eternal: "For the first time in her life, she felt the windows of her loneliness opening wide to the world. There was nothing she wanted to leave unframed" (175).

Young's description of Angelina's success with meditation – the achievement of "peace of mind ... all you can really count on ... what the gypsy was trying to tell me" (177) – seems almost too good to be true. Her's and her father's experiences however, seem based on Young's own "remarkable and continuing series of (non-drug induced) mystical experiences that I consider, thus far, to be the high points of my life";

> ... since the mid-sixties, I have been nourished by these intense and blissful interludes and, hence, have drawn much of my inspiration to write ... from what could be termed religious sources. I am not, of course, referring to church religion. Sometimes there is a vastness I feel growing within me that I could explore and delight in forever. No mere church could contain it. I cannot help but believe that all men have sensed this beautiful endlessness about themselves at one time or another. It is what I call soul.[22]

Angelina's success is also credible because we realize that she has mastered not an absolute state of mind, but a technique for achieving that state of mind; although her questions continue, Young demonstrates that his heroine can, of her own free will, temporarily dispel them. The chapter describing her success with meditation is entitled "Getting Over," and we are led to believe that Angelina has learned how to use meditation in order to get

22. *Natural Process*, ed. Ted Wilentz and Tom Weatherly (New York: Hill and Wang, 1970), pp. 180-181.

over. The final chapter in Book III suggests that she has learned to join the freedom which meditation gives her with the freedom of choice, to join the infinity of time with the finite nature of self, to create from the feeling of total release her own "soul space." Disgusted with the good times contrived by banalities of conversation and pretentious posturing between strangers, by sex and drugs, at Renee's New Year's party, Angelina leaves, choosing to welcome in a new year -- and a renewed commitment to life — by meditating in silence.

Angelina's choice to leave the party, a choice she would have been unable to make at the beginning of the novel, points to the third factor of which her sojourn in Detroit has made her conscious: her own free will. Although the gypsy had reminded her of its importance, in Books I and II, Angelina had passively let those changes happen to her whereas in Book III, she is able to distinguish between those changes which, being beyond her control, she must accept and those which she can both judge and control. In a letter to Curtis she once again reflects upon herself, this time setting forth her determination to create her own life, to make conscious choices:

> I love [my father] and yet at the same time I can't wait to get back to Berkeley to pick up my raggedy life where I left it hanging, flapping like some tattered garment hung out on a clothesline. I feel I'm at some kind of crossroads. I can go either this way or that. I can keep on being passive and taking whatever shit the world's dealing out and continue to get messed around at every turn, or I can do a turn-around and do a little dishing out myself ... I plan to start exercising a bit of my own free will ... you know that old blues lyric that goes: "Cried last night / and I cried the night before / I'm gonna change my way of living / so I won't have to cry no more?" (163-4)

Exercising a bit of her own free will, she does change her way of living; no longer passive, she chooses and she acts. At the conclusion of Book III, she not only identifies the pretentious intellectualizing of white Renee and the pretentious attitudinizing of black Ernest, but she also leaves Renee's party and leaves Detroit. Her departure from Berkeley and from Mexico had been determined for her by circumstances and by the generosity of friends; her departure from Detroit and from her beloved father is the result of a difficult decision, but one made with knowledge of the continuity

282

of time, the sanctity of solitude, and the necessity of her own "soul space."

In Book IV of *Who Is Angelina?* , Young brings Angelina full cycle. For his heroine as well as for the hero of *Invisible Man*, "the end is in the beginning." Angelina's life ia s spiraling rather than a stagnant circle; in returning to pick up her "raggedy life" where she left it hanging in Berkeley, she tests her newly acquired sense of time and self in the context of her recent past and her former acquaintances. To the extremes of terror and ecstasy, which freedom had brought before, she adds responsibility.

In the opening episode of Book IV, Young reveals the strength of his heroine's self, of her independence and integrity, as she chooses and acts in the familiar social context of a busy street corner in Berkeley. Witness to the robbery of a white acquaintance's purse, Angelina does not stand by passively. Reminded of previous robberies — her own apartment, her father's home, her aunt's purse — she determines to pursue, to catch, and to prosecute the thief. Her action above all suggests that she no longer will be victimized by circumstances, nor allow others to be victimized by them if she can choose. Her outrage, discussed earlier, at being identified as an " 'Uncle Tom collaborationist' " reflects her conviction that facile racist and political categories deny humanity; her insistence on pressing charges against the thief reflects her conviction that her decisions and actions can benefit humanity. In Young's novels, the protagonists are not ennobled by profound suffering or poverty, by desperate flights or murders, but rather by making what appear to be simple choices to defend simple principles of right and wrong. Thus if Angelina's pursuit of the thief, which involves her brandishing her umbrella like a samurai sword and her being assisted by a comic bulldog, is mock-heroic, it is also poignantly human.

In the course of Book IV, Angelina must make other choices. She applies for a job, recognizing the possibility of ther potential employer's humility as well as of her arrogance; she helps Margo, recognizing the necessity of adjusting her needs to Margo's. However, Young most clearly demonstrates Angelina's triumphant ability to retain her "soul space" as he describes her relationships with men. Not a self-conscious feminist, Angelina implicitly embodies an explicit feminist principle in these relationships; she knows that neither her sense of life's possibilities nor her sense of herself is dependent upon either sex or a man. In Mexico she had succumbed to Watusi; in Detroit, she had cared for her father; back in Berkeley, she is confronted by the memories of her former lover; the pressure and presence of Curtis, her epistolary lover; and the return of Watusi. She is troubled by her jealousy over her former lover; she yearns not to "get involved and all excited and lose this hard-earned spiritual high... [not] to go through all those changes again. It took too much out of her to be tempted that way" (234-35). She is able to put to rest her feelings about this man by realizing that " 'Cant no one person cause you to suffer if you make up your mind you dont want em to' " (250); she is able to put to rest her feelings for Curtis by insisting thath they can be "soul mates," by insisting that they can enjoy good food and the rain, music and the ocean together without having to have sex; she puts to rest her feelings about Watusi by determining to pay back the money he has given her and by recognizing that she can love him without being wedded to him:

> "That's the way I used to think ... either you do or you dont [love some-one]. But it isnt always that easy. Most of the time it's someplace in be-tween. It's taken me all my life to learn that. You can love somebody and not love em. You can hate somebody and not hate em. I love you ... but .. I mean, you have to understand how I mean that." (278).

Watusi understands; he leaves, but with appreciation for her and a promise of future meetings. Thus Angelina, by choosing to continue to define herself through her own mind and through multiple experiences rather than through the mind of another and a single relationship, continues to increase her sense of possibilities, the dimensions of her "soul space."

Coming to terms with the past in Detroit and in Berkeley, Angelina is at ease with the on-going present. Meditation had provided the means of attaining peace with time, and although it continues to do so, Angelina perceives that it is a means rather than an end. To meditate or not to meditate? Angelina chooses to meditate when it helps her – "Later for a movement! She loved being moved all alone this way; ablutions performed, meditation attended to, stomach empty, her entire body tingling with energy in the familiar seclusion of a newly cleaned cottage" (229). But she will choose not to meditate if it becomes as constricting as a movement: "Maybe she was being too uptight about meditation and the pursuit of serenity. The last thing she wanted to become was dull and inflexible like most people she saw around her lately — dreary, cheerless hippies and straights, whites and off-whites, blacks and browns, oldsters and youngsters" (237).

To her distraught friend, Margo, Angelina explains that while meditation has helped her, it has not resolved all her difficulties: " 'I still have hassles to work out. I still get headaches. I still get fed up with everybody and wanna go hide someplace. I'm saying that the change Ive been going through makes things a lot more interesting probably because I myself feel more in control and on top of stuff' " (263).

But even as she talks with Margo, an elderly neighbor dies. The event illuminates Young's conviction that the individual may choose his or her options and thus control the changes in his or her life within a framework of inevitable limitations which prohibit absolute free will or control. Although Angelina may, through meditation, believe she can transcend time, she must and does also realize that time passes, moving one closer to the last, inevitable change: death. In the novel's final chapter — "Time on Fire" — Young suggests that her heroine is aware of time's possibilities and its limitations; acknowledge the moment's passing: "Would [time] ever catch up with her ? ... [she went] for a head-clearing walk and let time continue to do what time does as it burns itself up with each moment" (280).

In the novel's penultimate chapter, Angelina makes two seemingly contradictory comments about freedom. When her neighbor dies, Angelina says, " 'Mama Lou is free' " (267). Thus death can be seen to represent both the final limitation and the ultimate liberation, a liberation from the restrictions of time and self into the eternity of time and selflessness. Mama Lou's death intrudes upon Angelina's pondering whether Margo longed "to be free, free of herself, free of being Margo" (262). We are reminded that Angelina had herself earlier longed for death, longed to be rid of "the stifling little cocoon of ... Self." The Angelina of the novel's conclusion, however, says emphatically, " 'I just wanna be me' " (279). Finally for Young, it seems therefore, as with Ellison, that liberation lies with self-knowledge, with the simultaneous acceptance of the limitations and responsibilities of time and self on the one hand and of choices and possibilities of time and self on the other hand. Explaining the title of his second book of poetry, *The*

Song Turning Back Into Itself (1971), Young expresses his belief that "In essence you're never anyone but yourself. You go through all these changes but in a sense you're always turning back into what you really are."[23] Thus in the conclusion of *Who Is Angelina?* , Angelina turns back into herself to discover "Possibilities ... beginning to trouble her again. choices, decisions! That was all her life had been" (278). Knowing herself, knowing at last who Angelina is, she knows, however, that she can choose and that in her choices lie both her freedom and her bondage. In the novel's final words, Young sets forth a range of possibilities for her life, possibilities which express choice and limitation, which in their openendedness express the full dimensions of her "soul space" and the continuation of her travels:

> Soon it would be time to either get up and get dressed and go to meditation, or lie in bed and feel guilty about skipping.
> This was order enough for her for now.
> There was tomorrow's drive down to Big Sur with Curtis. There would always be papers to correct. (280)

With Angelina, Young seeks to create a character who represents an individual, an Afro-American woman, at a particular moment in time — "I really was trying to write about a young woman and options in the 1970s in America. Just what was out there? But because she was Black that was something I wanted to deal with"; [this was] "my primary purpose in writing the book."[24] If he has succeeded in these ends, he has also succeeded in creating a heroine who can be identified with the heroines of classic American literature - Hester Prynne and Isabel Archer, who come to know themselves, their possibilities and limitations, through the choices they make — as well as certain heroines of Afro-American literature, created by Afro-American women writers. Mary Helen Washington describes these heroines Paule Marshall's Reena of the story by that name (1962), Alice Walker's Sarah Davis of "A Sudden Trip Home in the Spring" (1971), and Nella Larsen's Clare Kendry of *Passing* (1929) and Helga Crane of *Quicksand* (1928) — as anticipating the educated, middle-class black woman who has emerged as a force in American life in recent decades:

23. *Interviews with Black Writers*, p. 269.
24. *Melus* interview, p. 46.

286

As black women move further into areas that were once the private reserve of whites, those few of us — those fortunate few whose lives are not stunted and dreamless — are finding ourselves facing the tensions that Nella Larsen knew, and it is for us to do something about them, to take what she started further than she was able to go ... we are condemned to a new freedom.[25]

Al Young's Angelina Green finds, ultimately, triumph in being condemned to the dimensions of this "new freedom." She finds "soul space."

BIOGRAPHY

Al Young was born in Ocean Springs, Mssissippi, May 31, 1939, and grew up in Detroit, Michigan. He attended the University of Michigan from 1957 to 1961 and took his B.A. in Spanish at the University of California, Berkeley in 1969. He has worked at a variety of occupations: disc jockey, professional musician, lab. assistant, yard clerk for the Southern Pacific Railroad, medical photographer, Spanish tutor, personnel interviewer, book reviewer, actor, screenwriter. From 1969 to 1973, he held the Edward H. Jones Lectureship in Creative Writing at Stanford and has taught and lectured at universities across the United States. He has edited various periodicals and anthologies, including *Loveletter, Changes*, and, with Ishmael Reed, *Yardbird Reader* and *Y'bird*; with Reed, he also established Yardbird Publishing, Inc.

BIBLIOGRAPHY

Novels:
Snakes. New York: Holt, Rinehart and Winston, 1970.
Who Is Angelina? New York: Holt, Rinehart and Winston. 1975.
Sitting Pretty. New York: Holt, Rinehart and Winston. 1976.
Ask Me Now. New York: McGraw-Hill Book Company. 1980.

Poetry:
Dancing. New York: Corinth Books. 1969.
The Song Turning Back Into Itself. New York: Holt, Rinehart and Winston 1971.
Geography of the Near Past. New York: Holt, Rinehart and Winston,1976.

25. Mary Helen Washington, "Nella Larsen: Mystery Woman of the Harlem *Renaissance," Ms.* (December, 1980), p. 50.

PETER BRUCK

RETURNING TO ONE'S ROOTS: THE MOTIF OF SEARCHING AND FLYING IN TONI MORRISON'S *SONG OF SOLOMON* (1977)

> I have to *affirm* my forefathers and I *must* affirm my parents or be reduced in my own mind to a white man's inadequate conception of human complexity.
> Ralph Ellison, "A Very Stern Discipline" (1967)
>
> I mean to use the past to create the present.
> Statement by James Baldwin
> J. Baldwin / Margaret Mead, *A Rap on Race* (1971)

Unlike such early black feminine writers as Nella Larsen, who depicted the emotional anguish her heroines experience in a racial no-man's land, contemporary women writers strive towards female self-affirmation. Whereas Helga Crane, heroine of Larsen's *Quicksand* (1928) could never move beyond her self-destructive anger, writers of today such as Alice Walker, Gayl Jones and Toni Morrison work toward an assessment of black female expression that is no longer dominated by the painful encounter with a white world. Particularly the 1970s witnessed the emergence of a new range of subject matter[1] which, in keeping with Alice Walker, centers around the exposition of "the subconscious of a people, because the people's dreams, imaginings, ritual, legends etc. are known to be important, are know to contain the accumulated collective reality of the people themselves."[2] These requirements clearly apply

---

1. Cf., for example, the following anthologies: Toni Cade, ed., *The Black Woman*. New York: Signet, 1970; Mary Helen Washington, ed., *Black Eyed Susans. Classic Stories By and About Black Women*. Garden City: Anchor, 1975.

2. Statement by Alice Walker in John O'Brien, ed., *Interviews With Black*

to Toni Morrison's fictional universe whose four published novels to date not only probe into the inner life of black womanhood but, with the publication of *Song of Solomon* and *Tar Baby* (1981) are also increasingly concerned with Afro-American folklore. It is the very application of this new dimension which signals a significant departure from her earlier novels *The Bluest Eye* (1970) and *Sula* (1973), which portray the initiation experiences of their heroines.[3] In *Song of Solomon* Toni Morrison expands upon this pattern by fusing the theme of initiation with the quest for family roots, which, in turn, is linked to the search for Afro-American cultural heritage.

The narrative material used in the novel comprises more than half a century of family history. The present action relates Macon (Milkman) Dead's personal history from the time of his birth in 1931 up to his death in 1963. This narrative strand is framed by the stories of his aunt Pilate, his sister Corinthians as well as of his cousin Hagar, grandchild of Pilate, with whom Milkman has a love affair. These personal histories are interspersed with accounts of the past of Milkman's parents Macon Dead and Ruth Foster, all of which provide the reader with insight into the various layers of black experience. The narrative presentation of the complex material shows Morrison to be employing the strategy of multiple selective omniscience, the various narrative perspectives being arranged by the explicit presence of authorial intelligence. The coexistence of the author's textual presence and of the various personalized perspectives guides the reader's understanding of the action, usually preparing him for the intermittant changes from one character's perspective to another as well as for the frequent alterations in the temporal structure. The informing principle behind these shifting layers of presentation seems to be a reflection of the protagonist's indecision "to make up his mind whether to go for-

Writers. New York: Livewright, 1973, p. 202. For a thematic survey of contemporary black female writers see Faith Pullin, "Landscapes of Reality: The Fiction of Contemporary Afro-American Women," in A. Robert Lee, ed., *Black Fiction: New Studies in the Afro-American Novel Since 1945.* London: Vision Press, 1980, pp. 173-203.

3. For an extensive analysis of this theme see Jane S. Bakerman, "Failures of Love: Female Initiation in the Novels of Toni Morrison," *American Literature*, 52 (1981), 541-563.

ward or to turn back." (70)[4] Indeed, in order to learn to go forward, i.e. grow up, Milkman is forced to discover his family roots. Both the process of growing up as well as the narrative arrangement of this process are thus reminiscent of the image of history as spiral and recall James Baldwin's famous dictum "that the past is all that makes the present coherent."[5]

The theme of growing up is introduced early in the novel. Note the follwing authorial comment which foreshadows central aspects of the action to come: " ... at twelve Milkman met the boy who not only could liberate him, but could take him to the woman who has as much to do with his future as she had with his past." (35) The boy Milkman meets is his life-long friend Guitar who leads him to Pilate's house, a place Milkman is not supposed to go to. It is this first encounter with an alien world which anticipates Milkman's later quest in a nutshell. Being at Pilate's makes him "more alive than he'd ever been" (44) and induces in him for "the first time in his life" a feeling of "being completely happy." (47) It is also here that he listens for the first time to a song sung by Pilate, her daughter Reba and her grandchild Hagar that will later play a crucial role in his self-discovery. And it is also this forbidden visit which prompts his father to relate to Milkman the story of how his grandfather, a former slave, came by the name of "Dead":

> He [a northern soldier] asked Papa where he was born. Papa said Macon. Then he asked him who his father was. Papa said, 'He's dead.' ... Well, the Yankee wrote it all down, but in the wrong spaces ... in the space for his name the fool wrote, 'Dead',comma 'Macon.' But Papa couldn't read so he never found out what he was registered as till Mama told him.(53)

Significantly, Macon Dead II does not know the real name of his father, nor does this seem to bother him. The apparent lack of interest in one's genealogical history is here indicative of the rootless world of Milkman's father, a prominant owner of houses in an unnamed city in Michigan, whose philosophy of life is summed up by the following advice to his twelve year old son: "Own things. And let the things you own own other things. Then you'll own

4. Page numbers in brackets refer to the following edition: Toni Morrison, *Song of Solomon*, New York: Signet, 1978.

5. James Baldwin, "Autobiographical Notes," *Notes of a Native Son*. London: Corgi, 1965, p. 4.

yourself and other people too." (55) Yet, as Milkman is to discover, owning oneself involves not material possession but the unravelling of both one's distorted past as well as of one's roots.

The next major event to occur in the protagonist's life happens ten years later. After his father ended an argument with his wife by slapping her, Milkman rushes to his mother's aid and knocks down his father. This act, which sets in motion his gradual process of initiation, triggers off his first step toward self-knowledge:

> My mother nursed me when I was old enough to talk, stand up, and wear knickers, and somebody saw it and laughed and — and that is why they call me Milkman and that is why my father never does and that is why my mother never does, but everybody else. And how did I forget that? And why? (78)

Characteristically, this unexpected recollection comes about only after his father has told him an incident relating to his mother's past. By implication, then, Milkman's self-discovery involves not only his facing up to his own past but, more importantly, his grappling with different versions of his family's past, all of which are reminiscent of the oral tradition in folklore.

Earlier mention was made of the overt authorial control over the distribution of the shifting dramatized perception of the action through the various characters. As regards Milkman's process of initiation, these shifts in perspective serve a vital function. They accompany the protagonist's attempt at self-determination, thus shedding additional light on his search for his family history. The first narrative account to interrupt the story of Milkman's beginning self-awareness is a retrospective tale about Pilate's youth and her growing maturation. This highly compressed narrative strand introduces the theme of rootlessness.[6] The reasons for this situation in Pilate's life consist in her never having known her mother's last name (she died during childbirth) as well as in the peculiar circumstances of her birth: "she had come struggling out of the womb without help from throbbing muscles or the pressure of swift womb water. As a result ... her stomach was ... at no place interrupted by a navel."(28) After her father, a prosperous Pennsylvania farmer, was killed by white people, Pilate began a "wandering life" (148) for some twenty years, only to find out that her

6. Cf. Jane S. Bakerman, op.cit., p.554.

physical uniqueness "isolated her from her people" (149), thus providing her with only a marginal existence within the black community. Despite her isolated, rootless existence, her life is marked by a genuine "compassion for troubled people" and "a deep concern for and about human relationships." (150) This attitude distinctly sets her apart from the middle class world of Ruth and Macon Dead, which is characterized by lovelessness and artificiality. As Milkman's friend Guitar once put it: "Your father ... behaves like a white man, thinks like a white man." (225)

The antagonism between the two worlds is further expressed on the level of name symbolism. Indeed, the second generation Macon Dead turns out to be "living dead," as his interest in life is reduced to mere property-mindedness. A similar sterility applies to his wife Ruth, né Foster, whose maiden name alludes to her role as Milkman's foster mother. Bearing in mind that it was Pilate who instigated a new, though brief sexual relationship between Macon and Ruth and that it was she who prevented Ruth from having an abortion, we come to realize that she in fact not only saved Milkman's life but has also always watched over him as if he were her own. By extension, then, Pilate emerges as Milkman's pilot,[7] guiding him, as it were, out of the deathworld of his parents towards his true destiny, i.e. the discovery of his African heritage. Significantly, Pilate's role as genealogical guide also involves her final restoration to her origin through the aid of Milkman, who will prove to be able to provide the rootless Pilate with original family roots.

Prior to their symbiosis, Milkman has as yet to learn to separate himself from the property-centered world of his parents. Ironically, it is his father who brings about Milkman's dissociation from his parental ties. After Macon Dead has learned from his son of the existence of a green sack at Pilate's house which he believes to contain those gold coins he as an adolescent took from a man he killed, he urges Milkman to "get the gold." (173) In order to organize the theft, Milkman secures the help of Guitar, promising him one third of the share. Their attempt proves to be unsuccessful, however, as the sack contains only a dead man's bones. Again, Milkman follows his father's instruction, this time leaving for Danville, Pennsylvania, where Macon Dead believes the gold to be

7. Cf. the play on the words "Pilate" and "pilot" on pages 19 and 286 of the novel.

buried in a cave which Pilate and he fled to after the killing of their father. Milkman's journey to Danville and later to Shalimar, Virginia, sets in motion his final initiation, the treasure hunt turning into a parable of self-discovery.

The first stage of his odyssey takes him to a certain Reverend Cooper, who remembers both Milkman's father and grandfather. This initial confrontation with his family's past makes him realize for the first time that "he hadn't known what it meant: links." (231) His newly gained insight is, however, still overshadowed by his obsession to find the treasure. Following Reverend Cooper's advice, he visits an old black woman, Circe, who once provided his father and aunt with a hide-out and helped them to escape a white lynching mob. This second encounter with a person familiar with his family supplies him with important new information. It is from Circe that he learns that his grandmother's first name was "Sing," that the original first name of his grandfather was "Jake" and that Virginia was their geographical home. Moreover, Circe not only directs him to the mysterious cave where, however, he only finds "rocks, boards, leaves, even a tin cup, but no gold" (255); she also informs him that "old Macon's body" was once dumped there. Even though at this point Milkman is not able to digest this intelligence, it does persuade him to follow Pilate's former tracks to Virginia, to where, as he thinks, she must have taken the gold.

The initial stage of Milkman's journey introduces several elements which clearly place *Song of Solomon* in the tradition of the novel of initiation. Thus the departure from his home stands for the familiar exit pattern, and his first confrontation with a world hitherto unknown resembles the traditional period of transition, where the initiante moves from a state of naive self-assurance to a provisional state of insight. In terms of genre conventions, Circe emerges as Milkman's first mentor whose advice guides him both literally and figuratively in the right direction. Yet, what distinguishes *Song of Solomon* from the classical initiation pattern is the very absence of the figure of the tempter. This variation from genre conventions signals an expressive Afro-American quality of the initiation device. For unlike the common mainstream initiante, Milkman's process of maturation centers around the discovery of one's roots. Consequently, his transition from innocence to experience does not involve an experience of disillusionment nor does it imply the customary shock of recognition. Rather, in *Song of*

Solomon the mode of painful entrance into the adult world has been replaced by the notion of uncovering one's ancestry.

The second and final stage of Milkman's transition from rootlessness to the disclosure of his genealogy occurs at rural Shalimar, an all black community. Here the northern urban black protagonist finds himself confronted with rural southern brethren, whose hostility bewilders him. Note the following authorial explanation which precedes a violent encounter between Milkman and a Shalimar inhabitant: "They [the Shalimar blacks] looked at his skin and saw it was black as theirs, but they knew he had the heart of the white men who came to pick them up in trucks when they needed anonymous, faceless laborers." (269) The color metaphor, while underscoring the protagonist's racial rootlessness, suggests at the same time a new stratification of meaning with regard to Milkman's search, this additional meaning being the values associated with black urban and rural culture. Significantly, it is only after having entered the rural South that Milkman has learned to "stop evading things, sliding through, over, and around difficulties." (274) For the first time in his life he has taken a stand, i.e. successfully defended himself. Similar to his first violent encounter with his father, the store fight leads him to a new state of self-awareness. Whilst the fight with his father made him discover the origin of his nickname, the violent confrontation now paves the way to his being initiated into the grass-roots black community. In terms of geographical symbolism, traditional values are thus reversed, for it is the exit from the North and the concomitant entrance into the South that conditions the hero's losing "the heart of the white men."

Milkman's *inire* takes place during a nocturnal coon hunt to which he has been invited by some of Shalimar's inhabitants. Soon after the hunting party has set out, Milkman feels tired, begins "to limp and hobble" (278) and falls behind the group. Alone in the darkness of the Blue Ridge Mountains, he begins to wonder what he is doing there: "He had come here to find traces of Pilate's journey, to find relatives she might have visited, to find anything he could that either lead him to the gold or convince him that it no longer existed." (279) Similar to Faulkner's *Go Down Moses* Milkman's participation in the hunt returns him to his sources. Just as in "The Old People" and "The Bear" hunting is seen as a traditional action in which man unites himself through shared activities and a reverence for the wilderness with both his ancestors and his fellow men. Milkman thus learns to confront his essential self in the solitary wilderness of the woods. The moment of confrontation is clearly reminiscent of the Faulknerian notion of hunting as a training in brotherhood, since it involves the elemental recognition of belonging. He suddenly realizes "that he was with other people [and] his self — the cocoon that was 'personality' — gave way." (280) The newly gained feeling of togetherness lets him forget his physical pain, making him, as it were, a part of the rural southern grass-roots:

> ... he found himself exhilarated by simply walking the earth. Walking it like he belonged on it; like his legs were stalks, tree trunks, a part of his body that extended down down down into the rock and soil, and were comfortable there ... on the earth and on the place where he walked. And he did not limp. (284)

The discovery of his geographical roots prepares Milkman for the ultimate discovery of his genealogical ancestry. His aroused interest in his people together with his novel state of communal susceptibility now emotionally reconnects him to Pilate's house. This reminiscence ("he was homesick for her" (303)) includes the recollection of the old blues song "O Sugarman don't leave me here" which Pilate always used to sing. As the children of Shalimar sing a similar song, "O Solomon don't leave me here", as, moreover, their song includes the line: "Jake the only son of Solomon" (306), Milkman is finally able to piece together the various bits of previously collected information. His grandfather, as he learns from Susan Byrd, another inhabitant of Shalimar, is indeed the Jake the children sing about, for "he was one of those flying African children ... one of Solomon's children." (325) As Mrs. Byrd informs him further:

> Jake was supposed to be one of Solomon's original twenty-one children. ... According to the story he [Solomon] wasn't running away. He was flying. He flew. You know, like a bird. ... He ... was lifted up in the air. Went right on back to wherever it was he came from. (326)

The reference to this legend introduces a new layer of meaning which is crucial to an adequate appreciation of the novel. The application of the motif of flying, a traditional topos in Afro-American folklore and literature, suggests, in the present instance, a significant departure from earlier literary expressions. Particularly in the 1940s, the motif of flying was used to convey the notion of escape, freedom and, ultimately, of the at that time socially unattainable. Thus Jake in Wright's *Lawd Today*[8] and Bigger Thomas and his friend Gus in *Native Son* are fascinated with the idea of flying airplanes: " 'If you wasn't black and if you had some money and if they'd let you go that aviation school, you *could* fly a plane,' Gus said."[9] Similarly, Ajax, lover of Sula in Morrison's *Sula*, is lured by airplanes: "This woman Ajax loved, and after her - airplanes. There was nothing in between. And when he was not sitting enchanted listening to his mother's words, he thought of airplanes, and pilots, and the deep sky that held them both."[10] The preoccupation of black writers with this theme goes back to the segregated air force of World War II. By the 1940s, black men were trained at Tuskegee airfield, but for a long time, they were barred from combat duty. The idea of flying thus denotes a frontier of segregation, which almost obsessed the writers of the 1940s and even found a contemporary expression in James Wylie's novel *The Homestead Grays* (1977). However, flying has not only served as a symbol of social exclusion; rather, as a wishing game it has also been used to express a collective experience. As Ralph Ellison once remarked with regard to the airplane scene in *Native Son*: "[It is] a naive form of unrecorded literature ... in which the individual dream and wish is dramatized verbally and shared collectively."[11]

Indeed, Ellison himself was to explore this aspect in detail in such stories as "Mister Toussan" (1941), "That I Had the Wings" (1943) and "Flying Home" (1944). Note the following dialogue between the two boys Riley and Buster in "Mister Toussan":

'What would you do if you had wings?' he said.
'Shucks, I'd outfly an eagle, I wouldn't stop flying till I was a million, billion, trillion, zillion miles away from this ole town.'
'Where'd you go, man?'
'Up north, maybe to Chicago.'
'Man, if I had wings I wouldn't never settle down.'
'Me neither. Hecks, with wings you could go anywhere, even up to the sun

8 Richard Wright, *Lawd Today*. New York: Avon, 1963, p. 58.
9. Richard Wright, *Native Son*. New York: Signet, 1964, p.20.
10. Toni Morrison, *Sula*. New York: Bantam, 1975, p.109.
11. Ralph Ellison, "The Great Migration," *New Masses*, Dec. 2, 1941, p.23.

if it wasn't too hot. ...'
' ... I'd go to New York. ...'
'Even around the stars. ...'
'Or Dee-troit, Michigan. ...'
'Hell, you could git some cheese off the moon and some milk from the Milkyway ...'
'Or anywhere else colored is free ...'
'I bet I'd loop-the-loop ...'
'And parachute ...'
'I'd land in Africa and git me some diamonds ...'[12]

What appears to be a collective dream of freedom here gives way to a strategy of demasking this dream as false in the other two stories. Thus when Buster and Riley "play flying" by trying to teach a chicken to fly from the roof of the house down to the ground, their game only results in the chicken's death. In both "That I Had the Wings" and "Flying Home" the failure to achieve a state of flying is indicative of the urge to deny one's group experience and, in particular, those collective experiences referring to the past. Thus Riley in "That I Had the Wings" shouts at Aunt Kater after having been reprimanded by her for having killed the chicken: "I hate yuh ... I wish you had died back in slavery times,"[13] and for Todd, the protagonist in "Flying Home", flying becomes "the most meaningful act in the world" as it is a means of leaving behind "the shame the old man [Jefferson] symbolized."[14] Both Riley's dead chicken as well as Todd's airplane crash serve as ironic comments on the black's wish to escape his collective past.

Whilst flying in Ellison's short fiction is employed to unmask the attempt to leave behind one's group heritage as false, flying in black folklore has also been used to express the collective desire to

12. Ralph Ellison, "Mister Toussan," *New Masses*, Nov. 4, 1941, p.19.
13. Ralph Ellison, "That I Had the Wings," *Common Ground*, 3 (1943), p. 37; for detailed analyses of these stories in the light of Ellison's use of folklore see Dorothea Fischer-Hornung, *Folklore And Myth In Ralph Ellison's Early Works*. Stuttgart: Hochschulverlag, 1979, and Robert G. O'Meally, *The Craft of Ralph Ellison*. Cambridge, Mass.: Harvard UP, 1980.
14. Ralph Ellison, "Flying Home," in Langston Hughes, ed., *The Best Short Stories by Negro Writers*. Boston: Little, Brown and Company, 1967, pp.154-155; for a detailed discussion of this story see Bernhard Ostendorf, "Ralph Ellison, 'Flying Home'," in Peter Freese, ed., *Die amerikanische Short Story der Gegenwart*. Berlin: Erich Schmidt, 1976, pp.64-76.

return to one's roots. During the time of slavery legends of people who could fly were widespread throughout the South.[15] The common denominator of these folk tales consists in their voicing a longing to go back to one's original home, i.e. Africa, or, as Langston Hughes folk hero Simple put it, to the Caribbean:

> Ah, but I would fly! in winter I [would] live on baby oranges in Florida — if I did not go further to the West Indies and get away from Jim Crow. In fact, come to think of it, I believe I would just fly *over* the South, stopping only long enough to spread my tail feathers and show my contempt.[16]

It is the very notion of flying as a return to one's roots which underlines the action in *Song of Solomon*. Significantly, the novel opens with the account of a black insurance agent, who has announced to the black community that "at 3.00 P.M. on Wednesday the 18th of February, 1931, I will take off from Mercy and fly away on my own wings." (3) At first glance, the telling of this event would seem to be completely unconnected to the central action to follow, were it not for the fact that this event constitutes a major device of foreshadowing. Thus, one day after the agent has leaped into the air, Milkman is born in that very hospital from whose roof the flyer has taken off. The intimate connection between the two events is emphasized by the following narrative comment:

> Mr. Smith's blue silk wings must have left their mark, because when the little boy discovered, at four, the same thing Mr. Smith had learned earlier — that only birds and airplanes could fly — he lost all interest in himself. To have to live without that single gift saddened him and left his imagination so bereft that he appeared to be dull ... (9)

From the very beginning, then, Milkman's existence is closely linked to the motif of flying. It is said of him, for example, that he feels an "unrestrained joy at anything that could fly" (179), and while on the airplane that takes him to Pennsylvania he experiences a feeling of freedom: "In the air, away from real life, he felt

15. For accounts of "People Who Could Fly" see Langston Hughes/Arna Bontemps eds., *The Book of Negro Folklore*. New York: Dodd, Mead & Company, 1958; for the cultural background of this motif see Laurence W. Levine *Black Culture and Black Consciousness*. New York: Oxford UP, 1978, p.87.
16. Langston Hughes, *The Best Of Simple*. New York: Hill & Wang, 1961, p.124.

free, but on the ground ... the wings of all those other people's nightmares flapped in his face and constrained him." (222) The increasing use of the imagery of flying during Milkman's journey clearly alludes to his growing insight and anticipates on the level of symbolism his final self-discovery. After he has uncovered his heritage, the protagonist returns home, only to go back to Shalimar with Pilate, who, having learned that the bones in her green sack are those of her father, buries them at the site of Jake Solomon's legendary flight. While this act reconciles Pilate to her roots and, at the same times, provides Milkman with the ultimate knowledge of "why he loved her so: without ever leaving the ground, she could fly," (340) it also involves their death. For Milkman's friend Guitar, believing that Milkman did find the gold and cheated him, mistakenly shoots Pilate in the darkness and instigates the hero's taking a leap like his great-grandfather:

> As flat and bright as a lodestar he wheeled toward Guitar and it did not matter which one of them would give up his ghost in the killing arms of his brother. For now he knew what Shalimar knew: If you surrendered to the air, you could *ride* it. (341)

The symbolic fusion of the two friends with which the novel closes is reminiscent of the classical *Doppelgänger*-motif, which Morrison has previously put to use in *Sula*.[17] Such a reading, which is corroborated by various textual references, also helps to put into perspective the different political views of the two figures and the author's implicit criticism thereof.

Guitar's role as *alter ego* is already alluded to in the first chapter. He is witness to Mr. Smith's flight from the hospital roof and, unlike Milkman, he seems to grasp the implications inherent in Pilate's singing as his eyes show "a slow smile of recognition." (49) Just as with the female character Nel and Sula in *Sula*, Milkman and Guitar represent two sides of one aspect: the alienation of black man from himself and his people. Their state is emphasized by the different philosophies they adhere to, both of which turn out to be inadequate within the context of the action. Guitar, for instance, embodies the displaced rural Southerner who has become a member of the working-class in the North. Milkman, by contrast,

17. Cf. Morrison's own account in her interview with Robert B. Stepto, "Intimate Things In Place: A Conversation With Toni Morrison," *The Massachusetts Review*, 18 (1977), p. 476.

originally identifies himself completely with the middle class ideology of his father which, as he later realizes, "distorted life": "Owning, building, acquiring – that was his [father's] life, his future, his present, and all the history he knew." (304) By the same token, Guitar's guerilla stance on racial politics and his membership in the assassination squad the "Seven Days" reveal a distorted view of life as it constitutes an offense against humanity. Thus Guitar's assertion: "What I'm doing ain't about hating white people. It's about loving us" (160), shows his perverted ethnic philosophy, for, as Milkman points out to him: "Guitar, none of that shit is going to change how I live or how any other Negro lives. What you're doing is crazy. ... You can off anybody you don't like." (161/162)

The merger of the two friends is initially foreshadowed by their encountering a white peacock while investigating the surroundings of Pilate's house prior to their attempt to steal the green sack: "the bird had set them up ... They began to fantasize about what the gold could buy when it became legal tender." (180) Significantly, their individual reveries underscore their respective states of alienation, since both dream about material possessions. Translated into terms of the bird symbolism, the immaculate whiteness of the peacock is indicative of their identity as yet unachieved. Moreover, the inability of the bird to fly off ("Wanna fly, you got to give up the shit that weighs you down" (180)), clearly alludes to their racial rootlessness, which, in turn, derives from their white middle class aspirations. The use of the *Doppelgänger*-motif is further apparent on the level of the hunting metaphor. Since Guitar follows his friend throughout the latter's journey, he emerges as the hunter with Milkman becoming the hunted. The theme of the intimate relationship of the hunter to the hunted, which is again reminiscent of Faulkner, distinctly points towards the final communion of the two characters. Given such a context of associations, the textual interplay of the three central motifs falls into place. Just as Milkman's journey to Virginia in search for the gold finally leads to his recognition of his family chronicle, Guitar's following his friend's tracks signals his return to his geographical roots. And just as Milkman comes to achieve his own sense of racial identity in the wilderness of the southern woods, he comes to accept his *alter ego*: "This was what Guitar had missed about the South – the woods, hunters, killing.

But something had maimed him. ... He felt a sudden rush of affection... and ... within the sound of men tracking a bobcat, he thought he understood Guitar. Really understood him." (282) Thus their symbolic fusion at the end not only reintegrates them into the family of flying Africans; it also points to their having left behind their 'whitewashed' lifestyles, acquiring, as it were, their true identity by figuratively returning to Africa.

While the use of the flight symbolism would seem to imply that the black male can only become a complete person be returning to his racial heritage, it also includes a significant comment on black male-female relations. As Toni Morrison once stated:

> [Black men] are moving. ... That going from town to town or place to place or looking out and over and beyond and changing and so on — that, it seems to me, is one of the monumental themes in black literature about men. ... Although in sociological terms that is described as a major failing of black men — they do not stay home and take care of their children, they are not there — that has always been to me one of the most attractive features about black male life.[18]

In both *Sula* and *Song of Solomon*, the idea of moving is associated with male activities. Consequently, when women attempt to follow this pattern, they isolate themselves from the sustaining qualities of the black community and become "pariahs." Thus Sula's attempt to refuse to adopt the predetermined role of the black woman as wife and mother in the community of Medaillon cuts her off from the life-giving nature of the neighborhood. For when she returns to town after a long absence she finds herself unable to talk to any of the other women whose conventional lifestyle reminds her of death: "Those with husbands had folded themselves into starched coffins." (105) [19] After she is left by Ajax, the one man with whom she consented to have a steady relationship, she feels she has no more to experience: "I have sung all the songs there are," (118) and literally lies down to die.

Sula's failure to live as an autonomous woman casts a significant light on the possibilities Morrison envisages for black womanhood. If mobility, both in a geographical and sexual sense, is seen as a male metaphor, it follows the feminine experience demands an original expression of its own. In *Song of Solomon*, Morrison explores

18. *Ibid.*, pp. 486-487.
19. Page numbers in brackets refer to the Bantam edition.

three alternate versions of female existence. Similar to Sula, Hagar ·
embodies the theme of the deserted woman who cannot come to
terms with having been left behind by her lover. And just as Sula,
she dies, having been unable to find forms of expression that
would sustain her. The motif of the disillusioned woman permeates the whole novel. In terms of female genealogy, the first woman
to suffer from the experience of having lost her lover is Ryna, wife
of the legendary flyer Solomon: ... "she's supposed to have screamed out loud for days. And there's a ravine near here they call Ryna's Gulch, and you can hear this funny sound by it that the wind
makes. People say it's the wife, Solomon's wife crying. ... They say
she screamed and screamed, lost her mind completely." (326-27)
Ryna's wailing, which recalls the African custom of imploring the
spirits, constitutes one archetypal expression of the history of
black womanhood. The traditional African phrase "Go not away
from me"[20] finds its contemporary variant in Pilate's song "O Sugarman don't leave me here." Singing, then, serves as a female metaphor which counterbalances the male metaphor of flying. Both
singing and flying, i.e. moving, thus describe characteristic female-
male activities which have also often been expressed in various
black songs. Note, for example, the following lines:

> When a woman takes the blues,
> She tucks her head and cries;
> But when a man catches the blues,
> He catches er freight and rides.[21]

Within Toni Morrison's fictional universe, only those women who
manage to decipher the code of the blues "Don't you leave me
here"[22] are able to transcend the pain of disappointed love. Those
that prove to be unable to avail themselves of the cathartic effect
of singing either die of grief like Sula and Hagar or fall victim to
the sterility of the rootless black bourgeoisie like Ruth and her
daughter Lena.

In *Song of Solomon*, the possibility of female self-realization
rests on a rejection of the whitewashed lifestyles of black middle

20. This phrase is reported by Levine, op.cit., p.58.
21. These lines are printed in Levine, p.262.
22. "Don't you leave me here" is an old blues number by Jelly Roll Morton, recorded in1939; a recent version is sung by Big Joe Williams, *Storyville*,
(6.23702 AG)

class behavior. The only character to achieve a new sense of "self-esteem" (202) is Corinthians who falls in love with the yardman Porter and finally brings herself to leave her parents' house and move to Porter's place. Even though this act implies a new life as, for example, it involves leaving behind the fabrication of artificial roses with which her mother and sister occupy themselves and which "spoke to Corinthians of death" (200), Morrison carefully refrains from suggesting that Corinthians' choice will entail a promising future. As one critic has recently remarked: ..."to both Hagar and Corinthians, life *has* no worth without the men they love; they have no identity save the reflection of themselves in the eyes of those men."[23] Thus Corinthians' new life ultimately involves another state of bondage as she submits herself to Porter. This act of subjugation brings to mind the teaching of *The First Book of Corinthians* (I, 14:34-35) which stresses the submissive role of women.

What may appear to be a pessimistic depiction of black womanhood does, on the other hand, also make for a note of hope. For an alternative possibility of a new relationship between black men and women may finally be seen in the second meaning of the title, which leads back to the *Song of Songs*, where both Solomon and his beloved sing together: "Behold, you are beautiful my love; ... behold, you are beautiful my beloved."[24] Translated into terms of the novel, the celebration of mutual love and sensuality is given expression in the quasi-cultic encounter between Milkman and Sweet, which is reminiscent of a fertility rite. In *Song of Solomon* Morrison thus argues for the life-giving force of an affirmative sensuality which, if set against the deathworld of Ruth Foster, the disappointed love of Hagar and the submissive love of Corinthians, entails the promise of feminine selfhood.

23. Jane S. Bakerman, op.cit., p.563.
24. *Song of Solomon*, 1:15-16.

BIOGRAPHY

Toni Morrison was born in Lorain, Ohio, in 1931. She attended Howard University and Cornell University. From 1971-1972 she was professor at the State University of New York at Purchase. Since 1965 Morrison is editor at Random House.

BIBLIOGRAPHY

The Bluest Eye. New York: Holt, 1970.
Sula. New York: Alfred Knopf, 1973.
Song of Solomon. New York: Alfred Knopf, 1977.
Tar Baby. New York: Alfred Knopf, 1981.

1945 Burnham, Frederick Russell, *Taking Chances*. Los Angeles: Haynes.
Caldwell, Lewis A.H. (Abe Noel), *The Policy King*. Chicago: New Vistas
Himes, Chester, *If He Hollers Let Him Go*. New York: Doubleday, Doran.
Micheaux, Oscar, *The Case of Mrs. Wingate*. New York: Book Supply.
Wood, Odella Phelps, *High Ground*. New York: Exposition.
1946 Gross, Werter L., *The Golden Recovery*. Reno, Nev.:By the Author.
Henderson, George Wylie, *Jule*. New York: Creative.
Lucas, Curtis, *Third Ward Newark*. Chicago: Ziff Davis.
Micheaux, Oscar, *The Story of Dorothy Stanfield*. New York: Book
Supply.
Petry, Ann Lane, *The Street*. Boston: Houghton Mifflin.
Yerby, Frank, *The Foxes of Harrow*. New York: Dial.
1947 Blair, John Paul, *Democracy Reborn*. New York: By the Author.
Bland, Alden, *Behold – – A Cry*. New York: Scribner.
Himes, Chester, *Lonely Crusade*. New York: Knopf.
Jenkins, Deaderick Franklin, *Letters to My Son*. Los Angeles: Deaderick F. Jenkins.
Micheaux, Oscar, *The Masquarade, a Historical Novel*. New York: Book
Supply.
Motley, Willard, *Knock on Any Door*. New York: Appleton-Century.
Petry, Ann Lane, *Country Place*. Boston: Houghton, Mifflin.
Rasmussen, Emil Michael, *The First Night*. New York: Wendell Malliet.
Thomas, Will (William Smith), *God Is for White Folks*. New York: Creative Age, (also published under title: *Love Knows No Barriers*. New
York: New American Library, 1951).
Yerby, Frank, *The Vixens*. New York: Dial.
1948 Hurston, Zora Neale, *Seraph on the Suwane*. New York: Scribner.
Smith, William Gardner, *Last of the Conquerors*. New York: Farrar,
Straus.
West, Dorothy, *The Living Is Easy*. Boston: Houghton, Mifflin.
Yerby, Frank, *The Golden Hawk*. New York: Dial.
1949 Cooper, Alvin Carlos, *Stroke of Midnight*. Nashville, Ten.: Hemphill.
Hunter, Hermann L., *The Miracles of the Red Altar Cloth*. New York:
Exposition.
Jarrette, Alfred Q., *Beneath the Sky*. New York: Weinberg Book Supply.
Savoy, Willard W., *Alien Land*. New York: Dutton.

Yerby, Frank, *Pride's Castle*. New York: Dial.
1950 Adams, Alger Leroy (Philip B. Kaye), *Taffy*. New York: Crown Publ.
Demby, William, *Beetlecreek*. New York: Rinehart.
Redding, J. Saunders, *Stranger and Alone*. New York: Harcourt, Brace.
Smith, William Gardner, *Anger at Innocence*. New York: Farrar, Straus.
Yerby, Frank, *Floodtide*. New York: Dial.
1951 Bridgeforth, Med, *Another Chance*. New York: Exposition, publ. 1927 under title: *God's Law and Man's*.
Brown, Lloyd Louis, *Iron City*. New York: Masses & Mainstream.
Dodson, Owen, *Boy at the Window*. New York: Chatham Bookseller, published under title: *When Trees Were Green*.
Morris, Earl J., *The Cop*. New York: Exposition.
Motley, Willard, *We Fished All Night*. New York: Appleton - Century-Crofts.
Rosebrough, Sadie Mae, *Wasted Travail*. New York: Vantage.
Turner, Allen Pelzer, *Oakes of Eden*. New York: Exposition.
Yerby, Frank, *A Woman Called Fancy*. New York: Dial.
1952 Demby, William, *La Seffimana Della Fede*. Rome: Atlante.
Dickens, Dorothy Lee, *Black on the Rainbow*. New York: Pageant.
Easterling, Renee, *A Strange Way Home*. New York: Pageant Press.
Ellison, Ralph, *Invisible Man*. New York: Random House.
Himes, Chester, *Cast the First Stone*. New York: Coward-McCann.
Joseph, Arthur (John Arthur), *Volcano in Our Midst*. New York: Pageant.
Lucas, Curtis, *So Low, So Lonely*. New York n.p.
Roach, Thomas E., *Samson*. Boston: Meador Publishing Co.
Ward, Matthew, *The Indignant Heart*. New York: New Books.
Williams, Chancellor, *Have You Been to the River?* New York: Exposition.
Yerby, Frank, *The Saracen Blade*. New York: Dial.
1953 Arnold, Ethel Nishua, *She Knew No Evil*. New York: Vantage.
Baldwin, James, *Go Tell It on the Mountain*. New York: Knopf.
Brooks, Gwendolyn, *Maud Martha*. New York: Harper.
1953 Fisher, William, *The Waiters*. Cleveland: World.
Hough, Florenz H., *Black Paradise*. Philadelphia: Dorrance.
Kennedy, Mark, *The Pecking Order*. New York: Appleton.
Lucas, Curtis, *Angel*. New York: Lion.
Lucas, Curtis, *Forbidden Fruit*. New York: Universal.
Petry, Ann Lane, *The Narrows*. Boston: Houghton, Mifflin.
Scott, Anne, *Case 999, A Christmas Story*. Boston: Meador Publ. Co.
Wamble. Thelma, *All in the Family*. New York: New Voices.
Ward, Thomas Playfair. *The Right to Live*. New York: Pageant.
Wright, Richard, *The Outsider*. New York: Harper & Brothers.
Yerby, Frank, *The Devil's Laughter*. New York: Dial.
1954 Buster, Greene, *Brighter Sun: An Historical Account of the Struggles of*

a Man to Free Himself and His Family from Bondage, By His Grandson. New York: Pageant.

Chantrelle, Seginald, *Not Without Dust.* New York: Exposition.

Corbo, Dominic R., Jr. *Hard Ground.* New York: Vantage.

Crump, George Peter, Jr. *From Bondage They Came.* New York: Vantage.

Diggs, Arthur, *Black Woman.* New York: Exposition.

Himes, Chester, *The Third Generation.* Cleveland: World.

Jones, William H., *The Triangle's End.* New York: Exposition.

Jordan, Elsie, *Strange Sinner.* New York: Pageant.

Killens, John Oliver, *Youngblood.* New York: Dial.

Offord, Carl R. (Charles Ruthaven), *The Naked Fear.* New York: Ace.

Smith, William Gardner, *South Street.* New York: Farrar.

Smythwick. Charles A. Jr., *False Measure. A Satirical Novel of the Lives and Objectives of Upper Middle-Class Negroes.* New York: William-Frederick.

Spence, Tomas H. and Eric Heath, *Martin Larwin.* New York: Pageant.

Wallace, Elizabeth West, *Scandal at Daybreak.* New York: Pageant.

Ward, Thomas Playfair, *The Clutches of Circumstances.* New York: Pageant.

Wiggins, Walter, Jr., *Dreams in Reality of the Undersea Craft.* New York: Pageant.

Wright, Richard, *Savage Holiday.* New York: Avon.

Yerby, Frank, *Benton's Row.* New York: Dial.

1955 Browne, Theodore, *The Band Will Not Play Dixie: A Novel of Suspense* New York: Exposition.

Himes, Chester, *The Primitive.* New York: New American Library.

Humphrey, Lillie Muse, *Aggie.* New York: Vantage.

Lucas, Curtis, *Lila.* New York: Lion.

Ward, Thomas Playfair, *The Truth that Makes Men Free.* New York: Pageant.

Yerby, Frank, *The Treasure of Pleasant Valley.* New York: Dial.

1956 Baldwin, James, *Giovanni's Room.* New York: Dial.

Carrere, Mentis, *Man in the Cane.* New York: Vantage.

Harris, Elbert L., *The Athenian.* Daytona Beach, Fla.: College Publ. Co.

Sydnor, W. Leon, *Veronica.* New York: Exposition.

Vanderpuije, Nii Akrampahene, *The Counterfeit Corpse.* New York: Cornet.

Warner, Samuel Jonathan, *Madam President-Elect: A Novel.* New York: Exposition.

Woods, William B., *Lancaster Triple Thousand: A Novel of Suspense.* New York: Exposition.

Yerby, Frank, *Captain Rebel.* New York: Dial.

1957 Bosworth, William, *The Long Search.* Great Barrington, Mass.: Advance

Branch, Edward, *The High Places.* New York: Exposition.

English, Rubynn M., Sr. *Citizen U.S.A.* New York: Pageant.

Himes, Chester, *For Love of Imabelle.* Greenwich, Conn.: Fawcett.

Jackson, W. Warner, *The Birth of the Martyr's Ghost: A Novel.* New York: Comet.

Mayfield, Julian, *The Hit.* New York: Vanguard.

Montague, W. Reginald, *Ole Man Mose: A Novel of the Tennessee Valley.* New York: Exposition.

Shaw, Letty M., *Angel Mink.* New York: Comet.

Simmons, Herbert Alfred, *Corner Boy.* Boston: Houghton, Mifflin.

Smith, Joe, *Dagmar of Green Hills.* New York: Pageant.

Turpin, Waters Edward, *The Rootless.* New York: Vantage Press.

Yerby, Frank, *Fairoaks.* New York: Dial.

1958 Austin, Edmund O., *The Black Challenge.* New York: Vantage.

Bellinger, Claudia, *Wolf Kitty.* New York: Vantage.

Coolidge, Fay Liddle, *Black Is White.* New York: Vantage.

Dreer, Herman, *The Tie That Binds.* Boston: Meador.

Gibson, Richard, *A Mirror for Magistrates.* London: A. Blond.

Hodges, George Washington, *Swamp Angel.* New York: New Voices.

Hughes, Langston James, *Tambourines to Glory.* New York: John Day.

Kytle, Elizabeth, *Willie Mae.* New York: Alfred A. Knopf.

Lipscomb, Ken, *Duke Casanova.* New York: Exposition.

Mayfield, Julian, *The Long Night.* New York: Vanguard.

Motley, Willard, *Let No Man Write my Epitaph.* New York: Random House.

Pretto, Clarita C., *The Life of Autumn Holliday.* New York: Exposition.

Screen, Robert Martin, *We can't Run Away from Here.* New York: Vantage.

Wells, Jack Calvert, *Out of the Deep.* Boston: Christopher.

Williams, Jerome Ardell, *The Tin Box: A Story of Texas Cattle and Oil.* New York: Vantage.

Wright, Richard, *The Long Dream.* Garden City, N.Y.: Doubleday.

Yerby, Frank, *The Serpent and the Staff.* New York: Dial.

1959 Brown, Frank London, *Trumbull Park.* Chicago: Regnery.

Cook, Douglas, *Choker's Son.* New York: Comet.

Davis, Joseph A., *Black Bondage: A Novel of a Doomed Negro in Today's South.* New York: Exposition.

Dunham, Katherine, *A Touch of Innocence.* New York: Harcourt Brace

Harris, Leon R., *Run Zebra, Run! A Story of American Race Conflict.* New York: Exposition.

Himes, Chester, *The Crazy Kill.* New York: Avon.

Himes, Chester, *The Real Cool Killers.* New York: Avon.

Hooks, Nathaniel, *Town on Trial. A Novel of Racial Violence in a Southern Town.* New York: Exposition.

Lee, James F., *The Victims.* New York: Vantage.

Marshall, Paule, *Brown Girl, Brownstones.* New York: Random.

Pollard, Freeman, *Seeds of Turmoil: A Novel of American PW's Brainwashed in Korea.* New York: Exposition.

Potter, Valaida (Pseud.W.J.McCall), *Sunrise Over Alabama.* New York: Comet.

Puckett, G. Henderson, *One More Tomorrow*. New York: Vantage.
Vaught, Estella, *Vengeance Is Mine*. New York: Comet.
West, John B., *An Eye for an Eye*. New York: New American Library.
White, E.H. (Lydia Watson), *Our Homeward Way. A Novel of Race Relations in Modern Life*. New York: Exposition.
Wooby, Philip, *Nude to the Meaning of Tomorrow: A Novel of a Lonely Search*. New York: Expositon.
Yancey, A.H., *Interpositionulification, What the Negro May Expect*. New York: Comet.
Yerby, Frank, *Jarrett's Jade*. New York: Dial.
1960 Cooke, W.C., *The Rungless Ladder*. New York: Exposition.
Cooper, Clarence L., Jr. *The Scene*. New York: Crown.
Cotton, Ella Earls, *Queen of Persia: The Story of Esther Who Saved Her People*. New York: Exposition.
Cox, Joseph Mason Andrew, *The Search*. New York: Daniel S. Mead.
Cunningham, George, *Lily-Skin Lover: His Passion for Light-Complexioned Women Leads Him to Destruction*. New York: Exposition.
Himes, Chester, *All Shot up*. New York: Berkley.
Himes, Chester, *The Big Gold Dream*. New York: Avon.
Shores, Minnie T., *Publicans and Sinners*. New York: Cornet.
West, John B., *Bullets on My Business*, New York: New American Library.
West, John B., *Cobra Venom*. New York: New American Library.
West, John B., *A Taste for Blood*. New York: New American Library.
Williams, John Alfred, *The Angry Ones*. New York: Ace.
Also published as *One for New York*.
Yerby, Frank, *Gillian*. New York: Dial.
1961 Anderson, Henry L.N., *No Use Cryin'*. Los Angeles: Western.
Broadus, Robert Deal, *Spokes for the Wheel*. Muncie: Kingsman Press.
Cooper, Clarence L., Jr., *Weed*. Evanston, Ill.: Regency.
Du Bois, William Edward Burghardt, *The Black Flame: A Trilogy*. New York: Mainstream, 1957-61.
1. *The Ordeal of Mansart*. 1957.
2. *Mansart Builds a School* 1959.
3. *Worlds of Color* 1961.
Farrell, John T., *The Naked Truth*. New York: Vantage.
Hercules, Frank, *Where the Hummingbird Flies*. New York: Harcourt.
Himes, Chester, *Pinktoes*, Paris: Olympia Press.
Also published as: *Nowhere Street*. New York: Warner Paperback Libr.
Mayfield, Julian, *The Grand Parade*. New York: Vanguard.
West. John B., *Death on the Rocks*. New York: New American Library.
West, John B., *Never Kill a Cop*. New York: New American Library
Williams, John Alfred, *Night Song*. New York: Farrar, Straus & Cudahy.
Wilson, Pat, *The Sign of Keloa*. New York: Carlton.
Yerby, Frank, *The Garfield Honor*. New York: Dial.

1962 Baldwin, James, *Another Country*. New York: Dial.

Brown, Mattye Jeanette, *The Reign of Terror*. New York: Vantage.

Chastain,Thomas, *Judgment Day*. Garden City, N.Y.: Doubleday.

Clinton, Dorothy Randle, *The Maddening Scar: A Mystery Novel*. Boston: Christopher.

Cooper, Clarence L., Jr., *The Dark Messenger*. Evanston, Ill.: Regency.

Cooper, William, *Thank God for a Song: A Novel of Negro Church Life in the Rural South*. New York: Exposition.

Crump, Paul, *Burn, Killer, Burn*. Chicago: Johnson.

Delany, Samuel R., *The Jewels of Aptor*. New York: Ace.

Ferguson, Ira Lunan, *Ocee McRae, Texas*. San Francisco: Lunan-Ferguson—Library.

Gaines, Edwina, *Your People Are My People*. London: Great Western Publishing Co.

Kelley, William Melvin, *A Different Drummer*. New York: Doubleday.

Perkins, Charles, *Portrait of a Young Man Drowning*. New York: Simon & Schuster.

Simmons, Herbert Alfred, *Man Walking on Egg Shells*. Boston: Houghton, Mifflin.

Skinner, Theodosia B., *Ice Cream from Heaven*. New York: Vantage.

Talbot, Dave, *The Musical Bride*. New York: Vantage.

Teague, Robert L., *The Climate of Candor*. New York: Pageant.

Voglin, Peter, *Now You Lay Me Down to Sleep*. Dallas, Tex.: Royal Pub.

Yerby, Frank, *Griffin's Way*. New York: Dial.

1963 Cooper, Clarence L., Jr., *Black! Two Short Novels*. Evanston, Ill: Regency.

Davis, Russell F., *Anything for a Friend*. New York: Crown.

Delany, Samuel R., *Captives of the Flame*. New York: Ace.

Edwards, Junius, *If We Must Die*. New York: Doubleday.

Janssen, Milton W., *Divided*. New York: Pageant Press.

Killens, John Oliver, *And Then We Heard the Thunder*. New York: Knopf.

Mays, Willie and Jeff Harris, *Danger in Center Field*. Larchmont, N.Y.: Argonaut.

Parks, Gordon, *The Learning Tree*. New York: Harper & Row.

Rogers, Joel Augustus, *She Walks in Beauty*. Los Angeles: Western.

Smith, William Gardner, *The Stone Face*. New York: Farrar & Straus.

Vroman, Mary Elizabeth, *Esther*. New York: Bantam.

Williams, John Alfred, *Sissie*. New York: Farrar, Straus & Cudahy.

Wright, Charles Stevenson, *The Messenger*. New York; Farrar, Straus.

Wright, Richard, *Lawd Today*. New York: Walker.

1964 Boles, Robert E., *The People One Knows*. Boston: Houghton, Mifflin.

312

Flemister, John T., *Furlough from Hell: A Fantasy*. New York: Exposition.

Forte, Christine (Christine Forster), *A View from the Hill*. New York: Vantage.

Gaines, Ernest J., *Catherine Carmier*. New York: Atheneum.

Gunn, Bill, *All the Rest have Died*. New York: Delacorte.

Hunter, Helen, *Magnificent White Men*. New York: Vantage Press.

Hunter, Kristin, *God Bless the Child*. New York: Bantam.

James, Beauregard (pseud.), *The Road to Birmingham*. New York: Published for Society of Racial Peace of Washington, D.C., by Bridgehead Books.

Lahon, Vyola Therese, *The Big Lie*. New York: Vantage.

Patterson, Orlando. *The Children of Sisyphus*. London: Hutchinson, also published as *Dinah*. Elmhurst, N.Y.: Pyramid Books 1968.

Smith, Arthur Lee, *The Break of Dawn*. Philadelphia: Dorrance.

Sublette, Walter (S.W. Edwards, pseud.), *Go Now In Darkness*. Chicago, Baker.

Washington, Doris V., *Yulan*. New York: Carlton.

Webb, Charles Lewis, *Sasebo Diary*. New York: Vantage.

West, William, *Cornered*. New York: Carlton.

Williams, Richard Leroy, *Parson Wiggin's Son*. New York: Carlton.

Wilson, Carl Thomas David, *The Half Caste*. Ilfracombe, England: A.H. Stockwell.

Yerby, Frank, *The Old Gods Laugh: A Modern Romance*. New York: Dial.

1965 Anderson, Alston, *All God's Children*. Indianapolis: Bobbs.

Baraka, Imamu Amiri (LeRoi Jones), *The System of Dante's Hell*. New York: Grove.

Battles, Jesse Moore, *Somebody Please Help Me*. New York: Pageant.

Brown, Claude, *Manchild in the Promised Land*. New York: Macmillan.

Delany, Samuel R., *The Ballad of Beta – 2*. New York: Ace.

Demby, William, *The Catacombs*. New York: Pantheon Books.

Fair, Ronald L., *Many Thousand Gone: An American Fable*. New York: Harcourt.

Felton, James A., *Fruits of Enduring Faith*. New York: Exposition.

Fiore, Carmen Anthony, *The Barrier*. New York: Pageant.

Himes, Chester, *Cotton Comes to Harlem*. New York: Putnam.

Horsman, Gallan, *The Noose and the Spear: A Tale of Passion, Adventure and Violence*. New York: Vantage.

Johnson, Evelyn Allen, *My Neighbour's Island*. New York: Exposition.

Johnson, Joe, *Courtin', Sportin' and Non-Supportin'*. New York: Vantage Press.

Jones, Ralph H., *The Pepperpot Man*. New York: Vantage.

Kelley, William Melvin, *A Drop of Patience*. Garden City, N.Y.: Doubleday.

Martin, Chester, *He Was Born, He Died and He Lived*. New York: Carlton.

Motley, Willard, *Tourist Town*. New York: Putnam.

Ottley, Roi, *White Marble Lady*. New York: Farrar, Straus & Giroux.

Paulding, James E., *Sometime Tomorrow*. New York: Carlton.

Rhodes, Hari, *A Chosen Few*. New York: Bantam.

Robinson, John Terry, *White Horse in Harlem*. New York: Pageant.

Rollins, Lamen, *The Human Race a Gang*. New York: Carlton.

Van Dyke, Henry, *Ladies of the Rachmaninoff Eyes*. New York: Farrar, Straus & Giroux.

Wright, Richard. "Five Episodes from an Unfinished Novel." In Hill, Herbert (ed.), *Soon, One Morning: New Writing by American Negroes. 1940-1962*. New York: Alfred A. Knopf.

Yerby, Frank, *An Odor of Sanctity: A Novel of Medieval Moorish Spain*. New York: Dial.

1966 Barrett, Nathan N., *Bars of Adamaunt: A Tropical Novel*. New York: Fleet.

Bennett, Hal, *A Wildernes of Vines*. Garden City, N.Y.: Doubleday.

Blackwood, Granby, *Un Sang Mal Mele*. Paris: Editions Denoël.

Carrere, Mentis, *It's All South*. Los Angeles: John Hurry and Mary Louisa Dunn Bryant Foundation.

Cooper, John L., *Opus One*. New York: Maelstrom.

Davis, Charles, *Two Weeks to Find a Killer*. New York: Carlton.

Delany, Samuel R., *Babel – 17*. New York: Ace.

Delany, Samuel R., *Empire Star*. New York: Ace.

Fair, Ronald L., *Hog Butcher*. New York: Harcourt Brace Jovanovich.

Forte, Christine (Christine Forster). *Young Tim O'Hara*. New York: Vantage.

Guy, Rosa, *Bird at My Window*. Philadelphia: Lippincott.

Himes, Chester, *The Heat's On*. New York: Putnam.

(Also published as: *Come Back, Charleston Blue*. New York: Dell.)

Himes, Chester, *Run Man, Run*. New York: Putnam.

Hunter, Kristin, *The Landlord*. New York: Scribner.

Koiner, Richard B., *Jack Be Quick*. New York: Lyle Stuart.

Motley, Willard, *Let Noon Be Fair*. New York: Putnam.

Phillips, Jane, *Mojo Hand*. New York: Trident Press.

Shores, Minnie T., *Americans in America*. Boston: Christopher.

Thorup, Lester W., *Came the Harvest*. New York: Carlton.

Walker, Claude, Jr., *Sabih*. New York: Carlton.

Walker, Margaret (Mrs. F.J.Alexander), *Jubilee*. Boston: Houghton, Mifflin.

Wright, Charles Stevenson, *The Wig: A Mirror Image*. New York: Farrar, Straus & Giroux.

1967 Attaway, William, *Hear America Singing*. New York: Lion.

Beck, Robert (Iceberg Slim), *Pimp: The Story of My Life*. Los Angeles: Holloway.

Beck, Robert, (Iceberg Slim), *Trick Baby*. Los Angeles: Holloway.

Coleman, James Nelson, *Seeker from the Stars*. New York: Berkley.

Cooper, Clarence L., Jr., *The Farm*. New York: Crown.

Delany, Samuel R., *The Einstein Intersection*. New York: Ace.

Gaines, Ernest J.,*Of Love and Dust*. New York: Dial.

Hercules, Frank, *I Want a Black Doll*. New York: Simon & Schuster.

Jackson, J. Denis (Julian Moreau), *The Black Commandos*. Atlanta: Cultural Institute Press.

Johnson, Jesse J., *Ebony Brass: An Autobiography of Negro Frustration Amid Aspiration*. New York: William Frederick Press.

Johnson, William Matthews, *The House on Corbett Street*. New York: William-Frederick Press.

Kelley, William Melvin, *dem*. Garden City, N.Y.: Doubleday.

Killens, John Oliver, *Sippi*. New York: Trident.

Kirk, Paul, *No Need to Cry*. New York: Carlton.

Parrish, Clarence R., *Images of Democracy (I Can't Go Home)*. New York: Carlton.

Patterson, Orlando, *An Absence of Ruins*. London: Hutchinson.

Polite, Carlene Hatcher, *The Flagellants*. New York: Farrar, Straus & Giroux.

Ramsey, Leroy L., *The Trial and the Fire*. New York: Exposition.

Reed, Ishmael, *The Free-Lance Pallbearers*. Garden City, N.Y.: Doubleday.

Rollins, Bryant, *Danger Song*. Garden City, N.Y.: Doubleday.

Vroman, Mary Elizabeth, *Harlem Summer*. New York: Putnam.

Watson, Roberta Bruce, *Closed Doors*. New York: Exposition.

Wideman, John Edgar, *A Glance Away*. New York: Harcourt, Brace, World.

Williams, John Alfred, *The Man Who Cried I Am*. Boston: Little Brown.

Yerby, Frank, *Goat Song: A Novel of Ancient Greece*. New York: Dial.

1968 Baldwin, James, *Tell Me How Long the Train's Been Gone*. New York: Dial.

Bennet, Hal, *The Black Wine*. Garden City, N.Y.: Doubleday.

Boles, Robert E., *Curling*. Boston: Houghton, Mifflin & Co.

Delany, Samuel R., *Nova*. New York: Doubleday.

Heard, Nathan C., *Howard Street*. New York: Dial.

Lee, Audrey, *The Clarion People*. New York: McGraw.

Morrison, C.T., *The Flame in the Icebox: An Episode of the Vietnam*

War. New York: Exposition.

Smith, Bernard S., *Born for Malice.* New York: Vantage Press.

Smith, Maurice L., *Who Cares.* New York: Carlton.

Van Peebles, Melvin, *A Bear for the FBI.* New York: Trident.

Warren, Alyce, *Into These Depths.* New York: Vantage Press.

Whitney, Jim E., *Wayward O'er Tuner Sheffard.* New York: Carlton.

Yerby, Frank, *Judas, My Brother: The Story of the Thirteenth Disciple.* New York: Dial.

1969 Beck, Robert (Iceberg Slim), *Mama Black Widow*, Los Angeles: Holloway.

Beckham, Barry, *My Main Mother.* New York: Walker.

Brown, Cecil M., *The Life and Loves of Mr. Jiveass Nigger.* New York: Farrar, Straus & Giroux.

Brown, Frank London, *The Myth Maker.* Chicago: Path Press.

Cannon, Steve, *Groove, Bang and Jive Around.* New York: Ophelia Press.

Carvalho, Grimaldo, *The Negro Messiah.* New York: Vantage.

Coleman, Merton H., *That Godless Woman.* New York: Vantage Press.

Coleman, James Nelson, *The Null-Frequency Impulser.* New York: Berkley.

Farmer, Clarence, *Soul on Fire.* New York: Belmont.

Gilbert, Herman Cromwell, *That Uncertain Sound.* Chicago: Path.

Greenlee, Sam, *The Spook Who Sat by the Door.* New York: R.W. Baron.

Ferguson, Ira Lunan, *The Biography of G. Wash Carter, White.* San Francisco: Lunan-Ferguson—Library.

Himes, Chester, *Blind Man with a Pistol.* New York: Morrow.

Johnson, Hubert E., and Loretta Johnson, *Poppy.* New York: Carlton.

Kimbrough, Jess, *Defender of the Angels.* New York: Macmillan.

Lee, Audrey, *The Workers.* New York: McGraw.

Mahoney, William, *Black Jacob.* New York: Macmillan.

Major, Clarence, *All-Night-Visitors.* New York: Olympia.

Marshall, Paule. *The Chosen Place, The Timeless People.* New York: Harcourt Brace Jovanovich.

Pharr, Robert Deane, *The Book of Numbers.* Garden City, N.Y.: Doubleday.

Reed, Ishmael, *Yellow Back Radio Broke-Down.* Garden City, N.Y.: Doubleday.

Robinson, Rose, *Eagle in the Air.* New York: Crown.

Simpson, Rawle. *Adventures into the Unknown.* New York: Carlton.

Spence, Raymond, *Nothing Back But a Cadillac.* New York: Putnam.

Van Dyke, Henry, *Blood of Strawberries.* New York: Farrar, Straus & Giroux.

Verne, Berta (pseud.), *Elastic Fingers*. New York: Vantage.

Wamble, Thelma, *Look Over My Shoulder*. New York: Vantage.

Williams, Edward G., *Not Like Niggers*. New York: St. Martin's Press.

Williams, John Alfred, *Sons of Darkness, Sons of Light: A Novel of Some Probability*. Boston: Little Brown.

Wright, Sarah E., *The Child's Gonna Live*. New York: Delacorte.

Yerby, Frank, *Speak Now: A Modern Bovel*. New York: Dial.

1970 Battle, Sol, *Mélange in Black*. New York: Panther House.

Bennett, Hal, *Lord of Dark Places*. New York: Norton.

Bond, Odessa, *The Double Tragedy*. New York: Vantage.

Cain, George, *Blueschild Baby*. New York: McGraw-Hill.

Carson, Lular L., *The Priceless Gift*. New York: Vantage.

Delany, Samuel R., *The Fall of the Towers*. New York: Ace.

1. *Out of the Dead City*. 1963, rev. 1966.

2. *The Towers of Toron*, 1964, rev. 1966.

3. *City of a Thousand Suns*, 1965.

Fairley, Ruth Ann, *Rocks and Roses*. New York: Vantage.

Greene, Joe (B.B.Johnson), *Superspade No. 1: Death of a Blue-Eyed Soul Brother*. New York: Paperback Library.

Greene, Joe (B.B.Johnson), *Superspade No. 2: Black is Beautiful*. New York: Paperback Library.

Greene, Joe (B.B.Johnson), *Superspade No. 3: That's Where the Cat's At, Baby*. New York: Paperback library.

Greene, Joe (B.B.Johnson), *Superspade No.4: Mother of the Year*. New York: Paperback Library.

Greene, Joe (B.B. Johnson), *Superspade No. 5: Bad Day for a Black Brother*. New York: Paperback Library.

Groves, John Wesley, IV., *Shellbreak*. New York: Paperback Library.

Jackson, Emma Lou, *The Veil of Nancy*. New York: Carlton.

Jarry, Hawke, *Black Schoolmaster*. New York: Exposition.

Kelley, William Melvin, *Dunfords Travels Everywheres*. Garden City, N.Y.: Doubleday.

Meriwhether, Louise M., *Daddy Was a Number Runner*. Englewood Cliffs, N.J.: Prentice-Hall.

Morrison, Toni, *The Bluest Eye*. New York: Holt, Rinehart and Winston.

Robinson, J. Terry, *The Double Circle People*. New York: Suzanna.

Royal, A. Bertrand, *Which Way to Heaven?* New York: Vantage.

Russ, George B., *Over Edom, I Lost My Shoe*. New York: Carlton.

Scott-Heron, Gil, *The Vulture*. New York: World Publ.

Smith, George Lawson, *Transfer*. New York: Vantage.

Stern, Harold, *Blackland*. Garden City, N.Y.: Doubleday.

Stone, Chuck (Charles Summer Stone), *King Strut*. Indianapolis:

Turner, Peter, *Black Heat*. New York: Belmont.

Turnor, Mae Caesar, *Uncle Ezra Holds Prayer Meeting in the White House*. New York: Exposition Press.

Walker, Alice, *The Third Life of Grange Copeland*. New York: Harcourt Brace, Jovanovich.

White, Thomas J., *To Hell and Back at Sixteen*. New York: Carlton.

Wideman, John Edgar, *Hurry Home*. New York: Harcourt, Brace, World.

Young, Al (Albert James Young), *Snakes*. New York: Holt, Rinehart & Winston.

1971 Atkins, Russell, *Maleficium*. Cleveland: Freelance.

Bambara, Toni Cade, *Gorilla, My Love*. New York: Random.

Beck, Robert (Iceberg Slim), *Naked Soul of Iceberg Slim*. Los Angeles: Holloway.

Beckham, Barry, *Runner Mack*. New York: Morrow.

Davis, George B., *Coming Home*. New York: Random.

Davis, Nolan, *Six Black Horses*. New York: Putnam.

Gaines, Ernest J., *The Autobiography of Miss Jane Pittman*. New York: Dial.

Goines, Donald, *Dopefiend, The Story of a Black Junkie*. Los Angeles: Holloway.

Greene, Joe (B.B. Johnson), *Superspade No. 6: Blues for a Black Sister*. New York: Paperback Library.

Haskins, LeRoi R., *The Weak Arm of Justice*. New York: Vantage.

Killens, John Oliver, *Cotillion: Or One Good Bull Is Half the Herd*. New York: Trident.

McWhortle, A.C., *Lena*. New York: Grove Press.

Mason, B.J., *The Jerusalem Freedom Manufacturing Co*. New York: Paperback Library.

Pharr, Robert Deane, *S.R.O.* Garden City, N.Y.: Doubleday.

Smith, Odessa, *The Flame*. Detroit: Harlo Press.

Shears, Carl L., *Niggers and Po's White Trash*. Washington, D.C.: Nu-Classics & Science Publishing Co.

Smith, Daniel, *A Walk in the City*. New York: World.

Stewart, John, *Last Cool Days*. London: Andre Deutsch.

Van Dyke, Henry, *Dead Piano*. New York: Farrar, Straus & Giroux.

Van Peebles, Melvin, *Sweet Sweetback's Baadasss Song*. New York: Lancer.

Walker, Drake, *Buck and the Preacher*. New York: Popular Library.

Wylie, James, *The Lost Rebellion*. New York: Trident Press.

Yerby, Frank, *The Dahomean*. New York: Dial.

1972 Awoonor, Kofi, *This Earth. My Brother*. Garden City, N.Y.: Doubleday

Beckham, Barry, *Runner Mack*. New York: Morrow.

318

Colter, Cyrus, *The River of Eros*. Chicago: Swallow.

Cotton, Donald J., *Sore Foots*. Washington, D.C: Libratterian Books.

Davis, Charles W., *The Nut and Bolt*. New York: Vantage Press.

Fair, Ronald L., *We Can't Breathe*. New York: Harper-Row.

Goines, Donald, *Black Gangster*. Los Angeles: Holloway.

Goines, Donald, *Whoreson, The Story of a Ghetto Pimp*. Los Angeles: Holloway.

Hawkins, Odie, *Ghetto Sketches*. Los Angeles: Holloway.

Heard, Nathan C., *To Reach a Dream*. New York: Dial.

Kemp, Arnold, *Eat of Me, I Am the Savior*. New York: Morrow.

Love, D.C., *The Sheriff*. New York: Vantage.

Lubin, Arthur, *Wampala on the Hudson*. New York: Vantage.

McKenzie, William P., *The Solemn Hour*. New York: Carlton.

Overstreet, Cleo, *The Boar Hog Woman*. Garden City, N.Y.: Doubleday.

Patterson, Orlando, *Die the Long Day*. New York: Morrow.

Reed, Ishmael, *Mumbo Jumbo*. Garden City, N.Y.: Doubleday.

Scott-Heron, Gil, *The Nigger Factory*. New York: Dial.

Skinner, Theodosia B., *Dilemma of a College Girl*. Philadelphia: Dorrance.

Webster, Bill, *One by One*. Garden City, N.Y.: Doubleday.

Williams, John Alfred, *Captain Blackman: A Novel*. Garden City, N.Y.: Doubleday.

Yerby, Frank, *The Girl from Storyville*. New York: Dial.

1973 Ashley, Martin, *Checkmate and Deathmate*. New York: Vantage.

Briscoe, Lawrance, *Fisher's Alley*. New York: Vantage.

Brown, Josephine Stephens, *The Way of the Shadows*. New York: Exposition.

Bullins, Ed, *The Reluctant Rapist*. New York: Harper & Row.

Cain, Johnnie Mae, *White Bastards*. New York: Vantage.

Childress, Alice, *A Hero Ain't Nothing But a Sandwich*. New York: Coward.

Colter, Cyrus, *The Hippodrome*. Chicago: Swallow.

Dee, John, *Stagger Lee*. New York: Manor Books.

Delany, Samuel R., *The Tides of Lust*. New York: Lancer.

Drummond, Mary, *Come Go With Me*. Philadelphia: Dorrance.

Forrest, Leon, *There Is a Tree More Ancient Than Eden*. New York: Random.

Goines, Donald, *Black Girl Lost*. Los Angeles: Holloway.

Goines, Donald, *Street Players*. Los Angeles: Holloway.

Goines, Donald, *White Man's Justice: Black Man's Grief*. Los Angeles: Holloway.

Greenlee, Sam, *Bagdad Blues*. New York: Emerson Hall.

Harris, James Leon, *Endurance*. New York: Vantage.

Hathorn, Christine, *The Undoing of Abagail Wrigley.* New York: Vantage Press.

Jackson, Blyden, *Operation Burning Candle.* New York: Third Press.

Lewis, Ronald, *The Last Junkie.* New York: Amurn.

Major, Clarence, *No.* New York: Emerson Hall.

Mallory, Roosevelt, *Radcliff, No. 1: Harlem Hit.* Los Angeles: Holloway.

Mitchell, Loften, *The Stubborn Old Lady Who Resisted Change.* New York: Emerson Hall.

Nazel, Joseph Jr., *My Name Is Black.* New York: Pinnacle Books.

Palmer Jon, *House Full of Brothers.* Los Angeles: Holloway.

Shears, Carl L. (Sagittarus), *The Count-Down to Black Genocide.* Washington D.C.: NuClassics and Science Publishing Co.

Smith, Lois A. (Jezebelle), *The Most Precious Moments.* Washington, D.C.: Nu Classics and Science Publishing Co.

Underwood, Bert, *A Branch of Velvet.* New York: Vantage Press.

Van Peebles Melvin, *Ain't Supposed to Die a Natural Death.* Toronto, New York: Bantam.

Van Peebles, Melvin, *Don't Play Us Cheap. A Harlem Party.* Toronto, New York: Bantam.

Wideman, John Edgar, *The Lynchers.* New York: Harcourt, Brace, World.

Williams, Dennis, A., and Spero Pines, *Them That's Not.* New York: Emerson Hall.

1974 Baldwin, James, *If Beale Street Could Talk.* New York: Dial.

Bennett, Hal, *Wait Until Evening.* Garden City, N.Y.: Doubleday.

DuBois, Shirley Graham, *Zulu Heart.* New York: Third Press.

Easley, Nivi-Kofi A., *The Militants.* New York: Carlton Press.

Garrett, Beatrice, *Welfare on Skid Row.* New York: Exposition Press.

Goines, Donald (Al. C. Clark), *Crime Partners.* Los Angeles: Holloway House.

Goines, Donald (Al. C. Clark), *Cry Revenge!* Los Angeles: Holloway House.

Goines, Donald, *Daddy Cool.* Los Angeles: Holloway House.

Goines, Donald, *Death List.* Los Angeles: Holloway House.

Goines, Donald, *Eldorado Red.* Los Angeles: Holloway House.

Goines, Donald, *Never Die Alone.* Los Angeles: Holloway House.

Goines, Donald, *Swamp Man.* Los Angeles: Holloway House.

Hagans, Willie, *The Black Tarnished Image.* New York: Vantage Press.

Heard, Nathan C., *A Cold Fire Burning.* New York: Simon & Schuster.

Hernton, Calvin, *Scare-Crow.* Garden City, N.Y.: Doubleday.

Johnson, Charles, *Faith and the Good Thing.* New York: Viking Press.

Leonard, Mack, *Cover My Rear.* New York: Vantage Press.

320

McCluskey, John, *Look What They Done to My Song.* New York: Random House.

Mallory, Roosevelt, *Radcliff, No. 2: San Francisco Vendetta.* Los Angeles: Holloway House.

Mills, Alison, *Francisco.* Berkeley, Calif.: Reed, Cannon and Johnson.

Morrison. Toni, *Sula.* New York: Knopf.

Murray, Albert, *Train Whistle Guitar.* New York: McGraw-Hill.

Nazel, Joseph, *The Black Exorcist.* Los Angeles: Holloway House.

Nazel, Joseph, *Black Is Black.* New York: Pinnacle Books.

Nazel, Joseph, *The Iceman, No. 1: Billion Dollar Death.* Los Angeles: Holloway House.

Nazel, Joseph, *The Iceman, No. 2: The Golden Shaft.* Los Angeles: Holloway House.

Nazel, Joseph, *The Iceman, No. 3: Slick Revenge.* Los Angeles: Holloway House.

Nazel, Joseph, *The Iceman, No. 4: Sunday Fix.* Los Angeles: Holloway House.

Nazel, Joseph, *The Iceman, No. 5: Spinning Target.* Los Angeles: Holloway House.

Nazel, Joseph, *The Iceman, No.6:. Canadian Kill.* Los Angeles: Holloway House.

Olden, Marc, *Black Samurai.* New York: New American Library.

Olden, Marc, *Black Samurai, No. 2: Golden Kill.* New York: New American Library.

Olden, Marc, *Black Samurai, No. 3: Killer Warrior.* New York: New American Library.

Olden, Marc, *Black Samurai, No. 4: The Deadly Pearl.* New York: New American Library.

Olden, Marc, *Black Samurai, No.5: The Inquisition.* New York: New American Library.

Perry, Richard, *Changes.* Indianapolis: Bobbs-Merrill.

Readus, James-Howard, *The Death Merchants.* Los Angeles: Holloway House.

Reed, Ishmael, *The Last Days of Louisiana Red.* New York: Random House.

Ross, Fran, *Oreo.* New York: Greyfalcon House.

Shears, Carl L. (Sagittarus), *Before the Setting Sun: The Age before Hambone.* Washington, D.C.: NuClassics and Science Publishing Co.

Shockley, Ann Allen, *Loving Her.* Indianapolis: Bobbs-Merrill.

Smith, Verne, *The Jones Men.* Chicago: Henry Regnery.

Teague, Robert L., *Agent K-13 the Super Spy.* Garden City, N.Y.: Doubleday.

Yerby, Frank, *The Voyage Unplanned.* New York: Dial.

1975 Bottoms, Timothy L., *Mr. Schutzer.* New York: Carlton Press.

Bradley, David, *South Street.* New York: Grossman.

Byer, Reggie, *Nobody Gets Rich.* New York: Vantage Press.

Delany, Samuel R., *Dhalgren.* New York: Bantam Books.

Du Bois, David Graham, *... And Bid Him Sing.* Palo Alto, Calif.: Ramparts Press.

Faulkner, Blanche, *The Lively House.* Los Angeles: Crescent Publications.

Gay, Kathlyn and Ben E. Barnes, *The River Flows Backward.* Port Washington, N.Y.: Ashley Books.

Goines, Donald, *Inner City Hoodlum.* Los Angeles: Holloway House.

Goines, Donald (Al. C. Clark), *Kenyatta's Escape.* Los Angeles: Holloway House.

Goines, Donald (Al. C. Clark), *Kenyatta's Last Hit.* Los Angeles: Holloway House.

Hart, Marcus A., *The Lover with a Killer's Instinct.* New York: Exposition Press.

Hunter, Kristin, *The Survivors.* New York: Scribner's Sons.

Jackson, Blyden, *Totem.* New York: Third Press.

Johnson, Eugene D., *Of Human Kindness.* New York: Vantage Press.

Jones, Gayl, *Corregidora.* New York: Random House.

Leonard, Mack, *From Love to Love.* Reseda, Calif.: Mojave Books.

Major, Clarence, *Reflex and Bone Structure.* New York: Fiction Collective.

Mallory, Roosevelt, *Radcliff, No.3: Double Trouble.* Los Angeles: Holloway House.

Mays, James A., *Mercy Is King.* Los Angeles: Crescent Publications.

Moore, Marie E., *Little White Shoes.* Hicksville, N.Y.: Exposition Press.

Nazel, Joseph, *The Iceman, No.7: The Shakedown.* Los Angeles: Holloway House.

Nazel, Joseph, *The Black Gestapo.* Los Angeles: Holloway House.

Nazel, Joseph, *Death for Hire.* Los Angeles: Holloway House.

Nazel, Joseph, *Killer Cop.* Los Angeles: Holloway House.

Olden, Marc, *Black Samurai, No.6: The Warlock.* New York: New American Library.

Olden, Marc, *Black Samurai, No.7: Sword of Allah.* New York: New American Library.

Olden, Marc, *Black Samurai, No. 8: The Katana.* New York: New American Library.

Pharr, Robert Deane, *The Soul Murder Case: A Confession of the Victim.* New York: Avon Books.

Polite, Carlene Hatcher, *Sister X and the Victims of Foul Play.* New York: Farrar, Straus & Giroux.

Readus, James-Howard, *The Big Hit*. Los Angeles: Holloway House.

Readus, James-Howard, *The Black Assassin*. Los Angeles: Holloway House.

Robinson, Arthur, *Hang That Nigger*. New York: Vantage Press.

Rudolph, Christopher, *The Boy Who Cursed God*. New York: Carlton Press.

Shackleford, Frank, *Old Rocking Chair*. New York: Vantage Press.

Stampede, Herman, *Of Melancholy Male*. New York: Vantage Press.

Taylor, Mildred D., *Roll of Thunder, Hear My Cry*. New York: Dial Press.

Tillman, Carolyn, *Life on Wheels*. Los Angeles: Crescent Publications.

Williams, John Alfred, *Mothersill and the Foxes*. Garden City, N.Y.: Doubleday.

Williams-Forde, Bily, *Requiem for a Black American Capitalist*. New York: Troisieme Canadian.

Yerby, Frank, *A Rose for Ana Maria*. New York: Dial Press.

Yerby, Frank, *Tobias and the Angel*. New York: Dial Press.

Young, Al, *Who Is Angelina?* New York: Holt, Rinehart & Winston.

1976 Bennett, Hal, *Seventh Heaven*. Garden City, N.Y.: Doubleday.

Boullon, J.M., *Surrender the Dream*. Philadelphia: Dorrance.

Butler, Octavia E., *Patternmaster*. Garden City, N.Y.: Doubleday.

Cheatwood, Kiarri, *Lighting in the Swamp*. Detroit: Agasha Productions.

Delany, Samuel R., *Triton*. New York: Bantam Books.

Dickens, Al., *Uncle Yah Yah*. Detroit: Halo Press.

Dumas, Henry, *Jonoah and the Green Stone*. New York: Random House.

Gilmore, J. Lance, *Hell Has No Exit*. Los Angeles: Holloway House.

Girard, James P., *Changing All Those Changes*. Berkeley, Calif.: Yardbird Wing Editions.

Guy, Rosa, *Ruby*. New York: Random House.

Harris, Charlie Avery, *Macking Gangster*. Los Angeles: Holloway House.

Harris, Charlie Avery, *Whoredaughter*. Los Angeles: Holloway House.

Jefferson, Roland S., *The School on 103rd Street*. New York: Vantage Press.

Jones, Gayl, *Eva's Man*. New York: Random House.

Lawson, William, *Zeppelin Coming Down*. Berkeley, Calif.: Yardbird Wing Editions.

Leonard, Mack, *Another Front: A Novel of World War II*. Reseda, Calif.: Mojave Books.

Lyons, Charles (Js Said), *Street Justice*. Columbus, Ohio: Lyons Productions.

Mallory, Roosevelt, *New Jersey Showdown*. Los Angeles: Holloway House.

Nazel, Joseph, *Black Fury*. Los Angeles: Holloway House.

Nazel, Joseph, *Black Prophet*. Los Angeles: Holloway House.

Newton, Leon Thomas, *Veritus, the Nirvana from the East*. New York: Carlton Press.

Olden, Marc, *Harker File, No. 1*. New York: New American Library.

Olden, Marc, *Harker File, No. 2: Dead and Paid for*. New York: New American Library.

Readus, James-Howard, *Black Renegades*. Los Angeles: Holloway House.

Reed, Ishmael, *Flight to Canada*. New York: Random House.

Van Peebles, Melvin, *Just an Old Sweet Song*. New York: Ballantine.

Van Peebles, Melvin, *The True American: A Folk Fable*. New York: Doubleday.

Walker, Alice, *Meridian*. New York: Harcourt, Brace Jovanovich.

Young, Al, *Sitting Pretty*. New York: Holt, Rinehart and Winston.

1977 Barker, Ben, *The Time of the Terrorists*. Los Angeles: Crescent.

Dodson, Owen, *Come Home Early, Child*. New York: Popular Library.

Forrest, Leon, *The Bloodworth Orphans*. New York: Random House.

Jefferson, Xavier, *Blessed are the Sleepy Ones*. Port Washington, N.Y.: Ashley Books.

Morrison, Toni, *Song of Solomon*. New York: Alfred A. Knopf.

Wylie, James, *The Homestead Grays*. New York: Putnam.

Yerby, Frank, *Hail the Conquering Hero*. New York: Dial.

1978 Andrews, Raymond, *Appalachee Red*. New York: Dial Press.

Brown, Wesley, *Tragic Music*. New York: Random House.

Gaines, Ernest J., *In My Father's House*. New York: Knopf.

Glass, Frankcina, *Marvin & Tige*. New York: St. Martin's Press.

Guy, Rosa, *Edith Jackson*. New York: Viking Press.

Hunter, Kristin, *The Lakestown Rebellion*. New York: Scribner's.

De Jongh, James and Charles Cleveland, *City Cool*. New York: Random House.

Jourdain, Rose, *Those, the Sun Has Loved*. Garden City, N.Y.: Doubleday.

Lee, Helen Jackson, *Nigger in the Window*. Garden City, N.Y.: Doubleday.

Mays, James A., *Chameleon*. Los Angeles: Crescent Publishers.

Meaddough, R.J., *The Retarded Genius*. New York: Troisième-Canadian Publishers.

Pharr, Robert Deane, *Giveadamn Brown*. Garden City, N.Y.: Doubleday.

Smith, Patrick, *Angel City*. St. Petersburg, Florida: Valkyrie Press.

Walker, Wilbert L., *The Pride of our Hearts*. Hicksville, N.Y.: Exposition Press.

1979 Baldwin, James, *Just Above My Head*. New York: Dial Press.

Butler, Octavia E., *Kindred*. Garden City, N.Y.: Doubleday.

Childress, Alice, *A Short Walk*. New York: Coward, McCann & Geoghehan.

Douglas, Ellen, *The Rock Cried Out*. New York: Harcourt, Brace, Jovanovich.

Guy, Rosa, *The Disappearance*. New York: Delacorte Press.

Pugh, Charles, *The Hospital Plot*. New York: Ashley Books.

Riboud, Barbara Chase, *Sally Hemings*. New York: Viking Press.

Southerland, Ellease, *Let the Lion Eat Straw*. New York: Scribner's.

Thelwell, Michael, *The Harder They Come: The Story of Rhygin*. New York: Grove Press.

Yerby, Frank, *A Darkness in Ingraham's Crest*. New York: Dial Press.

1980 Andrews, Raymond, *Rosiebelle Lee*. New York: Dial Press.

Bambara, Toni Cade, *The Salt Eaters*. New York: Random House.

Speed, Carol, *Inside Black Hollywood*. Los Angeles: Holloway House.

Young, Al, *Ask Me Now*. New York: McGraw.

LIST OF CONTRIBUTORS

Dr. Peter Bruck, Fachbereich 23/Englisch, Universität Münster, Scharnhorststrasse 100, D-4400 Münster/W

Dr. Klaus Ensslen, Amerika-Institut, Universität München, Schellingstrasse 3, D-8000 München

Professor Dr. Michel Fabre, Université de Paris III, Sorbonne Nouvelle, U.E.R. Des Pays Anglophones, 5, rue de l'Ecole-de-Médecine, Paris (VIe)

Professor Dr. Klaus P. Hansen, Philosophische Fakultät-Amerikanistik, Universität Passau, Postfach 2540, D-8390 Passau

Professor Dr. Wolfgang Karrer, Fachbereich VII, Universität Osnabrück, Neuer Graben/Schloss, D-4500 Osnabrück

Privatdozent Dr. Eberhard Kreutzer, Englisches Seminar, Universität Bonn, Regina-Pacis-Weg 5, D-5300 Bonn

Dr. Deborah Schneider, Institut für Anglistik und Amerikanistik, Universität Erlangen-Nürnberg, Bismarckstr. 1, D-8520 Erlangen

Professor Dr. Elizabeth Schultz, Department of English, University of Kansas, Lawrence, Kansas 66045

Professor Dr. Albert Wertheim, Department of English, Indiana University, Bloomington, Ind. 47405